Killester Garden Village

Killester Garden Village Committee (l-r): Mr Aaron Crampton (Airman, Air Corps), Mr Tommy Crampton, Mrs Ali Fields, Mr Aodhán Ó'Ríodáin TD, Mr Gerry Leigh, Mrs Ciara Ryan, Mrs Avril Stephenson, Mr Kevin Martin (Comdt. Retd, Army Reserve), Mrs Linda Byrne.

KILLESTER GARDEN VILLAGE

The Lives of Great War Veterans and Their Families

Killester Garden Village Committee

The Liffey Press

Published by
The Liffey Press Ltd
'Clareville'
307 Clontarf Road
Dublin D03 PO46, Ireland
www.theliffeypress.com

A catalogue record of this book is
available from the British Library.

ISBN 978-1-7397892-8-2
Second printing

Printed in Dublin by SprintPrint.

Contents

Contents

Contents

Homes for Irish Heroes

One hundred years ago this year, the largest Irish WWI ex-servicemen housing estate on the island of Ireland was completed, the Killester Garden Village. Comprising 247 bungalows, the estate was the flagship estate for returning Irishmen from what some dubbed 'the war to end all wars'.

I write this preface for this unique and fascinating book thinking of my late Grandmother, Effie Brophy of 90 Abbeyfield, who instilled great values of life into me from my childhood in Killester, and especially in 90 Abbeyfield, which have influenced my life greatly. I always wondered about the unique layout and countryside feel of the Killester estate when growing up, and then I began listening to the family stories from my grandmother, about the houses being for ex-soldiers and sailors after the Great War, and then about my great grandfather, John Brophy, who was veteran of both the Great War and the Second World War. I was shown his medals and war memorabilia in a tin box, one of the Princess Mary Christmas gift boxes distributed to all members of the armed forces of the British Empire on Christmas day 1914. This is where my story began, and the passion grew to find out more about the Killester estate and about the ex-servicemen who lived there. Growing up in a WWI ex-servicemen housing estate influenced my decision to join the Irish Defence Forces, with whom I have now been serving for seven years.

I was eager from then to do something to recognise the service that these soldiers, sailors and airmen gave in the Great War and, more importantly, to recognise that they still suffered after the war from physical defects and/or mental health issues. I was also keen to recognise the Killester Garden Village itself, as there was nowhere to go or no easily accessible resource to find out about the area and its ex-servicemen.

Fast forward to 2013 and the former Legion Hall in Killester was under threat from developers. I wrote a letter to a local TD, Aodhan Ó Ríordain, asking to save the hall and I was inspired to do something to help in this regard. A group of locals got together at an inaugural meeting in Killester where the 'Save the Legion Hall' campaign started. Later we went by the name, 'the Killester WWI Memorial Campaign', which I founded. We hosted a historical exhibition in the local parish centre called 'Killester on Show' which sparked huge interest locally. Fast forward again to 2021 and a group of locals came together to revive the efforts of the previous group and hosted the first annual 'Killester Remembrance Ceremony' at the Legion Hall. In 2022, the 'Killester Garden Village Committee', of which I am the current Chairman, was formed and in November 2022, the committee engaged Mr Michael Nugent and Mr Nigel Henderson to research the original WWI ex-servicemen of the Killester Garden Village. This was the origin of this book with its outstanding research of the Killester veterans.

Michael and Nigel, kudos to both of you for all your hard work and diligent efforts in creating this book. I would also like to pay thanks to Mr Tom Burke MBE for his advice and wisdom, and to Mr Eamonn Delaney for his support throughout and great interest. I would like to say thanks to all on our committee and especially Gerry Leigh, Kevin Martin, Marion Martin, Linda Byrne, Ciara Ryan, Francis Chance and, of course, my mam and dad (Tommy and Avril) for all their work on all things Killester. I also want to thank the Killester Sports and Social Club at Hadden Park for allowing us to use it as a 'HQ' over the years. After all, it is named after a prominent Killester resident – Staff Sergeant Bill Hadden MM, Royal Army Medical Corps and 77 Abbeyfield.

Lastly, thank you to everyone in the community of Killester for their interest, support, kind words, passion, and submissions which all helped make this book happen and our other projects in Killester over the years. We have a unique community and one of which we can rightly be very proud.

The first Armistice Day ceremony in Killester occurred on 11th November 1923, with a huge turnout by the community. The ceremony took place on the greens at Abbeyfield and Middle Third, with the ex-servicemen under the control of Sergeant Major John Arthur McBrien, formerly of the Royal Irish Fusiliers and the Leinster Regiment. He marched the men onto parade and the officers, including Captain James De Lacy MC, formerly of Royal Inniskilling Fusiliers (and the Superintendent of Killester), fell in. The event included the Last Post, one minute's silence, Reveille, and a speech by the guest speaker, Major Bryan Cooper TD MC, late of the Connaught Rangers, was emotive and resonates with us today in some ways. In his speech, Major Cooper said:

> We have met here today on the fifth anniversary of the Armistice, for three reasons. First to render humble and hearty thanks to Almighty God for our victory. Secondly to hold, for a brief space, in loving remembrance those of our comrades who are no longer with us. And thirdly, we have come together today to confirm our own faith, to recall our deeds and to take courage for the future and from the recollection of the past.
>
> For it is no small thing we have accomplished. Together with our Allies, we have broken the strength of the greatest military power that the modern world has ever known – an Empire whose purpose was solely directed to securing supremacy in war.
>
> And wherever the battle was fiercest, there was the Irish soldier to be found. Irishmen stood in the gap at Mons, Irishmen shattered the power of Turkey in Gallipoli and Palestine, Irishmen were foremost on the blood-drenched steeps of the Somme, and Irishmen North and South stood side by side victorious on the ridge of Messines.
>
> Turn where you will, read what history you choose, no one can say that in the day of battle – Irishmen did less than their duty.
>
> And now that the day of battle is past and we are in civilian clothes again, our duty is not at the end. We have come back to a world which was utterly changed, wherein the old landmarks have vanished, but the old orders stand. ''Look to your front'', ''hold your head up'', obey the orders of those in authority: above all, have courage. That is what Ireland needs to-day and if we are strong

enough to do that we shall once again be rendering a supreme service to our country, and Ireland will have the cause to be proud of us not only as soldiers, but as citizens.

His words have inspired the preparation of this book that provides a brief history of Killester Garden Village but, rightly, focuses on the men who served in the Great War and came home, some to serve their new country in the armed forces and police force of the Irish Free State. Some of these men gave service in the Boer War and Second World War, both at home and with British forces abroad. Some of the descendants of the early occupants also gave service, at home and abroad, with British and Irish forces, in the Second World War and after. Maybe their stories will be collated and related at some stage.

In the meantime, I hope you will enjoy reading this book to remember the men and women of the Killester Garden Village.

Acknowledgements

As Chairman of the Killester Garden Village Committee I would like to take this opportunity to thank and acknowledge the following people and organisations for supporting or helping the Killester Garden Village Committee over the years and especially to those who assisted in making this book a reality.

I would like to thank all committee members, Mr Gerry Leigh, Mr Kevin Martin, Ms Marion Martin, Ms Linda Byrne, Ms Ciara Ryan, Mr Francis Chance, my mother Ms Avril Stephenson and my father Mr Tommy Crampton.

I would like to thank the supporters of our committee, Mr Tom Burke MBE Mr Eamonn Delaney, Ms Jan Glover, Mr Patrick Hugh Lynch, Ms Bronwen Maher, Mr Peter Purdue, Mr Gary Hanway and the committee at the Killester Donnycarney Football Team and staff at the Killester Sports and Social Club as well as Mr Frank Farrell.

I would like to thank the Royal Dublin Fusiliers Association and Mr Brian Moroney, Prince of Wales Leinster's Regiment Association and Mr Ken Geary, 18th Regiment of Foot Royal Irish (and South Irish Horse) Regiment Association and Ms Mary Anne Maher, the Connaught Rangers Association and Senator Gerard Craughwell, and the Munster Fusiliers Association.

I would like to thank the Royal British Legion Republic of Ireland Branch and its Chairman Mr Brian Duffy MBE, the Irish Military Heritage of Ireland Trust and its Chairman Mr Paul Fry (Retd. Brig Gen), the Irish Military Heritage Foundation and Mr Wesley Bourke, the Dublin Military Veterans group and Mr Anto Kenna, and the ONE for their support.

I would like to thank all our local TDs who have supported us over the years and a special thanks to our local Councillors who have done outstanding work for us over the years.

Lastly I would like to thank all residents in the Killester Garden Village for being involved in some way, helping out, supporting us, and inspiring us with the stories, passion and love for our community, its history and heritage. We truly do live in amazing and special community and we all should take a bow as we have done Killester and our families proud with this book and our efforts over the years.

Go raibh míle maith agat agus lest we forget.

Aaron Crampton, Chairman
Killester Garden Village Committee

Aaron's family – 90 Abbeyfield, Sgt John Brophy, a veteran of WWI and WWII

Introduction:
Nobody's Children

Tom Burke MBE

Sitting on a hillside looking down into a dusty valley at a mounted possie led by the legendary lawman of the American Old West, Joe Lefors, heading towards him, the outlaw Butch Cassidy, somewhat perplexed and in wonder, asked his fellow outlaw, The Sundance Kid beside him, 'Who are those guys?' I once lived on Killester Avenue, and knowing a little about the history of Killester, I often asked myself a similar question about the old men who lived in Middle Third, Abbeyfield, The Demesne and The Orchard of the Killester Garden Village, 'who were those guys?'

They weren't always old men. As young men back in the 1920s and 30s, they were the lucky men who moved into the bungalows and cottages of Killester to build a new life. All of them though had one thing in common; they were mostly if not all, Irish veterans of Irish regiments and other British forces who fought in The First World War.

Under the Irish Land (Provision for Sailors and Soldiers) Act of 1919, up to 31 December 1923, a sum of £2,071,000 had been spent by the British government on land purchase and the construction of 1,508 houses in the Irish Free State and 408 in Northern Ireland, i.e. a total of 1916 houses.[1] Under British administration, building was initiated by the Irish Local Government Board and continued after Irish independence by the Irish Sailors and Soldiers Land Trust which had members appointed by the Dublin, Belfast and London Governments. The actual target set by the Trust up to the end of 1923 was 2,626 houses in the Irish Free State and 1,046 in Northern Ireland, i.e., a total of 3,672.[2] In order to complete its target of house building and indeed carry-on building, the Trust received from the British Government in March 1925, a final grant of £1,300,000 'over and above the sum of £2,071,000 which had been spent under the Act of 1919 in full and final settlement of all claims on his Majesty's Treasury.'[3] By March 1926, the Trust had completed 1,692 cottages in the Irish Free State of which 289 were built in Killester and 733 in Northern Ireland making a total of 2,425 cottages.[4]

Even if the Trust had reached its target of building cottages in the Irish Free State for the ex-servicemen and their families who lived there, sadly the target of 2,626 houses split between 150,000 Irish ex-servicemen who were demobilised from the British forces between 1918 and 1920 was inadequate and would leave thousands out in the cold.[5]

The piquet fenced bungalows of the Killester Garden Village were a far cry from the squalor of tenement dwellings that the vast majority of the Irish ex-service men came home to after the war. Out of a study sample of 2,150 WWI Irish ex-servicemen who lived in Dublin, the majority of them lived in the Dublin 8 and Dublin 1 postal districts, i.e., between the canals. Some 28 percent lived in Dublin 8, and 20 percent in Dublin 1. The balance was spread across other poor areas of the city. The highest number of Royal Dublin Fusiliers killed in WWI came from Dublin 8 at 28 percent and Dublin 1 at 14 percent.[6] Their average age on enlistment was between 21 and 25 and most were unskilled labourers. For example, William Breen from Abbeyfield served in the East Lancashire Regiment; before he enlisted at the age of 20, he was general labourer.[7] Essentially, they left the social and economic misery of Dublin tenement life to go to war in 1914 and those who survived returned to the same tenement life after the war. The same can be said for ex-servicemen from Cork, Limerick and the main towns throughout the Irish Free State. The secretary of the Royal British Legion in Cork stated in *The Irish Times* in November 1927 that, 'fifty percent of the cases which we have to handle are those of families from three to five in number who are absolutely destitute and how they manage to exist at all is a complete mystery.'[8]

There were streets within these tenement districts which had a high concentration of ex-servicemen and their families living as neighbours. For example, in Dublin 8, Francis Street, had 18 ex-service families and 11 families with men killed who served in the Dublin Fusiliers. In Dublin 1, Summerhill had 27 ex-service families with 9 Dublin Fusiliers men killed in the war. There were some ex-servicemen who lived in the same tenement house. For example, John Cunningham served in the Surrey Regiment, John Aherne served in the Leinster Regiment, Thomas Buckley in the Royal Irish Fusiliers, Patrick Bolger in the Royal Army Service Corps.

All four men and their families lived in a tenement house at No. 27 Golden Lane off Bride Street. Some 62 of the sample were homeless and lived either in The Iveagh Trust or Molyneux Hostel in Peter Street.[9]

Unemployment amongst ex-servicemen in Ireland was approximately four times higher than in Britain. In Dublin alone, one estimate put the number of unemployed British ex-servicemen in 1927 at 30,000.[10] The lucky ones got menial jobs such as porters or night watchmen. Men who worked in Jacobs and the Banks got their pre-war jobs back. Capt. Dick Burke from The Demesne who served in the 6th Royal Irish Regiment and was awarded the Military Cross returned to his job at the National Bank in Camden Street, Dublin.[11] About 540 men returned to their jobs in Guinness.[12] The economy of these tenement inner-city streets in the post war years was very much dependent on British military pensions and British funded charities.

The tragedy of unemployment, destitution and chronic lack of housing among ex-servicemen in the Irish Free State came to a head in 1927 when the Cosgrave government commissioned the Lavery Committee to examine allegations of discrimination in state employment schemes, housing and war pensions. An alleged employment discrimination example presented to the Lavery Committee was that of Daniel Slyne from Inniskeane, County Cork, who wrote to the

Lavery Committee on 23 January 1928. He enlisted in the Irish Guards in 1915, 'In response to a personal appeal by the British Postmaster General, Mr Herbert Samuels.' After the war he applied to get his job back in the Post Office. He was threatened and told that:

> ex-British soldiers were a thing of the past.... My chances of securing an established appointment are now nil, as with the change of government, vacancies will only be given to telegraph messengers who are ex-National Army men.[13]

Nothing much came of the Lavery Report. The British ex-servicemen and women fell between the two stools of British abandonment and Irish indifference or rejection. In November 1927, the Parliamentary Secretary to the Irish Ministry of Posts and Telegraphs, Mr. M. Heffernan, referred to the Irish ex-servicemen and women of WWI as being 'nobody's child.'[14]

The recession in the 1930s didn't help with unemployment in the Free State running between 90,000 and 100,000. It is important to note, that unemployed and destitute Irish ex-servicemen in the 1930s did not have the monopoly on the misery of unemployment and lack decent housing. They suffered the same fate as their unemployed fellow citizens.

However, unlike their fellow citizens who fell on hard times, the ex-service man or woman had many ex-service charity nets to catch them when they fell. One such net was The Joint Committee of The British Red Cross and The Order of St. John's Ambulance Brigade working from No. 14 Merrion Square, Dublin funded by the headquarters in London. It was a sort of St Vincent de Paul Society for British ex-service personnel formed in 1914. Their charity work was later taken on by The Not Forgotten Society who gave help to ex-servicemen and war widows with items such as clothing, furniture, fuel, medical and funeral expenses. Over the years, mainly between the 1920's and late 1960's thousands of Irish ex-servicemen applied to this society for charitable help. Some 94 ex-service residents of Killester availed of help from The Joint Committee.

An example of an ex-service man who received help from The Joint Committee was that of a veteran from Cork who had served in The

Royal Munster Fusiliers at Gallipoli in April 1915; was married and had six children. In 1944 and 1959, he applied to the Society for a suit of clothes and a pair of boots. A Society report noted:[15]

> This man is most deserving; he has a wife and 6 children under 15 years. He has a job as a temporary postman, not regularly employed. He finds it impossible even to get shoes for the children and he badly needs clothes himself. In fact, clothes or shoes for any member of the family would be most helpful.

Men who had suffered the effects of malaria or the loss of a limb such as Daniel Brady from Abbeyfield in Killester who served in The London Regiment were helped. Those who suffered shell shock or mental trauma collectively known as neurasthenia attributed to or aggravated by their war service presented some appalling cases of destitution to the Joint Committee. Following a visit by a committee volunteer in early February 1960 to a hostel in Cork, a report was sent to Merrion Street on an ex-Dublin Fusilier who gave his address as St Vincent's Hostel, Merchant's Quay, Cork. He was a tragic case of neglect and poverty. He was discharged from the Dublin Fusiliers on 1 March 1917 as 'a manic.' He had a son in England in an Industrial School and a daughter with the nuns in a convent who ended up in a mental hospital.

The report noted:[16]

> This man is a widower, aged 64 and a half years is a bad neurotic, he lives at the above hostel where he pays 11 shilling and 3 pence per week for bed and light and breakfast. He has to buy his other meals outside, I am sure he rarely has a decent meal.When interviewed, this pensioner was wearing the suit given to him in April 1959, he had no overcoat, and I'm sure he feels the cold very much. A warm overcoat would be of great comfort to him. He also needs a warm pullover, underclothing, and if possible, two size 4 shirts with collars attached. This is a very neurotic man and I'm sure he is not very popular with charitable organisations here. I believe he is blacklisted by Shanakiel Hospital. Despite his manner, I do feel he should be helped as no doubt all his failings are a result of his war service.

Despite the poverty and destitution the ex-service man suffered once a year each November, for as long as he physically could, donned his Sunday suit, took his medals from the cupboard to pin on his chest and marched off to meet his old comrades at the annual remembrance parade in the cities and towns of Ireland. For many years after the war ended, he faced challenges here too.

It must be remembered that the Irish ex-servicemen and women who served in the British forces during WWI came home to an Ireland that had politically changed. During their absence in the battlefields of France, Flanders and Gallipoli, a terrible beauty had been born. During the War of Independence, Irish ex-servicemen kept their heads down. Of the 196 civilians killed, executed, murdered, take your pick, by the IRA between 1919 and 1921 for alleged spying activities for the British forces, at a minimum, 97 were ex-servicemen; at a maximum there was 120.[17]

On Sundays before 11 November, Catholic ex-servicemen paraded to Mass at the Pro-Cathedral in Dublin.[18] After the Mass, they would parade across O'Connell Bridge to assemble at St. Stephen's Green where they would be dismissed.[19]

Killester veterans regularly attended the annual remembrance parades in Dublin. Departing from Killester Railway Station, while on their way to the annual remembrance services in the Phoenix Park, Killester veterans would hold a remembrance ceremony at Amiens Street (Connolly) Station before heading over to Beresford Place and assemble for the parade to the Wellington Monument in the Phoenix Park. Ex-service employees of The Great Southern Railway gathered at the Remembrance Tablet in Kingsbridge (Heuston) Station to hold a service.[20] Estimates of up to 40,000 would assemble in the Phoenix Park.[21]

The parades were contentious and often dangerous, ending in violence between Sinn Féin and the Gardai and indeed between Sinn Féin and the ex-servicemen. The parades presented an annual difficulty for the Cosgrave administration. However, it's important to state that men like Éamon de Valera and Sean Lemass were compromising and had no problems with the ex-servicemen and women remembering and honouring their dead comrades. However, they felt the occasion was being mis-used by the upper echelons of the British Legion to flaunt their latent allegiance to the past regime of British rule in Ireland. Typical republican sentiments in the late 1920s were expressed at a public meeting in Foster Place on 8 November 1927 when Sean Lemass told the crowd:[22]

> They had no objection to any section of the people honouring their dead but they did object to the alien section in their midst, whose headquarters were situated in the building opposite (pointing to Trinity College) availing itself of these occasions.

He believed that:

> The vast majority of the British ex-servicemen themselves objected to the demonstrations being used for such purpose…

The Vice President of the Dáil, Kevin O'Higgins, had every reason to commemorate the Irish dead of WWI as two of his brothers had served in Flanders. Michael was killed and Jack served as a Surgeon-Commander on Admiral Beaty's flagship. He expressed concern with the politicising of the remembrance weekends. He hoped:

> . . . there would be respectful admiration . . . for the men who went out to France and fought there and died there, believing that by doing so they were serving the best interest of their country.

However, he did not want to see, 'the eleventh of November being turned into the twelfth of July.'[23]

By the outbreak of WWII in 1939, the focal point for Remembrance of WWI in the Republic of Ireland was at The National War Memorial Gardens at Islandbridge. The removal of the annual remembrance parade from the centre of Dublin to the southern outskirts, defused much of the volatility of the occasion.

The concept of a First World War National War Memorial in Dublin dates back to a meeting held in the Vice-Regal Lodge on 17 July 1919.[24] The construction of The National War Memorial Gardens continued on during the change of government in 1932 from Cosgrave to de Valera who was, 'quite well disposed towards the memorial'. He wanted work on a memorial to be continued:

> . . . in the same spirit of toleration, cooperation and mutual good will which it had been inaugurated.

He had agreed to attend the opening in April 1939. However, the formal opening was postponed owing to the outbreak of WWII.[25] The cost of the project was shared between the Trustees of the Memorial and the Irish Government; the latter putting up £50,000 authorised in 1931.[26] This was an extremely kind gesture of the Irish government at a time of widespread economic depression, unemployment and the national finances in need of more important expenditure.

So who were those old men who lived in Abbeyfield, Middle Third, The Demesne and The Orchard of the Killester Garden Village? In their mid-twenties, more than likely poor, living in tenement or urban dwellings, unskilled or working as a casual labourer, enlisted into the British forces at the outbreak of WWI. Having survived the terror of that war, they came home to a hostile Ireland that had politically changed in their absence. In the immediate years after the war, many like Capt. Dick Burke faced life-long treatment of their physical and mental war wounds. Some faced hostility, discrimination, unemployment, life-long destitution and harassment in remembering their fallen comrades. Unlike thousands of their ex-service comrades who returned to the squalor of tenement life, the Killester ex-serviceman got lucky in getting a house and a space to rear his family and live out his life with dignity.

As the Irish ex-service men and women died off, mainly in the late 1960s, so too did their tragic story and place in the narrative of modern Irish history. They were forgotten. In a speech titled, '1916 and the Ethics of Memory' at The Glencree Centre for Peace and Reconciliation on 27 June 2015, President Michael D. Higgins quoted the French philosopher Paul Ricqeur who warned us of the dangers in forgetting the past.

As Ricqeur put it, 'to be forgotten is to die twice.'[27] And die twice they did; once on the Western Front and Gallipoli and once in Ireland.

As a young man growing up in Killester, I was never told their story. That being so, I can be forgiven for my ignorance once, but not twice, because unlike Butch Cassidy and The Sundance Kid, I now know who those guys were.

Tom Burke
28 April 2023

Endnotes

1. First Report of the Irish Sailors and Soldiers Land Trust for Period 1st January 1924 to 31st March 1926. (London: HMSO, 1927). p. 15.

2. Report Issued by the Committee on British Ex-Servicemen. (Dublin: The National Archives of Ireland, 1927-1928.). p. 18.

3. Ibid. p. 19.

4. Garrett, A., *Down through the Ages. The History of Killester Church and Parish.* (Dublin: Available from Killester R.C. Church., 1996.). p. 16. See also Aalen, F. H. A., *Homes for Irish Heroes: Housing under the Irish Land (Provision for Soldiers and Sailors) Act 1919,* and the *Irish Sailors' and Soldiers' Land Trust, The Town Planning Review.* Liverpool University Press 59, no. 3, (July 1998), p. 316. I would like to offer my sincere congratulations to Patrick Hugh Lynch for his pioneering work in researching the history of the Killester Garden Village.

5. Report Issued by the Committee on British Ex-Servicemen. Section 1.

6. Burke, Tom, 'Whence Came the Royal Dublin Fusiliers?', *The Irish Sword* XXIV, no. 98, Winter (2005), p.453.

7. Not Forgotten Society Archive. Card Index. (In possession of Mr Tom Burke).

8. Poppy Day Record at Cork – 'Unbelievable Amount of Destitution', *The Irish Times.* 24 November 1927.

9. Burke, Tom, 'All His Failings Are a Result of War Service.' The Quest of WW1 Irish Ex-Service Personnel for Help. (Seminar: The National Library of Ireland, 17 September 2022).

10. Ireland's Ex-Service Men, *The Irish Times,* 15 November 1927.

11. Burke, Capt. Richard – Dick, 6th Royal Irish Regiment. (Dublin: RDFA Archive Dublin City Library and Archive).

12. Roll of Guinness Employees Who Served in His Majesty's Naval, Military and Air Forces, 1914–1918. (Dublin: Arthur Guinness and Sons, 1920).

13. Report Issued by the Committee on British Ex-Servicemen. File F. 50.

14. Appeal for Whips to Be Removed, *The Irish Times*, 17 November 1927.

15. Not Forgotten Society Archive. (Dublin: RDFA Archive Dublin City Library and Archive). As of date of publication, these files are not available for public scrutiny.

16. Ibid. The file reference and name of the ex-serviceman is not for publication.

17. Dr. O'Ruairc Padraig Og, 'Spies and Informers Beware!': I.R.A. Executions of Alleged Civilian Spies During the War of Independence 1919 – 1921, https://www.theirishstory.com/2017/06/04/spies-and-informers-beware-ira-executions-of-alleged-civilian-spies-during-the-war-of-independence-1919-1921/#.YyhsVLTMK00. See also Leonard, Jane, Getting Them at Last. The I.R.A. and Ex-Servicemen. Revolution? Ireland 1917-1923. (Dublin: Trinity History Workshop, 1990), pp. 119-129.

18. Remembrance Day in Dublin. Ex-Service Men Entering the Pro-Cathedral Dublin., *The Irish Times* 5 and 12 November 1934.

19. Ex-Service Men's Parade in Dublin – Youths Attempt to Snatch Medal, *The Irish Times*, 5 November 1934.

20. The Railwaymen – Parades at Three Stations, *The Irish Times*, 13 November 1933.

21. Great Gatherings in Dublin and Belfast, *The Irish Times*, 13 November 1933.

22. The Union Jack Denounced – Republicans and Armistice Day – Threats at Dublin Meeting, *The Irish Times*, 9 November 1927.

23. Jeffery, K., *Ireland and the Great War* (Cambridge: Cambridge University Press, 2000), p. 114.

24. History of the Irish National War Memorial 1919 to 1937. RDFA/20/06. (Dublin: RDFA Archive Dublin City Library and Archive, 1939), p. 1.

25. Jeffery, K., p. 122.

26. History of the Irish National War Memorial 1919 to 1937, pp. 4-5. See also Jeffery, K., pp. 120-121.

27. Higgins, President Michael D, '1916 and the Ethics of Memory', Aras an Uchtarain.

Chapter 1

A Brief History of Killester Garden Village

Nigel Henderson

As this chapter relates to the estate built for war veterans, the natural starting point is the post-war era, although the Killester area has a long history. It is worth noting that before the outbreak of the Great War, Killester was a small rural village just over three miles from Dublin city centre. It had a population of less than 200 people and was characterised by small farms and labourer's cottages, with some detached properties on the Howth Road. All that was to change in the early 1920s and plans showing the layout of the estate in 1926 and in the 1930s are included at the end of the chapter.

Around the time of the Great War, Dublin Corporation had purchased Killester House and its estate and, from 1917, the Killester Farm Colony trained disadvantaged inner-city girls in modern market gardening and farming techniques under instructors approved by the Department of Agriculture. However, Killester House was destroyed in an arson attack by Republicans in the Spring of 1921.

In 1919, the Houses of Parliament in London passed the Irish Land (Provision for Sailors and Soldiers) Act which provided funding for the erection of cottages across Ireland for veterans of the Great War. By 1924, a total of 1,614 cottages had been provided for war veterans in the Irish Free State. The most ambitious project was to provide low density housing in a semi-rural district close to Dublin city centre but

Killester Farm Colony
(source: Irish Life Magazine)

distant enough from the hustle and bustle of inner-city life. The plan was to build bungalows to a high standard based on a concept developed by Ernest Albert Aston who had presented imaginative and radical proposals for a comprehensive plan for the city. Aston's proposals included a joint housing authority to coordinate extensive rebuilding in the inner city, the development of garden suburbs on the outskirts, and 'plantations for city workers in convenient rural areas' connected by rail and tram. Killester Garden Village was, in essence, a garden suburb plantation with large gardens for each dwelling and open spaces for recreation. As there were already similar agricultural training schemes at Marino, Fairview, and Clontarf, Sir Henry McLaughlin purchased the estate, 39 acres in total, and donated the land to the Irish Local Government Board for the creation of an ex-servicemen's estate. Although the bungalows were built by IFS Commissioner for Public Works, all the funding came from the British Exchequer.

Site clearance and construction commenced in 1921 and ex-servicemen were employed in the construction of the buildings, with some of the workers later being allocated bungalows in the estate. During the construction phase, the estate was visited by Local Government Board (LGB) officials and other interested parties. In September 1921, the Freeman's Journal reported that the High Sheriff of Dublin and the

President of Dublin Rotary Club visited some of the nearly completed bungalows. The following month, delegates attending the Industrial Development Conference in Dublin visited the site to inspect the buildings. The first occupants moved into the new estate, which was still a muddy building site, in 1922. The construction was completed in 1923, with 247 bungalows being available for war veterans in three zones – The Demesne, Middle Third, and Abbeyfield. Over the following ten years, Killester Garden Village expanded to comprise 289 dwellings, with two-storey semi-detached houses being built in The Demesne (2) and Abbeyfield (6), and two detached bungalows being built in Middle Third. In addition, 32 two-storey houses were built at The Orchard, where there was a mixture of six-house blocks (24 dwellings), a four-house block, and two sets of semi-detached houses.

Bungalow Styles and Facilities

In 1923, the estate was a mixture of detached bungalows and semi-detached bungalows in three styles.

The Type A bungalow was semi-detached and had a floor area of 675 square feet. The ground floor comprised a living room (178 square feet), a scullery kitchen (86 square feet), and a bathroom/toilet (35 square feet). The first floor had two bedrooms measuring 152 square feet and 110 square feet.

The Type G bungalow was also semi-detached and had a floor area of 841 square feet. The ground floor comprised a living room (172 square feet), a scullery kitchen (95 square feet), and a bathroom/toilet (44 square feet). The first floor had three bedrooms measuring 147 square feet, 118 square feet, and 83 square feet.

The Type E bungalow was detached and had a floor area of 1007 square feet. The ground floor comprised a parlour (121 square feet), a living room (162 square feet), a scullery kitchen (89 square feet), and a bathroom/toilet (55 square feet). The first floor had three bedrooms measuring 160 square feet, 107 square feet, and 80 square feet.

In 1923, the estate contained 38 Type A bungalows, 176 Type B bungalows, and 32 Type G bungalows. There were 73 dwellings in The Demesne (13 being detached), Middle Third had 49 dwellings (11 being detached), and Abbeyfield had 125 dwellings (3 being detached).

Unfortunately, the available documentary evidence does not facilitate breakdowns of the number of Type A and Type G bungalows in each of the sections.

In anecdotal accounts and some publications, it has been recorded that only officers were allocated dwellings in The Demesne, with Middle Third being for Warrant Officers and Non-Commissioned Officers, and Abbeyfield being for the other ranks. It has also been suggested that all the detached bungalows were allocated to commissioned officers. The research carried out by Michael Nugent and Nigel Henderson shows that, even in 1925, there was a mixture of officers, Warrant Officers, Non-Commissioned Officers, and other ranks occupying bungalows in each of the segments.

Killester Garden Village (289 dwellings)

The Demesne (75 dwellings)

- 19 detached bungalows

- 54 semi-detached bungalows

- 2 semi-detached two-storey houses

Middle Third (51 dwellings)

- 13 detached bungalows

- 38 semi-detached bungalows

Abbeyfield (131 dwellings)

- 3 detached bungalows

- 122 semi-detached bungalows

- 6 semi-detached two-storey houses

The Orchard (32 dwellings)

- 24 two-story houses in blocks of four

- 4 two-story houses in a block of four

- 4 semi-detached two-storey houses.

Armistice Day, 1923
(source: British Pathe Newsreel)

Armistice Day 1923

In reporting on the Armistice Day commemoration held at Killester on 11th November 1923, *The Irish Times* reported that 1,500 people, 600 being children, were living in Killester Garden Village. The newspaper also reported that 300 men formed up in military order, wearing their medals, and that many women and children wore the medals awarded to their dead – husbands, sons and fathers. The newspaper also noted that many of the men, including two buglers, wore the uniform of the Irish National Army.

The Legion Hall

The veterans living in the estate formed a branch of the British Legion and a former military hut was obtained and erected in the estate. It was a wooden structure and was destroyed in an arson attack in April 1928, with the Guards finding three empty petrol tins nearby. A report in *The Ballymena Weekly Telegraph* of 27th April recorded that the hall was used for concerts and social events and concluded:

> *. . . the wanton outrage is universally condemned. In the building were a piano and a billiard table, both of which, of course, were destroyed. The last* [final] *instalment on the piano was paid only a few days ago.*

Undeterred by this attack on the community, the Killester Branch of the British Legion erected a hall of brick construction, which was opened in 1932. Whilst its exact location of the original wooden hall is not known, it might have been at the site of the current building, which is still known as the Legion Hall. Whilst the new hall was primarily a

British Legion Hall

place where the veterans could mix and reminisce, it was also used for community events. In 1942, James Martin of 124 Abbeyfield, in his role as Secretary of the Killester Branch of the British Legion, applied for a 'Public Dance Licence', as required by the Public Dance Halls Act of 1935. The hall was used for the annual children's Christmas party and for family events to mark milestones, such as significant birthdays and wedding anniversaries. With the passage of time, the British Legion branch closed and the hall later became the home of a martial arts club. However, the opposition to the proposed demolition of the hall demonstrates that it still holds a place in the affection of the descendants of the Killester veterans.

Difficulties in Killester

The estate was not perfect and there were a series of letters published in the Dublin newspapers highlighting problems in Killester Garden Village and complaining about the excessive rents. In a letter published in the *Dublin Evening Telegraph* on 6th December 1923, one correspondent reported that the houses were, miles away from civilisation, where you could not procure a box of matches, should you forget them in town.

He went on to say that the estate had been without a water supply for three weeks and that people had to wade through mud to get to their homes. He also said that after four each evening, 'no woman dare pass this way (without escort) without being molested' because no provision had been made for street lighting. The letter recorded, 'Oh how I sigh for a back kitchen in the slums and civilisation.' His statement that, 'Those houses that were built by funds raised voluntarily' highlights a lack of knowledge on his part. It was not until October 1924 that consideration was given to providing street lighting in Killester.

December 1923 also featured a court case in which the LGB sought to have James J. Fitzsimmons ejected from the bungalow that he had been allocated in April 1922 as he had failed to observe the conditions of the tenancy agreement. James Fitzsimmons had not only sub-let part of the bungalow but he had also placed a caretaker in possession of the premises. District Justice George P. Cussen granted the LGB possession of the bungalow.

In June 1924, Mr Frederick Owen Roberts, the Minister for Pensions in Ramsay McDonald's Labour government, visited Killester at the invitation of the Legion of Irish Ex-Servicemen. He was accompanied by Sir Henry McLaughlin and other dignitaries. During the visit, he inspected 130 veterans on parade, and, during the march past, he took the salute from a platform over which the Tricolour and Union Jack flew. The purpose of his visit was to gain first-hand information

Mr F.O. Roberts, British Minister of Pensions, chatting with ex-servicemen's children. Major Evans and Major Lefroy are joyous spectators.
(source: Rob Buchanan)

with regard to the conditions surrounding the Pensions administration and to determine whether there was any justification for the complaints which had reached him. Mr Roberts also toured the estate and had high praise for the residents and the improvements they had made to their gardens and interiors.

Trust and Tenants

The relationship between the occupants and the ISSLT was often fractious and resulted in several court cases being taken against the Trust by groups of residents and individual residents.

As a result of increased rents and evictions, the Killester Tenants' Rights Association (KTRA) was formed, with Daniel Patrick McAuliffe of 41 Middle Third being elected as its President. On 18th April 1930, the Saturday Herald reported on a meeting of the KTRA at which a motion was passed, stating that

> *. . . the cottages are the property of the tenants and consequently are free of all rent charges*

and

> *We base our claim on the promises made by the British Government through its agents during the War.*

The ISSLT had recently issued Robert George Butler of 38 Abbeyfield with an eviction notice as he owed £30 in rent, which equates to approximately £1,580 in current terms. As a consequence of this meeting and resolution, Robert Leggett of 100 Abbeyfield, Robert Butler of 38 Abbeyfield and James Haugh initiated a class action in the High Court against the ISSLT which was to have widespread ramifications for ex-servicemen across the Irish Free State. The tenants sought a High Court declaration that:

> *. . . the Irish Sailors and Soldiers Land Trust was not entitled to accumulate a reserve fund for the purpose of building new cottages out of the proceeds of the cottages provided for the accommodation of men who served in any of His Majesty's naval, military or air forces in the late war or for any purpose other than the repair and the insurance of the existing cottages, and to pay the debts and expenses of managing the Trust.*

They also sought to have it declared that:

. . . the existing rents are excessive and should only be sufficient to cover necessary outlay.

Whilst this court case was under way, the eviction notice against Robert George Butler was suspended. In August 1933, the Supreme Court of the Irish Free State ruled in favour of the litigants and newspapers reported that the Chief Justice, Gerald Fitzgibbon QC, in giving judgement, said:

The Irish Sailors' and Soldiers' Land Trust was to provide houses in which the victims of the Great War could live during their lives. In his opinion, there was no power whatsoever to charge those objects of this trust any rent for such residences.' (Source: *Belfast Weekly Telegraph*, 5th August 1933).

In the aftermath of the Supreme Court decision, Hugh Callan, who was allocated 119 Abbeyfield in August 1923, initiated a personal claim against the ISSLT in the courts. Whilst serving a prison sentence for fraud, Hugh Callan had been ejected from his bungalow, which was then allocated to Joseph McCann in January 1927. Hugh Callan took the ISSLT to court in 1934 claiming repayment of the rent that he had previously paid and sought to have Joseph McCann evicted and himself reinstated as the tenant. His case was unsuccessful.

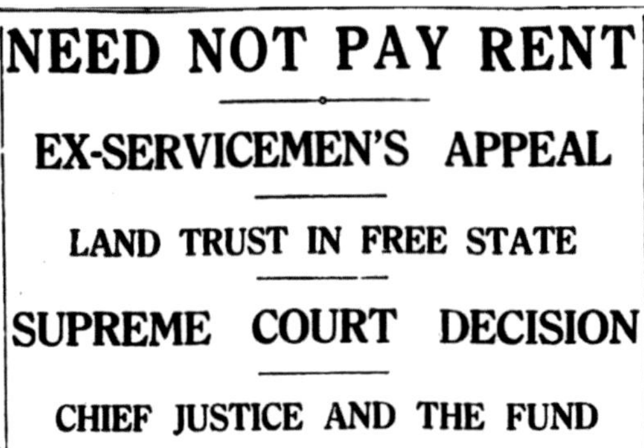

Belfast Weekly Telegraph, 5 August 1933

In 1939, Peter Markey of 85 Abbeyfield and Daniel Patrick McAuliffe of 41 Middle Third were part of a group of ex-servicemen from various parts of the Irish Free State who brought a court case against the ISSLT to determine who was responsible for executing repairs on the ISSLT properties.

There were also court cases in which the tenants challenged the levying of rates.

In 1952, the Houses of Parliament in London passed a law which granted the ISSLT the right to sell its properties to sitting tenants, whether the tenant was an ex-serviceman or the widow of an ex-serviceman. Daniel Patrick McAuliffe, as Honorary Secretary of the Land Trust Beneficiaries Association, took the ISSLT to court to determine whether it had the right to sell its properties in the Republic of Ireland.

These latter cases were unsuccessful.

Facilities and Transportation

The Great Northern Railway, whose tracks separated The Demesne from Middle Third, established a station at Killester in December 1923. This facility not only gave improved access to the city centre but opened the opportunity for family day trips to places like Howth and Malahide. From 1923, residents of the estate were providing transport to the city centre and, in 1924, Kathleen Gilbert of Clontarf started the Old Contemptible Omnibus Company, many of whose drivers came

Transport

from Killester Garden Village. The name comes from Kaiser Wilhelm's description of the original British Expeditionary Force as 'General French's contemptible little army.' The Kaiser's sneer became a badge of honour amongst British troops. The company's initial route ran from Eden Quay to Abbeyfield, but it later introduced routes to Philipsburgh Avenue, Howth, and Dollymount. The company used 26-seater and 32-seater buses manufactured by Guy Motors in Wolverhampton. In July 1925, the Dublin United Tramway Company initiated a bus service (Route 43) from Eden Quay at O'Connell's Bridge to Killester.

As the majority of the Killester residents were Catholic, the lack of a local church was a great inconvenience. In 1924 Very Reverend Father James McCarroll was appointed as Parish Priest of Coolock, Raheny and Killester. He recognised the need for a new church and the foundation stone for St Brigid's Church was laid on 5th July 1925. The estimated cost was £12,000 (approximately £588,450 in current terms) and the construction work was to be carried out by local residents. St Brigid's Church was solemnly blessed and dedicated by His Grace the Most Reverend Doctor Edward Byrne, the Archbishop of Dublin, on Sunday, 26th September 1926. At the ceremony, the Superintendent of Killester Garden Village, Captain De Lacey, seconded a motion by Mr Hugh Kennedy for the opening of a subscription list to assist in the clearance of any outstanding costs.

Sunday Independent, 19 and 26 September 1926

Irish Press, 7th August 1933

Whilst there were long-established shops on the Howth Road, several Killester residents established shops within the community at Middle Third. They were called the 'tin shops', because the roofs were made of corrugated iron. James Joseph and Ellen Mary Byrne of 49 Middle Third ran a grocery and general merchandise shop which became a lively meeting place for members of the community. John Patrick Banahan of 27 Middle Third had a butcher's shop, Joseph McCabe of 59 Abbeyfield ran a bookshop, and John McCrystal of 42 Middle Third provided a shoe making and repair service. The local Post Office and shop was run by Mrs Mary Ellen Donnellan of 43 The Demesne, following the death of her husband, Bernard in 1928. The local chip shop, which also became a very popular meeting place for young and old alike, was run by a war veteran called O'Rourke, but as there were several residents with that surname, it is difficult to link to a specific family. There was also a sweet shop run by a lady called Carmel, but the absence of a surname makes it impossible to link to a specific family. The tin-roofed shops supplied the community with just about everything they needed and are still fondly remembered by the descendants of the Killester families.

Competitions

The residents of Killester Garden Village took pride in their gardens, whether they were beautifying them with flowers or supplementing their income by growing fruit and vegetables. Residents were frequently listed as winners in local and city-wide competitions. In July 1931, Thomas and Christina Millner of 112 Abbeyfield were the overall winners in the Garden Competition organised by the Killester Branch of the Dublin Garden and Window Box Guild. The runners up were Patrick McCormack of 83 Abbeyfield, Richard Lindsay of 28 Middle Third, and Daniel Thomas Brady of 20 Abbeyfield.

Irish Press, 7th August 1933

Saturday Herald, 12th September 1939

In August 1933, the first Annual Flower Show and Garden Fete was held in the grounds of St Brigid's Schools and was hailed as a success by *The Irish Press* which reported a large attendance and a high standard of exhibits. The opening ceremony was performed by the Lord Mayor, Alderman Alfie Byrne TD, who was introduced by the Reverend J Kenny of Killester Parish Church. There were also competitions for home-made bread, knitting, crochet work, and needlework. There was a competition for Best Bunch of Wild Flowers which children under 15 could enter. First place was taken by E Lindsay of 28 Middle Third, with Nora and James White of 70 Abbeyfield taking second and third places. The following is a full list of the prize-winners:

The Milners won the 'Herald' Championship Cup in 1936 and they won the Darker Memorial Cup for 'Best Front Garden' in a competition organised by the Killester Horticultural Society and the Killester Branch of the National Garden Guild in 1939.

In September 1928, James Walsh won the substantial sum of £3,333 (approximately £261,000 in today's terms) in a newspaper football competition. John James Timmins of 32 The Orchard was a winner in the annual singing contest of the Irish Roller Canary Club in January 1953.

In October 1969, Mrs Elizabeth Arkins of 20 Middle Third won second place in a Home-Made Jam Competition organised by the Dublin Gas Company in its theatre on D'Olier Street. Elizabeth's prize was a gas fire.

Mrs Eileen Doran of 29 Abbeyfield was the winner of the Boland's Biscuits Popularity Poll in 1961, receiving an Austin 7 Mini car as her prize.

Editor's note: On the following pages are maps showing the Killester Garden Village plan in 1926 and in the 1930s.

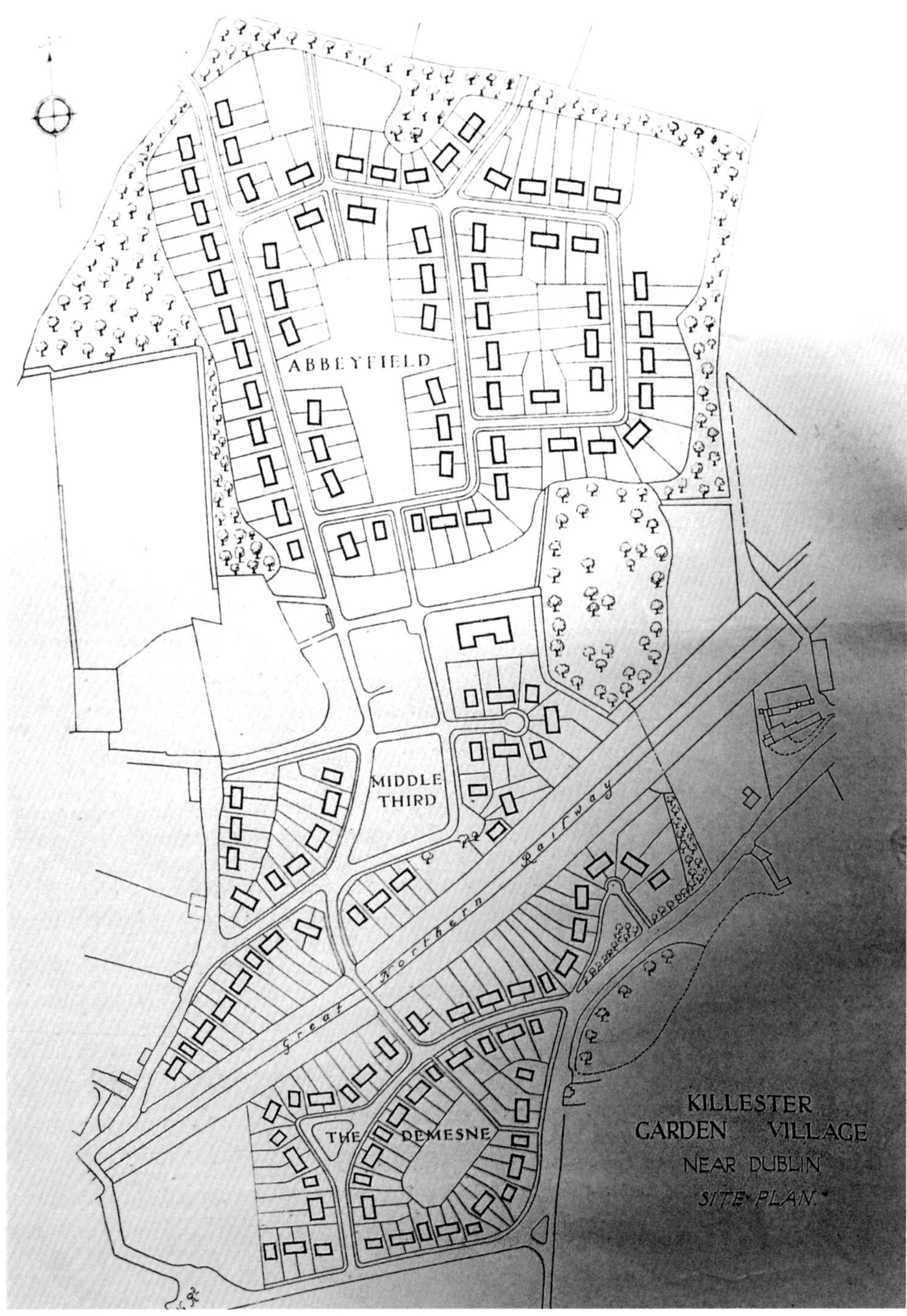

Killester Garden Village plan in 1926 (source: Irish Sailors' and Soldiers' Land Trust Report, 1924-1926)

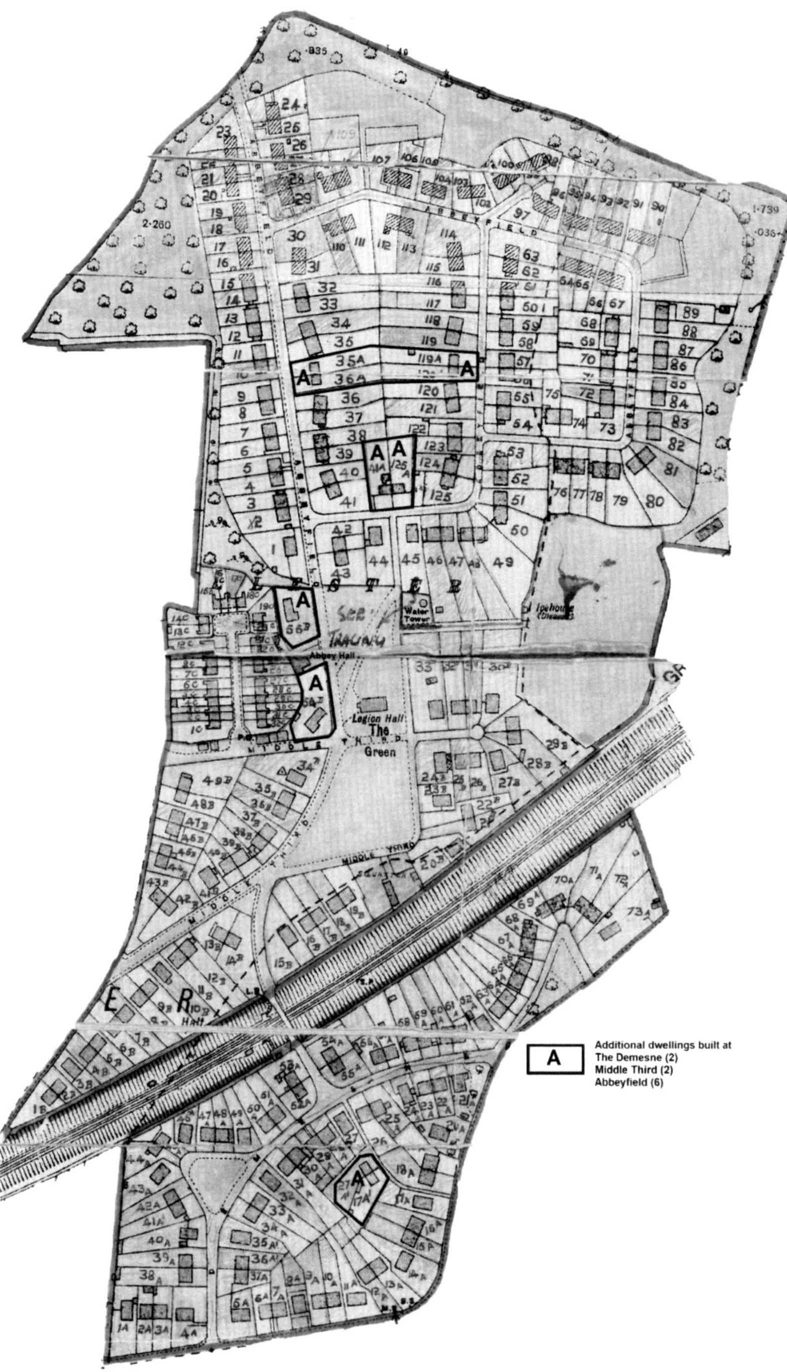

Killester Garden Village plan in the 1930s (source: believed to be from a later Irish Sailors' and Soldiers' Land Trust Report)

Chapter 2

Research Process Overview

Nigel Henderson and Michael Nugent

The Killester Garden Village Commemoration Committee engaged Michael Nugent (ww1researchireland) and Nigel Henderson (History Hub Ulster) to undertake research on the Great War Veterans and to write up biographies for this publication. The following provides an overview of the process by which the research was performed.

The earliest record of the occupants of the bungalows in The Demesne, Middle Third, and Abbeyfield was the 1926 Thom's Directory and this source was the basis for the list of men to be researched. The Thom's Directory generally only recorded the Surname and the initial of a forename (and occasionally not even an initial), which presented a major difficulty for the researchers. During the research, it was found that the Thom's directories sometimes contained typographical errors in surnames and incorrect forename initials. Another difficulty was that several of the 1926 occupants left Killester Garden Village within five years. Where sufficient information could not be identified for the 1926 occupant, the researchers extended the research to a subsequent occupant. A few men who were allocated a bungalow in one section of Killester Garden Village subsequently moved to one of the other sections – for example, Lieutenant Osmond Thomas Taylor moved from Abbeyfield to The Demesne in 1945.

Anecdotal evidence and some published sources record that each of the three sections of the original Killester Garden Village were allocated to veterans on the basis of rank groupings – i.e. The Demesne for commissioned officers, Middle Third for non-commissioned officers, and Abbeyfield for other ranks. However, the researchers very quickly determined that this was not the case, with each section having veterans from each of the rank groupings in 1926, and probably from 1922/1923.

As the Thom's Directory did not usually have full forenames, the initial identification of the occupants involved using Irish Genealogy and the Irish Newspapers Archive to identify matches in the Registers of Deaths for surname and initial, where the place of residence/death was the associated Killester Garden Village address. The newspaper archives were also searched for death notices and obituaries to identify the names of the man's wife/widow and place of burial. The researchers then used the information to backtrack to identify marriage and birth details and military service details.

The searches of the newspaper archives also frequently turned up additional information relating to the occupants, e.g. accidents involving the occupants or members of their families, winners of competitions, etc.

The research performed by Tom Burke on the records of the 'Not Forgotten Society' enabled the researchers to identify military details for some of the occupants, as did the interviews with descendants that were carried out by Jan Glover. The latter also turned up nuggets of information about occupants, for example, their occupations or trades. Another valuable source of background information on the occupants came from descendants who contacted the project through the Killester website, Facebook page, and Twitter.

In addition, searches for family trees and searches on the Dublin Cemeteries Trust and www.findagrave.com websites enabled the researchers to prepare more rounded biographies for veterans and their families. The family trees on Ancestry frequently included photographs of the veteran and/or family and the findagrave website frequently included photographs of gravestones, from which the death dates for a veteran's wife/widow were obtained. Whilst death notices referred to 'Dean's Grange Cemetery', this burial ground is now called

'Deansgrange Cemetery'. However, the historic name has been used in the occupant biographies.

The census returns held by the National Archives of Ireland provided information on where the veterans lived before the war, the names of their parents, occupations, and spouses. This facilitated the identification of birth and marriage details.

Information relating to military service was primarily identified from searches on various genealogy websites – Ancestry, FindmyPast, Fold3, and Forces War Records.

Medal entitlement documentation identified when the veteran went to a Theatre of War, the units with which he served, and when he was discharged from military service. For those men with pre-war army service, it was possible to identify the medals awarded and associated campaign clasps. Some of the veterans allocated bungalows in Killester had been awarded medals for service in conflicts in South Africa and India.

The attestation/service and/or discharge/pension documentation provided pre-enlistment occupations, next-of-kin details, as well as details when men were wounded or taken sick. These documents often pointed to service prior to the Great War and, in particular, in the Second Anglo-Boer War (1899-1902).

The register of admissions to medical facilities provided details on when a man was hospitalised, the reason, the location(s) at which he was treated, and the period of treatment.

For those men who were discharged as being no longer physically/medically fit for war service, the Silver War Badge Register (see below) provided enlistment dates, reason for discharge, and the discharge date. In some cases, the register recorded the age at discharge.

The Western Front Association's archive of pension cards provided information on the disability pensions awarded, including allowances for wives and children, where appropriate. The cards also recorded the claimant's post-discharge home address and, where the veteran pre-deceased his wife, details of the widow's forename and address.

For those Killester veterans who had been awarded gallantry medals, *The London Gazette* website was used to identify when the award was announced and, where relevant, the citation of the deed for which the award was made.

Whilst most of the occupants of Killester had served in the army, some had served in the Royal Navy or the Royal Naval Reserve and the National Archives website was used to obtain records for these men.

Several of the men allocated bungalows at Killester had been taken prisoner during the war and the online records of the International Committee of the Red Cross were accessed, which provided details of when and where they were captured, where they were held prisoner, birth dates, and next-of-kin details. Some of the ICRC records included details of transfer to internment camps in neutral counties and/or repatriation to the United Kingdom.

A visit to the National Archives resulted in access to the files for several commissioned officers who were allocated bungalows in Killester Garden Village. During the visit, ISSLT files relating to some of the occupants were accessed, with photographs being taken of original documents.

As several of the Killester veterans continued in army service after the war, the registers of the Irish regiments that were disbanded in 1922 provided valuable information.

Some of the Killester men signed up for the National Army in 1922 and the Army Census Records for that year also provided valuable information.

The biographies include reference to two military terms which necessitate explanation.

As military personnel were being discharged as being no longer medically or physically fit for war service, the Silver War Badge was instituted in 1916 and retrospectively awarded those who had been discharged from the start of the war. The inscription on the badge read, 'For King and Empire ~ Services Rendered' and, in most instances, accompanied by a personalised King's Certificate which included the following inscription, 'Served with honour and was disabled in the Great War. Honourably discharged on ...'.

During the negotiations that followed the temporary Armistice signed in November 1918, it was necessary to maintain a military presence on the Western Front. However, as the British military authorities did not want to have large numbers of men stationed in France and Belgium, the Class Z Army Reserve was created in December 1918. Soldiers who were transferred to this reserve force were liable for immediate recall to active service if the negotiations had failed and fighting re-commenced. Fortunately, this scenario did not materialise, and the Class Z Army Reserve was abolished in March 1920.

The Theatre of War recorded as 2A on Medal Index Cards covered engagements in the Balkans and one of the areas in which Irishmen served can be spelt as either Salonika or Salonica – the biography chapters use the Salonika spelling.

As a consequence, the range of sources accessed and searched has resulted in some very detailed biographies. Unfortunately, for some of the Killester occupants, the paucity of available records has resulted in less expansive biographies.

The Killester Garden Village Commemorative Committee wishes to extend its thanks and appreciation to the two researchers and to everyone who has provided input to the project.

RAHENY.   1865

Killester Garden City. Demesne.	Middle Third-street.	
1 McGowan, H.	1 Collins, M.	26 Smith, P.
2 Mates, C.	2 Hickey, D.	27 Phelan, R.
3 Duffley, P.	3 McGrath, T.	28 Mayne, A.
4 Crosbie, J.	4 Kerton, G.	29 McDowell, J. E.
5 McDonald, C.	5 Byrne, D.	30 Doyle, R.
6 Sadler, G.	6 Walker, A.	31 Murray, F.
7 Pailey, A.	7 Browne, J.	32 Byrne, Jas.
8 Nolan, J. H.	8 Kerns, D.	33 Pattison, G.
9 Bushe, Wm.	9 Costello, J.	34 Trebble, A
10 Derwin, C.	10 Dunne, J.	35 Bickford, C.
11 Garbutt, —	11 Raddy, F.	36 Parkes, R.
12 Graham, Wm.	12 Clarke, S.	37 Fitzgerald, P.
13 Carroll, J.	13 Healy, R.	38 Butler, R.
14 Storey, W.	14 Caird, J. D.	39 Lawrence, R.
15 Keegan, J.	15 Buchanan, Dr.	40 Clarke, V.
16 Galvin, Wm.	16 Kelly, M.	41 Cox, J.
17 Holt, C.	17 Gibson, Wm.	42 Keane, Mrs. M.
18 McDonald, M. J.	18 Murphy, C.	43 Murphy, J.
19 Lockhart, V.	19 Kirwin, H.	44 Woodman, A. J.
20 Liddy, J.	20 Farrell, P.	45 Keating, M.
21 De Lacey, J. C., Capt.	21 Larby, R.	46 Aston, R.
22 Austin, Wm.	22 Quigley, T.	47 Cummins, —
23 Nolan, M. J.	23 O'Regan, P.	48 Walsh, J.
24 Stack, P.	24 Croke, T.	49 Halpin, W. J.
25 Byrne, P.	25 Chapman, E.	50 Lawrie, E.
26 Downes, J.	26 Browne, G.	51 Garrahan, J.
27 Sharkey, J. C.	27 Banahan, J.	52 Harvey, J. R.
28 Gaffney, E.	28 Lindsay, E.	53 Waters, J. A. H.
29 Barnwell, Wm.	29 Tracey, Wm.	54 Pope, T.
30 Dale, F.	30 Pelham, G.	55 Woodhead, —
31 Lee, T.	31 Foster, —	56 Devereux, J. W.
32 Hursey, A.	32 Phoenix, C.	57 Hankey, F.
33 Mullins, G.	33 Mahon, R.	58 McCam, P.
34 Ratcliffe, B.	34 Osborne, G.	59 Reddin, R.
35 Rich, T.	35 Hendrick, P.	60 Reevey, C.
36 Wills, R. T.	36 Griffin, P.	61 Breen, W.
37 Nicholason, R.	37 Woods, R.	62 Halpin, J.
38 Fagan, J.	38 Keenan, J.	63 Prestage, T.
39 McDowell, E.	39 Nulty, J.	64 Cooney, T.
40 Earls, T. C.	40 Kennedy, J.	65 McCarthy, —
41 Merrigan, G.	41 Dowling, —	66 Johnston, J.
42 Flood, J.	42 McCrystal, J.	67 Reynolds, P.
43 Donnellan, B.	43 McGuirk, M.	68 O'Donnell, P.
44 Cobbledick, Wm.	44 Tracey, F.	69 McGrath, —
45 Meehan, J.	45 Somerville, Wm.	70 Allen, —
46 Makeling, A.	46 Stanley, Wm.	71 O'Brien, P.
47 McClean, W. D.	47 Byrne, John	72 McMullen, J.
48 Senier, T.	48 Forde, A.	73 Burrett, —
49 Flanagan, N. A.	49 Byrne, James	74 Taylor, —
50 Adair, E.		75 Browne, J.
51 Ward, J.		76 Brennan, —
52 Byrne, Wm.		77 Fletcher, —
53 Higginbotham, —		78 Kinahan, T.
54 Barrington, P. J.	Abbeyfield.	79 Phelan, J.
55 Kinsella, M.	1 Callan, J. J.	80 Murphy, —
56 Mahon, D. C.	2 Atkin, L.	81 O'Connor, —
57 Heffernan, T.	3 Higgins, J.	82 Collins, —
58 English, A.	4 Keogh, R.	83 McCormick, —
59 Wayte, W.	5 Brennan, J.	84 O'Loughlin, P.
60 Leech, S.	6 Desmond, J.	85 Markey, —
61 Phelan, T.	7 Gillard, T.	86 Graham, —
62 Ingrim, R.	8 Griffiths, B.	87 Masterson, J.
63 Breen, G.	9 Ridge, S.	88 Cannon, —
64 Black, E.	10 O'Rourke, J. J.	89 Darker, J.
65 Lynch, T.	11 Murphy, P.	90 Marks, —
66 Field, R.	12 Naughton, J.	91 Duffley, J.
67 Cavanagh, M.	13 O'Rorke, C.	92 Farrell, —
68 Brady, P.	14 O'Rourke, M.	93 Murphy, —
69 Long, C.	15 Martin, P.	94 Mullett, —
70 Kearns, R.	16 McGrane, Wm.	95 Eavans, —
71 Lambe, L.	17 Bowen, J.	96 Ryan, —
72 Switzer, W.	18 Burrows, Wm.	97 O'Reilly, H
73 Pyke, R.	19 Jennings, Wm.	98 Bridge, —
	20 Farrelly, —	99 Doyle, C.
	21 Farrell, J.	100 Leggett, R.
	22 Wallace, J.	101 Church, —
	23 Clifton, J.	102 Nolan, —
	24 Hyland, P.	103 Whelan, J. J.
	25 Proudfoot, C	104 Briggs, W. E.

1866   COUNTY DUBLIN DIRECTORY.

105 Coady, Wm.	112 Milner, T.	119 Callan, H.
106 Stafford, J.	113 Lomansey, P.	120 Connor, J.
107 Wade, T.	114 Redmond, W.	121 Harrison, W.
108 Warnock, J.	115 Lawlor, F.	122 Freeney, Wm.
109 Drea, P.	116 Cummins, W.	123 Nolan, K.
110 Murphy, J.	117 McKenna, J.	124 Martin, J.
111 Smith, F.	118 Sharpe, F.	125 O'Kane, B.

1926 Thom's Directory

Chapter 3

Occupants of The Demesne

At the completion of construction in 1923, The Demesne consisted of 73 dwellings, with twenty-one being Type G detached bungalows and the remainder being semi-detached bungalows. As there were two types of semi-detached bungalows built in Killester Garden Village, it is not possible to determine whether the semi-detached bungalows built in The Demesne were Type A, Type G, or a mixture of both.

Two additional dwellings were added to The Demesne in the early 1930s –occupants were recorded for 27a in 1931 and 17a in 1932. These were semi-detached two-storey houses, the latter becoming 220A Howth Road in 1938.

In the mid-1930s, The Demesne bungalows fronting onto Howth Road were given new addresses. In the 1938 Thom's Directory, Numbers 1 to 21 The Demesne had become 188 to 230 Howth Road and Numbers 62 to 73 The Demesne had become 232 to 254 Howth Road.

1 The Demesne/188 Howth Road – Hubert McGowan

Hubert was born on 18th May 1896 at 19 Naples Street, Belfast, the eldest child of David and Clementine McGowan, née Pattinson. Both David and Clementine had been born in England, and at the time of the birth, David was employed as a musician. Shortly after Hubert's birth, the family moved to Dublin, resident in Tranquil Lane in 1901 and at Quarry Lane, Glasnevin in 1911. At that time, Hubert was still in full time education. It is believed that Hubert enlisted in the Royal Field Artillery later in the war and was attached to No 428 Battery, Royal Field Artillery, with the regimental number 970306,

Hubert McGowan
1 The Demesne
(source: Jan Glover)

and serving in the rank of Bombardier. On 4th July 1922, he married Teresa O'Toole at Aughrim Street Roman Catholic Church. At that time, Hubert was in employment as a civil servant and was resident at Woodville, Cabra Road, Dublin. Hubert became active in the Ex-Servicemen's Tenants Rights Association (Eire) and was appointed Vice-Chairman in 1938. Hubert died aged 65 on 13th August 1961 at Jervis Street Hospital, Dublin, of cancer. Following a service at St Brigid's, Killester, Hubert was buried at St Fintan's Cemetery, Sutton (Section J Grave 108). Teresa McGowan was living at 188 Howth Road, Killester, when she died on 3rd December 1976, aged 83, and is buried alongside her husband in St Fintan's Cemetery. Also buried in the plot is Edward McGowan who was living at 188 Howth Road, Killester, when he died on 28th November 2011, aged 85.

2 The Demesne/190 Howth Road – Claude Augustus Mates

Claude was born on 24th September 1891 at 14 Grand Canal Place, Dublin, the eldest son of George and Annie Mates, née Lucas. George Lucas was in employment as a storekeeper. The 1901 Census shows the family as resident at York Street, in the Mansion House area of Dublin and by 1911, they had moved to Denmark Street. At that time, Claude was employed like his father as a painting contractor. Shortly after this he enlisted in a cavalry regiment, the 5th (Royal Irish) Lancers, regimental number 3658. Based at Marlborough Barracks, Dublin, he married Mary Christina Flanagan at Dublin Registrar's Office on 24th March 1913. Following the outbreak of War, Claude embarked for France on 15 August 1914. He served throughout the war and transferred to the Army Reserve on 15 March 1919. A holder of the 1914 or 'Mons' Star, Claude's medals were sent to his home, 'Georgina', Howth Road, Killester. His wife Mary died in childbirth at the family home aged 33, on 31st August 1927. The following year on 15th September 1928, Claude remarried, marrying Emily Mills at St John the Baptist Parish Church, Dublin. A report in the *Irish Independent* of 8th April 1957 stated that two of Claude's daughters, Elizabeth and Olive, were emigrating to Canada and that Claude and his wife hoped to follow them.

3 The Demesne/192 Howth Road – Patrick Joseph Duffley

Patrick was born at Ramore, Elphin, County Roscommon, on 23rd October 1895, the son of Patrick and Ellen Duffley, née Neary. At the time of his birth Patrick's father was a National School Teacher. His name does not appear on either the 1901 or 1911 Census, however it is known that he enlisted in the 4th (Queen's Own) Hussars, a cavalry regiment, on 15th August 1912, when he was aged 16. He was issued with the regimental number H9219. Following the outbreak of war, he embarked for France on 15th August 1914. He served throughout the war attaining the rank of Corporal and was awarded a gallantry certificate by the Commander 2nd Division for brave conduct at Sirault, northwest of Mons, Belgium, on 10 November 1918, the day before the Armistice. He was demobilised on 17th September 1919 in the rank of Corporal. On demobilisation, his address was 3 Seaview Terrace, Baldoyle. On 26th April 1922, he married Mary Hand at Baldoyle Roman Catholic Church. At the time of the marriage, Patrick was working for a gas company and was resident at Howth. An initial occupant of 3 The Demesne, Patrick died aged 85 on 18 February 1977 and is buried at St Fintan's Cemetery, Sutton.

4 The Demesne/194 Howth Road – John Crosby

John was born on 17th November 1883 at Navan, County Meath, the son of Patrick and Alice Crosby, née McArdle. At that time, Patrick McArdle was employed as a land steward. No entry is available for John on the 1901 Census however it was known that he was living at Ranelagh, Dublin, in 1906. On 28th November 1906, he married Margaret Kane at St Andrew's Roman Catholic Church, Dublin. At that time, John was employed as a motor mechanic and was resident at 21 Ranelagh Road, Dublin. The 1911 Census shows John resident with his wife and three children at Milltown Road, Rathmines. At that time, he was employed as a chauffeur. John enlisted in the Army on 9th December 1915 and, given his trade, unsurprisingly joined the Army Service Corps Mechanical Transport, with the regimental number, M2/201812. John embarked for service in Salonika, and remained there until he was honourably discharged with the Silver War Badge on 15 June 1918, due to general paralysis. A medical examination in January 1919 assessed that John was 40% disabled and he was in receipt of a pension of £2 per week for himself and 29 shillings and sixpence for his wife and four dependant children. John's medals were forwarded to his home address, which was given as 37 Killester Gardens, off Howth Road, Raheny. John died aged 71 on 23 March 1955 at his home address of heart failure.

5 The Demesne/196 Howth Road – Charles MacDonald

Charles was born on 1st October 1883 at Ulverston, Lancashire, the son of James and Elizabeth MacDonald. The 1901 Census of England shows him as resident with his family at 65 Moorhey Street, Oldham, Lancashire. Later that year on 15th September, he enlisted in the Manchester Regiment, being issued with the regimental number 6984. He made the military his career, serving in Singapore, St Helena, South Africa, and India, and by 1911 held the rank of Sergeant. On 9th August of that year, he married Delia Woods at St Mary's Chapel, Oldham. Following his marriage, he extended his service to complete 21 years. Charles embarked for Gallipoli with 11th battalion Manchester Regiment on 18th July 1915 and in June of the following year was awarded the Distinguished Conduct Medal, the citation reading, 'For consistent good work and devotion to duty.' By that time Charles held the rank of Temporary Regimental Sergeant Major. He was also Mentioned in Despatches in November 1916 for excellent duty. On 23rd April 1918, Charles was awarded the Military Cross, published in *The London Gazette* of that date, the citation reads:

> For conspicuous gallantry and devotion to duty under heavy shell fire. When the regimental aid post was being heavily bombarded and the medical officer and several stretcher-bearers had been killed, he at once set to work to reorganise the post and assist in moving the wounded. This warrant officer's gallantry and coolness undoubtedly saved many of the wounded. He also displayed great courage in getting ammunition and rations up to the line.

The following month on 27th May, he was appointed to a temporary commission as Second Lieutenant and was attached to 1st Battalion East Yorkshire Regiment. Following the Armistice, Charles served for a period of six months with the Auxiliary Division, Royal Irish Constabulary, before resigning his post and enlisting again in the Manchester Regiment in April 1921 for 90 days Emergency Service. In October 1922, he wrote to Infantry Records to obtain details of his service to enable him to apply for a house. At that time, he was employed in a Post Office Sorting Office. Charles was allocated the bungalow at 5 The Demesne/196 Howth Road, which he named, 'Wood Villa'. He died at St Mary's Hospital, Phoenix Park, Dublin, on 2nd October 1969 aged 86 of pneumonia.

6 The Demesne/198 Howth Road – George James Sadlier

George was born on 6th August 1881 at 17 New Lodge Road, Belfast, the son of George and Mary Ann Sadlier, née McDonald. George senior was a soldier at the nearby Victoria Barracks, Depot of the Royal Irish Rifles. George enlisted in the Royal Irish Rifles at Belfast in June 1897 aged fifteen and a half and was issued with the regimental number 5124. He served in South Africa from 1897 to 1900 whilst attached to the regiment's 2nd battalion. No campaign medals are recorded for his service in South Africa. On 9th January 1903, he married Mary Jane Skey at St Patrick's Chapel, Donegall Street, Belfast, and by 1911, the couple had six children. In 1909, George had successfully applied to extend his service to 21 years and the 1911 Census shows him in the rank of Sergeant, attached to 2nd battalion at Dover Castle, Kent. Service in India from 1912 to 1914 followed and following the outbreak of war, George embarked for France on 6th November 1914, and sustained a gunshot wound

George James Sadlier
6 The Demesne
(source: Ancestry family tree)

to the abdomen and liver on 9th April 1916. In the same year, he was awarded the Long Service and Good Conduct Medal.

Following convalescence, George was attached to the regiment's 5th (Reserve) battalion at Holywood, County Down as an Instructor, in the rank of Acting Company Sergeant Major. On 13th December 1918, George applied to be discharged from the Army, having served for 21 years. He was discharged on 12th May 1919, his address on discharge being given as 5 Tyrone Street, Belfast. By 1921, George had moved to Victoria Road, Clontarf, and having been assessed as 20% disabled was in receipt of a pension of five shillings and sixpence per week for himself and ten shillings and eightpence for his wife and seven eligible children. George obtained employment as a clerk at the Ministry of Pensions and moved into 6 The Demesne/198 Howth Road in 1924. He died aged 62 at his home address on 15th December 1943, the cause of death given as, 'cholesterolosis and gall stone as the result of old war wounds.' Following a funeral service at St Brigid's, Killester, George's remains travelled by train to Belfast for burial.

7 The Demesne/200 Howth Road – Arthur Patrick Paley

Arthur was born on 13th March 1887 at Lark Lodge, Naas, County Kildare, the son of David and Ellen Paley, née Disney. David Paley

Arthur Patrick Paley
7 The Demesne
(source: Ancestry family tree)

was a respected veterinary surgeon at The Curragh. Aged 17 and a shop assistant, Arthur enlisted in the Royal Artillery on 21st June 1894, and was issued with the regimental number 4519. Between 1894 and 1906, Arthur had completed postings to Malta, Bermuda, Halifax Nova Scotia, and British Columbia. By 1900, he held the rank of Sergeant and in the same year married Alice Ward at St George's, Bermuda. In a military reorganisation in 1902, he was attached to 58th Company, Royal Garrison Artillery and in the same year, he extended his service to complete 12 years. In 1905, he further extended his service to complete 21 years. A further posting to Bermuda followed and Arthur returned to the United Kingdom in February 1914.

Tragically, Alice died in November 1914, leaving Arthur with eight children, the youngest being three years old. Arthur remained in the United Kingdom in a training capacity until 1917, when he embarked for the Western Front, serving there with 532 Siege Battery, Royal Garrison Artillery. Arthur was discharged from the Army on 1st February 1920 on his own application in the rank of Regimental Sergeant Major, having completed over 25 years' service. Following discharge, Arthur applied for a disability pension, citing neurasthenia, deafness, and septal deviation. He was assessed as 40% disabled and was awarded eleven shillings per week for himself and seven shillings and a penny per week for five eligible children. Arthur gained employment as a Harbour Constable at Dublin Port and remained working until his death at Grangegorman Mental Hospital of heart failure on 19th September 1941, aged 54. Following a funeral mass at St Brigid's Killester, Arthur was buried at Glasnevin Cemetery.

8 The Demesne/202 Howth Road – John Henry William Nolan

John Henry William Nolan was born on 21st July 1879, at Corbally townland, Nenagh, County Tipperary, the eldest son of Robert and Kate Nolan, née Ralph. Robert Nolan was a Constable in the Royal Irish Constabulary. In the course of the marriage the couple were to have 14 children. John enlisted in the Royal Army Medical Corps on 14th September 1906, regimental number 726, and he was resident at 10 John Street West, Dublin, on 19th June 1911, when he married Annie Kinsella, at the Church of St Agatha, Dublin. At the time of the marriage, John's occupation was recorded as 'accountant'. No occupation is listed for Annie who was from Clonmore Terrace in the city.

John Henry William Nolan
8 The Demesne
(source: Ancestry family tree)

41

John next appears in available records on 7th June 1915 when he returned from working as a clerk for the RAMC in the Gold Coast, Africa. He then embarked for active service on 22nd July 1915. The medal index card for John Nolan records his first theatre of war as '2a' which covered engagements in Greek Macedonia, Serbia and Bulgaria, generally called the Salonika Campaign. However, as the British troops were only deployed to that part of the Balkans after attacks were launched by the Central Powers in October 1915, it is probable that John Nolan participated in the Autumn 1915 phase of the Gallipoli Campaign before being re-deployed to Salonika. The Salonika campaign was notable for extremes of heat in the summer and cold in the winter. Twenty times more men fell ill and died through sickness, than were killed or injured by enemy action. Unsurprisingly, John contracted malaria during his time on active service and, although he continued to serve until May 1919, when he was discharged with the Silver War Badge due to sickness. This badge was issued to those who had served with honour and had been discharged due to wounds or sickness and was accompanied by a commemorative scroll.

John's address on discharge was given as 9 Clonmore Terrace, Dublin. He was assessed as 40% disabled from debility following malaria and was in receipt of a pension of 16 shillings for himself and 14 shillings and twopence for his four children, Gladys Edna, Violet Maud, Letitia Kathleen, and Desmond Clarence. Two further children, Patricia and Irene, were born in the 1920s. John was allocated the bungalow at 8 The Demesne/202 Howth Road and tragically, Annie died on 25th May 1927 at Dr Steeven's Hospital, Dublin, of kidney disease. John married Julia Anna O'Brien on 19th July 1930 at Kilgarvan, Kenmare, County Kerry. Their only son, Vincent, was born on 11th February 1932. John died of old age aged 84 on 3rd October 1963 at his home and is buried in Glasnevin Cemetery.

9 The Demesne/204 Howth Road – William Bushe

A Londoner, William was born on 5th December 1881 at 3 Victoria Place, Maine Street, Bermondsey, the son of John and Henrietta Bushe, née Fenlon, and was baptised at Christ Church, Bermondsey, on 5th March 1882. William enlisted in the Royal Army Medical Corps on

22nd February 1901 at Aldershot. He served in South Africa from March 1901 until April 1905, during which time he extended his service twice, firstly to complete eight years and then, in 1905, to complete 12 years. For his service, he was awarded the Queen's South Africa Medal with a clasp for the Cape Colony, and the King's South Africa Medal for 1901 and 1902. On his return from active service, William married Mary Margaret Barratt on 20th November 1905 at the Registrar's Office Dublin. In 1909, in the rank of Sergeant, William again extended his service to complete 21 years.

William Bushe
9 The Demesne (204 Howth Road)
(source: Ancestry family tree)

The 1911 Census of Ireland indicates that William, Mary, and their three children were resident at 183 Old Youghal Road, Cork. At the outbreak of war, William was promoted to Staff Sergeant and embarked for the Western Front on 15th August 1914. He was Mentioned in Despatches in June 1915 and remained on active service until February 1919, by which time he was an Acting Sergeant Major. William was awarded the Long Service and Good Conduct Medal in April 1919 and in June of that year was awarded the Meritorious Service Medal for long and valued service. William was discharged from the Army having served for 21 years on 28th February 1922. By that time, his service number had changed in an Army renumbering scheme to 7245047. On discharge, his address was 39 Ard-Righ Road, Arbour Hill, Dublin. A disability pension claim indicates that William was suffering from defective vision and varicose veins, aggravated by his war service. William was allocated the bungalow at 9 The Demesne but had left Killester by 1932. The 1939 England and Wales Register shows William and Mary resident at 115 Abbey Road, Hampstead, London. At that time, William was employed as a clerk in the War Office. William died in January 1973 aged 91 at Marylebone, London, and is buried at Camden, London.

10 The Demesne/206 Howth Road – Christopher Joseph Derwin

Christopher, known as Christy, was born on 16th December 1884 at Hollybank, Drumcondra, the son of James and Kate Derwin, née Garaghan. The 1901 Census of Ireland shows Christy as resident with his parents and siblings at Drumcondra Road, Dublin. At that time, Christy, then aged 16, was still in full-time education. By 1911, Christy was resident with Margaret Lawler at Hutton's Lane, Dublin, and Christy was employed as a timekeeper in a timber yard. The 1911 Census indicates that Christy and Margaret had had three children, one of whom was still alive. Alice Maud had been born in 1906 and had died on an unknown date. Mabel had been born in 1908 and had died of bronchitis on 21 November 1910 aged two. Records indicate that Christy and Margaret married on 19th March 1912 at St Mary's Pro-Cathedral, Dublin.

Following the outbreak of war, Christopher enlisted in the South Lancashire Regiment with the regimental number 50701. In September 1917, he transferred to the Labour Corps with the corps number 364707 as he was unfit for front line duty. He was attached to 361st (Reserve) Employment Company, which was based at Tipperary. In September 1918, he was court-martialed for desertion, and was found not guilty. Christopher was demobilised on 24th November 1919. He applied for a disability pension citing gastritis and defective teeth and was initially awarded a pension of 15 shillings per week. This was changed in 1923 to 12 shillings per week for himself and 12 shillings and fivepence for Margaret and one dependant child. Christopher gained employment as a cabinet maker and was resident at 65 Killester Gardens in 1923 when a son, Francis Frederick died aged 16 months on 2nd April of Pneumonia. Around that time, Christopher was awarded a grant of £50 from the Not Forgotten Association, which he repaid. Margaret died at the couple's home at 206 Howth Road aged 59 on 16th March 1950, of coronary thrombosis. Christopher survived her for 16 years and died at Leopardstown Park Hospital aged 79 of a brain haemorrhage on 8th January 1966. The couple are buried at Section CB Grave 22 in Kilbarrack Cemetery, Sutton.

11 The Demesne/206 Howth Road – Arthur William Garbutt

Arthur was born early in 1887 at Aston, Warwickshire, the son of William Henry and Fanny Maria Garbutt, née Burgess. At the time of the birth, William Henry Garbutt was employed as a journalist. The 1901 Census shows William as resident with his parents and younger sister Edith, at 35 Weatheroak Road, Yardley, Birmingham. By 1911, Arthur had moved to Ireland and was resident as a boarder in the home of Ralph Mecredy, a medical student. At that time, Arthur was one of four boarders in the house who all identified as Buddhist. Like his father, Arthur was in employment as a journalist, taking up positions with *The Limerick Chronicle* and then *The Dublin Evening Mail* before becoming the Music Critic for *The Irish Times*, writing under the nom de plume, 'Obligato'.

On 10 July 1913, Arthur married Marion Jane Cooper at St Stephen's Green Presbyterian Church. At that time, Arthur was resident at Victoria Street, Dublin, whilst Marion was a florist from Ranelagh Road in the city. A son, Nevil Jack was born on 25th November 1915 at 10 Holles Street, Dublin, where Arthur and Marion were then resident. Military records indicate that Arthur enlisted in the Royal Garrison Artillery with the regimental number 169478. He did not enter a theatre of war prior to 1916. His medal records indicate that he served with Base Details of the RGA, indicating that he was most likely in a support role and would have been involved in bringing ammunition and supplies to batteries at the front. Records indicate that Arthur served until after the Armistice and on returning to civilian life, resumed his employment as a journalist with *The Irish Times*. Arthur and Marion were allocated the bungalow at 11 The Demesne, which Arthur named 'Elgar' after the composer, Sir Edward Elgar. In addition to his journalistic skills, Arthur was also an accomplished musician. Never in great health, Arthur's conditions including failing eyesight and rheumatism deteriorated, and he died aged 47 at his home on 18th December 1933 of chronic rheumatism and arthritis. Following a funeral service at Clontarf Parish Church, Arthur was buried at St Fintan's Cemetery, Howth (Section G Grave 29).

12 The Demesne/210 Howth Road – William Henry Graham

It is believed that William was born around 1889 in Dublin, his father also being named William Henry. A bottle-maker by profession, records indicate that William married Elizabeth Oliver on 11th March 1907 at St Matthews Church of Ireland, Dublin. William enlisted with the Royal Irish Fusiliers on 18th June 1913, being posted to 1st battalion with the regimental number 11266. He embarked for the Western Front with his battalion on 22nd August 1914 and saw much action in the early months of the war. He sustained serious gunshot wounds to the throat and was discharged from the Army with the Silver War Badge for honourable service being no longer fit for Military Service, on 20th May 1915. On discharge his address was given as 17 St Michael's Hill, Dublin. William was assessed as being 50% disabled and was in receipt of a disability pension of 20 shillings per week, reduced in 1922 to 16 shillings per week for life. William was employed as a house painter when he moved into 12 The Demesne. He died aged 65 at his home address on 21st December 1954 of gastritis and arteriosclerosis, his wife Elizabeth being present at the death.

13 The Demesne/212 Howth Road – Francis Patrick Colgan

No identifiable records can be found for the initial occupants of 13 The Demesne, named as J Carroll in the 1926 Thom's Directory. The 1932 Directory names the occupant as W Colgan. This man has been identified as Francis Colgan. Francis was born in Dublin around 1873 and his father's name was Patrick, but his mother's forename and maiden name are unknown. He enlisted in the Royal Dublin Fusiliers at Dublin on 14th October 1891. Prior to enlisting, he had been employed as a groom. Issued the regimental number 4512, Francis served with the regiment's 1st battalion in the East Indies and having completed eight years' service, was transferred to the Army Reserve on 14th January 1899. On 17th September 1899, he married Margaret Ivory at St Michan's RC Church, Dublin. At the time of the marriage, Francis was resident at 128 Guinness Buildings, Dublin. On 9th October of the same year, he was recalled to duty and was posted to South Africa as the Boer War had commenced. He served in South Africa until 12th March 1902 and on return home was discharged on 13th October 1903.

For his service in South Africa, he was awarded the King's South Africa Medal with clasps for 1901 and 1902 and the Queen's South Africa Medal with clasps for the Orange Free State, The Transvaal, Tugela Heights, the Relief of Ladysmith, and Laings Nek.

The 1911 Census shows Francis and Margaret as resident at house 27 Great Charles Street, Dublin, with three surviving children. At that time, Francis was employed as a postman. Following the outbreak of war on 4th August 1914, Francis enlisted six days later and, on this occasion, joined the Army Service Corps with the corps number SS/652. The SS prefix to his number indicates that he was attached to a Supply Section. On enlistment, Francis claimed to be 35 years of age when he was in fact 41. He served on the Western Front from 5th October 1914 and by January 1915 was in the rank of Acting Sergeant. At that time, he was court-martialed for drunkenness whilst on active service and having been found guilty, was reduced to the rank of Private. Francis was compulsorily transferred to 6th battalion Royal Dublin Fusiliers on 20th October 1917 and travelled to join them in Egypt. His regimental number at that time was 30912. Eight weeks later, he was transferred to 1st (Garrison) battalion Royal Irish Regiment with the regimental number 20659. Francis served with them in Egypt until after the Armistice and was demobilised on 11th March 1919.

On demobilisation, his character was described as, 'very good.' Francis returned to Dublin and resumed his occupation as a postman, his address at that time being 14 Belvedere Road, Dublin. He applied for a disability pension and was assessed as 30% disabled and was awarded a pension of eight shillings and thruppence per week for himself and seven shillings and thruppence per week for Margaret and five eligible children. Francis resided at 13 The Demesne/212 Howth Road from around 1930 and as a postman, was attached to Pearse Street Post Office. His son Joseph, as a member of Malahide Red Cross patrol, was commended in August 1944 for rescuing two girls from the sea at Malahide who were in danger of drowning. Francis died aged 86 at Leopardstown Park Hospital on 3rd July 1958, of myocardial degeneration. He is buried at Glasnevin Cemetery.

14 The Demesne – William Story

William's surname is spelt Storey in the relevant Thom's Directories. Born at Francis Street, Wexford, on 30th December 1890, William was the second son of William and Catherine Story, née Cullen. William senior was employed as an iron moulder at the time of the birth. By 1901, the family had moved to Dublin, and William was resident with his parents and five siblings at Arnott Street in the city. The 1911 Census shows William as resident as a boarder with the Eustace family at Bloomfield Avenue, Dublin. At that time William, then aged 20, was employed as a clerk in the Canadian Government Office. William enlisted with the South Irish Horse on 7th September 1914 with the regimental number 74019. He did not embark for active service until 19th May 1917, when he joined his unit attached to the 16th Divisional Train.

As the South Irish Horse was dismounted in September 1917 and redesignated as infantry, William joined the majority of his comrades in the 7th (South Irish Horse) battalion Royal Irish Regiment, being issued with the regimental number 25832. On 8th February 1918, he was promoted to the rank of Lance Corporal and in June of that year was transferred back to the cavalry, joining the Corps of Hussars and reverting to his original regimental number with the prefix H to denote his attachment to the Hussars. On 10th July 1918, William returned to Ireland and was posted to the South Irish Horse at Cahir, County Tipperary. William was demobilised on 16th February 1919. On demobilisation, he gave his address as 4 Welbeck Avenue, Liverpool, his father at that time being resident in the city. On 29th June 1921, William married Mabel Christina Dowling at St Mark's Parish Church Dublin. At the time of the marriage, William was resident at Great Brunswick Street, Dublin and Mabel was the daughter of a Master Butcher from 5 St Lawrence Road, Clontarf. The marriage register indicates that William had resumed his employment with the Canadian Government. A son, John Cullen Story, was born on 4th March 1922. At that time, the couple were resident with Mabel's parents at St Lawrence Road, Clontarf. Allocated the newly built bungalow at 14 The Demesne, William and his family resided there until William's death aged 81 on 25th September 1972. He died at St Mary's Hospital, Phoenix Park, of bronchopneumonia.

15 The Demesne/216 Howth Road – John Keegan

John was born around 1879 and enlisted with the Royal Garrison Artillery in 1896. After a period of service, he returned to civilian life and became a Post Office employee. At the outbreak of war, he re-enlisted with the Royal Garrison Artillery with the regimental number 20005. He embarked for active service on the Western Front on 25th September 1914 with 6th Siege Battery. John served throughout the war, rising to the rank of Sergeant. Following demobilisation he resumed employment with the Post Office, remaining in this employment until 1934. He died at Leopardstown Park Hospital, Stillorgan, on 4th July 1939 aged 60 of valvular disease of the heart.

16 The Demesne/218 Howth Road – William Patrick Flynn Galvin

William was born on 7th July 1874 at the Workhouse, Strokestown, County Roscommon, the son of Mary Flynn. On 18th August 1897, William married Mary Collins (known as Molly) at St Laurence O'Toole Roman Catholic Church, Dublin. At the time of the marriage, William's occupation is given as a civil servant. His father's name was given as Daniel Galvin, a Constable in the Royal Irish Constabulary. The 1901 Census records William and Mary as resident at house 3 in Drishogue, Millmount Place, Drumcondra. At that time, they had three children under the age of two and William was employed as a telegraphist in the GPO. By 1911, the family was resident at St Malachy's Road, Glasnevin, and had eight children. William is recorded as being a telegraph clerk in the GPO, Dublin. He enlisted towards the end of 1914, and given his occupation, unsurprisingly joined the Royal Engineers' Signallers, with the regimental number 75360. He embarked for active service in Egypt on 1st August 1915 and served past the Armistice, being demobilised on 15th April 1919. He applied for a Disability Pension and was assessed as being 30% disabled due to the effects of malaria. He was awarded a pension of 12 shillings per week. Allocated the bungalow at 16 The Demesne, Mary tragically died there aged 49 on 29th June 1924 of tuberculosis. William resided there until his death aged 64 at his home on 6th March 1938 of myocardial degeneration. Following a service at St Brigid's Killester, he was buried at Glasnevin

Cemetery. A son, James Galvin, served with the National Army, with the service number VR4795.

17 The Demesne/220 Howth Road – Charles William Holt

Charles was born on 17th April 1892 at Roanmore, Waterford, the son of William and Jessie Caroline Holt, née Stacey. At the time of the birth, William Holt was a Soldier. The 1901 Census of Ireland shows Charles as resident with his mother and siblings at 4 Government Terrace, Letterkenny, County Donegal. By 1911, the family had moved again to house 11 Tully West, County Kildare. At that time, Charles was an unemployed book-keeper. His father, William, was a foreman in the Army Ordnance Department. On 8th June 1915, Charles married Florence Annie Mills at St John the Baptist Church of Ireland, Drumcondra. At that time, Charles had enlisted in the army and was a Private in the Army Cyclist Corps. It is not known when Charles embarked on active service however, he was attached to XVIII Corps Army Cyclist Battalion, when he received burns and was hospitalised in August 1917. He served until after the Armistice and then, in the early 1920s, took up a post with the Irish Sailors and Soldiers Land Trust. He remained in this role until his death at his home address on 18th July 1957, aged 65 of heart disease and cancer. He is buried at St John the Baptist Cemetery, Clontarf. He was predeceased by his wife, Florence, who had died on 13th May 1954.

17A The Demesne/220A Howth Road – Robert Charles Taylor

The son of a Royal Irish Constabulary Constable, Robert was born in Kilkelly townland, County Mayo on 23rd July 1898. His parents were Robert and Mary Jane Taylor, née Cooke. Robert senior had enlisted in the Royal Irish Constabulary in 1882 (Force number 50590) and retired on 1st January 1914. The 1901 Census saw Robert with his family resident at Croghan townland, County Roscommon and by 1911, the family had moved to Connaught Street, Athlone, County Westmeath. Robert obtained a commission as Temporary Second Lieutenant in the Royal Irish Regiment and was posted to the Regiment's 2nd battalion on the Western Front on 15th June 1918. He also served with the 3rd battalion Royal Dublin Fusiliers at Grimsby as part of the Humber Garrison. Following discharge, Robert followed his father and was appointed as a Constable in the Royal Irish Constabulary (force number 70383) on 9th March 1920. Initially posted to Kinlough, County Leitrim, he then served with the Dublin Castle Clerical Company until he was discharged on disbandment of the Force in 1922. On discharge, Robert was awarded a pension of £54 per year.

On 29th March 1922, he married a widow, Margaret Theresa Murray, née Gaffney, at St Paul's Roman Catholic Church, Dublin. Margaret (known as Peg) was a Doctor's daughter from Carrick-on-Shannon, County Leitrim. She had previously been married to Samuel Murray, a Customs Officer from Clones, County Monaghan. Samuel had died aged 32 in 1919. Following the marriage, the couple were resident at Summerville Park, Rathmines when Robert enlisted in the National Army (Service number VR 2890) in August 1922. The National Army Census of 1922 shows Robert in the rank of Sergeant, stationed at The Curragh. Robert and Margaret moved to the newly built house at 17A The Demesne in the early 1930s and at that time Robert was employed by the Revenue Commissioner's Office. Margaret died aged 52 on 30th July 1947 at the Mater Hospital of intestinal obstruction. Robert continued residing at his home until his death aged 70, on 16th February 1969 at St Laurence's Hospital of respiratory and cardiovascular failure. The couple are buried at Glasnevin Cemetery.

18 The Demesne/222 Howth Road – Robert Murphy

The resident listed in the 1926 Thom's Directory was an M J McDonald however, no identifiable records can be found for this man. The occupant by 1932 was listed as a J Murphy. The correct forename was Robert. Robert was born on 14th March 1879 at Cappowhite, County Tipperary, the son of Robert and Mary Ann Murphy, née McConnell. Robert senior was a Constable in the Royal Irish Constabulary (force number 4058) stationed in Tipperary. He retired on 1st April 1891 and died four months later on 8th September at Corn Mow Street, Dublin. Robert enlisted in the Royal Inniskilling Fusiliers on 23rd July 1895. He claimed to be 18 but was in fact 16. He was posted to the regiment's 1st battalion (regimental number 5009) and saw service in South

Robert and Bridget Murphy
18 The Demesne (222 Howth Road)
(Source: www.findagrave.com)

Africa from November 1899 to February 1903 when he was transferred to the Army Reserve. For his service in South Africa, he was awarded the Queen's South Africa Medal and the King's South Africa Medal with clasps for 1901 and 1902.

On 7th January 1906, he married Bridget Dunne at Aughrim Street Roman Catholic Chapel. At the time of the marriage, Robert was a carpenter and was resident at 58 Great Charles Street. Bridget was the daughter of a carpenter from 12 Mount Temple Road. The 1911 Census shows the couple as resident at Ostman Place, Arran Quay, Dublin, with three surviving children. As a reservist, Robert was mobilised at the outbreak of war in 1914. He reported to the Regimental Depot at Omagh and was posted to 2nd battalion, retaining his regimental number. He embarked for the Western Front on 12th September 1914 and sustained a gunshot wound to the left forearm on 6th November 1914 at Ploegsteert, Belgium. The wound was severe enough that Robert was assessed as being no longer fit for military service. He was discharged with the Silver War Badge on 7th May 1915, having served in excess of 19 years with the Inniskillings.

On discharge, Robert's address was given as The Lodge, Claremount House, Claremount Avenue, Glasnevin. Allocated the bungalow at 18 The Demese around 1930, Robert resided there with his family. On the afternoon of 26th August 1939, Robert was at home when he disturbed a burglar, attempting to force the gas meter. Robert grappled with the man who attempted to stab him with a screwdriver. With limited power in his left arm, Robert shouted for help and was assisted in restraining the burglar by 16 years old Evelyn Lockhart, the daughter of his next-door neighbour, Victor Lockhart who was a Guard. The burglar, Patrick Byrne, was sentenced to three month's imprisonment and Evelyn Lockhart was commended for her actions by the judge. Bridget

Murphy died aged 70 at Adelaide Hospital on 22nd November 1954 of a heart attack. Robert survived her for four years and died at Meath Hospital on 21st July 1958 aged 79, of a spinal tumour. The couple are buried in the cemetery of St John the Baptist, Clontarf.

19 The Demesne/224 Howth Road – Victor Stanley Clement Lockhart

Victor was born on 4th October 1897, at Rathfarnham, County Dublin, the son of William James and Mary Ann Lockhart, née Dunphy. At the time of the birth, William Lockhart was a retired coastguard. Tragically, William died aged 63 in January 1901 and the 1901 Census of Ireland shows Victor as resident with an elder brother, Leslie, as boarders with the Loftus family at Knockeen, County Wicklow. The 1911 Census shows Victor as resident with the same family as a boarder. Victor enlisted in the Irish Guards on 22nd August 1913 and was attached to the regiment's 1st battalion with the regimental number 4525. Victor served throughout the war, rising to the rank of Sergeant and was discharged on 24th March 1919 with the Silver War Badge, as being unfit for further military service due to sickness. Victor applied for a disability pension and was assessed as being 20% disabled due to trench fever. He was awarded a pension of eight shillings per week.

On 13th August 1919, Victor married Johanna Scanlon at St Werburgh's Parish Church, Dublin. At the time of the marriage, Victor was employed as a caretaker and was resident at Chancery Lane, Dublin. Victor and Johanna were allocated the bungalow at 19 The Demesne, and Victor was appointed to An Garda Siochana in the 1920s and posted to Clontarf. Just after midnight on 18 October 1928, an armed robbery was carried out by three men at Corbett's Public House, 105 Howth Road. Victor responded to the report and after speaking to the publican, found three men hiding in a field. He pursued them and they opened fire on him with

Victor Lockhart
19 The Demesne (224 Howth Road)
(source: Garda Review)

revolvers, but Victor rushed and disarmed them and marched them at gunpoint to the Garda station. For his actions, Victor was awarded the Scott Medal for Valour, the highest bravery decoration available in the force and was also presented with a cheque by residents of Clontarf. In March 1935 whilst on foot patrol at Grafton Street, Dublin, Victor and another Guard were shot and wounded by two men, Victor receiving a gunshot wound to the leg. Victor resigned from the force on 6th March 1941, having served for over 16 years. During the Second World War it is believed that Victor served in the Royal Air Force, but not on active service in a theatre of war. In 1950, Victor and his wife emigrated to the United States, settling at 623 North Hobart Boulevard, Los Angeles, California, Victor becoming a naturalised US citizen in October 1951. No record of Victor's date of death is available.

20 The Demesne/228 Howth Road – James Thomas Liddy

James was born on 13th July 1881 at Enniskillen, County Fermanagh, the son of Benjamin Thompson and Isabella Liddy, née Elliott. The 1901 Census of Ireland shows him as resident with the Clarke family, also natives of Fermanagh, at Strand Road, Clontarf. At that time, James aged 16 was employed as a clerk. By 1911, James had moved with the Clarke family to Annesbrook Terrace, Clontarf, and was in employ-

James Liddy
20 The Demesne (228 Howth Road)
Source: Ancestry family tree

ment as an assistant solicitors clerk. The following year on 24th August, James married Rose Spicer at Sandford Parish Church, Dublin. Rose was the daughter of an army pensioner from Elm Park Avenue, Ranelagh, Dublin. It is not known exactly when James enlisted in the army however, he did not embark for a theatre of war before the beginning of 1916. He was appointed to the Machine Gun Corps and issued with the regimental number 36882. He served until after the Armistice and was demobilised on 30 May 1919. Allocated the bungalow at 20 The Demesne, James and Rose had moved to England by the late 1930s when the resident was a Robert Murphy. James died aged 81 at Ware, Hertfordshire, in October 1962.

21 The Demesne/230 Howth Road – James Christopher De Lacy

The Killester Garden Village had an on-site Supervisor who acted as a contact point for local issues. A retired Captain, who had been appointed as a Peace Commissioner by the Government of the Irish Free State, his name was James Christopher De Lacy and he lived at Number 21 Demesne, which had become 230 Howth Road by 1938.

James De Lacy was born in Cape Town, South Africa, on 12th December 1873 and was a shoemaker when he enlisted with the Royal Irish Rifles in London on 19th December 1887 at the age of 14, being posted to 1st Battalion. He served in Egypt, Malta, and India between 1888 and 1899. He served with 2nd Battalion in the Second Anglo-Boer War from October 1899 until February 1903, being awarded the Queen's South Africa Medal with the Cape Colony and Orange Free State clasps and the King's South Africa Medal with the 1901 and 1902 clasps. He was stationed at Richmond Barracks Inchicore, Dublin, when he married Rosaline Kearns of Wicklow on 16th February 1904 at St James' Roman Catholic Church. In the 1911 Census, James was a Colour Sergeant in the Royal Irish Rifles and was stationed at Victoria Barracks, Belfast. He was living at Cranburn Street in Belfast's Clifton Ward with his wife, their daughter, Bridget Christian De Lacy (5), and Rosaline's brother, Patrick Joseph Kearns (10). He was serving with 3rd (Special Reserve) Battalion when he was discharged in April 1913 with over 25 years' service and a gratuity of five pounds. James was nearly 41 when he re-enlisted with the Royal Irish Rifles on 21st September 1914, being posted to 7th Battalion and deployed to France with the 16th (Irish) Division in December 1915 as Regimental Quartermaster Sergeant with the regimental number 7/16397. RQMS De Lacy was awarded the Military Cross in the 1917 King's Birthday Honours and he received his commission on 20th July 1917, being posted to 1st Battalion, Royal Inniskilling Fusiliers. He was awarded a bar to the Military Cross in 1918, the citation being published in September:

For conspicuous gallantry and devotion to duty. When all senior officers had become casualties, he was put in command of the battalion. After the front line had been driven back, he personally went back into the line to clear up the situation, having three men killed. He showed a splendid example to all.

Rosaline De Lacy died of influenza and phthisis on 19th October 1918 at the Royal Dublin Lunatic Asylum, having been admitted from her home at Leitrim Place in Wicklow, and she is buried in Rathnew Cemetery, Wicklow. Captain James Christopher De Lacy relinquished his commission on 24th December 1919 and was living at Main Street in Wicklow when he was employed by the Imperial War Graves Commission in April 1920. He worked as a storekeeper in Italy until April 1922. Captain De Lacy had an official role at the ex-servicemen's estate at Balrothery for three months before his appointment as Supervisor at Killester Garden Village on 1st March 1923. He named his house in The Demesne as 'Innisfail' and used 'Innisfail, Howth Road' as his address in official records. He married Mabel Moorhead on 6th November 1924 at St Mary's Roman Catholic Church, Haddington Road, Dublin. A keen gardener, he was always encouraging the residents to make the most of their gardens. Presiding at a meeting of the Killester Branch of the Irish National Garden Guild in September 1939 just after the outbreak of the Second World War, Captain De Lacy addressed those present as follows:

> It is the duty of every person to assist in every way during the present crisis to help the Nation in the advancement of agriculture and to grow more vegetables and fruit so as to ensure that there will be no shortage during the critical periods before us.

James De Lacy's occupation was recorded as 'Army Reserve Officer' when he died of cancer at Hume Street Hospital, Dublin, on 24th April 1940, his age being registered as 65. Mabel De Lacy was living at Ely Place in Dublin when she died at 49 Wellington Road in the city on 28th September 1944, aged 67.

22 The Demesne/232 Howth Road – William Edward Austin

It is believed that William was born in Dublin around 1892. Following the outbreak of war, he enlisted in the Royal Inniskilling Fusiliers and was posted to the regiment's 6th battalion with the regimental number 12296. The 6th Inniskillings were attached to 10th (Irish) Division and William joined them at Gallipoli in September 1915. He served with the battalion in Salonika, Palestine, and in France where he was wounded on 8th November 1918, three days before the Armistice. He was demobilised on 6th December 1919 and at that time was resident in Clondalkin. Following demobilisation, William took up employment with the oil company, Shell Mex. Allocated the bungalow at 22 The Demesne, William only remained there a short time before moving with his family to 48 The Demesne. He died of cardiac failure aged 45 at Leopardstown Park Hospital, Stillorgan, on 2nd March 1937.

23 The Demesne/234 Howth Road – Mathew Joseph Nolan

Mathew was born in January 1892 at Stoke Damerel, Devon, the son of Matthew Joseph and Bridget Nolan, née Kenny. By 1901, the family had moved to Ireland and the census records Mathew as resident with his family at Mercer Street Lower, Dublin. By 1911, the family had moved to Primrose Avenue, Dublin, and Mathew was in employment as a clerk for booksellers. It is not known when Mathew enlisted in the Royal Army Medical Corps however, he embarked for duty in France on 27th August 1915. Mathew served throughout the war and was promoted to the rank of Sergeant. He was also awarded the Military Medal for gallantry in the field. He was demobilised on 8th May 1919 and on 19th October of that year, married Anastasia Meehan at St Agatha's Roman Catholic Church. At the time of the marriage, Mathew was resident at Fitzroy Avenue, Dublin, and was employed as a civil servant. He applied for a disability pension and was assessed as being 40% disabled due to malaria and a fracture of the skull. He was awarded a pension of 16 shillings per week. Mathew was allocated the bungalow at 23 The Demesne, but had moved to England by 1930. The next occupant was Thomas Bradley, formerly of the Connaught Rangers. Mathew died aged 53 at 243 Hedgemans Road, Dagenham, Essex on 4th October 1945.

24 The Demesne/236 Howth Road – Patrick Stack

Patrick was born on 7th March 1889 at Harmony Row, Dublin, the son of Edward and Marcella Stack, née Lynch. Records show that he enlisted in the Royal Garrison Artillery on 20th April 1911 at Dublin, having been a farm labourer prior to enlisting. He was initially posted to Hong Kong but was stationed in the United Kingdom on the outbreak of war. He embarked for France on 20th August 1915 and was hospitalised with mustard gas poisoning on 10th October 1917. He was discharged with the Silver War Badge as unfit for further military service due to wounds on 28th May 1919. On discharge his character was described as, 'very good, a steady and hardworking man.' Patrick applied for a disability pension and was assessed as 30% disabled due to gas poisoning and was awarded a pension of 12 shillings per week. On 25th January 1920, he married a nurse, Catherine Alice Dunk née Monaghan, at the Roman Catholic Church at the Catholic University. Catherine's first husband, Sergeant Philip William Dunk 9332, 1st battalion The Buffs (East Kent Regiment) had died of wounds aged 29 on 29th December 1917. He is buried at Rye Cemetery, Sussex. Patrick's brother, Private Edward Stack 678, 11th (Prince Albert's Own) Hussars had been killed in action on 31st October 1914 and is buried at Wulverghem-Lindenhoek Road Military Cemetery, Belgium. Allocated the bungalow at 24 The Demesne, Patrick gained employment at the Guinness Brewery. On 2nd July 1943, Patrick was dead on arrival at Jervis Street Hospital having been found dead seated in his kitchen with the gas turned on. The cause of death was given as, 'asphyxia following inhalation of coal gas, self-determined whilst of unsound mind.'

25 The Demesne/238 Howth Road – Patrick Byrne

No military details have been established for Patrick. He was married to Mary, née Hanlon, and was resident at 25 The Demesne from around 1925. Also resident at the house was Mary's father, Garrett Hanlon. Garrett had been born on 6th August 1865 at Monkstown, County Dublin. He enlisted in the Royal Navy aged 14 on 39th September 1879 and served until he was invalided on 9th May 1917. At that time, he had risen to the rank of Petty Officer 1st Class, and his final posting was at HMS *Impregnable*, a shore establishment at Devonport. He applied for a disability pension and was assessed as 30% disabled with shell shock and deafness. He was in receipt of a pension of 18 shillings and thruppence a week for life. Garrett died at 238 Howth Road on 20th January 1941 of cardiac failure aged 76. His daughter Mary died on 7th December 1960 aged 73 at 25 The Demesne. Her husband, Patrick Byrne died on 9th August 1967, at Sally Gap, Malahide Road, of a coronary thrombosis, aged 88.

26 The Demesne – John Joseph Murphy

Little is known of the life of John Downes who was living at 26 The Demesne in 1926 when his daughter Ellen married a soldier, also named John Downes. F Lees was recorded as the occupant in the Thom's directories from 1930 to 1933, with a J Murphy being recorded as the occupant in the Thom's directories from 1934 until at least 1947.

John was born on 30th May 1894 at 5 William Place, Dublin, the son of John and Anne Murphy, née Tunsted. At the time of the birth, John Murphy was employed as a bagman at the GPO. The family was resident at William's Place Upper in 1901. John's mother Anne died in childbirth aged 45 on 12th December 1908 and his father remarried in 1910. The 1911 Census shows John as resident with his family at Portland Place North. At that time John was employed like his father and three brothers at the GPO. John's occupation was as a store boy. Records indicate that he enlisted in the Royal Irish Rifles in Dublin on 8th April 1911, Regimental Number 9612 and was posted to 2nd battalion.

On 9th December 1911, John married Mary Donohoe at St Mary's Roman Catholic Pro-Cathedral, Marlborough Street. At the time of the marriage, John's occupation is given as a labourer. A son, also named John Joseph, was born in 1913 and John's occupation was given as a soldier. John embarked for active service on the Western Front on 23rd November 1914 and was discharged due to wounds on 18th March 1916 in the rank of Sergeant. He was awarded the Silver War Badge (28706). A daughter Mary Ann was born in 1916 at Newbrook, Rathfarnham, and this is the address given on John's Silver War Badge documentation. A daughter Frances Teresa was born in June 1917 and

John's occupation at that time is given as a postman. John applied for a disability pension and was assessed as 50% disabled due to gunshot wounds to the hand resulting in the loss of a thumb, and defective teeth. He was awarded a pension of 20 shillings per week and 5 shillings per week for Mary and one dependent child, rising to 23/9 and 8/9 in 1923. Two of John's brothers fell in the Great War within two months of each other. Corporal Michael Joseph Murphy (10269, 2nd Battalion Royal Irish Rifles) was killed on 9th June 1917 aged 20 and Corporal Laurence Leo Murphy (8962, 2nd Battalion Royal Irish Rifles) was killed aged 24 on 11th August 1917. John and Mary resided at 26 The Demesne for many years and Mary died aged 65 at St Kevin's Hospital on 6th July 1960. John survived her for eight years and died at his home on 7th July 1968 aged 74 of a coronary thrombosis, his occupation being given as a retired foreman. The couple are buried at Glasnevin Cemetery in the St Paul's section grave NE 81.

27 The Demesne/240 Howth Road – Thomas Christopher Sharkey

Thomas was born in 1873 at Low Road, Lisburn, County Antrim, the son of Hugh and Susan Sharkey. He enlisted in the Royal Irish Rifles on 10th September 1894 at Belfast, being issued with the Regimental number 4358. He was posted to the regiment's 1st battalion and was promoted to the rank of Lance Corporal in 1896 and Corporal in 1897. In April of that year, he embarked for South Africa, remaining there for two years, until the battalion was posted to India on 16th April 1899. Thomas was promoted to the rank of Sergeant in March 1900 however, in October 1902, he was court-martialed for being drunk on duty and was reduced in rank to Corporal. Thomas returned to the United Kingdom at the beginning of 1904 and was posted to the regiment's 2nd battalion, regaining the rank of Sergeant in March 1907.

On 23rd January 1909, he married Margaret Elizabeth Penrose at St Andrew's Roman Catholic Church, Dublin. The 1911 Census shows Thomas as attached to 2nd battalion Royal Irish Rifles who were the garrison battalion at Dover Castle, Kent. The following month, he was posted to the regiment's 3rd (Reserve) battalion and in May 1914, he was promoted to Company Sergeant Major. Thomas served at home throughout the war and in 1916, having served 21 years, was eligible to retire, but remained in service for the duration of the war, being discharged as 'time served' on 20th March 1919. Thomas, Elizabeth and three sons moved into 27 The Demesne and Thomas became a newsagent. They named their bungalow 'Rosevale' as Thomas' pension card records his address as 27 Rosevale, Killester. Elizabeth died of kidney disease aged 47 on 3rd January 1930 and is buried at Section E Grave 7055 in Kilbarrack Cemetery, Malahide. She was survived by Thomas who died aged 77 at his home address on 6th April 1951 of a heart attack and is buried in Yellow Walls Cemetery, Malahide (Section A Grave 499).

27A The Demesne – John Flahive

This property was constructed around 1930 after the initial construction of The Demesne was completed and was occupied initially by John Flahive and his family. Information indicates that John was born in Kilkenny in 1877, his father also called John, being a soldier. John enlisted with the Duke of Edinburgh's (Wiltshire) Regiment at Tralee, County Kerry, on 21st July 1891 the age of 14. His occupation on enlistment was recorded as musician. He was posted to the Regiment's 2nd battalion with the regimental number 2998 and served in India and then in South Africa during the Boer War, being awarded the Queen's South Africa Medal with clasps for Wittebergen, Cape Colony, and Transvaal. John was promoted Corporal in 1905 and Sergeant in the Regimental Band in 1907.

He was stationed at Portobello Barracks, Dublin, in 1910 when he married Mary Esther Thornton on 7th February, at the Church of Our Immaculate Lady of Refuge, Rathmines. Mary was the daughter of a hairdresser from Fitzgerald Street, Dublin. The 1911 Census shows John and Mary as resident in married quarters at Portobello Barracks. John continued to serve until 10th November 1912 when he had completed 21 years' service. He was discharged in the rank of Band Sergeant with his military character being described as, 'very good.' Following the outbreak of war in 1914, John enlisted with the Royal Munster Fusiliers at Kinsale, County Cork, on 28th September 1914. He was posted to the regiment's 9th (Service) battalion, part of 48th Infantry Brigade of the 16th (Irish) Division with the regimental number 9/1158. With his previous military service, John was promoted to the rank of Sergeant a week after enlisting. He embarked with the battalion for active service on the Western Front on 19th December 1915. In April 1916, the 9th Munsters were disbanded with most of the officers and men being posted to other battalions in the regiment. John, however, was posted to 2nd battalion Royal Irish Regiment with the regimental number 18051. He remained with this battalion for the remainder of the war, being promoted Colour Sergeant on 21st January 1917. On 21st May 1918, John was admitted to 149th Field Ambulance having sustained lacerations to his right ear. He was promoted Acting Sergeant Major on 10th November 1918, and served until demobilised on 12th March 1919.

On demobilisation, his address was given as 46 Upper Clanbrassil Street, Dublin. At that time, he and Mary had two sons and two daughters. A third daughter, Margaret, was born in July 1919. At that time, John was an Assistant Superintendent of Music. In 1923, John enlisted in the National Army on the foundation of the Army School of Music and was initially in charge of No 3 Band at The Curragh. In 1930, he was posted to Cork in charge of No 2 Band. Hhe was allocated the newly built bungalow at 27A The Demesne. John died aged 59 at Mercy Hospital, Cork, on 28th September 1936 of heart failure. The death register describes him as a Sergeant Major, Irish Free State Army. John's remains were escorted to Arbour Hill, Dublin, and his funeral proceeded from there with military honours to Mount Jerome Cemetery. In military service when he died, John had served in both the British and Irish armies for 39 years. Mary survived John for over 40 years, and died aged 88 at Harold's Cross Hospice, Dublin, on 24th February 1969.

28 The Demesne/242 Howth Road – Andrew Denis Gaffney

Thom's directory for 1926 shows the occupant as E Gaffney. The 1932 edition shows the occupant as R Gaffney. Born on 19th February 1884 at 63 Lower Mecklenburgh Street, Dublin, Andrew was the son of Michael and Eliza Gaffney, née Brien. Michael Gaffney was in employment as a labourer at the time of the birth. The 1901 Census shows Andrew as resident with his parents and siblings at Boardman's Lane, Dublin. At that time, Andrew was in employment as a clerk. On 28th

November of that year, Andrew enlisted with the Northamptonshire Regiment, being posted to 1st battalion with the regimental number 6482. Following this initial period of service, Andrew transferred to the Army Reserve and the 1911 Census shows him as resident with his family at Boardman's Lane. Andrew's occupation is given as a glue factory labourer and army reservist.

He married Ellen Byrne at St Andrew's Roman Catholic Church, Dublin, on 28th July 1912. Ellen was the daughter of a porter from 4 Back Lane, Dublin. Andrew was mobilised for duty with the Northamptonshire Regiment at the outbreak of war and embarked for France on 11th September 1914. He served throughout the war and was demobilised on 2nd September 1919 in the rank of Acting Company Quartermaster Sergeant. Andrew applied for a Disability Pension and was assessed as 20% disabled due to deafness and rheumatism. He was awarded a pension of 14 shillings per week for himself and seven shillings and a penny per week for Ellen and three eligible children. Following his demobilisation, Andrew gained employment as a clerk with the Navy, Army and Air Force Institute (NAAFI) based at Lord Edward Street, Dublin. By 1922, Andrew, Ellen and their three children were living in two rooms at 25H Iveagh Buildings, Bull Alley, Dublin, when he applied for a house at Killester Garden Village. His application successful, the family moved to 28 The Demesne on St Patrick's Day 1923 for an initial rent of 16 shillings per week.

Andrew opened a fruit and vegetable shop and also kept chickens at his home. He purchased his home from the Irish Sailors and Soldiers Land Trust in October 1955, paying the sum of £558 (approximately £11,838 in current terms). On 22nd December of that year, Ellen died at her home aged 71 of cardiac failure. Andrew passed his shop onto his son Michael, and on 18th November 1963, Michael was attacked by a man armed with an iron bar as he returned to 28 The Demesne with the day's takings from the family's 'tin shop'. The man ran off when Michael shouted for help and he was treated at Jervis Street Hospital for head injuries. Andrew died at his home address aged 81 on 30th October 1964, of bronchopneumonia. He is buried with Ellen at Glasnevin Cemetery.

29 The Demesne/244 Howth Road – William Barnwell

William was born at Beaumont, Coolock, Dublin on 18th December 1876, the son of Michael and Lucy Barnwell, née Hamilton. He enlisted in the Royal Irish Fusiliers at Dublin on 6th January 1896, being issued with the regimental number 5524. William was posted to the regiment's 1st battalion and embarked with them for South Africa for service in the Boer war. For his service in South Africa, he was awarded the Queen's South Africa medal with clasps for the Orange Free State, Transvaal, Talana, Defence of Ladysmith, and Laing's Nek, and also the King's South Africa Medal with clasps for 1901 and 1902.

On his return to Ireland, he was stationed at Wellington Barracks, Dublin, when on 6th February 1907, he married Margaret Roche at the Visitation Chapel, Fairview. Margaret was from Drumcondra and the daughter of a labourer. The 1911 Census shows William at St Lucia Barracks, Bordon, Hampshire, with his battalion. He embarked for active service on the Western Front on 22nd August 1914. He had returned from active service and was based at Glenfield Camp, Clonmany, County Donegal, when Margaret died on 25th August 1917 aged 32, of septic peritonitis. William then married Mary Kelly at the Church of the Three Patrons, Dublin, on 14th January 1918. The following month, on 8th February, William was discharged from the army, his term of engagement completed. He was awarded the Silver War Badge as he had been honourably discharged. On discharge, he gave his address as 28 Patrick Street, Kingstown, Dublin. William applied for a Disability Pension and was assessed as 60% disabled with neurasthenia. On 15th February 1919, he gained employment as a stableman at the Guinness Brewery, Dublin. William died aged 69 on 28th September 1951 at Drumcondra Hospital of cancer. Following a service at St Brigid's, Killester, he was buried at Glasnevin Cemetery.

30 The Demesne – Francis Henry Dale

Known as Henry, he was born on 12th July 1887 in the St Catherine's area of Dublin. His father's name was also Henry and his mother's name remains unknown. Henry enlisted with the 5th Battalion Royal Dublin Fusiliers on 29th November 1904 at Dublin with the regimental number 6168. This was a militia battalion which was intended for

Home Defence duties and soldiering with this unit was part-time. At the time of enlistment, Henry was in employment as a shoemaker, and resident at 4 Cornmarket, Dublin. He only remained with this unit for a number of weeks before enlisting in the Regular Army, joining the Royal Irish Rifles at Dublin on 20th January 1905 with the regimental number 7826 and being posted to the 2nd battalion at Belfast.

The following year, on 15th September, he married Mary Ward at the Church of St Michael and St John, Dublin. Henry served in India from March 1909 until January 1913, the 1911 Census showing him on detachment in Burma (Myanmar). On return from India, Henry was transferred to the Army Reserve as his contract stipulated. Following the outbreak of war, he was mobilised in August 1914 and embarked for France with 2nd battalion Royal Irish Rifles on 14th August with the regimental number 10912. Henry spent three periods on the Western Front in the duration of the war, along with periods at home, most likely in a training capacity with the 3rd (Reserve) Battalion. During one of his periods of overseas service, Henry received a gunshot wound to the left thigh. He was honourably discharged on 12th July 1918 with the Silver War Badge as, 'no longer fit for military service.' Henry held the rank of Lance Sergeant on discharge and was resident at Block 19H, Iveagh Buildings, Bride Street, Dublin. He was initially assessed as 40% disabled due to his leg wound and was in receipt of a pension of 17 shillings and fourpence per week for himself, and ten shillings and sixpence per week for his wife Mary and son, Albert. Henry gained employment at the Transport Department of the Guinness Brewery which he joined on 13th March 1920. He died on 28th August 1940 aged 52, at St Vincent's Hospital, Dublin, of the effects of a gastric ulcer. He is buried at Glasnevin Cemetery. Henry's home at 30 The Demesne, also appears in records as being named 'Frankfort'.

31 The Demesne – Edmund (or Edmond) O'Donnell

The original occupant of this address is listed in Thom's Directory as a T Lee. Research has not identified any relevant records for someone of that name. An E O'Donnell was the occupant in the 1930 Thom's Directory.

Edmond O'Donnell was born on 2nd March 1884 at 113 Brunswick Street to Edmund O'Donnell, a labourer, and Mary O'Donnell (née Cahill). Edmond O'Donnell was a labourer when he married Elizabeth Matthews on 23rd April 1909 at St Mary's Roman Catholic Pro-Cathedral. Three children were born at 7 Summer Place – Elizabeth Mary (1909), Francis James (1913), and Albert (1915). Thereafter, his forename was recorded as Edmund. He enlisted with the Irish Guards (Regimental Number 7340) on 5th April 1915, being discharged as medically unfit on 1st October 1916. Undeterred, he enlisted with the Royal Engineers (Regimental Number 15728) on 14th April 1916, giving his occupation as sailor and his home address as 6 North Great Charles Street. He served on the Western Front with the Inland Waterways and Transport section (later renamed as Inland Waterways and Docks) from 17th October 1916 to 19th April 1919. Corporal O'Donnell (now with Regimental Number WR/502486) was transferred to the Class Z Army Reserve on 18th May 1919 and was discharged on demobilisation on 31st March 1920.

The O'Donnell family was living at 28 St Joseph's Cottages on Church Road in 1925 when Edmund wrote to the Royal Engineers' Records Office to request his service medals. In this letter, Edmund records that his discharge was connected with being injured during a football match. In the letter he records that he was on the staff of the Harbour Master at the Port of Dublin before the war and that he had 'rendered all assistance in connection with the embarkation of troops and war materials for France.' He also reported that, 'I have distinguished myself in my employment under the Harbour Master, Capt. J. H. Webb, R.N.R., by Life-saving in the Dublin River.' One of the pension cards for Edmund O'Donnell records that he had also served with the Royal Garrison Artillery (Regimental Number 9717). Edmund O'Donnell was a berthing master when he died of gastric ulceration haematoma at 31 Abbeyfield on 29th May 1939, aged 54. His son, Francis, was present at death. Edmund is buried in Mount Jerome Cemetery and the funeral from St Brigid's Church was attended by members of the Dublin Port and Docks Board. A death notice in the Evening Herald recorded his forename as Edward. Elizabeth O'Donnell died of bronchopneumonia at 31 The Demesne on 28th March 1961, aged 83, her daughter, Elizabeth Tobin, being present. Elizabeth is also buried in Mount Jerome Cemetery. A death notice in the Irish Independent recorded Elizabeth as being the widow of Edward O'Donnell.

32 The Demesne – Arthur Hursey

Born on 4th April 1883, Arthur was educated at the Royal Hibernian School, Dublin, before following his father Henry and enlisting in the Royal Engineers aged 14 on 25th June 1897, being issued with the regimental number 930. Whilst stationed in Armagh in 1905, he married Annie Black on 12th December at Mullaghbrack Church of Ireland. Tragically, Annie died the following year at Markethill, County Armagh, of nephritis. Having served for 18 years, Arthur was discharged from the Army on 8th October 1912 and gained employment as a clerk. He enlisted with the 10th (Service) battalion Royal Dublin Fusiliers on 9th November 1915, with the regimental number 24712. The 10th Royal Dublin Fusiliers were known as, 'The Commercials' as their recruits were mainly drawn from trades in the city. On enlistment, Arthur gave his address as 20 Maud Street, Dublin. On active service, Arthur sustained a gunshot wound to the chest and, following treatment and convalescence, was compulsorily transferred to the Labour Corps on 28th May 1918. Following the Armistice, he was transferred again, to 2nd battalion Yorkshire Regiment with the regimental number 62716. On 4th April 1919, Arthur married Margaret Stubbs at St Brigid's Church of Ireland, Castleknock. He was discharged from the Army on 19th September 1919 and applied for a Disability Pension, being assessed as 20% disabled due to the effects of his chest wound. He resumed employment as a clerk, and he and Margaret were allocated the bungalow at 32 The Demesne. Arthur died aged 48 at his home on 7th January 1933, the cause of death given as, 'Fibrosis of the right lung following old gunshot wound of the chest.' Arthur and Margaret's son James, served in the Second World War as Rifleman 7018479, 2nd battalion Royal Irish Rifles. He was killed in action in France aged 22 on 9th June 1944, three days after D-Day, and is buried at Cambes-en-Pleine War Cemetery, near Caen, France.

33 The Demesne – Edward Joseph Campbell

The initial occupant of 33 The Demesne was a G Mullins. Research has not identified any relevant records for someone of that name. By 1945, the resident was Edward Campbell.

Edward Joseph Campbell was born on 18th May 1895 at Castle Street to John Campbell, a labourer, and Hannah Campbell (née MacMahon). In 1911, the family was living at the Corporation Buildings on Nicholas Street in Wood Quay and Edward was recorded as being a wine porter. It has not been possible to verify his war service but he was an asylum attendant at Portrane who married Kathleen McCollum on 13th October 1925 at St Agatha's Roman Catholic Church. In April 1957, Edward Campbell junior was climbing a spiked wall outside a shop on Howth Road, when he slipped and a spike pierced his jaw. Dr R Loughlan and Dr M Shrage, both of Howth Road, administered anaesthetic at the scene before a Dublin Fire Brigade ambulance took Edward to the Jervis Street Hospital, where he was later reported as being 'fairly comfortable' later the same night. Edward Campbell junior was variously recorded as being seven or nine in newspaper reports. Edward John Campbell's letter about road safety issues in Killester was published in *The Evening Herald* on 6th February 1964. 1973 was a tragic year for the Campbell family of 33 The Demesne. Gordon Philip Campbell died on 9th April 1973 at the age of three and is buried in Balgriffin Cemetery. Edward Joseph Campbell, formerly of 33 The Demesne, was living at 1 Dublin Street in Baldoyle when he died on 16th June 1973, aged 78, and Catherine Campbell was living at the same address when she died on 15th December 1973, aged 69. Edward and Catherine Campbell are buried in Balgriffin Cemetery (Section D Grave 18).

34 The Demesne – Bernard Joseph Ratcliffe

Bernard was born on 1st June 1886 at 6 Hender Place off Grand Canal Street, Dublin, the son of Joseph and Margaret Ratcliffe, née Murphy. The 1901 Census shows the family as resident at Verschoyle Place, Dublin. At that time, Bernard was employed as a telegraph messenger and he was also a member of the Dublin City Royal Garrison Artillery, a militia unit. On 2nd September 1904, Bernard enlisted in the Royal

Garrison Artillery for three years at Dublin, being issued with the regimental number 20852. On enlistment, he gave his occupation as postman. Posted to 22nd Company, he served in Sierra Leone before being transferred to the Army Reserve in October 1907.

On 25th April 1909, Bernard married Bridget Daniel at St Andrew's Roman Catholic Church, Dublin. At the time of the marriage, Bernard had resumed employment as a postman and was resident at Holles Row. Bridget was from Verschoyle Place. The 1911

Bernard and Bridget Ratcliffe
34 The Demesne
(source: Ancestry family tree)

Census shows the couple as resident at Primrose Street, Dublin, along with a son, Joseph, born in 1910. At the outbreak of war, Bernard was mobilised and rejoined the Royal Garrison Artillery at Great Yarmouth. He was posted to 31st Battery and embarked for France on 16th August 1914, serving on the Western Front until February 1917. He was attached to a home defence unit in East Anglia before being compulsorily transferred to the Labour Corps on 2nd October 1918. Bernard was posted to No 397 Employment Company and issued with the corps number 663072. He was demobilised on 14th March 1919, his military character being noted as, 'very good.' On discharge, Bernard resumed his occupation as a postman and was allocated the bungalow at 34 The Demesne. In 1939, he was one of a number of residents who took an action at the High Court against Dublin Corporation concerning the assessment of rates for the houses in Killester Village. Bernard later moved to London and died there in 1964 aged 78. Bridget had predeceased him the previous year.

35 The Demesne – Arthur Joseph Farrelly

The initial occupant of 35 The Demesne was a T Rich. Research has not identified any relevant records for someone of that name. Arthur Farrelly moved into the bungalow around 1930. Arthur had been born on 5th August 1894 at 5 Lower Gloucester Place, Dublin, the son of Thomas and Cecilia Farrelly, née Jordan. At the time of the birth, Thomas Farrelly was employed as a porter. By 1911, Arthur was still resident at 5 Lower Gloucester Place with his widowed Mother and six siblings. At that time, he was employed as a messenger.

He married Mary Kelly at St Agatha's Roman Catholic Church, Dublin on 29th August 1916 and by 7th September, had enlisted in the South Irish Horse with the regimental number H2211. He embarked for active service in late 1916 and along with most of his comrades in the South Irish Horse, was transferred to the 7th (South Irish Horse) battalion, Royal Irish Regiment, in September 1917, with the regimental number 25296. Arthur was discharged from the army as no longer fit for active service on 14th March 1918, suffering from bright's disease. He was awarded the Silver War Badge and on discharge, applied for a disability pension. He was assessed as 40% disabled and was awarded a pension of 16 shillings per week for himself and four shillings per week for Mary. On 20th June 1939, tragedy struck the family when their 18 years old son, Patrick, died at his home of tuberculosis. Arthur and Mary had moved from Killester by the late 1940s and were residing at 22 Lembay Road, Drumcondra. Arthur died aged 60 on 18th November 1954 at Leopardstown Park Hospital, of renal failure. He is buried at Glasnevin Cemetery.

36 The Demesne – Robert Francis Wills

Born in 1889 the son of an army pensioner in the St James' area of Dublin, Robert enlisted in a militia unit of the Royal Army Medical Corps on 4th August 1906 with the corps number 1994. At the time of enlistment, he was aged 18 and employed as a clerk with the Dublin branch of Blackie and Sons Publishers, whose headquarters were in Glasgow. On 29th October of the same year, he enlisted with the 5th (Royal Irish) Lancers with the regimental number 7497. On 15th January 1913, whilst stationed at Marlborough Barracks, Dublin, he married Frances Kelly at the Chapel of the Visitation, Fairview, Dublin. Frances was from Richmond Road, Dublin. Following the outbreak of war, Robert embarked with his unit to the Western Front on 8th October 1914. At some stage during the war, he transferred to the Guards Machine Gun Regiment, with the regimental number 4934. He was demobilised on

19th March 1919 with a pension of 12 shillings and 8 pence per week. On demobilisation, he gave his address as that of Frances' family, 187 Richmond Road, Dublin. Robert gained employment as a van man and died at his home at 36 The Demesne on 20th January 1964 of cancer, aged 75. At that time, his daughter, Maureen Keogh was resident at 15 The Demesne/216 Howth Road.

37 The Demesne – Richard Fisher Nicholson

The son of a Royal Irish Constabulary Constable, Richard was born at Dovea townland, near Thurles, County Tipperary on 29th November 1879. His parents were William and Fanny Martha Nicholson, née Fisher. The 1901 Census shows Richard as resident with his maternal Grandmother on her farm at Toberbeg, Dunlavan, County Wicklow. In June of that year, Richard married Hannah Stokes at Blackhall Place Methodist Church, Dublin. Hannah was from 20 Baggott Terrace and her father, deceased at the time of the marriage, had been a soldier. On 7th March 1902, Richard took up employment in the Traffic Department of the Guinness Brewery as a labourer on the firm's cross channel steamers. By 1911, Richard and Hannah were resident at Finn Street in the Arran Quay area of Dublin with six surviving children. It is not known when Richard enlisted in the army however, it is known that he joined the Royal Army Medical Corps with the number 100948.

Richard does not appear to have served in a theatre of war and therefore has no medal entitlement. He was demobilised after the Armistice in the rank of Acting Sergeant and applied for a Disability Pension citing pulmonary tuberculosis. He was assessed as 100% disabled and was awarded a pension of 46 shillings and eightpence per week for himself, and 47 shillings and sixpence for Hannah and six eligible children. When Richard left the army, he was resident at 56 Stella Gardens, Sandymount, Dublin.

Richard Nicholson
37 The Demesne
(source: Nigel Henderson)

In January of 1920, Richard and Hannah's eldest son William, enlisted in the Royal Army Medical Corps with the corps number 15177. He was however, discharged after three months service as medically unfit. Allocated the bungalow at 37 The Demesne, the family only remained there until 1930, the resident in 1931 being an M Brennan. By 1936, Richard and his family were resident at 16 St Aidan's Park Road, Marino. Sometime after this, the family moved to Northern Ireland. Two of Richard and Hannah's other sons also served in the Second World War. Richard Fisher Nicholson enlisted in the Royal Navy in 1926 with the Navy number MX 45792. He served until 1944 and was awarded the Long Service and Good Conduct Medal. Robert Fisher Nicholson served as PO/X100815 with 41 Commando Royal Marines. He died aged 22 on 13th January 1945. He is buried at Ballycairn Presbyterian Church, Ballylesson, County Down. Recognised as a war fatality by the Commonwealth War Graves Commission, his grave is maintained by relatives. Richard died at Belfast on 31st January 1959 and Hannah died on 23rd March the following year. They are both buried with their son Robert at Ballycairn Presbyterian Church.

38 The Demesne – John Joseph Fagan

John was born on 18th May 1881 at 23 Denzille Street, Dublin, the son of Abraham and Bridget Fagan, née Fogarty. At the time of the birth, Abraham Fagan was employed as a butler. John enlisted in the Royal Irish Rifles at Dublin on 23rd February 1899 with the regimental number 5822. He was promoted Lance Corporal in December 1901 and Corporal in February 1903. He was promoted Sergeant in February 1906 and in July of that year extended his service to complete 12 years. On 22nd July 1908, he married Elizabeth McCann at the Roman Catholic Cathedral, Dublin. Elizabeth was from North Frederick Street, Dublin. John was promoted Colour Sergeant on 10th April 1913 and following the outbreak of war, was promoted Sergeant Major and transferred to the newly raised 6th (Service) battalion Royal Irish Rifles, part of 29th Infantry Brigade, 10th (Irish) Division. John embarked for Gallipoli with his battalion on 10th July 1915, seeing service there and also at Salonika. He was awarded the Long Service and Good Conduct Medal on 29th March 1917, and on 20th November 1917 was compulsorily transferred to the Machine Gun Corps, with the corps number 120924. John was discharged on 9th March 1920 at his own request, having served for two weeks over 21 years. At the time of discharge, John gave his address as 26 Ilchester Street, Belfast, and an assessment of his military character described him as, 'Honest, sober, hardworking, reliable and intelligent.' John applied for a disability pension, citing malaria. He was assessed as 20% disabled and in addition to his military pension, was awarded a pension of five shillings and sixpence per week for himself and four shillings and eight pence for Elizabeth and two children. John gained employment as a clerk and was allocated the bungalow at 38 The Demesne. Tragically, Elizabeth died aged 40 at St Vincent's Hospital, Dublin, of septicaemia on 1st September 1927. John died on 17th June 1947 aged 66 at his home address, of bronchitis. He is buried with Elizabeth at Mount Jerome Cemetery, Dublin.

39 The Demesne – Edward McDowell

A Boer War veteran, Edward was born on 13th February 1881 at 2 Henrietta Buildings, Dublin, the son of Patrick and Eliza McDowell, née Courtney. He enlisted in the Royal Irish Fusiliers on 7th January 1899 and for his Boer War service was awarded the Queen's South Africa Medal with clasps for the Orange Free State and the Transvaal, and the King's South Africa Medal with clasps for 1901 and 1902. Edward transferred to the Army Reserve in the following years and the 1911 Census shows him as resident with his parents and brother at 16 Oriel Street Upper, Dublin. At that time, he was employed as a carter. The following year on 3rd June 1912, he married Bridget Bennett at St Catherine's Roman Catholic Church, Dublin. At the time of the marriage, Edward was residing at Killarney Street. Bridget was a laundry worker from 41 Pimlico, Dublin. As an army reservist, Edward was mobilised at the outbreak of war. He rejoined the 1st battalion Royal Irish Fusiliers and retained his regimental number, 6482. He embarked for the Western Front on 22nd August 1914 and was wounded in 1915, being discharged with the Silver War Badge due to wounds on 10th January 1916.

On discharge, Edward was resident at Bridget's family home at Pimlico. He applied for a disability pension and was assessed as

30% disabled, primarily due to disordered action of the heart. He was awarded a pension of 12 shillings a week for himself and five shillings and thruppence for Bridget and their children. Allocated the bungalow at 39 The Demesne, Edward gained employment as a drillmaster. A son, Patrick Joseph died at the family home aged 17 on 4th March 1933 of tuberculosis. Edward died at the City of Dublin Hospital aged 59 on 8th May 1942 of postoperative shock following a cancer operation. The death register records his occupation as a 'Physical Instructor'.

40 The Demesne – Thomas Cadden Earls

Thomas was born on 8th April 1890 at 15 Park Place, Cunningham Road, Dublin, the son of Thomas James and Emily Earls, née Cadden. At the time of the birth, Thomas Earls was employed as a tailor. By 1901, Thomas was resident with his family at 201 Clonliffe Road, Drumcondra, Dublin and was resident in the same house in 1911. At that time, he was employed as a clerk with the London and Northwestern Railway at Dublin Port. Thomas enlisted in the South Irish Horse in November 1916 with the regimental number 73769. On his departure from the

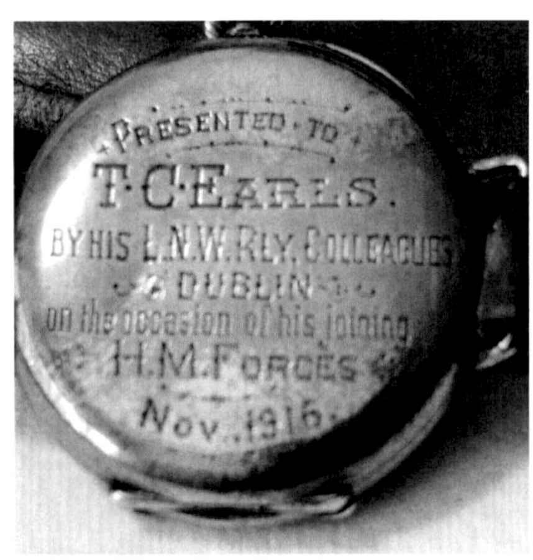

railway company, he was presented with a watch by his colleagues (image source: Ancestry Family Tree). The following year on 30th April 1917, he married Eleanor Virginia Dowling at St George's Parish Church, Dublin. Demobilised on 14th March 1919, Thomas resumed his occupation as a shipping clerk. He was also a Freemason, being a member of the Pyramid lodge in Dublin. Thomas died aged 82 on 30th June 1972.

41 The Demesne – George Joseph Merrigan

Born on 22nd October 1898 at Mount Prospect, Clontarf, George was the son of Laurence and Kate Merrigan, née Pearson. At the time of the birth, Laurence Merrigan was employed as a gardener. The 1901 Census shows the family resident at Snughborough, Clontarf. By 1911, they had moved to Carricklawn, County Wexford. Following the outbreak of war, George enlisted in the Royal Dublin Fusiliers with the regimental number 27620. It is known that he did not deploy on active service until 1916 at the earliest and was attached to the regiment's 1st battalion. At a later stage, he transferred to the 7th battalion Royal Irish Regiment, being issued the regimental number 26345. George was de-mobilised on 8th November 1919. Eligible for the British War Medal and Allied Victory Medal, information indicates that these medals were returned. George married Margaret Birmingham on 31st August 1921 at St Andrew's Roman Catholic Church, Dublin. Allocated the bungalow at 41 The Demesne, Margaret was resident there when she died at St Vincent's Hospital on 10th July 1933 of cancer. On 13th February 1934, George married a widow, Catherine Stephens née Finnis, at St Brigid's, Killester. At the time of the marriage, George was employed as a tram conductor. George died at Jervis Street Hospital on 4th January 1939 aged 40, when he was knocked off his bike by a car at Annesley Bridge, Dublin. The driver of the car, William Clarke, was charged with manslaughter however, it is not clear if he was convicted. In a sequel, George's mother and his wife both claimed damages for his death, the dispute being taken to the High Court which ruled that his mother had precedence.

42 The Demesne – James Joseph Flood

Born on 19th January 1888 at Drumcunnion townland on the border between Counties Monaghan and Cavan, James was the son of a farmer, Patrick, and his wife Catherine, née Caulin. James was resident at the family farm at Drumcunnion for both the 1901 census and 1911 census and was recorded as being a farm worker in the latter. Unfortunately, no military service records can be positively identified for James. It is known that post-war, he married Mary Ellen (Nellie) Caffrey on 28th August 1920 at St Joseph's Roman Catholic Church, Berkeley Street, Dublin. At that time, James was employed as a salesman and was resident at 165 Church Road, Dublin. Nellie was the daughter of a sanitary engineer from 48 Royal Canal, Dublin. The couple were the initial occupants of 42 The Demesne in 1923, residing there all their married lives and raising their family there. Nellie died at the family home aged 78 on 12th March 1972 of bronchopneumonia. James, a civil servant, survived her by three years and died on 1st February 1975 aged 87 also at his home address. They are both buried at Balgriffin Cemetery at Section R Grave 22.

43 The Demesne – Bernard Donnellan

Bernard was born on Tuesday, 17th June 1884 at Carrownaglearagh townland, near the town of Elphin, County Roscommon, the son of Bernard and Bridget Donnellan, née Butler. Bernard married Elizabeth Moran on Thursday, 29th October 1908 at St Mary's, Carrick-on-Shannon, County Leitrim. At that time, Bernard's was recorded as being a merchant and his address as Rooskey, County Roscommon. Elizabeth was from the townland of Tullylannan, County Leitrim. By 1911, the couple had two children who were born at Rooskey, County Roscommon – Bernard Vincent was born on 21st September 1909 and Thomas Gerard was born 8th September 1910. The 1911 Census shows Bernard and Elizabeth along with their son Thomas, resident with Elizabeth's parents at Tullylannan, County Leitrim. Their eldest son, Bernard, was resident with Bernard's parents at Carrownaglearagh. In the following years, Bernard and his family moved to Dublin, most likely for improved employment prospects for Bernard. Two further children were born to the couple, Teresa Veronica, born on 28th November 1914 at 7 Upper Baggot Street, Dublin, and an unnamed female, born on 27th September 1915, also at 7 Upper Baggott Street, Dublin. Tragically, this baby died within minutes of being born.

Available records indicate that Bernard enlisted in the Royal Army Medical Corps on 2nd September 1915, less than three weeks before the birth of his second daughter. He was issued with the corps number 68263 and it is known that he did not embark for the Western Front until at least the beginning of 1916. He was also wounded on two occasions, his name appearing on the War Office Daily Lists of 30th November 1917 and 2nd May 1918. It is known that on one of these occasions, Bernard received a gunshot wound to the foot.

Records indicate that Bernard was discharged on 21st August 1919 as medically unfit due to wounds and was in receipt of the Silver War Badge. Bernard applied for a disability pension on discharge and following a medical was assessed as 40% disabled due to his foot injury and bronchial problems and was awarded a pension of 16 shillings per week for himself, 14 shillings for Elizabeth and four shillings a week for his surviving children. Sometime in the early 1920s, Elizabeth tragically died, but no death register entry can be found for her. Bernard then married Mary Ellen Slowey at St Andrew's Roman Catholic Church, Dublin, on Monday 23rd April 1923. At that time, Bernard was employed as a civil servant and was resident at 38 Harrington Street, Dublin. Mary was resident at 40 Upper Fitzwilliam Street in the city. Bernard was allocated the bungalow at 43 The Demesne and opened a Post Office at one of the 'tin shops' established in Middle Third. Bernard and Mary Ellen had a son, John Joseph, born in 1926. Tragically, Bernard died at St Vincent's Hospital, Merrion Road, Dublin, on 27th December 1928 of bronchitis and kidney disease, aged 44. He is buried at Glasnevin Cemetery, Dublin.

Following Bernard's death, his pension was reassessed. Mary Ellen was deemed ineligible for a Widow's Pension, most likely as she was Bernard's second wife. A pension was instead awarded to Bernard's younger sister Teresa, as guardian of the children from his first marriage, resident at Carrick on Shannon, County Roscommon. Bernard's younger brother John Joseph (Jack) served with 2nd battalion Irish Guards, regimental number 8489. He was killed in action near Boesinghe, Belgium, aged 26 on 31st July 1917. He has no known grave and is commemorated on the Menin Gate Memorial, Ypres. It is believed that his younger sister Winifred served as a nurse in the Great War however, no nursing records relating to her from that time can be found. She died at the family home at Carrownaglearagh aged 25 on 15th March 1926.

44 The Demesne – William Alfred Cobbledick

William was born at Belderrig, County Mayo on 23rd May 1882, the son of John Francis and Lydia Esther Cobbledick, née Hope. At the time of the birth, John was employed as a coast guard. The 1901 Census shows William as resident as a boarder at 12 Eden Quay, Dublin. At that time, he was employed as a plumber. On 24th January 1905, William married Elizabeth Starkey at St Mary's Roman Catholic Pro-Cathedral, Dublin. At that time, he was employed as a gas fitter. The 1911 Census shows the couple and two children as resident with William's parents at 29 Alvington Street, Plymouth. Following the outbreak of war, William enlisted in the Royal Engineers with the regimental number 1193, later changed to 514437. He embarked for active service in France in June 1918 and was demobilised on 8th March 1919. Tragically, Elizabeth died aged 36 on 15th June 1920 at 11 Marlborough Street, Dublin, of tuberculosis. The following year, on 27th September 1921, William married Helena Louisa Lynch at the Church of St Laurence O'Toole, Dublin. At that time, William was resident at Harcourt Street and was employed as a clerk. Allocated the bungalow at 44 The Demesne, tragedy was to strike the family twice in 1932. Firstly, Emily, a daughter of William from his first marriage, died aged 20 as an inmate of a Magdalen Laundry at High Park Penitentiary, Drumcondra, of heart disease. On 11th October of the same year, Louisa was knocked down and seriously injured by a stolen car at Howth Road in an incident in which another pedestrian was killed. Louisa died aged 60 at her home address on 8th November 1950 of a coronary thrombosis. William survived her for two years, dying at Harold's Cross Hospice aged 70 on 18th December 1952 of cancer.

45 The Demesne – Edward Patrick Meehan

The son of Charles and Catherine Meehan, née Brennan, Edward was born on 17th September 1891 at 70 Marlborough Street, Dublin. Both the 1901 and 1911 Census show Edward as resident with his paternal grandmother at 88 North Strand Road in the city. In 1911, Edward was employed as a labourer. The following year on 17th January 1912, he married Sarah O'Reilly, the daughter of an engine driver, at St Agatha's Roman Catholic Church, Dublin. At the time of the marriage, Edward was residing at 17 King's Avenue, Dublin. Following the outbreak of war, Edward enlisted in the Royal Irish Rifles, serving with the regiment's 1st battalion, with the regimental number 8903. Around the time of the Armistice in 1918, Edward transferred to the Northumberland Fusiliers in the rank of Sergeant with the regimental number 42951. He continued to serve into the 1920s and was awarded the General Service Medal with clasps for Iraq and Northwest Persia. This medal was forwarded to him at his home at 45 The Demesne. Following his discharge from the Army, Edward gained employment as a clerk. He died aged 41 at his home address on 16th June 1933 of tuberculosis. Edward's younger brother, Private John Joseph Meehan 2036, 1st battalion Royal Irish Rifles was killed in action on 1st July 1916 aged 20. He is commemorated on the Thiepval Memorial to the Missing.

46 The Demesne – Albert Edward Wakeling

Albert was born on 7th April 1879 at 5 George Street, Bethnal Green, London, the son of William and Emma Wakeling, née Nye. At the time of the birth, William was employed as a bootmaker. Albert enlisted in the Army Ordnance Corps with the corps number S3704 towards the end of the century and served during the Boer War in South Africa, being eligible for the Queen's South Africa Medal with a clasp for the Cape Colony. The Army Ordnance Corps was responsible for the supply and maintenance of weaponry for the army in the field. On his return from South Africa, Albert was posted to Islandbridge Barracks, Dublin. Interestingly, Albert appears to have married the same woman twice in three years. On 1st November 1903, Albert Edward Wakeling married Mary Kearney, daughter of John Kearney, a cooper, at St Nicholas' Roman Catholic Church, Francis Street, Dublin. On 8th April 1905, Albert Edward Wakeling married Mary Kearney, daughter of John Kearney, a cooper, at the Registrar's Office, Dublin. No explanation can be found as to why this is the case. By 1911, the family was resident in married accommodation at The Curragh. At that time Albert and Mary had four children. A fifth child, Mary, died aged 2 of diptheria at Cork Street Hospital, Dublin, on 20th April 1908. During the Great War, Albert appears to have served within the United Kingdom and Ireland. At some stage in the late 1930s the family relocated from 46 The Demesne to England. Albert died aged 88 on 19th August 1968 at 23 Ewart Road, Portsmouth. A son, Gerard Christopher, served in the Royal Navy throughout the Second World War and having enlisted as a Stoker, attained the rank of Petty Officer.

47 The Demesne – William Donald McLean

Born on 2nd January 1866 at Queen's Terrace, Dublin, William was the son of Robert and Alice McLean, née McGrath. At the time of the birth,

Robert's occupation was recorded as a brass pounder. William was first married on 28th June 1896 at Trinity Church of Ireland, Dublin. His wife was Emily Lilian Williams, the daughter of a solicitor from Lower Gardiner Street. William's occupation is recorded on the marriage register as a shorthand writer. The 1901 Census of Ireland shows the couple as resident with four children at Clonliffe Road, Dublin. By 1911, the family had moved to St Michael's Road, Dublin, and were resident there with five surviving children. At that time, William was employed as a commercial clerk in the wine trade. William enlisted in the Royal Dublin Fusiliers on 1st September 1915 and served as Donald McLean with the regimental number 8765. On enlistment, William was 49 years of age.

Records indicate that he did not serve in a theatre of war and he was discharged on 19th June 1916 with the Silver War Badge due to sickness. On discharge, his address was given as 38 Cuffe Street, Dublin. Tragically, his wife, Emily died aged 41 on 29th May 1917 of heart disease. The following year, on 12th September, William married a widow, Lucy Taylor, née Greenslade, at St George's Church of Ireland, Dublin. The marriage register records William's occupation as 'Private in the Royal Dublin Fusiliers'. However, he had been discharged from the Army two years previously. Following the Armistice, William applied for a disability pension. He was assessed as 80% disabled due to melancholia and awarded a pension of five shillings per week backdated to June 1916, and this rose to 32 shillings per week in 1920. William resumed his employment as a commercial clerk and was struck by tragedy again when his second wife, Lucy died on 8th December 1922 aged 55 at the Adelaide Hospital, Dublin, of pneumonia. Allocated the bungalow at 47 The Demesne, William became the Secretary of the Killester Branch of the British Legion. William died aged 80 at his home address on 25th January 1947 of heart disease. He is buried at Mount Jerome Cemetery.

48 The Demesne – Walter William Alfred Austin

The initial occupant of 48 The Demesne was a T Senior. Research has not identified any relevant records for someone of that name. Walter Austin moved into this bungalow in 1928. Walter was born at St Saviour's, Southwark, London, on 15th April 1893, the son of Walter and Mary Jane Austin. He was educated at Knapp Road School, Tower Hamlets, London, and the 1911 Census shows him as resident with his family at 7 Smyrke Road, Old Kent Road, London. At that time, Walter was still in education. Following the outbreak of war, he enlisted in the Army Service Corps and was issued with the corps number M/29122. It is known that he did not embark for active service until at least the beginning of 1916. He served throughout the war and reached the rank of Sergeant, serving in the Transport Section. Walter and his wife, Annie, moved into 48 The Demesne in 1928 and Walter was in employment with the Shell/Mex Oil Company. He died on 2nd March 1937 at Leopardstown Park Hospital aged 45, of valvular disease of the heart and is buried at Mount Jerome Cemetery. Annie lived in Killester until 1956 when she died on 2nd April aged 67 at St Vincent's Hospital, of heart failure.

49 The Demesne – Nicholas Anthony Flanagan

The second son of Nicholas and Bridget Flanagan, née Carroll, Nicholas was born in Dublin in 1896. At that time his father was an auctioneer. The 1911 Census shows the family as resident at Hibernia Terrace, Kilmainham. At that time, Nicholas, then aged 15, was still in full time education. Nicholas enlisted with the 5th (Royal Irish) Lancers, with the number L/4829. He embarked for the Western Front on 17th October 1915 and the following year on 13th February 1916, he married a nurse, Philomena Richardson, at the Roman Catholic Church of the Golden Bridge, Kilmainham, Dublin. Nicholas served throughout the war and was demobilised on 16th August 1920. A daughter, Mary Agnes, was born on 16th November 1920 at Holles Street Hospital. Following discharge, Nicholas gained employment with the Irish Land Commission as a clerk, and he applied for a Disability Pension from the army, citing rheumatism and was assessed as 40% disabled. He was awarded a pension of 16 shillings per week for himself and seven shillings for Philomena and Mary. Tragically, Philomena died on 4th January 1931 aged 37 at Harold's Cross Hospice, of tuberculosis. Nicholas survived her for six years and died on 17th October 1938 at his home at 49 The Demesne of acute rheumatism. He is buried with Philomena at Mount Jerome Cemetery.

50 The Demesne – Ephraim (Edward) Adair

Both versions of the forename appear on available records. Edward was born at Larne, County Antrim, on 12th July 1889, the son of James and Elizabeth Adair, née McIntosh. The birth register records his forename as Ephraim. By 1901, the family were resident at 5 Circular Road in the town. Tragically, Elizabeth died aged 43 at her home on 30th October 1903 of melancholia. Following this, the family relocated to live with relatives in Dublin, and the 1911 Census shows them as resident at Bride Street in the city. At that time, Edward was in employment as a hot water fitter. He enlisted in the Royal Navy for the duration of the war as Edward, on 2nd June 1916 as an Able Seaman with the number K33669, however, he was redesignated in August 1916 as an Engine Room Artificer with the number M24803. In April 1917 at Medway, Kent, he married Ethel Florence Coller before returning to active service. He served on several ships, including the battleship HMS *Hannibal*, before being demobilised on 14th October 1919. He returned to Dublin and gained employment as a fitter and he and Ethel had two daughters, Ellen, born on 23rd May 1920, and Margaret Elizabeth born on 1st April 1922. He was allocated the bungalow at 50 The Demesne as Edward in 1923 and a son, Hugh, was born there in 1925. Tragically Hugh died aged seven on New Year's Day 1932 of diphtheria.

In the following years, Edward and Ethel appear to have experienced marital difficulties and Edward vacated the property and moved back to 68 Bride Street. In July 1937, the ISSLT took Edward to court in an effort to have him evicted from the property as he was no longer residing there. Edward indicated that if Ethel left the property, he would return and occupy it with his children. A stay on the eviction was ordered by the court, however, the situation does not appear to have been resolved in Edward's favour. The bungalow was vacant by 1939 and occupied by a P McConnell in 1940. Death records indicate that Ephraim Adair died aged 61 at Mercer's Hospital, Dublin, on 21st May 1950 of a heart attack. At that time, he was resident at 20 St Kevin's Parade. He and Ethel do not appear to have been reconciled, as she was resident at 41 Foster Terrace, Ballybrack, Dublin. Edward is buried at Mount Jerome Cemetery.

51 The Demesne – John Ward

Few details can be found for John. He is believed to have been born in 1878 and his wife was named Elizabeth. They were resident at 51 The Demesne from 1923. A son, Francis Joseph (Frank), an insurance agent and living at 51 The Demesne, died at the Jervis Street Hospital, aged 30, on 2nd November 1937. John died aged 73 at St Kevin's Hospital, Dublin, on 12th February 1952 of motor neurone disease. Elizabeth survived him for four years and died on 8th March 1956. The couple are buried at Glasnevin Cemetery.

52 The Demesne – William Byrne

A native of Dublin having been born in 1887, William was a Private in the Royal Army Medical Corps during the Great War having the corps number 68469. It is not known when he enlisted and he did not serve abroad until at least 1916. He was demobilised on 9th November 1919, and on demobilisation gave his address as 1 Temple Street, Dublin. He applied for a disability pension citing malaria and bronchitis. He was assessed as 50% disabled and was awarded a weekly pension of one pound per week for himself and 14 shillings and ninepence for his wife Josephine and three eligible children. Allocated the bungalow at 52 The Demesne, William gained employment as a commercial traveller. Josephine died at the family home on 9th April 1952 aged 57 of pneumonia. William survived her for five years and died aged 70 on 10th April 1957 at his home of cancer. William and Josephine are buried at Glasnevin Cemetery.

53 The Demesne – William Maurice Higginbotham

William was born at Glenmaurice, Clontarf, on 15th May 1884, the son of Maurice Fitzgerald and Kate Jane Higginbotham, née Harte. At the time of the birth, the birth register records Maurice as 'Gentleman'. Both the 1901 and 1911 Census shows the family as resident at St Laurence's Road, Clontarf. The 1911 Census records William as being in employment as a tramway company clerk. William enlisted with the Army Service Corps Mechanical Transport with the corps number M2/147859. Records indicate that he served in a theatre of war, but not before 1916. On 12th June 1918, he married Robina Harper at Clontarf

Parish Church. His occupation is recorded on the marriage register as a commercial clerk, however, he continued to serve in the military until 24th May 1919. He resided at 53 The Demesne until 1931 and then moved to Wales. He died aged 86 at St Asaph, Denbighshire, Wales in April 1971.

54 The Demesne – Patrick Joseph Barrington

Patrick was born on 25th February 1887 at the Rotunda Hospital, Dublin, to Patrick Barrington, a house painter by trade, and Margaret Barrington (née McMahon) of 76 Mary's Lane in the Inns Quay district of the city. Patrick enlisted with a militia battalion of the Royal Dublin Fusiliers (Regimental Number 6301) on 21st June 1908 at Maryborough in Queen's County. He was a house painter and living on Chancery Street when he married Bridget Malone at the Roman Catholic Church on Aughrim Street, Dublin, on 10th April 1910, and they were living at Charles Street West in 1911.

Patrick Barrington held the rank of Sergeant when he was posted to 1st Battalion Royal Dublin Fusiliers on the Western Front on 8th April 1917. He was taken prisoner at Malassise Ferme near Ronssoy on 21st March 1918, on the opening day of the German Spring Offensive and spent eight months as a Prisoner of War at Gustrow POW camp on the coast of the Baltic Sea in northern Germany and was repatriated five weeks after the Armistice. He re-enlisted or extended his service on 4th March 1919 at Naas. He was demobilised on 5th July 1922, with his discharge address being at North King Street. He then enlisted with the National Army and was stationed at Stewart Barracks at The Curragh, County Kildare, on the night of 12th/13th November 1922. However, a pension card records his address as 68 Abbeyfield in 1924 and he is recorded as being the occupant of 54 The Demesne in the 1926 Thom's Directory. Brigid Barrington died of tuberculosis at the Lourdes Hospital, Dublin, on 22nd June 1926 at the age of 36. Although the 1928 and 1929 Thom's directories record Patrick as the occupant of 54 The Demesne, he was recorded as living at Moore Street when he married Mary Broughal on 4th November 1928 at St. Joseph's Catholic Church. In the 1931 Thom's Directory, the occupant of 54 Demesne was recorded as 'A Buttenshaw'. Patrick and Mary were living at 63 Glenshesk

Park in the Whitehall district when Mary died on 15th December 1938 at the age of 32. Patrick then married Margaret Kelly on 3rd November 1940 at the Church of Our Lady of the Visitation in Fairview. Patrick died of chronic bronchitis and cardiac failure at Leopardstown Park Hospital in Stillorgan on 2nd January 1945, aged 57 (although his age is recorded as 48 in the Register of Deaths). Although he is recorded as being a painter in the marriage registers, his occupation was recorded as 'British ex-soldier' in the Register of Deaths.

55 The Demesne – James Joseph Kinsella

The 1926 and 1932 Thom's directories record the occupant as M J Kinsella. James was born on 1st February 1894 at 7 Upper Gloucester Street, Dublin, the son of James and Mary Kinsella, née Maher. The 1901 Census shows James as resident with his mother and siblings as a lodger with the Strom family at Lower Gloucester Street. By 1911, James was resident with his parents and siblings at Rutland Street Upper, Dublin. At that time, James was in employment as a porter. Records indicate that James was an employee of Dublin Corporation before leaving to serve in the Great War. It has not been possible to identify James' military records however it is known that following his return from the Great War, he joined the Dublin Fire Brigade, initially being stationed at Tara Street. On 21st April 1925, James married Rebecca Lawlor, the daughter of a labourer from Hamilton Row at St Andrew's Roman Catholic Church, Dublin. At the time of the marriage, James' address was given as Fire Brigade Headquarters. James and Rebecca brought up a family of six sons and a daughter at 55 The Demesne. James died aged 60 at St Luke's Hospital, Rathgar, on 21st October 1954 of cancer. Following a service at St Brigids Killester, James' remains were conveyed to Mount Jerome

James Kinsella
55 The Demesne
(source: Ancestry family tree)

Cemetery on a Fire Engine, the coffin draped with the Municipal flag on which rested his helmet and axe. A son, James was also a member of the Fire Brigade.

56 The Demesne – Daniel Mahon

Born at 19 Summerhill, Dublin, on 7th November 1885, Daniel was the son of Daniel and Elizabeth Mahon, née Martin. The 1901 Census shows Daniel as resident with his family at Britain Place, Dublin. At aged 15, Daniel had completed his education and was an apprentice. On 13th August 1909, Daniel married Mary Hill at St Mary's Roman Catholic Pro-Cathedral, Dublin. The 1911 Census shows Daniel and Mary as resident at Portland Row, Dublin. At that time the couple had a son, Edward William. A daughter named Maureen had been born prematurely on 11th December 1910 and had died the same day. The 1911 Census shows Daniel in employment as a boilermaker's helper. Daniel enlisted in the South Wales Borderers on 9th December 1915. He was posted to the Regiment's 3rd battalion with the regimental number 59755. This was a reserve battalion and was based at Liverpool as part of the Mersey Garrison. Daniel did not serve in a theatre of war and was discharged on 9th January 1919 with the Silver War Badge as unfit for service due to sickness. Daniel applied for a disability pension citing heart problems and varicose veins. He was assessed as 30% disabled and was in receipt of a pension of 16 shillings for himself and 11 shillings and tenpence for Mary and three eligible children. Following discharge, Daniel gained employment as a clerk with the Department of Industry and Commerce and worked there from 1919 to 1934. He then obtained a post with the Headquarters Staff at Dublin Castle. Daniel died on 14th April 1936 aged 50 at Dr Steeven's Hospital of complications following an appendicitis operation. He is buried at Glasnevin Cemetery.

57 The Demesne – Thomas Heffernan

Thomas was born on 6th September 1875 at 10 Great Britain Street, Dublin, the son of William and Mary Heffernan, née Gore. At the time of the birth, William Heffernan was employed as a painter. Thomas enlisted in the Royal Navy on his 18th birthday on 6th September 1893 at Portsmouth, as a Boy, with the Naval Number 158031. At the time of enlistment, he was five feet and one inch tall. His initial posting was to HMS *Impregnable*, a training ship based at Devonport, Plymouth. Thomas served on several ships, including HMS *Terrible* which was involved in supporting the landings in South Africa at the outbreak of the Boer War. By 1901, Thomas had attained the rank of Leading Seaman. By 1905, Thomas had again been promoted to Petty Officer 1st Class, and was serving on the newly commissioned battleship, HMS *Lord Nelson*. At the outbreak of war in 1914, Thomas was serving at HMS *Excellent*, a shore establishment at Portsmouth.

The following year, on 9th September 1915, Thomas married Alice Charlotte Tait at St Stephen's Church of Ireland, Mount Street Crescent, Dublin. At the time of the marriage, Thomas' address was given as Temple Buildings, Upper Dominick Street, Dublin, and his occupation given as, 'Petty Officer RN'. Alice was the daughter of a plumber from Waterloo Road in the city. Thomas embarked on active service with HMS *Attentive* in August 1916. On 1st January 1917, he was awarded the Distinguished Service Medal for, 'War Services – Operations in Belgium' which involved the deployment of Naval Siege Guns. Later that year in May 1917, Thomas was promoted to Acting Chief Petty Officer. HMS *Attentive* was part of the Dover Patrol and participated in the Zeebrugge Raid in April 1918 when a joint Royal Navy and Royal Marines operation was launched to block the U-Boat pens at the Belgian port by sinking concrete filled ships at the port entrance. Although a failure and with heavy casualties sustained by the attackers, eight Victoria Crosses were awarded for gallantry. Following this raid, Thomas transferred to HMS *Victory I*, a shore establishment, and then to HMS *Fisguard*, a shore establishment, to train Engineers. He was discharged, 'time served' on 10th March 1920. In addition to his Distinguished Service Medal, Thomas was eligible for the 1914-15 Star, British War Medal, and Allied Victory Medal. Thomas and Alice were allocated the bungalow at 57 The Demesne and were resident there until Alice's death at her home on 17th September 1956 of cancer. Thomas died less than two years later at Meath Hospital, on 14th July 1958 of general paralysis. The Death Register records his occupation as a retired seaman.

58 The Demesne – Alfred English

The son of a shoemaker, Alfred was born on 13th June 1864 at the Coombe Hospital, Dublin. His parents, John and Mary, were resident at 1 Derby Square in the city. By the early 1890s, Alfred had enlisted in the Royal Navy. On 3rd January 1893, he married Sarah Ann Kemp at Castleknock Parish Church. At that time, Alfred's occupation was given as Seaman RN. A witness to the marriage was Sarah's Aunt, Dora Soxsmith. The 1911 Census of Ireland shows Alfred and Sarah resident with two children at West Rock, Ballyshannon, County Donegal. At that time, Alfred was a Petty Officer in the Coastguard and served throughout the war in that capacity. He retired in the rank of Chief Petty Officer (Coastguard) in April 1921 as he had reached the upper age limit and was allocated the bungalow at 58 The Demesne. He was also in receipt of a pension for gastritis and deafness. Sarah's Aunt Dora appears to have resided with the family as she died at 58 The Demesne on 20th October 1932 aged 83. A neighbour, Rose Liddy from 20 The Demesne was present at the death. Sarah English died aged 74 at her home address on 23rd November 1942. Alfred survived her for a year and died aged 79 on 8th August 1943 at the Mater Hospital, Dublin, of cancer.

59 The Demesne – Walter William Wayte

Walter Wayte was born on 29th April 1893 at 4 Walter Terrace, Dublin, the son of Albert and Agnes Wayte, née O'Neill. Albert Wayte was a well-known motorcycle engineer and took part in motorcycle racing events. The 1901 Census shows Walter as a resident with his parents at Richmond Road, Drumcondra. By 1911, Walter was resident with his parents and seven siblings at Walter Terrace, Drumcondra. On 27th October 1915, Walter enlisted in the Royal Flying Corps as a Fitter with the corps number 12261. He embarked for active service on 5th October 1916 and transferred to the Royal Air Force on its formation on 1st April 1918. Walter was demobilised on 11th March 1919 and on demobilisation gave his address as, 'The Homestead', Iona Road, Glasnevin. He became a motor engineer and on 1st November 1922, married Eileen Henrietta Hopkins at St George's Parish Church, Dublin. Allocated the bungalow at 59 The Demesne, Walter was arrested in March 1928 for a series of unspecified offences involving females on train journeys between Amiens Street and Killester. Released on bail after a period in custody, there are no records to indicate if Walter was ever convicted. He left Killester by 1931 and moved to England. He died in Harrogate, North Yorkshire in 1975. Eileen also died at Harrogate in 1978.

60 The Demesne – Samuel Arthur Leech

Samuel was born in Dublin around 1879, the son of Bernard and Sarah Leech, née Sharpe. Bernard Leech was in employment as a building contractor. Samuel enlisted in the 8th (King's Royal Irish) Hussars at Dublin on 21st June 1898. At the time of enlistment, he was employed as a carpenter. He joined the Hussars at Cahir, County Tipperary, on 24th June as Private 4141. Tragically, Samuel's mother died at Sir Patrick Dun's Hospital Dublin, aged 42, on 16th December 1899 of cancer. The Hussars were deployed to South Africa to serve in the Boer War and Samuel embarked for South Africa on 13th February 1900, serving there until 17th January 1901. Family information indicates that he was wounded at Geluk's Farm on 13th October 1900 and he was invalided back to the United Kingdom. For his service in South Africa, he was awarded the Queen's South Africa Medal with clasps for Johannesburg, Diamond Hill, Belfast, Cape Colony, and the Orange Free State. The 1901 Census shows Samuel as resident with his father and siblings at London Bridge Road, Dublin, the census recording his occupation as, '8th Hussars'. He was promoted Lance Corporal on 1st June 1901 and Corporal in October of that year.

In July 1903, due to a reduction in strength, Samuel was transferred to the Army Reserve. Records indicate that he continued to reside with his family and took up employment as a painter. On 4th December 1906, Samuel married Anna Harley at Sandymount

Samuel Leech
60 The Demesne
(source: Stephen Leech)

Chapel, Dublin. At the time of the marriage, Samuel was resident at 9 Serpentine Terrace, Sandymount, and was employed as a painting contractor. Anna was from Lambert Terrace Sandymount and was employed as a Lady's Companion. Samuel enlisted in the South Irish Horse on 25th January 1908 with the regimental number 73006. This was a part-time Yeomanry unit and soldiering included a two-week camp each year to hone military skills. The 1911 Census shows Samuel as resident at Vergemont Hall, Dublin. At that time, he and Anna had five children. By the outbreak of war in 1914, Samuel had been promoted to the rank of Regimental Quartermaster Sergeant. He served throughout the war in Ireland, being promoted to Regimental Sergeant Major on 2nd May 1917. He was demobilised from the army on 2nd June 1919 and resumed his trade as a painting contractor. Allocated the bungalow at 60 The Demesne, Samuel resided there until his death of heart failure aged 86, at St Kevin's Hospital, Dublin, on 7th August 1964. He is buried at Section G Grave 78 in Balgriffin Cemetery, Dublin. Two of the children born to Samuel and Anna Leech died in 1989 and 1990 and are buried in the same plot as Samuel. Eileen Margaret (76) was an invalid and living at the Verville Retreat in Clontarf when she died on 30th December 1989. Samuel Leech (81), a retired painter, was living at Ringsend Street in Inchicore when he died on 24th December 1990.

61 The Demesne – Thomas Whelan

The Thom's Directory for 1926 indicates that the resident of 61 was a T Phelan. The 1932 Directory shows the resident as B Whelan. Further research shows the resident from 1923 to be Thomas Whelan. In addition, James Joseph (Jim) Crowley was resident there when he died on 18th March 1936 aged 56 of pernicious anaemia. Jim had been born at Kinsale, County Cork, on 4th May 1879, the son of John and Margaret Crowley, née Sheehan. John Crowley was a coastguard at Kinsale. Jim enlisted in the Royal Navy in 1902, Naval Number 351167, and had served in the Far East prior to the outbreak of war. During the war, he served on several ships including the battleship, HMS *Ramillies*. He was discharged on 31st December 1920 in the rank of Chief Signal Boatswain. His younger brother, John Francis, was also a member of the Royal Navy in the rank of Petty Officer, Naval Number 353697. He was drowned aged 29 on the 16th January 1914, when the Submarine A7 was lost with all hands during a training exercise off Whitsands Bay, Cornwall.

It has not been possible to positively identify Thomas Whelan from civilian and military records. From press reporting, he appears to have been involved in dealing in cars. On 3rd August 1939, he was involved in a serious road traffic accident when the car he was driving struck another vehicle on the Howth Road. His 16 years old daughter, Eileen, was a passenger. On 16th May 1942, press reporting indicates that Thomas was sentenced to 18 months imprisonment for receiving stolen goods, being part of a ring involved in the theft and resale of bicycles. In court, he claimed to have forfeited his British Army pension as he had been a Despatch Rider for Michael Collins during the War of Independence, during which he was wounded. As a result of his imprisonment, he was evicted from 61 The Demesne, the resident in 1944 being a J Garraghan. Records indicate that Thomas Whelan died aged 60 on 18th March 1955 at 44 Church Dublin. This may be the same Thomas Whelan.

62 The Demesne/232 Howth Road – Robert Ingram

The son of a carpenter, Robert was born on 3rd September 1879 at 9 Cow Parlour, Dublin, his parents being William and Ann Ingram, née Brennan. Tragically, Robert's father died when he was five and he was raised along with three siblings by his mother. At the age of 15, Robert was employed by the Guinness Brewery however, this does not appear to have been a long-term commitment. The 1901 Census shows Robert as resident with his widowed mother at Hamilton Street, Dublin. At that time, he was employed as an apothecary's assistant. On 22nd August 1905, he married Sarah Curtis at Dalkey Parish Church. At the time of the marriage, Robert was resident at Adelaide Terrace, Kilmainham and Sarah was from Montalto, Dalkey. The 1911 Census shows the couple as resident at Foyle Road, Clontarf, with two daughters. Robert was still in employment as an apothecary's assistant. He enlisted in the Royal Navy on 2nd August 1914 for a year however, with the outbreak of war coming two days later, he was engaged for the duration of the War. He was posted to the Royal Naval Air Service as a Medical Attendant with the number M9417. He served throughout the war, including two years in France, and was demobilised on 12th April 1919. He was allocated the bungalow at 62 The Demesne and gained employment as a clerk. He died at his home address on 27th February 1942 aged 62 of tuberculosis.

63 The Demesne/234 Howth Road – George Brien

George was born on 12th October 1873 at Rockbrook, Rathfarnham, Dublin, the son of John and Mary Anne Brien, née Fitzgerald. He married Mary Jenkinson at Rathgar Roman Catholic Church on 9th January 1899. At that time George was a labourer and resident at 49 Upper Rathmines, Dublin. Mary was a tradeswoman, resident at 15 Upper Rathmines. The 1901 Census shows George and Mary as resident at house 474 Upper Rathmines. They were both servants of the householder, Lisette Gahagan. In 1911, the family were resident at house 105 Upper Rathmines. At that time George and Mary had three daughters and a son, and George was employed as a labourer.

George enlisted with the Royal Dublin Fusiliers on 2nd February 1915. He was posted to the 8th battalion with the regimental number 18793 and embarked for France on 19th December 1915. He was wounded on 28th May 1917 and on recovery was transferred to the Labour Corps, with the corps number 478858. He was posted to No 18 Company, Labour Corps and continued to serve until demobilised on 27th March 1919. On demobilisation, his military character was described as, 'Good'. George's forwarding address on demobilisation was 45 Rathmines Road, Dublin. He applied for a disability pension in relation to his wounds and was initially assessed as 20% disabled and awarded a pension of eight shillings per week for himself and three shillings and sixpence for Mary and one dependant child under 16. George resumed work as a labourer and he and Mary were allocated the bungalow at 63 The Demesne/234 Howth Road in the mid-1920s. Mary died at her home on 7th October 1954 aged 82 of heart failure. George survived her for seven years and died at St Kevin's Hospital, Dublin on 24th September 1961 aged 87 of pneumonia and complications of a broken leg. George and Mary are buried at Mount Jerome Cemetery.

64 The Demesne/236 Howth Road – Edward Joseph Black

The son of a Mercantile Marine Mate, Edward was born on 23rd April 1888 at 48 Charlesville Avenue, Dublin. His father was also named Edward and his mother was Bridget Black, née Storey. The 1901 Census shows Edward as resident at the Monastery Boarding School, Clondalkin. On completion of his education, Edward followed his father and joined the Mercantile Marine. The 1911 Census shows Edward as an Able Seaman in Portsmouth. He did not continue his career at sea and, following the outbreak of war in 1914, enlisted in the Army Service Corps Mechanical Transport with the corps number M2/082530. He embarked for France on 10th September 1915, and served throughout the war being demobilised on 27th June 1919. During his service, Edward appears to have been wounded and treated at a hospital in Birkenhead, Liverpool. On 2nd February 1920, Edward married Brigid Donohoe at the Church of Our Immaculate Lady of Refuge, Rathmines. At the time of the marriage, Edward was residing at 21 Dunville Avenue, Rathmines, and was in employment as a motor engineer. Brigid was from 41 Lower Mountpleasant Avenue, Rathmines. The couple moved into 64 The Demesne/236 Howth Road in the mid-1920s and Edward continued in his occupation as a mechanic. He died aged 78 on 23rd October 1966 at the Mater Hospital, Dublin of the effects of cancer. He is buried at Mount Jerome Cemetery.

Edward Black
64 The Demesne
(source: Ancestry family tree)

65 The Demesne/238 Howth Road – Thomas Lynch

No military records can be positively identified for Thomas. It is known that he was born around 1860 and on 9th November 1879, he married Kathleen McDermott at St Andrew's Roman Catholic Church, Dublin. At the time of the marriage, Thomas was employed as a billiard marker. The 1901 Census shows him as a widower, living with his daughter

Theresa, at Upper George's Street, Dublin. Thomas was in business as a tobacconist at that time. In 1911, he was still resident with his daughter at George's Street, Dublin and was still a tobacconist. Thomas died of chronic nephritis on 18th March 192, aged 65, at 24 The Demesne, which was the home of Patrick Stack. His daughter Theresa of the same address was present at the death. The Thom's directories record Thomas as the resident at 65 The Demesne in 1926 through to the 1929 edition, with 'O'Hanlon, G' being the occupant in 1930. Osmond Thomas Taylor, previously of 71 Abbeyfield, became the occupant of 65 The Demesne in 1945.

66 The Demesne/240 Howth Road – Richard Joseph Field

Richard was born on 9th June 1873 at Kilbarrack Junction, Dublin, the son of John and Margaret Field, née Flood. John Field was employed as a railway pointsman at the time of the birth. Richard enlisted in the Royal Garrison Artillery at Dublin on 14th April 1891 with the regimental number 84446. He served in Malta and Jamaica until October 1898, when he was transferred to the Army Reserve, only to be recalled to duty in 1899 due to the Boer War. Following his recall to duty, he appears to have served within the United Kingdom and Ireland. On 26th January 1900, he married Mary Foran at St Joseph's Roman Catholic Church, Rathdown, County Wicklow. Richard served until April 1903 when he was discharged having completed his period of engagement. He did, however, remain in the Special Reserve of the RGA which meant part-time soldiering with a two-week residential camp each summer.

The 1911 Census shows Richard and Mary and four surviving children resident at Crampton Quay, Dublin. At that time, Richard was employed as a storeman. On 8th March 1915, Richard re-enlisted in the Royal Garrison Artillery with the regimental number 281470. At the time of enlistment, he was resident at 1 Rutledge Cottages, off Meath Street, Dublin. On 9th January 1916, he was posted to Egypt, serving there until April 1917 war before serving in England in the rank of Gunner until he was demobilised on 11th March 1919. On demobilisation, Richard's address was given as 142 Cope Street, Dublin. He applied for a Disability Pension citing rheumatism which had been aggravated by his war service. He was assessed as 20% disabled and awarded a pension of eight shillings per week for himself and eight shillings and fourpence per week for Mary and six eligible children. Richard resumed his employment as a storeman and was allocated the bungalow at 66 The Demesne in the mid-1920s. He resided there until his death aged 76 on 9th May 1950. The death register records his cause of death as, 'chronic valvular disease of heart 33 years, rheumatic infection 1914-1918 War. Cardiac & respiratory failure 24 hours certified'.

67 The Demesne/242 Howth Road – Michael Frederick Wild Cavanagh

Michael was born on 5th July 1892 at Mount Vernon, Ballymount, Dublin, the son of John and Mary Louisa Cavanagh, née Wild. At the time of the birth, John Cavanagh was a journalist. By 1901, John Cavanagh had died, and Michael was resident with his widowed mother, an aunt and three siblings at Shelbourne Road, Dublin. By 1911, Michael, then aged 18, was still resident with his family at Shelbourne Road and was employed as a clerk in a warehouse. Michael enlisted in the Royal Engineers, most likely in 1915, and was issued with the regimental number 282211. He embarked on active service around 1916 and was awarded Engineer pay on 26th May 1917. He served for the remainder of the war and on his return to Dublin, took up employment as an electrician. On 28th April 1919, he married Clare Gladys Cleary at Fairview Roman Catholic Chapel, Dublin. At that time, Michael was employed as a telephone engineer and was resident at St James' Terrace, Sandymount. Clare was from Brighton Avenue, Fairmount, and the daughter of a journalist. The couple were resident at Sandymount Road in 1922 when their daughter, Clare Gladys was born on 17th April. Michael was allocated the bungalow at 67 The Demesne in 1923 and resided there with his family, continuing in employment as a telephone engineer. His wife, Clare, died aged 57 at her home on 22nd July 1948 of biliary colic. In March 1962, Michael was badly injured when his motorcycle skidded on Howth Road and struck a lamppost. Following convalescence from his injuries, he continued to reside at 67 The Demesne, until his death aged 73 at his home address on 21st February 1966, of toxaemia and exhaustion. The couple are buried at Dean's Grange Cemetery, Dublin.

68 The Demesne/244 Howth Road – William John Pearston Jamieson

The Thom's Directory for 1926 and 1932 indicates that the resident of 68 was a P. Brady. No identifying records can be found based on this information. It is believed that William Jamieson and his family were resident at Killester from the late 1940s. William had been born at 95 Church Road, Dublin, on 19th September 1897, the son of William and Agnes Jamieson, née Pearston. At the time of the birth, the family had recently moved from Scotland. William Jamieson senior was a grocer. The 1901 Census shows the family as resident at Northcourt Avenue, Dublin and by 1911, they were resident at 7 Anglesea Street in the city. On the available information, it has not been possible to identify William's military service. However, from 13th August 1919, he was employed at Guinness' St James' Gate, Brewery. On 16th October 1926, he married Elizabeth Mary Glennon at St Michan's Roman Catholic Church, Dublin. At the time of the marriage, William was resident at Anglesea Street, Dublin, and Elizabeth was from Anglesea Road in the city. William worked for Guinness for over 39 years becoming a senior tap man. He died at the Company's Dining Room on 18th March 1959 of a coronary thrombosis. Elizabeth survived him for 22 years and died on 6th January 1982. The couple are buried at Mount Jerome Cemetery.

69 The Demesne/246 Howth Road – Charles Robert Long

Charles is believed to have been born around 1886 and most likely enlisted in 1915 with the 16th (The Queen's) Lancers, a cavalry regiment, with the regimental number L1075. He embarked for the Western Front in 1916 and was hospitalised in July 1917 with a severe gunshot wound to the left thigh. He was discharged from the army in 1919 and applied for a disability pension. On discharge, his address was given as 34 Montpelier Hill, Dublin. He was assessed as 30% disabled and was awarded a pension of thirteen shillings per week for himself and three shillings per week for his wife, Bridget. Charles gained employment as a lithograph operator and was allocated a house at 69 The Demesne, which he named, 'Lancer Villa'. He resided there until his death aged 71 on 4th December 1958. He collapsed with a coronary thrombosis at the bus stop, Howth Road, Killester, and was found to be dead on arrival at Jervis Street Hospital.

70 The Demesne/248 Howth Road – James Whelan

The resident of this address is recorded in the 1926 Thom's Directory as an R Kearns. No civilian or military records of anyone of this name can be identified for the address. James Whelan is recorded as the occupant in the 1930 Thom's Directory. Few biographical details can be found for James who was born around 1890. He initially enlisted in the Royal Engineers (regimental number 50733) and embarked with them to Gallipoli on 4th July 1915. He was medically evacuated to the island of Mudros on 10th September with dysentery. Following recovery, James was transferred to the Bedfordshire Regiment with the regimental number 32475, and he served with that regiment until de-mobilised on 29th March 1919. James applied for a Disability Pension, citing dysentery. He was assessed as 20% disabled and awarded a pension of eight shillings per week. His address on demobilisation was recorded as 22 Lower Gardiner Street, Dublin. James gained employ-ment as a shop assistant and he and his wife Mary (née Brophy) moved into 248 Howth Road (formerly 70 The Demesne) around 1940 – his wife's forename is sometimes recorded as Marie or Maria. Five years after moving into 70 The Demesne, their son Anthony, died aged 15 at Baggott Street Hospital of septicaemia. In addition to Anthony, records indicate that the couple had four other children – Joseph, Gerard, Eric, and Teresa. James appears to have been active in St Brigid's Parish, or-ganising a seven-a-side football tournament for the parish fete. James, a retired shop assistant, died at 248 Howth Road on 2nd November 1965 aged 74 of cirrhosis of the liver. Mary died aged 81 at her home on 25th August 1972 of a coronary thrombosis. In the death register, Mary is described as the widow of a painter. The couple are buried at Kilbarrack Cemetery, Sutton (Section BG Grave 4).

71 The Demesne/250 Howth Road

Although there were at least four residents of 71 The Demesne between 1923 and 1973 research has been unable to positively identify civilian or military records for any of the four. What is known is that the resident in the 1926 Thom's Directory was an L Lambe. By 1930, this had changed to a C Reavy. At that time, a kennel for breeding greyhounds appears to have operated from the premises. By the early 1950s a family by the name of Desmond resided at 71 The Demesne as Bridget Desmond died there on 30th September 1953. Unfortunately, there are no details of her husband. By the early 1970s, the residents were Patrick Joseph McAlister and his wife, Margaret. Patrick had been a Customs & Excise Officer and he died at Sir Patrick Dun's Hospital on 29th August 1973, aged 77. Margaret McAlister was living at 250 Howth Road when she died on 6th September 1987, aged 89. Patrick and Margaret McAlister are buried at Balgriffin Cemetery (Section D Grave 104).

72 The Demesne/252 Howth Road – Robert Frederick Switzer

Robert was born on 11th June 1884 in the townland of Cloonshanbilla, Boyle, County Roscommon, the son of John Thomas and Matilda Switzer, née Sparling. At the time of the birth, John Switzer was employed as a land servant. The 1901 Census shows Robert as resident with his parents and elder sister, Edith, at Cooleshill, Kings County (now County Offaly). Available information indicates that Robert had been a member of the South of Ireland Imperial Yeomanry (later the South Irish Horse) since September 1903. By 1910, Robert had moved to Dublin and was employed as an office worker in the Brewhouse of the Guinness Brewery. The Census of the following year shows Robert as resident with relatives at North Dock Street, Dublin. At that time, his occupation was given as a general labourer. At the outbreak of the war, Robert was a Sergeant in C Troop, S Squadron, South Irish Horse with the regimental number 37, and, having been mobilised for active service, embarked for the Western Front on 17th August 1914. By 1916, Robert was an Acting Sergeant Major. In September 1917, the South Irish Horse was dismounted due to military necessity and became an infantry battalion, the 7th (South Irish Horse) battalion Royal Irish Regiment. At that time, Robert's regimental number changed to 25824. On 17th October of that year, Robert was awarded the Meritorious Service Medal for valuable services rendered during the course of the war. He was posted to No 7 Officer Cadet Battalion at Fermoy, County Cork in February 1918 and was commissioned as a Second Lieutenant in the 7th battalion Royal Irish Regiment on 25th June 1918. A report on him on completion of the course stated:

> A good solid type of fellow with good experience. His theoretical knowledge is not quite on a par with his practical work. Nevertheless, he will make a good officer.

An astute assessment. He was awarded the Military Cross for an action on the night of 21st/22nd October 1918, the citation reading:

> For conspicuous gallantry and able leadership. During the night of 21st/22nd October 1918, previous to the attack on Bossuyt Chateau Wood east of St Genois, under heavy machine gun fire, he made three reconnaissances of the ground to be covered in the advance bringing back valuable information. In the attack he penetrated the enemy lines to the furthest point reached near the village, and when surrounded by the enemy, counter-attacked, inflicting heavy losses and held his position for ten hours, finally getting into touch with his Company.

Robert relinquished his commission on 27th August 1919 and on his return home, married Catherine Fulham, the couple initially residing at 23 Harman Terrace, Dublin. In the early 1920s the couple were allocated the bungalow at 72 The Demesne (which became 252 Howth Road in the mid-1930s). In February 1925, newspaper reports indicate that Robert sued his neighbour, Charles Edward Pyke of 73 The Demesne, for injuries received by his son, John William Switzer, who had been knocked down by Mr Pyke's motor vehicle. The following month, tragedy was to strike the family when their son James Albert, died aged three weeks of bronchitis. Further tragedy was to strike the family on 21st July 1934, when John Switzer, who had been injured in the previous motor accident, was knocked down and

Robert and Catherine Switzer
72 The Demesne (252 Howth Road)
(source: Ancestry family tree)

killed by a tram car during a thunderstorm. At the inquest, Robert told the coroner that his son had had defective eyesight from the initial accident. A keen gardener, Robert won many prizes for his displays at his home. Employed as a timekeeper, he died at his home on 23rd August 1942 aged 52, of kidney disease. He was buried in the cemetery of St John the Baptist, Clontarf. His war service is commemorated on the Roll of Honour at the St James' Gate Brewery.

73 The Demesne – Charles Edward Pyke

Charles was born on 13th January 1898 at Ardeevan, Glasnevin, Dublin, the son of Charles Lloyd and Maggie Pyke, née Cinnamond. His father, Charles was employed as a commercial traveller. The 1901 Census shows Charles as resident with his parents and three elder siblings at Church Hill, Naul Road, Glasnevin. By 1911, the family were resident at Church Hill Terrace, Glasnevin. Charles senior and his eldest son Percival were both agents for a Tea and Sugar Company. Charles enlisted in the North Irish Horse, a Yeomanry Cavalry Unit, in April 1916 with the regimental number 2149. This unit recruited mainly in the north of Ireland and Charles had family connections there as his mother was from County Down. He joined his unit on the Western Front in 1916 and in June 1917, transferred to the South Irish Horse, his regimental number being 3145. When the South Irish Horse was dismounted in September 1917, Charles and most of the regiment were transferred to the 7th (South Irish Horse) battalion Royal Irish Regiment. Charles' regimental number changed again, this time to 25712. Charles served for the remainder of the war and was demobilised in February 1919. On discharge, his address was given as 5 Seafield Terrace, Clontarf. Charles followed his father's career path and became a commercial traveller and was resident at 73 The Demesne when he was involved in an accident with his neighbour's son in February 1925. On 9th February 1931, Charles married Helen Buchanan Matthews, the daughter of a farmer at St Ann's Church of Ireland, Dublin. Records indicate that following his marriage, Charles changed careers, becoming a Customs and Excise agent. He and Helen also moved to Ard na Mara, Malahide. Helen died aged 73 at St Joseph's Nursing Home on 17th May 1969.

Chapter 4

Occupants of Middle Third

At the completion of construction in 1923, Middle Third comprised 49 bungalows, most being semi-detached but there were eleven of the larger, detached bungalows. The 1931 Thom's Directory records that two additional dwellings – Number 50 and Number 51 – had been added to Middle Third. They were detached bungalows and the Abbey Hall had been built between the two plots by 1930. In the late 1940s, some of the bungalows in Middle Third were re-addressed as Killester Avenue, retaining their original house numbers – for example, 3 Middle Third had become 3 Killester Avenue by 1946.

1 Middle Third – Michael J Collins

Michael J Collins was born around 1873 to Francis Collins, a carpenter, and Bridget Collins (née Verso) and was a carpenter and living at Bride Street when he married Elizabeth McBride of Carter's Lane on 17th June 1888 at St Paul's Roman Catholic Church. They were living at Nicholas Avenue in Arran Quay in 1901. *The researchers have not been able to identify war service details for the occupant.*

Michael and Elizabeth Collins were living at Killester when their daughter, Julia, married a soldier called James Callaghan in 1923. Elizabeth Collins died at the Dublin Union Workhouse on 6th December 1933, aged 59. Julia and James Callaghan were living at 1 Middle Third when Julia died on 21st December 1945, aged 46. Michael was living at 1 Middle Third when he died of cardiac failure and emphysema at St Kevin's Hospital on 3rd October 1945, his age being registered as 72, and is buried in Glasnevin Cemetery. The 1947 Thom's Directory records the occupant as 'Flynn, S'.

2 Middle Third – Daniel Hickey and Patrick Brennan

Daniel Hickey took possession of the bungalow in June 1925. In 1939, Daniel Hickey was one of seventeen tenants from Killester Garden Village who brought an action in the courts against the ISSLT and Dublin Corporation seeking a declaration that the cottages were *'exempt from rates as being used for charitable purposes'*. In his evidence at the hearing, Daniel stated that he was married with two children and was working as a debt collector. In the court papers his occupation was recorded as 'commercial agent'.

The second occupant was **Patrick Brennan** in 1944. He was born on 28th February 1881 at Ballon near Carlow to John Brennan, a blacksmith, and Ellen Brennan (née Maher). In 1901, Patrick was a blacksmith but he was an RIC Constable stationed in County Mayo when he married Bridget Burke on 14th April 1904 at St Mary's Roman Catholic Church in Clonmel, and Patrick was a labourer when they were living at Roundwood Town in County Wicklow in 1911. Patrick enlisted with the Irish Guards (Regimental Number 11538) on 12th December 1915 in Birmingham and served on the Western Front. He was attached to 3rd Battalion and stationed at Warley Camp when he was reported as missing from 27th December 1917 in the Police Gazette

Patrick and Bridget Brennan
2 Middle Third
(source: www.findagrave)

dated 8th January 1918. The next edition of the Police Gazette reported that he had returned to duty. Patrick Brennan was discharged due to wounds on 16th July 1918 (aged 36 years and 7 months) with Silver War Badge Number 378993. He was living at 7 Christ Church Place when he was awarded a 30% Disability Pension in respect of gunshot wounds to the face, tinnitus, defective vision and deafness, and conjunctivitis, at the rate of eight shillings per week plus five shillings and tenpence per week for his dependants. Bridget Brennan died at 2 Middle Third on 9th January 1950, aged

70, and Patrick Brennan died at Leopardstown Park Hospital on 21st December 1974, aged 93 (although the gravestone records his age as 96). Patrick and Bridget Brennan are buried in Glasnevin Cemetery (VF 72 – St. Paul's Section).

3 Middle Third – Thomas John McGrath

Thomas John McGrath was born on 7th May 1892 at 3 Usher's Quay to Edward McGrath, a house painter, and Catherine McGrath (née O'Connell) and the family home was at Arran Quay in 1901 and Usher's Quay in 1911. *The researchers have not been able to identify war service details for the occupant.* Thomas was a soldier when he married Bridget Birmingham of 15 Lough Road in Cork on 30th April 1919 at St Finbar's West Roman Catholic Church at The Lough in Cork. Thomas McGrath was recorded as being a Soldier when their first child, Walter Edward, was born was born on 21st August 1920 at 15 Lough Road in Cork. Kathleen Pauline McGrath, a daughter of Thomas and Bridget, died at the age of 10 months in 1927. In late 1941, their son enlisted with Royal Air Force Volunteer Reserve for service in the Second World War under the name Edward Walter McGrath. Sergeant McGrath was the Flight Engineer on an Avro Lancaster Mark 3 aircraft (Serial Number PB465) of 103 Squadron which took off from RAF Elsham Wolds at 11:46 on 29th November 1944 for a day-time bombing raid on Dortmund.

*Thomas and Bridget McGrath
3 Middle Third
(source: www.findagrave)*

The aircraft was involved in a mid-air collision with an Avro Lancaster from 550 Squadron and crashed with the loss of six members of the crew – one man survived the crash and was taken prisoner. Edward Walter McGrath was 24 years old and is buried in the Reichswald Forest War Cemetery in Germany. Thomas John McGrath was living at 3 Killester Avenue when he died of dementia paralytica at Grangegorman Mental Hospital on 30th October 1946, aged 54, and Bridget McGrath died on 12th March 1976. Thomas, Bridget, and Kathleen Pauline McGrath are buried in the same plot in Glasnevin Cemetery (St Paul's Section – CG 28)

4 Middle Third – George Kerton

George Kerton was born on 6th October 1883 at Constitution Place in Clonmel to George Kerton, a Soldier and later a printer, and Ellen Kerton (née Tynan) and the family lived at Queen Street in Clonmel in 1901 and at Quinn Street in Clonmel in 1911. George enlisted with the Royal Irish Regiment in 1900 but was discharged after three days as he was under-age. George was a tailor when he enlisted with the 4th (Reserve) Battalion of the Royal Irish Regiment (Regimental Number 3992) on 28th January 1901 at the age of 18. In August 1901, he transferred to the Regular Army and attested with the Connaught Rangers (Regimental Number 7199), serving in South Africa from May 1902 to January 1903. He transferred to the 8th (King's Royal Irish) Hussars (Regimental Number 5196) in June 1903 and served at home until being transferred to the Army reserve in August 1909 and his twelve-year period of engagement terminated on 21st August 1913.

George was a waiter and living in Kildare when he married Catherine O'Leary of Brighton Place in Clonmel on 5th April 1910 at SS Peter and

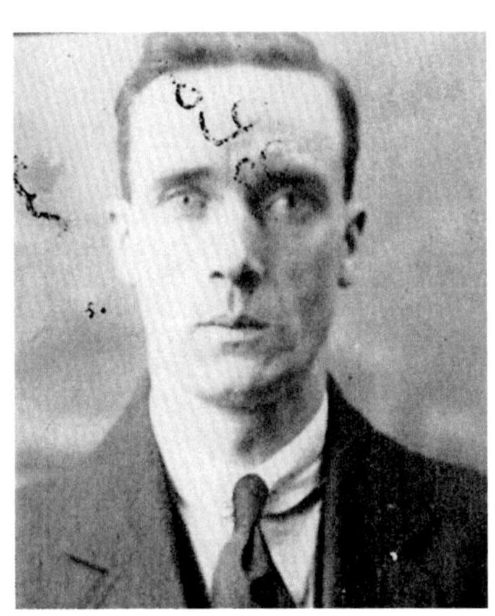

George Kerton
4 Middle Third
(sources: Merchant Navy Card)

Paul Roman Catholic Church in Clonmel. Their first child, George Christopher, was born on 29th June 1912 at Kildare and died of diptheria at the Cork Street Hospital on 24th August 1916. A second son, Alfred Patrick, was born on 10th March 1918 at Tilledon Cottages in Clontarf. George re-enlisted with 11th Hussars (Regimental Number 24141) on 29th September 1914, giving his occupation as a barman. He served on the Home Front throughout the Great War with the Hussars, 5th (Royal Irish) Lancers (Regimental Number 16197), 6th Reserve Regiment of Cavalry (Regimental Number 10589), and the Labour Corps (Regimental

Number 595145). He was an Acting Sergeant when he was transferred to the Class Z Army Reserve on 18th March 1919, his character being recorded as Very Good. He had undertaken a course of instruction in cooking in Dublin in January 1916 and subsequently joined the British Merchant Navy as a cook. In the 1926 Thom's Directory, George Kerton was listed as the occupant of 4 Middle Third and he remained at that address until he died of congestive heart failure at St Kevin's Hospital on 29th August 1963, aged 79, and is buried in St Fintan's Cemetery in Sutton (Section D Grave 61). Catherine Kerton was living at Shanbally in Cappoquin when she died at St Joseph's Hospital in Dungarvan on 15th July 1980 and is buried in St Declan's Cemetery in Cappoquin, County Waterford.

5 Middle Third – Daniel Byrne

Daniel Byrne was born on 29th March 1887 at 4 Denzille Place in Trinity Ward to Daniel Byrne, who was a porter and later a carpet planner/layer, and Sarah Byrne (née Doyle). The family lived at Boyne Street in 1901 and at Wentworth Place in 1911. Daniel Byrne enlisted with the Royal Munster Fusiliers (Regimental Number 8515) on 17th October 1905 and was stationed in England with 1st Battalion in 1911. Daniel was a waiter living at Marlborough Place when he married Mary Cleary of Queen's Terrace on 22nd November 1914 at St Andrew's Roman Catholic Church. He was recalled from the army reserve in August 1914 but discharged due to sickness on 1st September 1914 with Silver War Badge Number 77412. Daniel and Mary were living at 2 Wilson Place and Daniel was recorded as being an instructor when Sylvester was born in November 1916. It is possible that he was serving on the Home Front in a training capacity. Daniel and Mary were living at 20 Queen's Terrace when Daniel unsuccessfully applied for an army pension. They were living at 20 Queen's Terrace when Arthur Oliver Byrne was born in May 1920, Daniel's occupation being recorded as waiter. Daniel Byrne was recorded as a waiter when he died of cancer at 5 Middle Third on 3rd February 1947, aged 58, and Mary Byrne died at 5 Middle Third on 28th June 1961, aged 72. Daniel and Mary Byrne are buried in Dean's Grange Cemetery. When Sylvester Byrne died in Armagh in 1974, a death notice recorded that he was formerly of 5 Middle Third, Killester.

6 Middle Third – Alexander John Walker

Alexander John Walker was born on 22nd June 1874 at Thistle Street in Peterhead to Helen Walker. He enlisted in the Royal Naval Reserve on 7th April 1899 and in November 1902, embarked with William Spiers Bruce aboard the *Scotia* as a crew member on the Scottish Antarctic Expedition. The expedition explored the uncharted Weddell Sea, returning to Scotland in 1904. Alexander was a merchant seaman and living at Broad Street in Peterhead when he married Hannah Moult Cowap of Kirk Street on 23rd September 1904 at the North Eastern Hotel in Peterhead, according to the forms of the United Free Church of Scotland.

At the outbreak of war in 1914, Alexander was working as a rigger at the John Brown shipyard in Glasgow when he was recalled to active service and posted to the Far East, serving aboard HMS *Tamar* in Hong Kong, HMS *Empress of Asia* in Asia and the Middle East, being awarded the Royal Naval Reserve Medal whilst serving on the latter. He was serving on HMS *Dufferin*, supplying troops in the Middle East, when he was awarded the Royal Naval Reserve Long Service and Good Conduct Medal in 1917. Alexander was serving on HMS *Excellent* when he was awarded a £50 Royal Naval Reserve Gratuity in May 1918 and he served as an Acting Senior Gunner on a Defensively Armed Merchant Cruiser (attached to HMS *President II*) from the end of May 1918 until he was discharged on 29th January 1919 with the rank of Leading Seaman. Tragically, his wife Hanna died in 1919 and Ancestry family trees record that there were six children born to this marriage. Alexander later married Mary Alice Hayden and they would go on to raise eight children in Middle Third, although two died in infancy. Alice Patricia Walker died of bronchitis and cardiac failure at 6 Middle Third on 24th December 1928, aged seven weeks, and Kathleen Walker died of shock and respiratory failure during surgery at the Temple Street Hospital on 22nd September 1938, aged seven months. Alexander was a marine engineer when he died of cancer at 6 Middle Third on 23rd October 1946, aged 72, and is buried at St John the Baptist Cemetery, Clontarf, along with Alice Patricia.

7 Middle Third – John Browne

John Browne was born around 1878 at Golden, Cashel, and his father was also called John. *The researchers have not been able to identify war service details for the occupant.*

After being discharged, John joined the Guinness Brewery on 17th February 1919, aged 31, and was working as a vat washer in the Brewhouse Department when he died. He was living at the Rialto Buildings when he married Catherine Quigley from Grosvenor Road in Rathgar on 6th April 1921 at the Church of the Three Patrons in Rathgar. Catherine Browne died at 7 Middle Third on 28th March 1951, aged 57, and John Browne was living at 7 Middle Third when he died of pulmonary embolism and bronchopneumonia at Jervis Street Hospital on 13th May 1958, aged 71. John and Catherine Brown are buried in Mount Jerome Cemetery

8 Middle Third – Daniel Kearns

Daniel Kearns was born on 3rd July 1890 to Martin Kearns, a painter, and Bridget Kearns (née Robbins) and the family home was at 23 Coombe in the Wood Quay district. Daniel enlisted with the Royal Irish Rifles (Regimental Number 8604) on 13th April 1902 and was stationed with 1st Battalion in India in 1911. Daniel was recalled from the army reserve on the outbreak of the war and was posted to 1st Battalion on the Western Front on 5th November 1914 and later served with 2nd Battalion. He was stationed at Victoria Barracks in Belfast when he married Alice Comiskey of Regent Street in Belfast on 4th February 1917 at St Patrick's Roman Catholic Church. Corporal Daniel Kearns was serving with 1st Battalion when he was discharged due to wounds on 23rd June 1918 with Silver War Badge Number 423560. A son, Gerald Kevin Kearns, had been suffering from tuberculosis for eighteen months when he died of scarlet fever at the Cork Street Hospital on 16th June 1926 at the age of four. On 5th July 1938, Maureen Kearns (a tailoress with Todd, Burns & Company) was cycling home from work along Sean MacDermott Street when she was struck by a car that was on the wrong side of the road, having just passed a stationary bus. Maureen (19) was dead when she arrived at the Mater Hospital. The driver of the car, Martin Cussack, a merchant of Marlborough Street, was charged with manslaughter but was acquitted at trial in February 1939. Daniel was a retired labourer and living at 8 Middle Third when he died of cancer at St Joseph's Nursing Home in Raheny on 26th July 1970, aged 80. Alice Kearns was living at 8 Middle Third when she died at Beaumont Hospital on 9th January 1991. Daniel, Alice, Maureen, and Gerald are buried in Glasnevin Cemetery.

9 Middle Third – James Costello

James Costello was born on 19th February 1882 at 7 Upper Grand Canal Street to James Costello, a blacksmith, and Margaret Costello (née Flynn). In 1911, he was a Chief Engineer and was living on a house ship at Sir John Rogerson's Quay in South Dock. James was an engineer and living at Haddington Road when he married Kathleen Brannack of Lower Baggot Street on 21st August 1917 at St Andrew's Roman Catholic Church. He served with the Mercantile Marine, being awarded the Mercantile Marine Medal and the British War Medal. The Merchant Navy Card, introduced in 1918, records that James Costello was a fireman and he was later employed as a sea-going engineer for the Dublin Gas Company. James Costello died of cancer

James Costello
9 Middle Third
(source: Merchant Navy Card and Google Images)

at 9 Middle Third on 17th August 1950, aged 68, and Kathleen Costello died at 9 Middle Third on 15th March 1965, aged 80. James and Kathleen Costello are buried in Glasnevin Cemetery.

10 Middle Third – James Francis (Joseph) Dunne

The researchers have not been able to identify family or war service details for the occupant. Agnes Dunne died at 10 Middle Third on 27th February 1969, aged 70. Joseph Dunne was a retired harbour policeman and living at 10 Middle Third when he died of bronchopneumonia, chronic bronchitis, and paralysis at Leopardstown Park Hospital 9th December 1971. Joseph and Agnes Dunne are buried in Balgriffin Cemetery (Section I Grave 56).

11 Middle Third – Francis Augustine Roddy and Joseph Caprani

In the 1926 Thom's Directory, the occupant's surname is recorded as RADDY and in the 1928 Thom's Directory, the occupant is recorded as 'Caprani, J'.

Francis Augustine Roddy was born on 28th August 1878 at Eyrecourt near Portumna in County Galway to John Roddy, an RIC Constable, and Eliza Roddy (née Horan). Francis was a clerk and living at Emmett Street when he married Mabel Sutton of Charleville Avenue on 1st August 1900 at St Agatha's Roman Catholic Church. He enlisted with the Royal Fusiliers (Regimental Number STK/1350) and was deployed to France with 10th Battalion (aka Stockbrokers Battalion) on 13th October 1915 and served on the Western Front until 16th April 1918. Sergeant Roddy was transferred to the Class Z Army Reserve on 27th March 1919 and was living at North Dock Place in Sandymount when he was awarded a 20% Disability Pension at nine shillings and fourpence in respect of gunshot wounds to left thigh, bunions, and varicose veins. The Roddy family left the Killester bungalow in 1926 and Francis, a civil servant, was living at 35 North Brunswick Street when he died of lobar pneumonia at the Royal City of Dublin Hospital on 26th March 1946, aged 67. Mabel Roddy was living at Pearse Square when she died at St. Kevin's Hospital on 13th May 1957, aged 75. Francis and Mabel Roddy are buried in Glasnevin Cemetery.

Joseph Caprani was born on 2nd September 1897 at 3 Rose Terrace to Menotti Giovanni Caprani, a printer/compositor, and Margaret Mary Caprani (née O'Connor) and the family lived at East Wall in North Dock in 1901 and at Merville Terrace in Clontarf in 1911. Joseph enlisted with the Leinster Regiment (Regimental Number 3336) in July 1915 and landed at ANZAC Cove with 6th Battalion in August 1915. He was serving with 7th Battalion on the Western Front when he was admitted to Number 11 Stationary Hospital with gastritis in June 1916. He received a commission with 3rd Battalion Connaught Rangers on

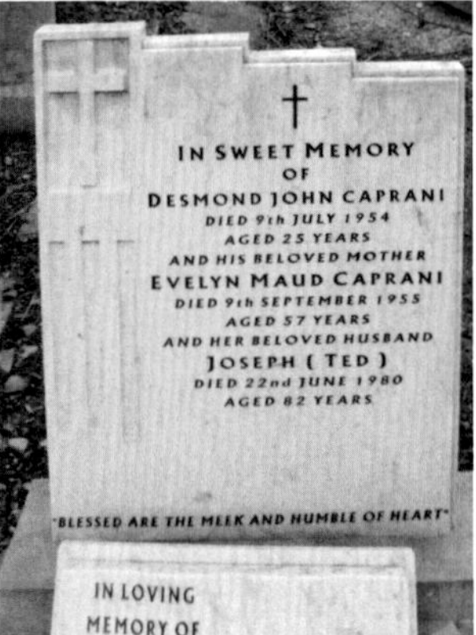

Joseph Caprani
11 Middle Third
(sources: Ancestry Family Tree and www.findagrave)

30th July 1918 and was living at Richmond Road in Fairview and Hillview Cottages in Shankill after leaving the army. Joseph was a civil servant and living at Crawford Avenue in Drumcondra when he married Evelyn Maud Wayte of Drumcondra on 1st July 1925 at St Columba's Roman Catholic Church in Drumcondra. Joseph and Evelyn Capraini moved into 11 Middle Third in December 1926 and their first child, Desmond John, was born there in 1929. Joseph took the ISSLT to court in 1935, seeking a repayment of the rent that he had paid up to the time of the Supreme Court decision in the case brought by Leggett, et al. He also sought a legal declaration that the rent agreement signed on 24th December 1926 was never valid in law. The case was still rumbling through the court system in 1937. His son, Desmond John Caprani, died of tuberculosis at Middle Third on 9th July 1954, aged 25, and Evelyn died at St Luke's Hospital in Rathgar on 9th September 1955, aged 57. Joseph (Ted) Caprani was still living at 11 Middle Third when he died at the Sacred Heart Residential Home on 22nd June 1980, aged 82. Joseph, Evelyn Maud, and Desmond John Caprani are buried in St John the Baptist Graveyard in Clontarf.

12 Middle Third – Samuel Clarke

Samuel Clarke was born on 10th February 1890 at 6 Lower Abbey Street to John Clarke, a tailor's porter, and Isabella Clarke (née Synnott). The family lived at Belvedere Road in Rotunda in 1901 and at Lower Abbey Street in North Dock in 1911. Samuel was a labourer and living at Cuffe Street when he married Catherine Watts of Mercer Street on 21st January 1912 at SS Michael and John Roman Catholic Church. Catherine Clarke gave birth to four daughters between 1914 and 1920, when the family was living at Marlborough Street. Samuel Clarke enlisted with the Royal Irish Regiment (Regimental Number 3/8206) and was posted to 2nd Battalion on the Western Front on 21st June 1915. He subsequently served with 6th Battalion before being transferred to the Labour Corps (Regimental Number 576779), serving with 953 Company. Sergeant Samuel Clarke was serving with 17th (Garrison) Battalion Worcestershire Regiment (Regimental Number 64677) when he was discharged on 3rd March 1919. In February 1922, Samuel Clarke received a £45 grant from the Military Service (Civil Liabilities) Department towards establishing a cabinet making business. The Clarke family was living in Killester when their eldest daughter, Martha Elizabeth, died of Tubercular Meningitis at St Mary's Hospice in Harold's Cross on 17th August 1924, aged 10. Joyce Ann Clarke had been suffering from bronchitis for four days when she died of convulsions at 12 Middle Third on 25th January 1931, twelve days after being born. Samuel Clarke was a carpenter when he died of pulmonary thrombosis and acute cardiac failure at Jervis Street Hospital on 5th August 1957, aged 67, and Catherine Clarke died at 12 Middle Third on 21st June 1969, aged 77. Kathleen Clarke was a machinist and living at 12 Middle Third when she died at St Laurence's Hospital on 11th July 1959, aged 50.Samuel and Catherine Clarke are buried in Kilbarrack Cemetery (Section CJ Grave 13). Also buried in the plot are their daughters, Martha Elizabeth, Joyce Ann, and Kathleen

13 Middle Third – Richard Healy

Richard Healy was born on 28th June 1886 at 8 Sackville Lane to Christopher Healy, a butcher, and Mary Healy (née Phillips). After Mary Healy died, Christopher married Maryann Harriet Behan on 29th August 1893 and the family home was in the Royal Exchange district – at Nassau Place in 1901 and at Chatham Street in 1911. Richard was a labourer and living at Great Britain Street when he married Maggie Kearney of Pitt Street on 7th February 1909 at St Andrew's Roman Catholic Church and they were living at 24 Stoneybatter in Arran Quay in 1911, Richard now being recorded as being a painter. Richard Healy enlisted with the Royal Dublin Fusiliers (Regimental Number 14705) on 26th September 1914, and he was deployed to France on

20th December 1915 with 8th Battalion. Sergeant Richard Healy was awarded the Distinguished Conduct Medal for his actions during the Battle of Hulluch in April 1916, with the citation being published in *The London Gazette* on 23rd June 1916. He sustained gunshot wounds to his left humerus on 12th May 1916 and was evacuated to England on HM Hospital Ship *St Omer* on 25th July 1916. The gunshot wounds significantly impaired the use of his left arm and Acting Company Sergeant Major Healy was discharged on 25th May 1917 with Silver War Badge Number 184106. His address on discharge was 16 Temple Street but the family was living at 40 Bessborough Avenue when Richard was awarded a 60% Disability Pension in respect of gunshot wounds to his left arm at the rate of thirty-two shillings per week. He received a supplement of twenty-four shillings and eleven pence in respect of his wife and five children. Richard was employed as a coal porter when a son, Christopher, died of meningitis at the Hardwicke Hospital on 25th August 1922 at the age of ten. Richard returned to work as a painter and died of tubercular laryngitis at Harold's Cross Hospice on 29th April 1932, aged 45, and a daughter, Eileen, was working in a factory when she died of pulmonary tuberculosis at the family home on 17th July 1940, aged 22. Margaret Healy died at 13 Middle Third on 30th October 1966, aged 78. Richard, Margaret, Christopher and Eileen are buried in Glasnevin Cemetery (St Paul's Section MD Grave 105), along with Margaret's mother, Mary Kearney, who died on 27th January 1925.

14 Middle Third – John David Crowe Caird

John David Crowe Caird was born on 16th February 1894 at Chapelizod in Castleknock to John Alexander Caird, a merchant, and Emmeline Caird (née Broadbent) and the family was living at Chapelizod in 1901 before moving to 13 Hibernian Terrace in New Kilmainham by 1911, when John was recorded as being a bookkeeper. John Caird enlisted with the South Irish Horse (Regimental Number 845) and was posted to the Western Front on 14th April 1915. In September 1917, when the South Irish Horse was dismounted, he was transferred to 7th Battalion Royal Irish Regiment (Regimental Number 25917). Private Caird was transferred to the Class Z Army Reserve on 15th March 1919 and was awarded a 15% Disability Pension at five shillings and sixpence per week, which terminated in November 1921. John was a commercial clerk and living at Hill View in Chapelizod when he married Alice Campbell of Charleville Road on 28th December 1920 at All Saints Church of Ireland. On Saturday 12th March 1921, the staff of Messrs. Brooks, Thomas and Company met in the Dining Hall at Sackville Place to present John Caird with a wallet of treasury notes to mark his marriage. In 1944, the Thom's Directory records that A W Johnston was the occupant of 14 Middle Third. John Caird was a retired cashier living at 92 Castle Avenue in Clontarf when died on 5th August 1958, aged 68. Alice Caird was living at 3 Greenore Avenue in Glasnevin when she died on 23rd February 1979, aged 73. John and Alice Caird are buried at Saint Fintan's Cemetery in Sutton (Section G Grave 8).

15 Middle Third – Dr George Buchanan

George Buchanan was born on 15th February 1891 at 61 Moyne Road in Rathmines to Francis Parke Buchanan, a boot merchant, and Rebecca Jane Buchanan (née Henchie) and the family lived at Upper Rathmines in 1901 and 1911, when George was a medical student. He graduated in medicine at Dublin University and served with the Royal Army Medical Corps in the Great War, being commemorated on the Roll of Honour for Adelaide Road Presbyterian Church. After the war he established a general medical practice in Clontarf and he was living at Upper Rathmines when he married Emily Stewart Kelso on 15th April 1919 at Letterkenny Presbyterian Church. Two occupants – Dr Buchanan and Mrs Brennan – are listed for 15 Middle Third in the 1932 and 1933 Thom's directories and, from 1934 to 1936, the Thom's directories record the occupants as Dr Buchanan and Mrs Lees. In December 1936, George and Emily were spending Christmas with friends and were also absent from the family home at 'Moyville' on Castle Avenue in Clontarf when it was burgled on Christmas night. The thieves ransacked all the principal rooms and made off with jewellery valued at £140 and £11 in cash. Dr Buchanan died of hyperpiesis (hypertension) and diabetes at 'Moyville' on 31st October 1963, aged 72.

The Thom's directories from 1937 to at least 1947 record the occupant Mrs F Lees, who had formerly lived at 26 The Demesne.

James Lees, a retired sales director of 'Balmoral' 15 Middle Third, died at St Joseph's Nursing Home on 30th March 1967, aged 71, his second wife, Dorothy, being present at death. The details of James' marriage to Dorothy have not been identified as the civil records for the 1960s are not available online. James was a commercial clerk living at Glasnevin when he married Georgina Wayte on 2nd November 1921 at St George's Church of Ireland, his father being recorded as Robert, a builder. Georgina Lees, who was a sister of Walter Wayte of 59 The Demesne, died at 15 Middle Third on 4th June 1960, aged 65. James and Georgina Lees are buried in St. Fintan's Cemetery (Section M Grave 79). Several Ancestry family trees record that James Lees was born on 20th May 1895 in Belfast to Richard Lees, a carpenter/builder, and Christine Lees (née McKelvey). In the 1911 Ireland Census, James' father's name is recorded as Robert Alexander Dickey Lees. The Roll of Honour for Fortwilliam Park Presbyterian Church in Belfast records that James Lees served with the Royal Engineers. No relationship has been established between James Lees and Mrs F Lees.

In July 1969, two youths appeared in the Children's Court having left a trail of destruction in the bungalow at 15 Middle Third, the property of Mrs Dorothy Lees. *The Evening Herald* reported that, 'The residence was completely wrecked, fittings were torn from the wall and irreplaceable china was smashed, windows were broken, food-stuff was scattered and telephone wires were cut. Damage amounted to £300.'

16 Middle Third – Michael Kelly

Based on the age recorded in the Register of Deaths, Michael was born around 1886 and, according to the Register of Marriages, his father, John Kelly, was a Sergeant in the Royal Irish Constabulary. Michael Kelly was an RIC Constable and living at Benedict's Gardens in Dublin when he married Mary Kelleher of Hardwicke Place on 26th December 1913 at the St Mary's Roman Catholic Pro-Cathedral on Marlborough Street. Michael enlisted with Irish Guards (Regimental Number 6588) in January 1915 and was posted to France on 16th August 1915. He was serving with 2nd Battalion when he sustained gunshot wounds to the hand and a flesh wound of the scalp in August 1916, being treated at Queen Alexandra's Military Hospital at Millbank in London for fourteen days. He was listed as wounded in the Casualty List issued by the War Office on 8th September 1916 and was entitled to one Wound Stripe. He later transferred to the Guards Machine Gun Corps (Regimental Number 1444) and was transferred to the Class Z Army Reserve on 16th March 1919. Michael was living at 46 North Strand Road when he was awarded a 20% Disability Pension in respect of rheumatism and pyorrhoea (also known as periodontitis) at eight shillings per week, with a supplement of three shillings and sixpence per week in respect of two children. Michael Kelly was a clerk and living at 46 North Strand Street when Michael Francis and Marie Evelyn were born in March 1919 and July 1920 respectively. Mary Kelly died at Our Lady's Hospice at Harold's Cross on 27th March 1946, aged 52. Michael, who had worked for the Dublin Port and Docks Board, was living at 16 Middle Third when he died of rheumatic fever at St Kevin's Hospital on 18th March 1952, aged 66. Michael and Mary Kelly are buried in St. John the Baptist Cemetery in Clontarf.

17 Middle Third – William Gibson

William Gibson was born on 10th October 1880 at 90 Upper Church Street to John Gibson, a labourer, and Margaret Gibson (née Cox). William was a postman and living at Murtagh Road when he married Margaret Finnegan of Benburb Street on 11th April 1910 at St Paul's Roman Catholic Church, and they were living at 22 Usher's Island in the Usher's Quay district in 1911. William enlisted with the Royal Army Medical Corps (Regimental Number 78216) and was posted to a Theatre of War after December 1915. Lance-Corporal William Gibson was transferred to the Class Z Army Reserve on 12th February 1919 and was living at 9 Hardwick Street when he was awarded a 20% Disability Pension at the rate of eight shillings per week, with a supplement of seven shillings and one penny for his wife and four children. One of their children, Margaret, died of hodgkin's disease at 17 Middle Third on 14th February 1940, aged 25. Their son, Thomas, married Margaret Mary McDonnell of Church Street in Dublin on 24th June 1935, and they were living at 17 Middle Third when Margaret Mary Gibson died of septicaemia puerperal at Hardwicke Hospital on 30th April 1936, aged 26. Thomas then married Elizabeth Rourke from St Helen's in Lancashire on 11th July 1940 and their daughter, Bernadette, died of a cerebral embolism at 17 Middle Third on 5th April 1959, aged 17. Thomas Gibson's first wife and daughter are buried in Glasnevin Cemetery. William Gibson's wife, Margaret, died of cancer at Hume Street Hospital on 18th September 1958, aged 77, and William died of cancer at 17 Middle Third on 30th March 1962, aged 81. William and Margaret Gibson, and their daughter Margaret, are buried in Glasnevin Cemetery (St. Patrick's AL 69). A son, Thomas Gibson, was an employee of the Dublin GPO and was living at 17 Middle Third when he died suddenly at the Mater Hospital on 24th July 1985.

18 Middle Third – Charles Stuart/Stewart Murphy

Charles Stuart/Stewart Murphy was born around 1885 and his father was Michael Murphy, a building contractor. Charles was a bricklayer and living at Sinnott Place when he married Mary Ellen McCarthy of Carnew Street on 13th July 1913 at the Roman Catholic Church on Aughrim Street. He enlisted with Royal Irish Rifles (Regimental Number 5948) in June 1915 and was posted to 2nd Battalion on the Western Front in March 1917 at the age of 35. Charles was an Acting Sergeant when he sustained gunshot wounds to the right leg and head in August 1917 and was transferred to a base hospital on Number 31 Ambulance Train. He sustained gunshot wounds to the face in May 1918 and was treated at the Croydon War Hospital and at the County of Middlesex War Hospital at Napsbury. Charles was subsequently transferred to the Labour Corps (Regimental Number 670652) and was transferred to the Class Z Army Reserve on 12th April 1919. The Murphy family was living at 28 Oxmanton Road in Dublin when he was awarded a 30% Disability Pension in respect of gunshot wounds to the jaw and head at the rate of thirteen shillings per week, with an allowance of eight shillings and ten pence for his wife and three children. Charles Murphy was a machine hand when he died at 18 Middle Third of a cerebral embolism and re-spiratory failure on 6th May 1930, aged 45, and is buried in Glasnevin Cemetery. The entry in the Glasnevin Cemetery Register records his age as 48. The occupant of 18 Middle Third was recorded as John H Evans in the 1944 Thom's Directory.

19 Middle Third – Henry Joseph Kirwan and James Joseph A Walsh

The 1926 Thom's Directory records the occupant as 'Kirwan, H' and the 1928 edition records the occupant as 'Walsh, J'.

Henry Joseph Kirwan was born on 18th January 1891 at Mark's Alley in Dublin to Peter Kirwan and Margaret Kirwan (née McBride). Tragically, Peter Kirwan died on Christmas Day 1890 of consumption, three weeks prior to Henry's birth. Henry enlisted in the Royal Army Service Corps in early 1915 as a Driver, with the Corps number T2/12384. He embarked for Egypt on 15th June 1915 and served throughout the war, being demobilised on 13th May 1919 in the rank of Sergeant. On 2nd November of that year, he married Marcella Cleary at St Catherine's Roman Catholic Church, Dublin. At that time, Henry was resident at

Henry Kirwan
19 Middle Third
(source: David Kirwan)

25 Sandwith Place, Dublin. Allocated a bungalow at 19 Middle Third, Henry's mother-in-law, Elizabeth Cleary, died there on 9th May 1924. The family moved to 42 Fairfield Avenue, Dublin in 1927 and Henry was recorded as being a labourer at the Guinness brewery when he died of cancer at Sir Patrick Dun's Hospital on 15th January 1938, aged 46. He was survived by Marcella and seven children. Marcella died on 11th November 1973 and both she and Henry are buried at Glasnevin Cemetery.

The second occupant was **James Joseph A Walsh** who was a Warrant Officer in the British Army and a Captain in the National Army. James was a Warrant Officer Class 1 when he was deployed to France with 1st Battalion Royal Irish Rifles (Regimental Number 6298) on 6th November 1914 and was reported as wounded in the Casualty List issued by the War Office for operations in April and May 1915, entitling him to one Wound Stripe. He was transferred to 1st Garrison Battalion Royal Irish Fusiliers (Regimental Number G/150) on 25th

James Joseph A Walsh
19 Middle Third
(source: www.findagrave)

September 1915. The battalion was posted to India in February 1916 and James was stationed there when a daughter, Mary Bridget Walsh, was born at Iveagh Buildings on Bride Street on 22nd May 1916. His wife, Kathleen, died at the age of 32 of post-partum haemorrhage and shock on the same day. James held the rank of Regimental Sergeant Major when discharged and was awarded the Long Service and Good Conduct Medal in 1920. In September 1928, James won the substantial sum of £3,333 (approximately £261,000 in today's terms) in a newspaper football competition. His second wife, Mary Bridget Walsh died at 19 Middle Third on 18th May 1933, aged 48, and is buried in Birr, County Offaly. Their daughter, Mary Brigid (Sheila) Walsh, died of pulmonary tuberculosis at 19 Middle Third on 7th April 1940, aged 17, and is buried in Glasnevin Cemetery. The entry for Sheila in the Register of Deaths records that James Walsh was employed in the Accountant's Branch at the General Post Office. James Joseph Walsh married Ellen/Helen Ward of Boyle in County Sligo on 24th October 1940 at St Brigid's Roman Catholic Church at Killester. In January 1962, James won £71-8-7 in a competition organised by MH Pools of Upper O'Connell Street. James Joseph A Walsh was living at 19 Middle Third when he died of congestive cardiac failure at St Kevin's Hospital on 5th April 1967, aged 83, and is buried in Glasnevin Cemetery (Plot YK 61, St. Patrick's Section). Helen Walsh was living at 19 Middle Third when she died at St Mary's Hospital, Phoenix Park, on 19th December 1968 and is buried in Balgriffin Cemetery.

20 Middle Third – Thomas Arkins

In the 1926 Thom's Directory, the occupant is recorded as 'Farrell, P' and in 1938 the occupant was 'Arkins, Thos'.

Thomas Arkins was born on 11th March 1887 at 2 Upper Jane Place in North Dock to Thomas Arkins and Ann Arkins (née Courtney). His mother died in March 1894 and the family was living at Lower Oriel

Street in North Dock in 1901 – Thomas senior was recorded as being a carrier and Thomas junior was recorded as being a stationer's messenger. Thomas Arkins was a van driver when he enlisted with the Royal Irish Rifles (Regimental Number 7255) on 2nd November 1903 in Dublin and was stationed in India with 1st Battalion in 1911. He was mobilised on 4th August 1914 and deployed to France on 6th November 1914 as a Private. In May 1915, he was a patient in the Rawalpindi British General Hospital in Marseilles and was subsequently transferred to 1st Garrison Battalion Royal Irish Fusiliers (Regimental Number G/72) on 18th September 1915 and served in India from February 1916 until 1918. He was transferred to the Leinster Regiment (Regimental Number 40022) and served on the Western Front with 2nd Battalion, achieving the rank of Acting Warrant Officer Class 2. He was posted to India with 1st Battalion in late 1919 and was allocated Army Number 7178265 in 1920. The battalion returned to the UK in April 1922 and, although the Leinster Regiment was formally disbanded in June 1922, the pension ledger card records that Sergeant Thomas Arkins was discharged on 15th August 1922.

In addition to the 1914 Star, British War Medal, and Victory Medal, Thomas was awarded the Indian General Service Medal with the Malabar 1921/22 Clasp. He was living at 17 Simmons Place in Summerhill when he was awarded a pension of seven shillings and sixpence for 52 weeks in respect of gunshot wounds to the right foot, with a terminal gratuity of £10. A younger brother, Bernard, was a Company Sergeant Major with 6th Battalion Royal Dublin Fusiliers when he was killed in action in Salonika on 9th December 1915 and is commemorated on the Doiran Memorial in Greece. Thomas was a bank porter and living at Fitzwilliam Lane when he married Elizabeth Halpin of Woodview in Stillorgan on 20th July 1930 at Donnybrook Roman Catholic Church. Thomas Arkins died at 20 Middle Third on 7th May 1973, aged 86, and Elizabeth Arkins died at the James Connolly Memorial Hospital in Blanchardstown on 28th November 1985. Thomas and Elizabeth Arkins are buried in Mount Jerome Cemetery.

21 Middle Third – Richard William Larby

Richard William Larby was born on 4th October 1881 at Aldershot Camp in Hampshire to Richard H Larby, a soldier, and Mary Agnes Larby (née Hamill). Richard Larby senior had enlisted in Portsmouth on 29th August 1870 with the 82nd Regiment of Foot, which became the Prince of Wales's Volunteers (South Lancashire Regiment) under the 1881 Childers Reforms. He was invalided from the Army with bright's disease in October 1895, with twenty-five years of service. In 1901, Richard Larby senior was a publican, and the family home was at Barrack Street West in Fermoy, County Cork. Richard Larby junior enlisted with the Army Service Corps (Regimental Number T/595 and later S/19030) around 1901 and his marriage to Bridget O'Donoghue was registered in Bradford in the second quarter of 1909. In the 1911 England & Wales Census, they were living with their son Richard (10 months old) at 265 High Street in Aldershot and Richard was recorded as being a Corporal with nine years and one month of army service. They were living at Victoria Barracks in Belfast when Bride Eileen Larby was born in February 1914. Richard Larby held the rank of Sergeant when he was posted to France with 1st Divisional Train (HQ Company) on 16th August 1914 and he held the rank of Quartermaster Sergeant when he was awarded the Long Service and Good Conduct Medal in 1920. Richard was stationed at Fermoy when Joseph Henry Larby was born in September 1919. Richard Larby was a clerk when he died of coronary thrombosis and cardiac failure at Sir Patrick Dun's Hospital on 29th November 1949, aged 68, and Bridget Larby died at 21 Middle Third on 23rd May 1966, aged 83. Richard and Bridget Larby are buried in Mount Jerome Cemetery. Maura Johnson (née Larby) was living at 21 Middle Third when she died at Jervis Street hospital on 15th July 1982 and Joseph Larby was living at 21 Middle Third when his wife Kathleen died on 13th September 1985.

22 Middle Third – Thomas Quigley

Thomas Quigley was born on 2nd May 1881 at 19 Queen Square in South Dock to Thomas Quigley, an RIC Constable, and Mary Anne Quigley (née Byrne) and the family lived at Sorrento Road in Dalkey (1901) and St. Patrick's Road in Drumcondra (1911). Thomas was a commercial traveller and merchant when he married Ann Johnson of Phibsborough Road on 26th April 1911 at St. Joseph's Carmelite Church on Berkeley Road. He enlisted with the Royal Engineers (Regimental Number WR/355033 and later number 151063) and served with the Inland Waterways and Transport branch, being posted to a Theatre of War after December 1915. Corporal Quigley was transferred to the Class Z Army Reserve on 12th March 1919 and was living at Mountjoy Square when he was awarded a 30% Disability Pension in respect of debility caused by malaria at the rate of twelve shillings per week, with a supplement of three shillings per week in respect of one child. Thomas Quigley died in 1958, aged 76, although the Register of Deaths is not available. Catherine Quigley was living at 22 Middle Third when she died at St Mary's Hospital, Phoenix Park, on 25th August 1967, aged 91. Thomas and Catherine Quigley are buried in Glasnevin Cemetery and the entry on the cemetery website records that Thomas was 86 when he died.

23 Middle Third – Donald O'Regan (Domhnal O'Riagain)

The 1926 Thom's Directory records the occupant as 'O'Regan, P', who also used the Irish version of his name, Domhnal O'Riagain. His daughter, Maureen Brigid Joseph O'Regan, died at 24 Middle Third on 22nd April 1925, aged 12. *The researchers have not been able to confirm family and military service details for this occupant.* William Burrows and his family moved to 23 Middle Third from 18 Abbeyfield in the early 1930s.

24 Middle Third – Thomas William Croke

Thomas William Croke was born on 28th July 1882 at Short Course in Waterford to Thomas Croke, a porter, and Ellen Coke (née Morrissey) and the family lived at Thomas Terrace in Waterford in 1901. Thomas enlisted with the Royal Irish Regiment around 1901 (Service Number 6906) and he was stationed at the New Barracks in Fermoy when he married Rachel Savage from High Street in Waterford, on 28th June 1904 at Waterford Roman Catholic Cathedral. In 1911, Thomas was stationed at Alderney Garrison in the Channel Islands and his occupation was recorded as a clerk. He held the rank of Sergeant when he was

Thomas and Rachel Croke
24 Middle Third
(source: Pauline O'Reilly)

deployed to France on 13th August 1914 with 2nd Battalion Royal Irish Regiment but was taken prisoner at Le Cateau on 26th August 1914 and was incarcerated at Sagan and Sprottau Prisoner of War camps. He held the rank of Company Quartermaster Sergeant when he was repatriated to England in January 1919, as reported in the Weekly Casualty List dated 21st January 1919. Thomas returned to active service and remained in the army after the war. He was a Regimental Quartermaster Sergeant and stationed in India with 2nd Battalion Royal Irish Regiment when he was transferred back to England in November 1920 on the hospital ship HMAT *Assaye*, the medical register records that he was suffering from paranoia. Thomas Croke (now with Army Number 7109026) was discharged on 31st October 1921, being awarded a 40% Disability Pension in respect of gunshot wounds and neurasthenia at the rate of eleven shillings per week. In addition to the trio of service medals, RQMS Thomas William Croke was also the holder of the Long Service & Good Conduct Medal and the Meritorious Service Medal, both being awarded in 1919.

The 1926 Thom's Directory records that Thomas William Croke was the occupant of 24 Middle Third, where he lived for the rest of his life. On 1st February 1931, John Aloysius Croke, a warehouseman, was injured during a football match at Kimmage but completed the game. He was taken ill after he returned to his parents' bungalow in Middle Third and was taken to Baggot Street hospital, where internal injuries were diagnosed. John Croke died of kidney related difficulties on 26th February at the age of 22. In 1934, the British Ministry of Pensions appointed Thomas to the Dublin, Donegal, and District Area Advisory Committee. Thomas Croke had been Secretary of the Irish Athletic Boxing Association for eighteen years when he and Rachel celebrated their Golden Wedding Anniversary in 1954. Thomas Croke died of chronic bronchitis, emphysema, and myocardial degeneration at 24 Middle Third on 10th January 1957, aged 74. The Register of Deaths records that Catherine Tracey of 29 Middle Third was present at death.

25 Middle Third – Edwin Chapman

Edwin Chapman was born on 31st October 1888 at Hackney in London to George Edwin Henry Chapman, a brass finisher, and Emily Chapman (née Randall). He was baptised at St Luke's Church on 18th November 1888 and the family was living at Domingo Street in West Finsbury in 1901. Edwin enlisted with 6th Battalion Royal Munster Fusiliers (Regimental Number 10468) and was stationed at Aghada Barracks in Cork when he married Mary Traynor of George's Street on 30th June 1915 at Saints Michael and John Roman Catholic Church in Dublin. Edwin was deployed to Gallipoli on 15th August 1915, and he was hospitalised with dysentery later the same month. He was also hospitalised with shell shock in April 1916, and gas poisoning in July 1916. He transferred to the Royal Flying Corps (Regimental Number 106551) on 31st August 1917 and was a cook with the rank of Corporal when he entered the Royal Air Force on its formation on 1st April 1918. He served with the Army of the Rhine in 1919 and 1920 and was transferred to the Class F Reserve on 20th March 1920. Edwin and his family were living at Hardwicke Street when he was awarded a 30% Disability Pension in respect of gas poisoning at the rate of thirteen shillings per week, with a supplement of three shillings per week for his wife and child. During the Second World War, his daughter, Evelyn, served with the Auxiliary Territorial Service. Edwin Chapman was living at 25 Middle Third when he died of myocarditis and chronic bronchitis at Portrane Mental Hospital in Donabate on 6th June 1956, aged 67.

26 Middle Third – Joseph Scully

In the 1926 Thom's Directory, the occupant is recorded as 'Browne, G' and in 1932 the occupant was 'Scully, J'.

Joseph Scully was born on 1st May 1898 at New Road, Maryborough in Queen's County to Joseph Scully, an asylum attendant, and Ellen Scully (née Lodge) and the family home was at Well Road (formerly

New Road) in Maryborough in 1901 and 1911. At that time, Joseph Scully senior was a builder's labourer. Joseph Scully enlisted at Naas with the 21st (Empress of India's) Lancers (Regimental Number L/11729) and served in India, being entitled to the British War Medal. Bernadette Scully, a grand-daughter, records,

> Joseph was stationed at the 21st Lancers garrison at Rawalpindi in the Punjab. In 1915 there was major unrest among the local Mohmad (Pathan) tribesmen along the North-West Frontier. Joseph volunteered to ride from the fort, scouting for any tribesmen encampments. He spotted one camp, and under fire, made it back to the fort to swiftly make his sightings. After listening, the Commanding Officer ordered him to attend to his horse. Joseph went back to Harry, and saw his rump was shot to pieces. Heartbroken, Joseph had to take out his gun and shoot the poor animal.

Whilst stationed in India, John Scully, an elder brother of Joseph who had enlisted at Naas along with him, lost his life on the Western Front. Private John Scully was serving with 2nd Battalion Leinster Regiment (Number 10132) when he was killed in action on 12th August 1915 and has no known grave, being commemorated on the Menin Gate Memorial to the Missing in Ypres. Whilst the medal entitlement documentation records entitlement to just the British War Medal, the photograph in the Scully family archive shows ribbons for two service medals. It is probable that Joseph served on the Western Front with the 21st Lancers Service Squadron which became part of the XIV Corps Cavalry Regiment. Private Scully was discharged from the 21st Lancers on 3rd March 1919 so that he could enlist with the 9th Lancers (Regimental Number L/20310). It is not known when Joseph Scully was demobilised, but he was appointed as a postman in Manchester in December 1920 and a marriage between Joseph Scully and

Joseph Scully
26 Middle Third
(source: Bernadette Scully)

May Boyton was registered in the second quarter 1921 in the Chorlton district of Lancashire. The Scully family returned to Dublin and Joseph was allocated the cottage at 26 Middle Third in the early 1930s. Bernadette Scully recalls:

In Dublin Joseph worked as a postman and rode everywhere on his bicycle. The couple loved to garden. The long back garden had gooseberries, blackcurrants, a plum tree, apple trees and long rows of seasonal vegetables, and potato drills. A large chestnut tree, planted by their youngest son, Joe, gave shade to the house. At the very end of the garden, backing onto the rail embankment was a chicken coup. Joseph supplied fresh eggs to one of local 'tin shops'. The chicken feed he kept in a big barrel in the side garage. It gave off a warm, earthy aroma next to the kitchen doorway. The front garden was all flowers for May. Lots and lots of roses. Joseph created a shell garden wall for May because of her love of the thatched shell cottage in Wexford. At one stage Joseph had a prize-winning greyhound too. As an elderly couple, May and Joseph attended mass every day in St. Bridget's church. They sat in the same third row seat in the front on the left. Every year, they would go on the parish pilgrimage to Lourdes where Joseph found solace helping help people in and out of the waters. After May died, Joseph went to mass every morning and then cycled out to Balgriffin to put fresh flowers on her grave.'

Their youngest son, also called Joseph, served with the Irish Guards and saw action in the Suez Crisis in 1956. Joe's last army posting was with the Queen's horse guards in the late 1960s. After leaving the army, Joe returned to Dublin and was living with his parents at 26 Middle Third when he died at the Mater Hospital on 17th September 1972, aged 46. Mary (or May) Scully of 26 Middle Third died at Mercer's Hospital on 30th May 1968, aged 68, and a death notice recorded her maiden name as Boynton. Joseph (Joe) Scully worked for the Post & Telegrams Office on Amiens Street and, when his health started to fail, he left Killester in 1977 to live with a son, Michael, in Blackrock. Joseph spent his final years at the Clevis Nursing Home, part of Leopardstown Park Hospital, where he died on 4th October 1983, aged 85. Joe and May Scully are buried in Balgriffin Cemetery.

It is interesting to note that the Leopardstown Park Hospital was established in October 1917 when Gertrude Dunning gifted Leopardstown Park, a magnificent country manor set in 100 acres of parkland, to the British Ministry of Pensions, with the stipulation that the house and its grounds were to be used to treat soldiers who had been disabled while serving with the British forces. It was only in the 1970s that the hospital started to treat people who had not served in the British armed forces and the first female patient was admitted in the 1980s. The hospital was administered and financed by the British government until it was transferred to the Irish Department of Health in 1979, although it retains its close connection with the British ex-service community. (Information from the hospital's website, www.lph.ie)

27 Middle Third – John Patrick Banahan

John was born on 30th August 1892 at Strokestown in County Roscommon to Francis Banahan and Anne Banahan (née Breslin) who farmed land at Cloonfree. On 12th February 1912, John was appointed to the Royal Irish Constabulary, with the force number 66430. He was initially stationed at Enfield, County Meath. At the outbreak of the Great War, many RIC men enlisted in the military with the blessing of their superiors, their jobs being held for them until their return. John, like many other RIC men enlisted in the Irish Guards and was posted initially to 1st battalion and then on its formation, to 2nd battalion,

regimental number 6757. He embarked with 2nd battalion for the Western Front in August 1915 and was wounded in action on 15th September 1916 during the Battle of the Somme, sustaining gunshot wounds to both hips. He was initially treated at No 34 Casualty Clearing Station and then was medically evacuated to

John Banahan
27 Middle Third
Sources: Ancestry Family Tree and
www.findagrave.com

the United Kingdom where he was treated at hospital in Harrogate, Yorkshire. Medically unfit for active service, John was discharged with the Silver War Badge on 11th January 1919, holding the rank of Lance Sergeant. He was assessed as 20% disabled and awarded a pension of eight shillings per week. He returned to Cloonfree and resumed his career in the RIC, being posted to Naas, County Kildare. On 16th February 1920, he married Jane Allen, a housekeeper and daughter of a farmer, at Dargan Roman Catholic Chapel in County Meath. John continued to serve in the RIC until it's disbandment. He was discharged on 26th May 1922 and was in receipt of a pension of £94 per year and became a butcher. John and Jane moved into 27 Middle Third in 1923 and raised a family of four in the bungalow. John ran a butcher's business from one of the 'tin shops' in Killester. Jane died aged 60 at her home address on 13th November 1955. Following this, John moved to Beech Park Grove, Foxrock, County Dublin, where he died aged 77 on 20th June 1969, of coronary thrombosis. Both John and Jane are buried at Glasnevin Cemetery.

28 Middle Third – Richard Lindsay

Richard Lindsay was born on 23rd January 1892 at the Rotunda Hospital to David Lindsay, a paper cutter, and Mary Lindsay (née Ives), who lived at 10 Grenville Street in Mountjoy. The family lived at 9 Upper Buckingham Street in 1901 and at 21 Annesley Avenue in 1911. Richard was an apprentice bookbinder when he enlisted with 3rd Battalion Royal Dublin Fusiliers (Regimental Number 5076) at Naas on 9th November 1910 but was discharged after 153 days service so that he could join the Regular Army. He enlisted as a Driver with the Royal Field Artillery (Regimental Number 65386) at Naas on 11th April 1911 and was posted to 45th Battery. He was stationed in India with the 66th Battery in December 1913. He was deployed to France on 4th October 1914 and served on the Western Front until July 1916. He was then posted to Salonika with the Mediterranean Expeditionary Force in October 1916, where he served until October 1918, when he was evacuated from Salonika onboard HM Transport *Arbroath* and subsequently admitted to the University War Hospital in Southampton. He was evacuated under the 'Y Scheme' and his documentation was endorsed with the following statement, *'Malaria case not to be sent to a theatre of war where Malaria is prevalent, except France and Italy'*. He was serving with 45th Battery, Royal Field Artillery when he was discharged due to war-related sickness on 10th February 1919, with Silver War Badge Number B201361. He was living at 21 Annesley Avenue when he was awarded a 40% Disability Pension in respect of disordered action of the heart and malaria at the rate of twenty shillings per week. Richard was a labourer and living at Annesley Avenue when he married Catherine Giles from North Clarence Street on 4th April 1920 at St Agatha's Roman Catholic Church. They were living at 13 Great Charles Street when their son, Michael, was born on 7th January 1921.

A son of Richard and Catherine died on 19th December 1925, aged two days, and Catherine subsequently died of puerperal septicaemia at 28 Middle Third on 24th December 1925, aged 33. Catherine and her infant child were buried in Kilbarrack Cemetery on St Stephen's Day. Richard was a cigarette operator when he married Elizabeth Leonard of Pigeon House Road on 21st April 1930 at Ringsend Roman Catholic Church. Richard Lindsay served as an ARP Volunteer during the Second World War and helped the injured after the German bombing of North Strand in May 1941. A son, Michael Lindsay, joined the Royal Air Force in 1942 and was posted to Belgium in 1944. At around 4pm on 22nd October 1944, ten airmen from Number 14 Personnel Transit Centre were playing football when a German rocket (either a V1 or a V2) landed in their midst. Six men were killed outright, two more died of their wounds and the remaining two were seriously injured. Sergeant Michael Lindsay (617313) died of injuries at Number 6 Canadian General hospital on 29th October 1944,

The Lindsay Family – Richard, Elizabeth, and Kathleen, 28 Middle Third
(sources: Patrick Turner and Jennifer Lindsay)

aged 23, and is buried in Schoonselhof Cemetery in Antwerp, Belgium. Richard was a machinist with W D & H O Wills, the tobacco company, when he died of pulmonary thrombosis and cardiac failure at 28 Middle Third on 25th June 1946, aged 54. Elizabeth Lindsay (née Leonard) was still living at 28 Middle Third when she died at Jervis Street Hospital on 13th January 1980. Richard and Elizabeth Lindsay are also buried in Kilbarrack Cemetery (Section DE Grave 15), along with Richard's first wife, Catherine, and their infant son. The grave is marked by a simple iron Celtic cross bearing the words, 'The Lindsay Family'..

29 Middle Third – William Henry Tracey

The surname is sometimes recorded as TREACY, particularly in the birth registrations for children born between 1916 and 1921.

William Tracey was born on 3rd December 1888 at 35 Lower Sherriff Street in North Dock to Robert Tracey, a sailor, and Margaret Tracey (née Dignan) but was living with his with grandmother, Jane Tracey, at Albert Road in Glasthule, Dublin in 1901 and at Longford Terrace in Kingstown in 1911, when his occupation was recorded as van man. William, who had served with 4th Battalion Royal Dublin Fusiliers (Regimental Number 7756) and had been discharged at the termination of his period of engagement, re-enlisted with the Royal Dublin Fusiliers (Regimental Number 11832) on 12th August 1914 and was initially posted to 6th Battalion. William was stationed at Curragh Camp when he married Catherine Keogh of Great George's Street North on 8th November 1914 at St Mary's Roman Catholic Pro-Cathedral on Marlborough Street. William was posted to 3rd Battalion in March 1915, whilst the 6th Battalion left Ireland bound for Gallipoli in May 1915. He was an Acting Sergeant when he was posted to the Western Front on 15th December 1916. He saw active service with 2nd Battalion and 8th Battalion and, following a period of home service, was posted to 9th Battalion on the Western Front on 10th June 1917. William was transferred to the Class Z Army Reserve on 3rd February 1919 and was living at 27 George's Street when he was awarded a 60% Disability Pension in respect of tubercle of lung at twenty-four shillings per week. The initial allowance of seventeen shillings and sixpence per week in respect of a daughter born in August 1916 (Annie) was uprated to twenty-three shillings and sixpence per week following the birth of a son, Frederick, in October 1919. A further son, William, was born at 27 George's Street in March 1921. His service record includes a letter dated 16th February 1920 from the Dublin Branch of the Comrades of the Great War requesting that William Tracey be finally discharged as being 'No longer physically fit for war service' (King's Regulations Paragraph 392 XVI). Catherine Tracey was a widow and living at 29 Middle Third when her son, William, died on 20th April 1978. Catherine Tracey died at 28 Middle Third on 7th December 1984, aged 90, and is buried in St Fintan's Cemetery in Sutton (Section L Grave 66).

30 Middle Third – George Henry Pelham

George was born George Henry Putnam on 22nd September 1885 at West Ham, Essex, the fifth child of Walter and Anna Putnam, née Tucker. At that time, Walter Putnam was employed as a cooper. The 1901 Census shows George as resident with his parents and ten siblings at 52 Melrose Road, Harrow Green, Essex. George, then aged 15, had completed his education and was in employment as an office boy for a tea merchant. George married Margaret Josephine May on 8th August 1906 at Walthamstow Parish Church and was a Clerk when he joined the 1st Lancashire Royal Field Artillery Reserve (Regimental Number 1444) in September 1908. He transferred to the Regular Army Royal Field Artillery in December 1908 and was issued with the regimental number 53733. For some unknown reason, George enlisted under the surname Pelham. Angelo Floyd Pelham was baptised on 26th November 1913 at the Church of St Finbarr in Cork. At the outbreak of war, then in the rank of Corporal, George embarked for the Western Front on 11th September 1914, attached to 24th Battery RFA. By 1917, George had risen to the rank of Battery Sergeant Major and for service in the field, he was commissioned as a Second Lieutenant, effective from 11th April 1917. George was posted to Ireland, serving in Cork and Athlone, with two sons being born to him and Margaret May, a baker's daughter from Newbridge, County Kildare. George was recorded as being a 'military officer' when George Floyd Pelham was born on 12th December 1918 at Trabeg Terrace, South Douglas Road, Cork. Lieutenant George Henry Pelham was living in Weybridge when he was discharged from the Army in 1919 suffering from neurasthenia and debility. He remained on the Reserve of Officers until 22nd September 1935. In 1919, the Pelham family was living at Ballybay House in Athlone and George's occupation was recorded as 'independent means' when Patrick Oliver Pelham was born on 15th August 1920. George Pelham was recorded as the occupant of 30 Middle Third in the 1926 Thom's Directory. In January 1927, another son, Walter, was born. George was recorded as being a 'car driver' when Walter tragically died of heart disease aged 3 months on 13th April 1927 at Temple Bar Hospital. Later that year, on 31st August, George married Margaret at Clontarf Parish Church. The marriage register records George, a motor mechanic, under his birth surname of Putnam. The occupant of 30 Middle Third was recorded as 'Armstrong, F' in the 1932 Thom's Directory, the Pelham family having moved to England around 1930 and another son, Terence, was born in Surrey in 1932. The 1953 Surrey electoral register shows George and Margaret, under the surname Pelham, resident at 54 School Lane, Chertsey, with their youngest son, Terence. George died at Chertsey in January 1969 aged 84. In the Great War, George's elder brother, Private William James Putnam (20856, 5th Battalion, King's Shropshire Light Infantry) was killed in action on 18th March 1917 and is commemorated on the Arras Memorial.

31 Middle Third – William Dupuy

The 1926 Thom's Directory records the occupant as 'Foster' and the 1927 directory records the occupant as 'Dupuy, W'.

William Dupuy was a son of James Dupuy and Caroline Dupuy and his birth was registered in the Sheffield district in the fourth quarter of 1881. In 1911, William was a coachman to the Reverend Charles William O'Hara Mease of Castleknock, Rector of Castle Tunnock Church of Ireland. He married Margaret Spotiswoode of Hammond Street on 31st January 1912 at St Nicholas Roman Catholic Church on Francis Street. William enlisted with the 3rd (Prince of Wales's) Dragoon Guards (Regimental Number 3DG/4724) but was deployed to

France with 6th (Carabiniers) Dragoon Guards on 8th September 1914. He later served with 3rd Dragoon Guards and the Corps of Dragoons (Regimental Number D/19896). He was transferred to the Class Z Army Reserve on 27th March 1919 and was living at Hammond Street when he was awarded a 30% Disability Pension in respect of myalgia at the rate of eight shillings per week, which was later increased to twelve shillings per week. Margaret Dupuy died at Mercer's Hospital on 10th October 1958, aged 73, and William Dupuy was a retired painter when he died of renal disease at 31 Middle Third on 13th March 1867, aged 85. William and Margaret Dupuy are buried in Glasnevin Cemetery.

32 Middle Third – Christopher Phoenix and James Frederick Chard

The 1926 Thom's Directory records the occupant as 'Phoenix, C' and the 1944 directory records the occupant as 'Hoare, A'.

Christopher Phoenix was a sawyer when he enlisted with the Royal Navy (Naval Number K33363) as a Stoker on 23rd May 1916 and his Royal Navy service sheet recorded that he was born on 12th November 1897 at North Dublin. There is no matching birth registration and there is no matching record in the Ireland Census Record for 1901 or 1911. He was serving on HMS *Africa* when he was invalided from the service on 28th August 1918 and was living at 100 Lower Gardiner Street when he was awarded an allowance of eleven shillings per week for 56 weeks.

The third occupant of 32 Middle Third was **James Frederick Chard**. He was born on 24th February 1889 at Patrick Street in Kilkenny to James E Chard, a house steward at the Kilkenny County Club, and Susan Chard (née Beaver). In 1901, the family was living at Usher's Quay in Dublin and James senior was a tipstaff (an officer of the courts). James enlisted with the 5th (Royal Irish) Lancers (Regimental Number 5L/7047) and was stationed at Marlborough Barracks when he married Emily Moore of Lower Dorset Street on 12th February 1912 at Dublin Registry Office. He was deployed to France on 15th August 1914 and later served with the Middlesex Regiment (Regimental Number D16949) before returning to the 5th (Royal Irish) Lancers and later being incorporated into the Corps of Hussars (Regimental Number L/12670). James Chard was transferred to the Class Z Army Reserve on 11th April 1919. The Chard family home was at Innisfallen Parade off the North Circular Road when Herbert Chard was born in May 1917 and Edith Chard was born in January 1920. The Chard family was living at 32 Middle Third when Emily Jane Chard died on 3rd October 1953, aged 65. James Frederick Chard was a retired labourer when he died of hypertension and a coronary thrombosis on 3rd May 1966, aged 76. James Frederick and Emily Jane Chard are buried in Mount Jerome Cemetery.

33 Middle Third – Richard Mahon

Richard Mahon was born on 29th August 1884 at 36 Belview Buildings in the Usher's Quay district to George Mahon and Elizabeth Mahon (née Roberts). Although his father's forename is recorded as **James** on the entry in the Register of Births for Richard, it is recorded as George in the Register of Births entry for his brother, Robert, and in the Register of Marriages entry for Richard. In 1911, Robert and Richard Mahon were living with their widowed mother at 48 Reuben Avenue, and both are recorded as clerks at St James' Gate Brewery. Robert had joined Guinness at the age of 14 on 22nd July 1895 and Richard had joined at the same age on 20th February 1899. Richard was a clerk in the Brewhouse Department when he married Elizabeth Bray on 15th September 1914 at the Church of Ireland Cathedral of the Holy Trinity (also known as Christ Church Cathedral). Richard enlisted with the South Irish Horse (Regimental Number 1474) and held the post of Sergeant when he was posted to the Western Front sometime after December 1915. In the September 1917 restructuring of the cavalry regiments, he was transferred to the 7th (South Irish Horse) Battalion of the Royal Irish Regiment (Regimental Number 25588). Richard was taken prisoner at Lempire on 21st March 1918 during the Battle of St Quentin, also known as the German Spring Offensive. Sergeant Mahon was repatriated to England in February 1919 and transferred to the Class Z Army Reserve on 8th April 1919. He was living at Reuben Avenue when he was awarded a 30% Disability Pension at fourteen shillings per week in respect of nervous debility, with a supplement of five shillings and threepence in respect of his wife and child. Richard Mahon was recorded as being a 'brewing chemist' in the 1920 birth register entry for his son, George Thomas (who would join Guinness on 31st January 1938 at the age of 18 and work in the Malthouse Department). Richard Thomas Mahon, who was born in 1923, joined Guinness on 8th June 1942, aged 19, and worked in the Brewer's Laboratory Department. Elizabeth Mary Mahon died at 33 Middle Third on 26th July 1948, aged 67. Richard Mahon senior was recorded as being a retired clerk and living at 33 Middle Third when he died of ventricular failure and myocardial infarction at the Mater Hospital on Eccles Street on 18th June 1970, aged 85.

34 Middle Third – William Mooney

In the 1926 Thom's Directory, the occupant is recorded as 'Osborne, G' and in 1940 the occupant was 'Mooney, W'.

William Mooney was born around 1892 and enlisted with the Royal Irish Regiment (Regimental Number 6/3591) on 22nd May 1915. He was deployed to France with 6th Battalion on 17th December 1915 and was discharged due to wounds on 28th August 1918 with Silver War Badge Number 442189. William Mooney was single and living at 23 Rialto Terrace off the South Circular Road when he was awarded a 30% Disability Pension in respect of gunshot wounds to the left knee at the rate of twelve shillings per week on a permanent basis. William enlisted with the National Army (Regimental Number 24638) on 13th July 1922, aged 26, and was stationed at the District Transport Post in Cork in November 1922. His next-of-kin was recorded as his mother of St Joseph's Terrace in Irishtown. William was stationed at Portobello Barracks when he married Kathleen Griffin from North Circular Road on 22nd July 1927 at St Agatha's Roman Catholic Church. In January 1949, Miss Monica Mooney of 34 Middle Third was awarded a 'Radio Reviewer' prize sponsored by Raleigh Cycles at the Publicity Club's Silver Jubilee Ball in the Metropole Ballroom. William Mooney was a retired corporation employee when he died of hypertension and coronary thrombosis at 34 Middle Third on 8th October 1960, aged 68, and is buried in Dean's Grange Cemetery.

35 Middle Third – Patrick Joseph Hendrick

Patrick Joseph Hendrick was born on 14th August 1888 at 49 Bride Street in the Mansion House district to John Henry Hendrick, a cooper, and Margaret Hendrick (née Kenny). In 1911, he was a hairdresser and living with his widowed mother at 31 Lower Stephen Street in Royal Exchange and he married Mary Agnes Doyle from Coleraine Street, on 7th August 1913 at St. Michan's Roman Catholic Church. Patrick and Mary were living at Grenville Street when Patrick enlisted with the Royal Dublin Fusiliers (Regimental Number 24864) on 11th November 1915, one month after the birth of his second child. He was initially posted to 4th Battalion before being posted to 9th Battalion on the Western Front on 30th March 1916. He was transferred to the 16th Division Infantry Base Depot at Etaples in early April 1916 and then attached to 18th Division Infantry Base Depot. Following a period of home leave in September 1917, Patrick was admitted to Number 24 General Hospital in Etaples on 26th October, being diagnosed as suffering from disordered action of the heart. Lance-Corporal Hendrick was evacuated to England onboard HM Hospital Ship *Brighton* on 14th November and was attached to 4th Battalion when he was discharged as being 'No longer physically fit for war service' on 25th February 1918, with Silver War Badge Number 320376. He was living at 139 Parnell Street after discharge, being awarded a weekly pension of twenty-seven shillings and sixpence with effect from 26th February 1918 before dropping to eight shillings and thruppence per week after four weeks. The pension was to be reviewed after 48 weeks. Patrick Joseph Hendrick was a Hairdresser when he died of valvular disease of the heart at 35 Middle Third on 10th April 1930, aged 41, and is buried in Mount Jerome Cemetery.

36 Middle Third – Patrick Griffin

Patrick was born on 26th November 1885 at Gartnaskagh near Knock in County Clare to John Griffin, a farmer, and Bridget Griffin (née O'Dea). No military details have been identified but he married Mary M Dillon in the first quarter of 1915 in the St Pancras district of London and two daughters were born in London – Margaret (c1917) and Kathleen (c1921). A son called Frank was born in Dublin in 1926. Patrick was

Honorary Treasurer of the Killester Tenants' Rights Association in 1931 and was Honorary Secretary of the Ex-Servicemen's Tenants' Rights Association (Eire) in 1937. He was also prominent in promoting Irish cultural activities along with Father Kenny of St Brigid's Church in Killester, using the Irish version of his surname, Griobhta. In June 1940, Margaret Griffin (21) was attacked in Clontarf at the junction of Castle Avenue and Blackheath Road on the way home from the tennis club. She was struck on the head and her legs were slashed by a sharp instrument. Patrick Griffin was a civil servant with the Revenue Commissioners when he died of cancer at 36 Middle Third on 26th June 1945, aged 59, and is buried in Dean's Grange Cemetery.

37 Middle Third – John Frederick Galbraith

The 1926 Thom's Directory records the occupant as 'Woods, R' and the 1927 directory records the occupant as 'Galbraith, S', but the initial is a printing error.

John Galbraith was born on 7th November 1874 at Market Street in Sligo to John Herbert Galbraith, a draper, and Sarah Galbraith (née Garrett). John was a clerk when he enlisted with the Connaught Rangers (Regimental Number 4110) at Galway on 5th February 1892. He served in India from December 1897 until November 1903 and married Elizabeth Claffey on 4th February 1899 at the Fort Chapel in Bombay. Their first child, Frederick Hewlitt Revington Galbraith was born at Meerut in November 1899. Their second child, James Robert Galbraith, was born at Meerut in January 1901 but died in July 1901 at Nasirabad. After returning from India, the Galbraith family was living at Boyle in Roscommon when three further children were born – Joseph in 1904, Ruby Elizabeth in 1906, and Mary Violet in 1907. Colour Sergeant Galbraith was serving with 4th Battalion when he was discharged at the termination of his second period of engagement on 4th February 1913 with 21 years of service. His address at discharge was 25 Treswell Crescent, Hillsborough, Sheffield. John re-enlisted with 5th Battalion Connaught Rangers (Regimental Number 5/461) on 26th August 1914, three months before he turned 40. He served with the Mediterranean Expeditionary Force from 9th July 1915 until 15th May 1919, having taken part in landings at Anzac Cove on 7th

August 1915. He was compulsorily transferred to the Labour Corps (Regimental Number 587710) on 15th June 1918 and was serving with 983 Company when he was transferred to the Class Z Army Reserve on 13th June 1919. Regimental Quartermaster Sergeant John Frederick Galbraith had served in the British Army for over 25 years. After his discharge, the Galbraith family lived at 20 Portobello Road in Wood Quay. John Frederick Galbraith, a retired civil servant, was dead on arrival at Jervis Street Hospital on 10th January 1942, aged 67. The entry in the register of deaths records 'Probably heart disease, no attendant, inquest unnecessary'. Elizabeth Galbraith of 37 Middle Third died at the Royal City of Dublin Hospital on Baggot Street on 25th August 1953, aged 80. John and Elizabeth Galbraith are buried in Grangegorman Military Cemetery.

38 Middle Third – James Keenan

James Keenan was born on 11th August 1884 at Blackrock to Bernard Keenan, a farmer, and Ellen Keenan (née Stewart) and he was a porter living at Royal Canal Bank when he married Ellen Goulding of Cottage Place on 24th October 1909 at St Agatha's Roman Catholic Church. In 1911, they were living at 8 Campbell's Row in Rotunda and James was working as a butcher. James was a van man when he enlisted with the Army Service Corps (Regimental Number M/337484) and was posted to a Theatre of War after December 1915. James and Ellen were living at Portland Street when Margaret was born in January 1915 and when James was born in December 1916. Private James Keenan was discharged on 17th April 1918 and the family was living at William Place when Bernard was born in February 1921. James Keenan was a retired van driver when he died of bronchitis, emphysema, and cardiac failure at 38 Middle Third on 11th January 1968, aged 83. Ellen Keenan was living at 38 Middle Third when she died at her daughter's home in St Pappin's Green on 20th November 1976. James and Ellen Keenan are buried in Balgriffin Cemetery (Section K Grave 319). James Keenan junior was living at 38 Middle Third when he died at Beaumont Hospital on 19th March 1989.

39 Middle Third – John Mangan

The Thom's directories for 1926 to 1929 record the occupant as 'Nulty, J' and the 1930 Thom's Directory records the occupant as 'Mangan, J'.

John Mangan was born on 11th July 1886 at 18 Smithfield in Arran Quay to Thomas Mangan, a car driver, and Mary Anne Mangan (née Mooney) and the family lived at Little Ship Street in Wood Quay in 1901 and at Brown Street in Arran Quay in 1911. *The researchers have not been able to confirm war service details for this occupant.* John was a labourer and living at Brown Street when he married Annie Daniel from Connaught Street on 11th January 1926 at St Paul's Roman Catholic Church, Arran Quay. His sister, Christina, had married John Thomas Daniel in January 1920 and their son, John Thomas Daniel (2), died at 39 Middle Third on 8th September 1928. Mary Anne Mangan's mother, Mary Daniel was 63 years old when she died at 39 Middle Third on 22nd August 1933. In the 1930s, John Mangan and his family shared the bungalow with his sister (Christina Daniel), his brother-in-law (John Thomas Daniel) and his mother-in-law (Mary Daniel). Anne Mangan died at 39 Middle Third on 20th June 1968, aged 70, and John Mangan, a retired law messenger, was living at 39 Middle Third when he died of pneumonia at 55 Rosemount in Dundrum (the home of his son, Thomas Francis Mangan) on 24th February 1970, aged 83. John and Anne Mangan are buried in Balgriffin Cemetery (Section H Grave 274).

40 Middle Third – Joseph Kennedy

Whilst most extant records indicate that Joseph Kennedy was born around 1878, the 1869 birth registration is the only one where there is a match with the father's forename and occupation as recorded in Joseph's marriage registration, which was verified from his army service papers.

Joseph Kennedy was born on 27th July 1869 at Townsend Street in Trinity Ward to Thomas Kennedy, a blacksmith, and Alice Kennedy (née Mathews), and was baptised on 23rd July 1869 at Westland Row Church. Joseph was a blacksmith when he enlisted as a Driver with the Royal Field Artillery (Regimental Number 1017) on 13th September 1899 in Glasgow – his age was recorded as 21 years and 7 months. He was appointed as a Shoe Smith in May 1901 and was living at Capel Street when he married Catherine/Kate French, a Dressmaker from Blessington Street, on 28th January 1908 at St Joseph's Roman Catholic Church. Joseph was posted to India in February 1908 and transferred to the Royal Garrison Artillery (Regimental Number 224886) as a Farrier Sergeant the following month. Kate Kennedy gave birth to two daughters in India – Kathleen on 15th May 1910 in Nowgong and Alice on 6th August 1911 at Klianspur. Joseph was deployed to Mesopotamia on active war service with 86th Company (Heavy Battery) in February 1915 and took part in the Siege of Kut-al-Amara, where an Ulsterman, Captain John Alexander

Joseph and Catherine Kennedy
40 Abbeyfield
(source: Ruth O'Connor)

Sinton of the Indian Medical Service, was awarded the Victoria Cross. He was posted back to India in September 1916 and remained on garrison duties until posted back to the United Kingdom in September 1917. He spent the remainder of his war service on the Home Front.

Farrier Quartermaster Sergeant Joseph Kennedy was serving with 2nd Reserve Battery when he was discharged due to illness on 18th November 1918 with Silver War Badge Number B42190. He had 19 years and 67 days army service and his age at discharge was recorded as 40 years and 9 months. His character was recorded as 'Exemplary' and he was described as being, 'A sober, steady, reliable, hardworking, and intelligent Warrant Officer.' His address at discharge was 53 Upper Gardiner Street, which was where Joseph was born on 23rd August 1919. Joseph was awarded a 50% Disability Pension in respect of Neurasthenia due to war service and defective vision aggravated by war service. The rate was twenty shillings per week with a supplement of eleven shillings and ninepence per week for his two children. He was also in receipt of a service pension of 33 pence per day for the rest of his life. His total weekly pension was 51 shillings and one penny (£2-11-01) which equates to just over £110 per week in current terms.

Joseph and Kate had a further two children and Joseph (born on 23rd August 1919) served with the Irish Guards in the Second World War. Joseph Kennedy was recorded as being a British Army pensioner when he died of neurasthenia, chronic bronchitis, and myocardial degeneration at 40 Middle Third on 6th May 1951, aged 81. His age at death is recorded as 73 in the Register of Deaths. Catherine Kennedy was living at 40 Middle Third when she died at Our Lady's Hospice at Harold's Cross on 28th September 1957, aged 73. Joseph and Catherine Kennedy are buried in Malahide New Cemetery (Section D Grave 1175). Ruth O'Connor, a grand-daughter of Joseph and Catherine Kennedy, recalls:

> By all accounts, Joseph was a great character. Unassuming but loved to play the fiddle which I have proudly acquired. He was also quite an inventor. Always creating things with his hands and he also made dentures for people at the kitchen table of Middle Third.

41 Middle Third – Daniel Patrick McAuliffe

The Thom's directories for 1926 records the occupant as 'Dowling' and in 1930 the occupant was recorded as 'McAuliffe, D'.

Daniel Patrick McAuliffe was born on 12th April 1884 at Edenhill near Ballydougan in County Cork to Maurice McAuliffe, a gardener, and Kate McAuliffe (née Kearney/Kenny). Although the family was living at Clooneen near Westport in County Mayo in 1901 and 1911, Daniel was not present in the household. Daniel was a member of the Hibernian Hurling and Football Club before he moved to London before the war to work in the newspaper business. Daniel enlisted with the Irish Guards and was stationed at Warley near Brentwood in Essex when he married Ellen (Nellie) Moriarty on 4th November 1916 at Mallow Roman Catholic Church. He subsequently served on the Western Front, being discharged in 1919. When he returned to Ireland after the war, Daniel worked as an insurance clerk and was living at 19 Upper Sheriff Street in Dublin when Ellen gave birth to Michael Maurice McAuliffe at the Holles Street Hospital in December 1920. He was later the office manager of the Irish National Insurance Company at College Green. Daniel was recorded as the occupant of 53 The Demesne in the 1928 and 1929 editions of the Thom's Directory before moving to 41 Middle Third in 1929. He was Honorary Secretary of the Killester Tenants' Rights Association in 1931 and, in 1939, he was one of a group of ex-servicemen from various parts of the Irish Free State who brought a court case against the ISSLT to determine who was responsible for executing repairs on the ISSLT properties. He later became the Honorary Secretary of the Land Trust Beneficiaries Association. In December 1952, Lord Carew of Castletown House in Cellbridge outlined the ISSLT proposals for the sale of its properties to sitting tenants, whether ex-servicemen or the widows of ex-service-men, at a meeting of the Tullamore Branch of the British Legion. In January 1953, Daniel McAuliffe wrote to the Leinster Leader challenging Lord Carew to debate 'the whole question with him in the Legion Hall, Killester, or in any central town in his own county to which all the tenants of the Trust's Schemes there can be invited'. Daniel McAuliffe subsequently took the ISSLT to court to determine whether the Trust had the right to sell its properties. Ellen (Nellie) McAuliffe died at St Kevin's Hospital on 17th January 1955, aged 67, and Daniel was living at 41 Middle Third when he died of a pulmonary embolism at the Jervis Street Hospital on 11th November 1964, aged 80. Daniel and Nellie McAuliffe are buried in Mount Jerome Cemetery. The obituary printed in the Irish Independent on 13th November 1964 recorded that:

> *. . . he figured in several incidents during the fight for independence. He had comparatively easy access to depots in which arms were deposited after the 1914-18 war, in which he served, and he obtained for Sam Maguire and other colleagues supplies of small arms. In the 1919/21 period he also succeeded in having a store of arms in a large ordnance depot inspected by Sam Maguire and other volunteers.*

The obituary also referred to Daniel's role as an Honorary Secretary of the Sam Maguire Memorial Committee which, in 1928, donated the trophy awarded to the winners of the All-Ireland football championship.

42 Middle Third – John McCrystal

John Peter Paul McCrystal was born on 30th June 1885 at 45 Upper Wellington Street in Inns Quay to John McCrystal, a bread van driv-er, and Maria McCrystal (née Corbett) and the family was living at

Primrose Street in Inns Quay. John was a bootmaker when he married Josephine Doyle, a dressmaker, on 28th September 1910 at St Joseph's Roman Catholic Church on Berkeley Road. In 1911, they were living at 2 Millmount Avenue in Drumcondra along with three of Josephine's siblings. John was living at Fountain Place off North Brunswick Street when he enlisted with the Royal Irish Rifles (Regimental Number 3/5750) in March 1916. and was initially posted to 3rd Battalion before being posted to 1st Battalion on the Western Front in June 1917. Exactly two months later, having sustained shrapnel wounds to his left shoulder, John was posted to Depot duties on the Home Front and subsequently transferred to 3rd Battalion on 25th January 1918.

Lance-Corporal McCrystal was living at Lower Northbrook Avenue when he was discharged due to wounds on 30th May 1918, with Silver War Badge Number 394291. He was awarded a 40% Disability Pension in respect of shrapnel wounds at the rate of twenty-seven shillings and sixpence from 31st May 1918 for four weeks and then dropping to eleven shillings per week for 48 weeks. John McCrystal returned to his boot making trade and had one of the 'tin shops' in the estate. He was living at 42 Middle Third when he died of uraemia and chronic nephritis at St Kevin's Hospital on 19th September 1948, aged 63. Josephine McCrystal was still living at 42 Middle Third when she died at Our Lady's Hospice at Harold's Cross on 28th February 1981, aged 97. John and Josephine McCrystal are buried in Glasnevin Cemetery.

43 Middle Third – Michael McGuirk

Michael McGuirk was born on 7th January 1876 at 21 Lower Jane Place in North Dock to Bernard McGuirk and Jane McGuirk (née Lawlor) and the family was living at Newcomen Court in Mountjoy in 1901. Michael was a carter and living at Newfoundland Street when he married Christina Elizabeth Cullen, a printing factory employee from Strandville Avenue, on 5th June 1905 at St Lawrence O'Toole Roman Catholic Church and they were living at 16 Cottage Place in Rotunda in 1911. Michael enlisted with the Royal Inniskilling Fusiliers (Regimental Number 26595) and was posted to 7th Battalion on the Western Front after December 1915. He was wounded in the head and back and taken prisoner on 23rd March 1918 during the German

Spring Offensive. He was held at Giessen POW camp near the Dutch border and his repatriation was reported in the Weekly Casualty List 5754 dated 31st December 1918. Private McGuirk was transferred to the Class Z Army Reserve on 10th June 1919. Part of Middle Third was renamed as Killester Avenue and Michael McGuirk was living at 43 Killester Avenue when he died of myocordial failure at Grangegorman Mental Hospital on 2nd March 1956, aged 80, and is buried in Glasnevin Cemetery.

44 Middle Third – Christopher Smith

The 1926 Thom's Directory recorded that 'Tracy, F' was the occupant and the 1930 directory recorded 'Smith, C' as the occupant.

Christopher Smith was born on 28th June 1898 at 50 Bride Street in Mansion House, to Patrick Smith and Ellen Smith (née Hanrahan). He was a driver and living at Fingal Street when he enlisted with the Forage Department of the Army Service Corps (Regimental Number F28026) on 30th March 1916. He was serving with Q Company at Bow Granary in Stratford when he was discharged on 27th September 1916 to facilitate his enlistment as a Driver with the Royal Field Artillery (Regimental Number 172227). Christopher was in the army and living at Talbot Street when he married Kathleen Lee from Frederick Lane on 16th November 1919 at St Andrew's Roman Catholic Church. He was demobilised on 31st March 1922 and was living at 7 South Frederick Lane when he was awarded a pension in respect of malaria at the rate of seven shillings and sixpence per week for 70 weeks. Christopher Smith was a motor mechanic with the Automobile Association and living at 44 Killester Avenue when he died of lobar pneumonia and femoral thrombosis at Grangegorman Mental Hospital on 17th March 1953, aged 56. Kathleen Smith died at 44 Killester Avenue on 15th April 1960, aged 65. Christopher and Kathleen Smith are buried in Glasnevin Cemetery.

45 Middle Third – Thomas O'Keefe

The 1926 Thom's Directory recorded that 'Somerville, Wm' was the occupant and the 1930 directory recorded 'O'Keefe, Thos' as the occupant. *The researchers have not been able to confirm birth, marriage, or military details for this occupant.*

In 1939, Thomas O'Keefe of 45 Middle Third was one of a group of ex-servicemen from various parts of the Irish Free State who brought a court case against the ISSLT to determine who was responsible for executing repairs on the ISSLT properties. Thomas was a labourer at the Guinness Brewery when he died of intestinal obstruction and toxaemia at Mercer's Hospital on 24th August 1960, aged 67, and is buried in Swords Cemetery. His widow, Bridget (Bridie) O'Keefe of 45 Middle Third, died at the Drumcondra Hospital on 20th February 1968, aged 67, and is buried in St Columcille's Cemetery

46 Middle Third – William Stanley

William Stanley was born around 1888 to John Stanley, a GPO linesman and storekeeper, and Ada Stanley (née Coulson) and the family home was at 1 Seville Place in the North Dock district in 1901 and 1911. He was a wireman for the GPO and living at Seville Place when he married Annie Lawler of Upper Rathmines on 18th July 1915 at the Church of the Three Patrons in Rathgar. He enlisted with the Royal Field Artillery (Regimental Number 100569) on 2nd August 1915 and was deployed to the Western Front after December 1915. Gunner Stanley was serving with 5c Reserve Brigade when he was discharged due to sickness on 12th July 1917, with Silver War Badge Number 211025. He was still a GPO employee when he died of cardiac disease at 46 Killester Avenue on 22nd January 1948, aged 52. Denis O'Rourke from 13 Abbeyfield was recorded as being present when William died. Ann Stanley died at 46 Middle Third on 18th February 1963 at the age of 80, her married daughter, Patricia Josephine McAuley, being present. William and Ann Stanley are buried in Glasnevin Cemetery.

47 Middle Third – John Byrne

John Byrne was recorded as the occupant in Thom's directories up to at least 1947. The *researchers have not been able to confirm birth, marriage, military, or death details for this occupant.* Ellen Mary Byrne of 49 Killester Avenue died at St Vincent's Hospital on 28th November 1937, aged 55

48 Middle Third – Andrew Forde

Andrew Forde was born on 16th April 1889 at Corban's Lane in Naas to Patrick Forde and Mary Forde (née Reilly) and was baptised on 23rd April 1889 at St David's Roman Catholic Church in Naas. In 1901, he was living with his maternal grandparents in Naas, and he enlisted with the Royal Dublin Fusiliers (Regimental Number 9577) on 24th August 1906. He was living at Harristown when he married Catherine Barry from Ballymun on 16th September 1914 at Glasnevin Roman Catholic Church. Andrew Forde was deployed to France with 2nd Battalion on 23rd August 1914 and he sustained gunshot wounds to the index and middle fingers of his right hand and right foot. He was serving with 1st Battalion when he was discharged due to wounds on

Andrew and Catherine Forde
48 Middle Third
(source: www.findagrave.com
and RDF Association)

28th August 1916 with Silver War Badge Number 20184. He was living at Beechview in Glasnevin when he was awarded a 30% Disability Pension in respect of gunshot wounds to the right hand at the rate of twelve shillings per week. He then enlisted with the Army Service Corps (Regimental Number F/27021) on 28th January 1918 and was posted to the Forage Department but was discharged as 'not likely to become an efficient soldier' on 12th February 1918. He was living at Dobbin's Cottages in Finglas when he enlisted with the National Army (Regimental Number 8932) on 3rd August 1922 at the age of 33 and was stationed at Beggars Bush Barracks in Dublin in the 1922 National Army Census.

In the 1928 Thom's Directory, 'Johnston, J' is recorded as the occupant of 48 Middle Third. The Forde family was living at Birkenhead in Cheshire in 1939. Andrew Forde was living at Woodward Road in Rockferry, Cheshire, when he sailed from Liverpool onboard SS *Britannic* on 19th May 1950, bound for New York. Andrew died in

New York on 30th May 1961, aged 72, and Catherine Forde died on 26th December 1989, aged 96. They are buried in the Most Holy Trinity Catholic Cemetery at East Hampton Cemetery in Suffolk County.

49 Middle Third – James Joseph Byrne

The oldest veteran who was a 1925 occupant and was living at the same bungalow when he died was James Joseph Byrne of 49 Middle Third, but the researchers have been unable to confirm war service details for this occupant. James was born on 16th May 1873 at 12 East James Street to Patrick Byrne, a railway signalman, and Mary Jane Byrne (née Boyle) and the family home was at Rugby Road in the Ranelagh district in 1901, when James was recorded as being a railwayman. He was recorded as being a clerk when he married Ellen Mary Plummer of Warren Street on 4th June 1901 at Saint Kevin's Roman Catholic Church. In 1911, James Joseph Byrne was a railway station master and the family home was at Lower Knockanrahan at Arklow in County Wicklow. James is consistently recorded as being a clerk in the Register of Births before and after 1911. The family was living at St Anthony's Road in Dublin in 1912 when a son, also named James, was born at Emerald Square in Dublin in May 1916. James was a clerk and living at St Anthony's Road in Rialto when another son, Oliver Manning Byrne, was born in August 1920. Ellen's mother, Anne Jane Plummer, died at 49 Middle Third on 30th December 1926, aged 67, and her father, David Plummer, died at Hollybank Road on 9th April 1927, aged 73. Ellen M Byrne, daughter, was recorded as being present at the deaths of Anne Jane Plummer and David Plummer, who are buried in Glasnevin Cemetery. Ellen Mary Byrne died at St Vincent's Hospital on 28th November 1937, aged 55, and James was recorded as being a shopkeeper when he died of pulmonary odema and myocardial degeneration at 49 Middle Third on 23rd November 1968, aged 95. James Joseph Byrne and Ellen Mary Byrne are buried in Glasnevin Cemetery. The Byrne family was still living at 49 Middle Third in 2023.

50 Middle Third – Michael Stacey and Patrick Michael Walsh

This dwelling was a detached bungalow and the 1931 Thom's Directory records the occupant as M Stacey and the 1936 directory records the occupant as Michael Stacey. The 1937 directory records the address as vacant, and the occupant is recorded as P Walsh in 1938.

Michael Stacey married Bridget Flynn (or O'Flynn) in England, the marriage being registered in the third quarter of 1901 at Windsor in Berkshire. In 1911, Michael Stacey, a Sergeant in the Irish Guards, was living at Mount Vernon Terrace in Cork with his wife Bridget (née Flynn/O'Flynn) and an infant daughter, Eileen Mary. Michael later enlisted with the Royal Munster Fusiliers (Regimental Number 10397) and held the rank of Regimental Sergeant Major when he landed at Suvla Bay, Gallipoli with 10th (Irish) Division on 7th August 1915. He was commissioned on 26th May 1916, remaining with the Royal Munster Fusiliers. Michael and Bridget Stacey were living at 8 St Clare's Terrace in Rathmines where three children were born – Michael William (1917), Margaret Elizabeth (1920), and Maurice Patrick (1922). His Medal Index Card records 'NCOs School of Instruction, Templemore, Ireland' as an address. This is scored out and replaced with an instruction that medals were to be sent to 'HQ, Dublin University OTC, Trinity College, Dublin'. In the 1937 Thom's Directory, Captain Stacey was recorded as the occupant of 119 Seafield Road in Clontarf. John Stacey, the son of an officer in the National Army, died at 119 Seafield Road on 17th September 1936, aged 22. Brigid Stacey from 119 Seafield Road died at the Meath Hospital on 19th January 1957, aged 72. Michael J Stacey, a retired army Captain, died of acute cardiac failure at his daughter's house at Kincora Road on 25th September 1961, aged 83, his son, Maurice Patrick Stacey, being present. Michael and Brigid Stacey are buried in Glasnevin Cemetery, along with their son, John.

In January 1936, **Patrick Michael Walsh** was the occupant of the bungalow at 50 Middle Third. Patrick was born on 14th September 1894 at Oughterard in County Galway to Michael Walsh, a

*Walsh Family Memorial
50 Middle Third
(source: www.findagrave.com)*

tailor, and Catherine/Kate Walsh (née Joyce). The family was living in Galway Town in 1901 (Market Street) and 1911 (Rosemary Lane). Unfortunately, no military records which positively identify Patrick's Great War service can be found. He married Elizabeth McLoughlin at St Mary's Roman Catholic Pro Cathedral, Marlborough Street, Dublin, on 14th April 1925. At that time Patrick was a teacher and resident at Gardiner Street. Elizabeth (known as Lilly) was from 34 Cresswell Street, Everton, Liverpool. A daughter, Mary Emilia was born on 31 July 1926 but tragically died two days later. Patrick was teaching at O'Connell School, a Christian Brothers school, named after the lawyer and advocate for Catholic emancipation, Daniel O'Connell, at North Richmond Street, Dublin. Patrick died aged 50 at the Mater Hospital, Dublin, on 23rd June 1944 of hypertension. Elizabeth continued to reside in the family home until her death aged 90 in March 1988. The couple are buried along with their infant daughter and Patrick's father, Michael, at Glasnevin Cemetery (Plot ML 282 – St. Patrick's Section).

51 Middle Third (later 56 Middle Third) – Joshua Alexander Gibson

The Thom's directories from 1931 to 1936 record the occupant as William O'Meara, with Mrs Gibson being recorded as the occupant from 1937 to at least 1947. This detached bungalow was given the name 'Dartrey' and was redesignated as 56 Middle Third in the early 1940s.

It is possible that William O'Meara was Captain Liam O'Meara, Irish Defence Forces, who died at 39 Blackheath Park on 22nd November 1944, aged 55,and buried at Kill-o-Grange Cemetery. He was survived by his widow, Kathleen O'Meara.

Joshua Alexander and Florence Gibson were the second occupants of the bungalow.

Chapter 5

Occupants of Abbeyfield

At the completion of construction in 1923, Abbeyfield comprised 125 bungalows, most being semi-detached but there were three of the larger, detached bungalows. In the very early 1930s, three pairs of semi-detached two-storey houses had been added to Abbeyfield and the 1933 Thom's Directory recorded 131 occupants. The additional dwellings were numbered 35A/36A, 119A/120A, and 41A/125A (later re-designated as 126 and 127 by 1938).

1 Abbeyfield – James John Callan

James Callan was born on 8th February 1873 at Corrybracken near Carrickmacross in County Monaghan to John Callan, a farmer, and Ellen Callan (née Keenan). He was a commercial traveller and living at Emor Street, Dublin, when he married Elizabeth Cleary of Upper Camden Street on 22nd November 1899 at St Kevin's Roman Catholic Church. James and Elizabeth were living at Mount Pleasant Avenue in 1901 and Elizabeth and their five children were living at Mountpleasant Buildings in 1911. James Callan was living in a furnished room at Pleasant Street in the Fitzwilliam district in 1911. James Callan enlisted with the Army Service Corps and was posted to the Western Front in September 1914 and was discharged on 23rd August 1919. He was living at 11 Shamrock Villa in the Harold's Cross district when he was awarded a 30% Disability Pension at twelve shillings per week in respect of malaria, disorderly action of the heart, and rheumatism. He was awarded a supplementary pension at the rate of twelve shillings and seven pence per week in respect of his wife and five children. James Callan junior was born on 22nd October 1919 at

Shamrock Villa in Rathmines and was serving as a Sergeant (Number 542701) with 138 Squadron Royal Air Force when he died on 14th April 1943, aged 23. He was an Air Gunner on a Handley Page Halifax Mark II aircraft that took off from RAF Tempsford on 13th April 1943 and was lost over the sea whilst engaged in an operation for the Special Operations Executive. He was one of nine crewmen who lost their lives, and he is buried in Brookwood Military Cemetery. James Callan was a commercial agent when he died on 16th December 1944, aged 71, of chronic bronchitis and heart failure at 1 Abbeyfield. Elizabeth Callan had been suffering from cancer for six months when she died of bronchopneumonia at 1 Abbeyfield on 29th August 1952. James and Elizabeth Callan are buried in Glasnevin Cemetery.

The next occupant was John Thomas Timpson, who had been allocated 10 The Orchard in the early 1930s.

2 Abbeyfield – Leonard Atkin

Leonard Atkin was born on 18th December 1896 in Bradford, Yorkshire, and was baptised at Holy Trinity Church in Bradford on 11th February 1897. His parents were Thomas Berrington Atkin, a railway guard, and Eliza Atkin (née Duke) and the family lived at 73 Kershaw Street in Bradford in 1901 and 1911, when Leonard was recorded as being an office boy. Leonard was 19 when he enlisted with a Scottish regiment in 1915 and, in his reminiscences, he records that he was appointed as batman to Major Douglas. However, he lost the Major's luggage on a cross-channel sailing to Ireland and a few days later he failed to wake the Major in time for a parade. Indeed, it was the major who had to wake Leonard, who was then placed in charge of the Orderly Room. He was stationed at Naas Camp when he married Margaret (Peg) Minto, a VAD administrator at Naas Hospital, on 24th August 1917 at the local Roman Catholic Church. Two days after the wedding he was posted to Scotland and was subsequently transferred to the Machine Gun Corps (Number 124341). Leonard records that he was a Corporal in charge of a Signal Section when he was posted to France. In his diary, Leonard records that he was gassed and that he was buried for three days when a bomb hit his trench. Whilst Leonard was in France, Peg travelled to Bradford to stay with his parents for the

birth of their first child, Eileen. In his
diary, Leonard details that she travelled to Great Britain on RMS *Leinster*
but when she arrived at Holyhead
for the return journey to Ireland, she
discovered that civilian sailings had
been curtailed after the sinking of
the *Leinster* by a German submarine.
After two days living in the Waiting
Room at Holyhead, a Red Cross officer, on being informed that Peg was
a VAD volunteer, arranged for her to
travel on a blacked-out Royal Navy

Leonard Atkin and Margaret Atkin
(née Minto), 2 Abbeyfield
(source: Jan Kelleher)

vessel, despite regulations prohibiting civilian passengers. The entry in
Leonard's diary ends: 'Peg faced this as she faced everything in life with
calm and courage. Thank God she arrived safely.'

Leonard Atkin was transferred to the Class Z Army Reserve on 13th
October 1919 and the gassing that he suffered would later cause stomach ulcers and subsequently contribute to his death. Leonard was a
clerk when Desmond Berrington Atkin was born at 3 Hibernian Terrace
in Chapelizod on 7th May 1921 and the family moved to Abbeyfield in
1922. Ken Kelleher, a grandson of Leonard and Margaret Atkin, provided the following information:

> They bought and rented out three small shops in Killester opposite
> the Killester Community Hall, one of which they ran themselves
> for a while. Leonard also operated as a self-employed film distrib-
> utor/agent for 20th Century Fox from circa 1920 to 1950 – a cutting
> edge new technology industry then.

Leonard and Peg raised four children – Eileen, Desmond, Doreen,
and Denise (the latter three being born in Dublin).

In the 1935 Thom's Directory, 'Atkin, L, Confectioner' is recorded
after British Legion Hall.

Margaret Atkins died of cancer at St Laurence's Hospital on
11th April 1961, aged 65 – the address is recorded as 20 Abbeyfield
in the Register of Deaths. Leonard Atkin died at 2 Abbeyfield on 4th

September 1972, aged 75. Leonard and Margaret Atkin are buried in Mount Jerome Cemetery.

3 Abbeyfield – John Anthony Higgins

John Anthony Higgins was born on 30th June 1898 at 34 Emerald Square in Dublin to Thomas Higgins, a cooper at the Guinness Brewery, and Mary Higginson (née Whittaker). The family home was in the Merchant's Quay district – at Dolphins Barn Lane in 1901 and at Raleigh Place in 1911. John Higgins was a cooper when he enlisted in the Royal Navy on 9th November 1915, and he served on the Cruiser, HMS *Bellona* until his discharge on 12th March 1919. He joined the cooperage department at Guinness on 26th May 1919 and was living at Cork Street when he married Margaret Josephine Farrell of Arden Street on 24th September 1923 at St Nicholas Roman Catholic Church on Francis Street. John Anthony Higgins was living at 3 Abbeyfield when he died on 31st May 1972 and Margaret Higgins was living at 41 Lower Camden Street when she died on 27th December 1981. They are buried in Glasnevin Cemetery.

4 Abbeyfield – Richard Keogh

Richard Keogh was born on 5th August 1883 at Loughall in Harold's Cross to Patrick Keogh, a labourer at the Guinness Brewery, and Margaret Keogh (née Davy) and the family lived at Darley's Buildings in Merchants Quay in 1901. Richard joined Guinness on 26th July 1898 at the age of 14 and worked as a labourer in the Victoria Quay Vathouse. He left Guinness on 3rd August 1901 aged 17, possibly to join the army. In the 1911 England & Wales Census, Richard was stationed in England as a Corporal in the 6th (Inniskilling) Dragoons (Number 6DN/5436) and he was posted to France on 16th December 1914. He transferred to the Corps of Dragoons (Number D/21092) and was a soldier when he married Alice Keogh on 30th August 1918 at St Catherine's Roman Catholic Church – both were living at 20 Harman Street in Merchants Quay. He was transferred to the Class Z Army Reserve on 21st February 1919. Richard Keogh was a GPO labourer when he died of pleurisy and myocarditis at the St Patrick's (County) Hospital in Waterford on 24th February 1945, aged 61, and is buried in Grangegorman Military Cemetery.

5 Abbeyfield – John James Brennan

John James Brennan was born on 17th May 1878 at High Hill, New Ross in County Wexford to James Brennan, a shoemaker, and Anastasia Brennan (née Comerford). John was a clerk when he enlisted with the Royal Irish Regiment (Number 6727) on 10th of October 1899 and served in the Boer War with 1st Battalion, being awarded the Queen's South Africa Medal (Transvaal, Cape Colony, and Orange Free State clasps) and King's South Africa Medal (1901 and 1902 clasps). He was stationed at Wexford when he married Margaret Marshall on 26th June 1905 at Wexford Roman Catholic Church. John held the rank of Sergeant when he was posted to 2nd Battalion Royal Irish Regiment on the Western Front sometime after December 1915.

John was transferred to the Corps of Accountants (Number 7733170) on 17th February 1920 and was an Acting Staff Sergeant when he was discharged on 28th March 1922. The National Army Museum's registers for the men serving with the Irish regiments disbanded in 1922 records John Brennan's Army Number as 7109021, which is within the range of numbers allocated to the Royal Irish Regiment. He was living at 40 Ard Righ Road in Arbour Hill when he was awarded a 20% Disability Pension in respect of neurasthenia, myalgia, and pyorrhoea at the rate of five shillings and sixpence per week, with a weekly supplement of nine shillings and sixpence for his wife and six children. He worked as a clerk for the British Ministry of Pensions in Dublin and was living at 5 Abbeyfield when his wife, Margaret, died at Dr Steeven's Hospital on 15th July 1925, aged 39. John then married Ellen Walsh at New Ross Roman Catholic Church on 17th August 1927, and her mother, Johanna Walsh, died at 5 Abbeyfield on 6th March 1941 at the age of 76. Ellen Walsh (26) was listed as living at High Hill Street in New Ross with her mother, Johanna (61), in the 1911 Census. Margaret Brennan (24), a daughter of John and Margaret, was living at 5 Abbeyfield when she married Donald Gillies in 1933. Although the Thom's Directories from 1933 onwards list the occupant of 5 Abbeyfield as Mrs Brennan, John Brennan was living at 5 Abbeyfield when he died of cancer on 10th February 1952, aged 73. Ellen Brennan was living at 5 Abbeyfield when she died at St Kevin's Hospital on 25th July 1961, aged76. John and

Ellen Brennan are buried in Kilbarrack Cemetery in Sutton (Section DD Grave 7), along with John's first wife, Margaret.

Additional information provided by Edward Culkin, a great grandnephew of John Brennan.

6 Abbeyfield – John Desmond

John Desmond was born on 28th April 1884 at Mark's Court in Dublin to Edward Desmond, a basketmaker, and Mary Desmond (née Dunsworth). Mary died on 30th August 1898 and Edward married Sarah Cleary on 17th June 1900 and the family lived at Jervis Street in 1901. John was a labourer and living at Chancery Street when he married Jane McCabe of Phibsborough Road on 28th January 1908 at St Paul's Roman Catholic Church in Arran Quay. In 1911, they were living at 15 Lower Dominick Street in the Rotunda district and John was recorded as being a dairy labourer. John Desmond was recalled from the army reserve on 4th August 1914, being attached to 5th Battalion Royal Dublin Fusiliers (Number 6343) before being posted to the regiment's 2nd Battalion on the Western Front on 23rd October 1914. He also served with 9th Battalion Royal Dublin Fusiliers (Number 32330) on the Western Front. The Active Service Certificate records that he was attached to the Royal Army Medical Corps and that he was wounded in 1914, 1915, and 1916. He was transferred to 2nd (Home Service) Garrison Battalion Royal Irish Regiment (Number 2G/2334) on 29th January 1917. John Desmond was demobilised on 24th February 1920 and was living at Commons Street when he was awarded a 30% Disability Pension in respect of abscess of jaw, injury to right thigh, and gunshot wound to shoulder. The rate was twelve shillings per week plus an allowance of fourteen shillings and three pence for his dependents – a wife and six children. Three of John's brothers served in the Great War with the Royal Dublin Fusiliers – Private

John Desmond
6 Abbeyfield
(sources: Ancestry Family Tree
and www.findagrave.com)

Edward Desmond was killed in action with 6th Battalion at Gallipoli on 10th August 1915, Private Joseph Desmond was killed in action with 2nd Battalion on 18th December 1915, and Private Gerald Desmond was serving with 2nd Battalion when he was taken prisoner on 27th August 1914 and repatriated in December 1918. John Desmond was living at 6 Abbeyfield in Killester when he died of cancer at St Kevin's Hospital on 8th June 1942, aged 57. Jane Desmond died at 6 Abbeyfield on 19th January 1950. John and Jane Desmond are buried in Glasnevin Cemetery.

7 Abbeyfield – Thomas Mitchell Gilliard

Thomas Mitchell Gilliard was born on 30th September 1887 to Henry Gilliard and Maria Gilliard (née Wilson) who farmed land at Ballyreaghan near Ballinalee in County Longford. Thomas enlisted with the Irish Guards (Number 12145) and was posted to the Western Front after December 1915. Thomas was a soldier and living at Ship Street in Dublin when he married Annie Eager of Athdown Manor in Kilbride on 11th June 1918 at Kilbride Church of Ireland in County Wicklow. He was a Lance-Corporal when he was demobilised on 22nd February 1920 and joined Guinness on 27th April 1920, becoming a foreman in the Brewhouse Department. He was living at 135 Summer Hill when he was awarded a 20% Disability Pension at 8 shillings per week in respect of arthritis in right elbow. The Gilliard family was liv-

ing at Mount Street in 1921 before they moved to Abbeyfield. On 13th December 1929, whilst walking home from school, their son, Thomas (6), was knocked down on Seafield Road in Clontarf by a bus and taken to the Children's Hospital on Temple Street, where he died of extensive injuries later the same day. John Laffan, the driver of the Dublin United Tramways Company bus, appeared in court charged with causing the death of Thomas Gilliard. Further tragedy was to visit the family in the Second World War. Joseph Gilliard was born at the Rotunda Hospital on 18th April 1921 and enlisted for war service with the Royal

Thomas Galliard
7 Abbeyfield
(source: www.findagrave.com)

Air Force. He was a Pilot Officer with 432 (Leaside) Squadron when he died on 16th February 1944, aged 22, and is buried in Harrogate (Stonefall) Cemetery. He was the flight engineer on a Handley Page Halifax Mark III aircraft from RAF East Moor which crashed near York during a night-time training flight. Thomas Gilliard died of myocarditis and cardiac failure at 7 Abbeyfield on 8th November 1945, aged 58, and is buried in St. John the Baptist Cemetery in Clontarf.

8 Abbeyfield – Benjamin Griffith

Benjamin Griffith was born on 6th October 1888 at Marble Lane in Waterford to John Griffith, an acting Sergeant in the Royal Irish Constabulary, and Grace Anne Griffith (née Swanton) and the family later lived at Annestown in Waterford. Benjamin was a painter when he enlisted with the Royal Field Artillery (Number 54584) on 25th January 1909 and was stationed in India in 1911. He was posted to D Battery 84 Brigade, part of the 18th (Eastern) Division, on the Western Front on 30th April 1915. Bombardier Griffith was discharged due to wounds on 13th March 1919 with Silver War Badge Number B261995 and *The London Gazette* (17th June 1919) reported that he had been awarded the Military Medal. Benjamin was living at Poleberry Street in Waterford when he was awarded a 30% Disability Pension in respect of asthma at the rate of thirteen shillings per week. The pension rate was reduced to eight shillings and eight pence per week (20% disability) in September 1921. Benjamin was a painter and living at Great Brunswick Street in Dublin when he married Mary Leonard on 31st May 1921 at Ringsend Roman Catholic Church. Mary was a sister of Elizabeth Leonard who married Richard Lindsay of 28 Middle Third in 1930. The 1939 Thom's Directory recorded that 8 Abbeyfield was vacant and the 1940 directory recorded the occupant as 'Thornton, J'. In 1939, Benjamin was a stereo-typer living at 24 Ayres Road in Stretford, Lancashire, with Mary and two of their children. Benjamin Griffiths died at Barton in Lancashire in December 1960, aged 72, and Mary Griffith died in Manchester on 15th March 1966. Benjamin and Mary Griffith are buried in Manchester Southern Cemetery.

9 Abbeyfield – Sydney Ridge and William Thomas Edwards

Sydney Ridge was born on 14th August 1887 at St Gennys in Cornwall to William Ridge and Elizabeth Ridge (nee Gist). Sydney was a soldier and stationed at the Curragh Camp when he married Mary Fenlon of Spencer Place on 6th November 1910 at St. Joseph's Carmelite Church on Berkeley Road, Dublin. Mary Ridge was living at 19 Dorset Row in the Inn's Quay district of Dublin in 1911. Sydney Ridge was posted to France with the 5th (Princess Charlotte of Wales's) Dragoon Guards (Number D/666) on 15th August 1914 and subsequently served with the Corps of Dragoons (Number 31447). He transferred to the Royal Tank Corps on 1st February 1919, being finally discharged on 17th March 1922 with the rank of Acting Farrier Sergeant. He was living at Derrynane Parade in the Inn's Quay district when he was awarded a 20% Disablement Pension at 8 shillings per week in respect of epilepsy, with a supplement of seven shillings and a penny for his dependants, a wife and four children. In November 1922, Sydney's degree of disablement was upgraded to 50%, with the pension rising to twenty shillings per week and the supplement rising to seventeen shillings and ninepence per week. Andrew Ridge of 9 Abbeyfield died of gastro-enteritis at Temple Street Hospital on 2nd October 1926, aged four months. There is no name recorded for 9 Abbeyfield in 1939 Thom's Directory and the 1940 edition records that W. T. Edwards was the occupant. On 1st April 1942, the Belfast Telegraph reported on a mortar explosion at Hilltown in County Down in which one soldier was killed and two injured, including a Private Sydney Ridge. It is possible that the Ridge family left Abbeyfield at the outbreak of the Second World War, with Sydney re-enlisting for war service.

In 1939, the bungalow was allocated to William Thomas Edwards, who was born in September 1891 at Shoeburyness in Essex, his father, James, being a serving soldier.

William Thomas Edwards
and Elizabeth Edwards
9 Abbeyfield
(source: Val Cronin)

William was a boatman with 287 days service with the 4th (Special Reserve) Battalion Royal Dublin Fusiliers (Regimental Number 8032) when he decided to join the regular army. He enlisted with the Connaught Rangers (Regimental Number 9718) on 24th July 1909 at the age of 17 years and ten months. He held the rank of Corporal when was deployed to France with 2nd Battalion on 14th August 1914 and was reported as 'Missing' on the Casualty List dated 15th September 1914. During a period of home leave, he married Elizabeth Barnes on 2nd May 1915 at St Andrew's Roman Catholic Church. He returned to overseas service and, now serving with 1st Battalion, was deployed to the Mesopotamian Expeditionary Force in December 1915. He sustained gunshot wounds to the neck on 18th April 1916, being reported in the Casualty List issued by the War Office on 31st May 1916. He remained in Mesopotamia (now called Iraq) for the remainder of 1916 and 1917 and part of 1918, when the battalion was transferred to the Egyptian Expeditionary Force for service in the Near East. A child, William Thomas, was born at 45 Charlemount Street on 7th July 1919 but died sixteen days later. Sergeant William Edwards remained in the army after the war and served in India, now with the Army Number 7143235, and was discharged on 13th December 1921, having completed twelve years of service. William was awarded a 20% Disability Pension in respect of malaria and nervous debility at the rate of nine shillings and fourpence per week with a weekly allowance of two shillings for his wife. After being demobilised, William worked for CIE at Inchicore and was a retired labourer when he died of cerebral thrombosis at 9 Abbeyfield on 13th January 1969, aged 78. Elizabeth had died of bronchopneumonia at the Mater Hospital on 7th April 1966, aged 69. William and Elizabeth Edwards are buried in Mount Jerome Cemetery. After William's death, the bungalow passed to his son, Cecil, who was well-known in Killester. Cecil's widow, Rita, still lives at Abbeyfield and a piece by Val Cronin, a daughter of Cecil and Rita Edwards, is included in Chapter 7.

10 Abbeyfield – John O'Rourke

John O'Rourke was born on 29th March 1893 (recorded as 12th February 1893 on POW documents) at Chapelizod in Dublin to James O'Rourke and Bridget O'Rourke (née Connolly), although the surname was registered as ROURKE. His father died at Chapelizod on 4th September 1895, aged 40, and Bridget married Henry Paterson, a sailor, on 17th June 1901. However, in 1911, she was a widow and living at 31 New Row in the New Kilmainham district with two sons from her first marriage and a daughter from her second marriage. John O'Rourke was an engineer's assistant with Mr Spence of Cork Street when he enlisted with the Royal Garrison Artillery (Number 56656) on 7th April 1915. He was transferred to the Royal Dublin Fusiliers (5/21745) on 3rd June 1915 and initially attached to 5th Battalion. He was posted to 9th Battalion in France on 28th August 1916 and was transferred to 8th Battalion nineteen days later. He was serving with 2nd Battalion when he was taken prisoner at Ronssoy on 21st March 1918 and was incarcerated at Cassel, Mannheim, and Limburg POW camps. He was repatriated on 11th December and received medical treatment at King George's Hospital at King's Cross in London before being transferred to 3rd Battalion Royal Dublin Fusiliers for Home Service.

John was living at New Row when he married Mary Cahill of Phoenix Street on 1st January 1919 at Golden Bridge Roman Catholic Church. The family home was in St Paul's Street in Dublin when John made a Statement of Disability at Grimsby on 25th February 1919. He specified his disability as rheumatism dating from June 1918 when wading a river to escape captivity. The Medical Officer determined that his disability was myalgia. John was posted to 1st Battalion Royal Dublin Fusiliers in August 1919 and was living at Redcar in Yorkshire when he was discharged as being 'Surplus to Military Requirements' on 7th January 1920. The family was living at Railway View in Roscrea when John was awarded a 20% Disability Pension in respect of neurasthenia at the rate of eight shillings per week. Mary Josephine O'Rourke died at Mercer's Hospital on 6th January 1953, aged 57, and John O'Rourke was living at 10 Abbeyfield when he died of myocardial infarction at St Kevin's Hospital on 19th May 1968, aged 75. The Register of Deaths records his age as 79.

11 Abbeyfield – Philip Murphy

Philip Murphy was born on 13th December 1884 at Kells Union Infirmary to Edward Murphy and Mary Murphy (née Cheevers). Philip was a labourer and living at Wall Square when he married Elizabeth Kavanagh on 5th August 1906 at St Mary's Roman Catholic Pro-Cathedral on Marlborough Street and they were living at 16 Lower Gloucester Street in Mountjoy district in 1911, Philip being employed as a quay labourer. He enlisted with the Royal Irish Regiment (Number 9083) in September 1914 and was posted overseas after December 1915. He was serving with 2nd Battalion when he was hospitalised with corneal opacity in July 1917 and was discharged to a Base Dept in Etaples. Private Philip Murphy subsequently transferred to the Labour Corps (Number 369707) and was discharged due to sickness on 16th January 1919 with Silver War Badge Number B183691. He was living at Mountjoy Place when he was awarded 40% Disability Pension in respect of defective vision at the rate of sixteen shillings per week, with a supplement of nineteen shillings per week for his wife and six children. He later received a £65 grant from the Military Service (Civil Liabilities) Department to start a greengrocers business. Elizabeth Murphy died on 17th December 1935, aged 50, and Philip Murphy was living at 11 Abbeyfield when he died of valvular heart disease at St Kevin's Hospital on 4th January 1940, aged 55. Philip and Elizabeth Murphy are buried in Glasnevin Cemetery.

12 Abbeyfield – Joseph Gerald Naughton

Joseph Gerald Naughton was born on 12th November 1893 at Ahascragh near Ballinasloe in County Galway to James Naughton, a builder, and Ellen Naughton (née Farrell or O'Farrell). James Naughton died on 17th April 1895, aged 64, and Ellen and Joseph were living with her parents at River Street in Ballinasloe in 1901. In 1911, Joseph was a bank porter and living with his widowed mother at Abbey Lane in Loughrea, County Galway. Joseph was a soldier when he married Janette Ballentyne Nicholson, a nurse, on 13th September 1918 at St Malachy's Roman Catholic Church in Belfast. In the marriage register, Joseph was recorded as serving with the Royal Army Medical Corps and he and Janette were both living at 11 Botanic Avenue. Joseph Gerald Naughton was the occupant of 12 Abbeyfield in the 1947 Thom's

Directory and his Golden Cocker Spaniel won first prize at the Bray Dog Show in 1950. Joseph died on 16th August 1960, aged 76, of epithelioma and anaemia at Galway Regional Hospital and is buried in Ahascragh Old Graveyard. Douglas James Naughton was born on 15th May 1918 at 74 University Street, with his parents being recorded as Joseph Gerard Naughton of Gray's Point in Bangor and Janette Ballantyne Naughton (née Nicholson). Douglas James Naughton was educated at St Andrew's College and at Trinity College Dublin where he graduated with a medical degree in 1941 before moving to a practice in England. Whilst at Trinity, he captained the Dublin University Boat Club in the 1939/40 season. He gained a commission with the Royal Naval Volunteer Reserve and was a Surgeon Lieutenant on HMS *Curacoa*, which sank on 2nd October 1942 with the loss of 337 men following an accidental collision with the ocean liner, RMS *Queen Mary*. Surgeon Lieutenant Douglas James Naughton was 24 years old when he died and is commemorated on the Chatham Naval Memorial in England.

13 Abbeyfield – Cornelius O'Rourke

Cornelius Joseph O'Rourke was born on 14th September 1883 at 9 Arran Quay to Cornelius O'Rourke, a car man and later a florist/fruiterer, and Elizabeth O'Rourke (née Maguire). Cornelius was a painter and lodging with the Haughton family at Parkgate Street in the Arran Quay district in 1911. Cornelius enlisted with the Royal Engineers (Number 10776) and was deployed to France as a Sapper with 7th Field Company on 23rd August 1914. During a period of home leave, he was living at Ellis Quay when he married Mary Bridget Barry of Benburb Street on 16th September 1915 at St Paul's Roman Catholic Church. Cornelius was reported as missing on 11th July 1918 (War Office Daily List No.5615) and was later confirmed as a Prisoner of War. He was repatriated to England on 23rd November 1918, arriving at Hull onboard SS *Stockport*, and was transferred to the Class Z Army Reserve on 15th March 1919. He was living at 15 Holles Street when he was awarded 20% Disability Pension for the Effects of Gas and Rheumatism at the rate of eight shillings per week. He also received a dependants' allowance of two shillings per week. Cornelius returned to his trade as a House Painter and Mary Bridget O'Rourke died at 13 Abbeyfield on

8th March 1924, aged 40. Cornelius then married Ellen Hill of Benburb Street on 9th February 1927 at St Paul's Roman Catholic Church. Cornelius O'Rourke died at 13 Abbeyfield of acute nephritis and myocardial failure on 20th August 1946, aged 52. Ellen Mary O'Rourke was living at 13 Abbeyfield when she died at St Mary's Hospital, Phoenix Park on 16th February 1965, aged 80. Cornelius Joseph O'Rourke and both his wives are buried in Glasnevin Cemetery.

Note: an Ancestry family tree records service in South Africa between 1899 and 1901 and there is a medal roll entry for a Lance-Sergeant C O'Rourke serving with 1st Battalion Royal Irish Fusiliers (Number 5106), being awarded the Queen's South Africa Medal with Orange Free State, Transvaal, Talana, and Relief of Ladysmith clasps. I am not convinced that this was Cornelius O'Rourke.

14 Abbeyfield – Michael O'Rourke

Michael O'Rourke was born around 1893 and enlisted with the Royal Dublin Fusiliers (Number 19974). He was deployed to France with 8th Battalion on 10th December 1915 and reported as wounded in the War Office Casualty List dated 19th May 1916. Corporal Michael O'Rourke was transferred to the Class Z Army Reserve on 7th March 1919 and was married when he was awarded a 20% Disability Pension in respect of gas poisoning at the rate of eight shillings per week. Michael was working as a railway porter when his son, Michael Patrick O'Rourke, died of cardiac failure on 7th November 1934. He had been diagnosed as having leukaemia for two months and was three years and five months old when he died. Michael later ran the chip shop in one of the 'tin shops' and was recorded as being self-employed when he died of cardiac and respiratory failure, and myocardial infarction, at Jervis Street Hospital on 7th February 1971, aged 79. Margaret was still living at Abbeyfield when she died on 12th January 1979, aged 87. Michael and Margaret O'Rourke are buried in Balgriffin Cemetery (Section K Grave 199).

15 Abbeyfield – Peter Martin

Peter Smith was born on 16th April 1878 at Rathdown Workhouse to Margaret Smith and later adopted the Martin surname. He joined Guinness as a labourer in the Brewhouse Department on 20th August

1908 and was living at Echlin Street in Usher's Quay when he married Catherine (Kate) Toole of Purcell's Terrace in Bray on 15th February 1903 at Bray Roman Catholic Church. His father's name was recorded as Peter Martin, a carpenter. In 1911, Peter, Kate, their two sons and two daughters were living at 70 Rialto Cottages in Usher's Quay. Peter enlisted with the Worcestershire Regiment (Number 8871) and held the rank of Sergeant when he was posted to 11th Battalion on the Salonika Front after December 1915. Peter and Catherine had a further four children between 1911 and 1922, although James Martin died in May 1914 at the age of one. The Martin family was still living at 70 Rialto Cottages when Ellen was born in July 1921. Philip Martin was a brewhouse foreman with Guinness when he died of mitral valvular disease at 15 Abbeyfield on 28th December 1938, aged 57, and Catherine Mary Martin died at 15 Abbeyfield on 8th February 1956, aged 74. Peter and Catherine Martin are buried in Saint Peter's Cemetery in Bray (Plot Number CA36). Their son Christopher, an Actor with the Unity Players, was living at 15 Abbeyfield when he died in December 1961, aged 45.

16 Abbeyfield – William J McGrane

William McGrane was born on 26th March 1892 at St. Margaret's townland in Finglas to Patrick McGrane and Kate McGrane (née Byrne) and the family later lived at Ballyfermott Lower in Palmerstown. William was a labourer when he enlisted with the Royal Irish Fusiliers (Number 10757) in 1911. He was living at Waterford Street when he married Julia Mary Cullen from Cumberland Street on 7th March 1914 at St Mary's Roman Catholic Pro-Cathedral on Marlborough Street. William was deployed to France with 1st Battalion on 22nd August 1914. He was admitted to Number 2 General Hospital on 3rd July 1916 with gunshot wounds to the face and discharged to a convalescence depot on the same day. He was reported as wounded in the War Office Casualty List dated 25th July

William and Julia McGrane
16 Abbeyfield
(source: M. Myers)

1916, entitling him to one wound stripe. He was treated for myalgia at 30th Casualty Clearing Station in October 1916. The medical admissions registers record that he had five years of army service in July 1916 but five years and six months service in October 1916. He was subsequently transferred to the Labour Corps (Number 417721, although some documents record 411727), serving with 911 Agricultural Employment Company and 254 Agricultural Employment Company. During the war he was also an orderly for the Reverend David Sloane Corkey, a Chaplain who had an arm amputated during the Great War.

The Reverend Corkey was Minister of Dundrod Presbyterian Church and when the war memorial tablet was erected, he ensured that William McGrane's name was included. He is probably the only Irish Roman Catholic to be commemorated on a war memorial tablet in a Presbyterian Church in Ireland. William and Julia McGrane were living at 35 Cumberland Street when Julia and Margaret were born in April 1920 and October 1921 respectively. After the war, he was employed as a chauffeur and as a lorry driver, his last employer being Irish Carton Printers. Julia McGrane's sister, Margaret Cullen, was living at 16 Abbeyfield when she died on 16th February 1941 at the Mater Hospital, aged 40, and is buried in Glasnevin Cemetery. Julia Mary McGrane died at Sir Patrick Dun's Hospital on 5th December 1968, aged 76. William McGrane was living at 16 Abbeyfield when he died at Jervis Street Hospital on 6th October 1981, aged 89. William and Julia Mary McGrane are buried in Balgriffin Cemetery (Section I Grave 39). Their youngest daughter, Claire Massey (née McGrane) lived in the bungalow until c2003.

17 Abbeyfield – William John Bowen

The 1926 Thom's Directory records the occupant as 'Bowen, J' and the occupant is listed as 'Bowen, Mrs' in the Thom's directories from 1935 to 1947. Tom Burke advised that William Bowen received assistance from the 'Not Forgotten Society' until 1960 and that the occupant of 17 Abbeyfield in the 1967 Thom's Directory was Frederick O'Connor.

William John Bowen was born around 1881/1882 to William Bowen, a coachman, and Hannah Bowen (née Garr) and the family lived at Crammer Lane in Baggotrath in 1901 and at Booterstown

Avenue in Blackrock in 1911. William served as a Steward at the Irish Hospital Corps during the Second Anglo-Boer War, being awarded the Queen's South Africa Medal with the Cape Colony, Orange Free State, and Transvaal clasps. William was a coachman when he married Elizabeth Allen, a lady's maid, on 10th July 1905 at Christ Church, Dublin. In 1911, William (now a butler) and Elizabeth (now a cook) were working for Thomas Norman Sample, a ship owner, and Kate Isabel Sample at Dunishal, Ballybeg, Wexford. The Census return recorded that William and Elizabeth had four children, but they were living with relatives in 1911. The children were Violet May Bowen (born in Rathdrum in May 1906), Lionel Allen Bowen (born in Cellbridge in August 1907), Hannah Annie Maria Bowen (born in Maryborough in November 1908), Elizabeth Bowen (born at Prospect Cottage in Ballytruckle in June 1910), and John William Bowen (born in Maryborough in June 1915).

William John Bowen was recorded as being a coachman or chauffeur in the birth register for the first four children but as a Soldier in the birth register for John William Bowen. William enlisted with the South Irish Horse (Number 1069) on 2nd September 1914 and was posted to France with A Squadron on 11th September 1915, joining the 21st Division. In September 1917, the South Irish Horse was disbanded and, whilst many men were re-allocated to 7th Battalion Royal Irish Regiment, William was re-allocated to the Corps of Hussars (Number 73085). Private William John Bowen was discharged on 8th February 1919 as being 'No longer physically fit for war service', with Silver War Badge Number 423847. His age at discharge was recorded as 36 years and five months, indicative of an 1882 birth year. The family was living at Ridge Road in Maryborough, Queen's County, when William was awarded a 20% Disability Pension in respect of synovitis (right knee) and disorderly action of the heart. The rate was eight shillings per week, with a supplement of eight shillings and tuppence for his wife and five children. The family later moved to 7 Merchants Cottages in the East Wall district of Dublin. Elizabeth Bowen was recorded as being the wife of a gatekeeper when she died at 17 Abbeyfield on 14th September 1926, aged 53, and is buried in St John the Baptist Cemetery in Clontarf. A Jane Bowen, recorded as being the wife of a storeman, was living at 17 Abbeyfield when she was admitted to 'The Rest' on Camden Row, where she died on 20th July 1952, aged 62. It is not known what the relationship was between Jane Bowen and William John Bowen.

18 Abbeyfield – William Joseph Burrows

William Burrows was born on 8th May 1888 at Kilcommon near Clogheen in County Tipperary to Charles Burrows, a caretaker, and Elizabeth Burrows (née Connor). His father died on 19th September 1891 and Elizabeth was a nurse and living at Nelson Street in Dublin when she married Charles Davis, a merchant from Wicklow, in April 1900. However, whilst Charles and Elizabeth Davis were living at High Street in Wicklow in 1901, William and his brother Henry (10) were recorded as being orphans and living in Cahir with Eliza Jane Wilson, a widow – there were two other 'orphaned' children in the household, Alicia Sloane (12) and Maria Morrison (2). William enlisted with the Irish Guards on 21st March 1908 and was living with his mother and step-father at High Street in Wicklow in 1911 – Henry (20) was also present in the household. William joined the staff of the Guinness Traffic Department on 29th May 1911 and was recalled to active service at the outbreak of the war, being posted to the 1st Battalion Irish Guards on the Western Front on 13th September 1914. He was taken prisoner at Sorrbeck in the Ypres Sector on 6th November 1914 and was held in POW camps at Giessen, Limburg, Celle, and Meschede before being transferred to an internment camp in Holland in June 1918. He was repatriated to England onboard SS *Willochra* on 18th November 1918 and discharged as being 'No longer physically fit for war service' on 17th February 1919 with Silver War Badge Number B130850. He was awarded a 20% Disability Pension at eight shillings per week in respect of gunshot wounds (that had caused defective vision) and debility. The degree of disability was increased to 30% in December 1920 (twelve shillings per week), then to 40% in January 1922 (sixteen shillings per week), and finally to 50% in January 1923 (twenty shillings per week).

Although William Burrows had been employed by Guinness before the war, his name is not recorded on the St James' Gate Roll of

Honour. William Burrows returned to work for Guinness after the war and was a mechanic and living at High Street in Wicklow when he married Rosanna Wall of The Mall in Wicklow on 23rd June 1920 at Rathdrum Roman Catholic Church. The Burrows family moved from 18 Abbeyfield to 23 Middle Third around 1931 and that was the family home when William died on 1st April 1965, aged 73, of respiratory failure and pneumonia at St Mary's Chest Hospital, Phoenix Park. He was buried in Kilbarrack Cemetery in Sutton, the funeral costs being covered by a grant from the Not Forgotten Society. Rosanna Burrows and their daughters were living at 23 Middle Third when an In Memoriam Notice was published in the Irish Independent newspaper on 1st April 1974. Rosanna Burrows died at 23 Middle Third on 10th October 1976 and is buried in Kilbarrack Cemetery in Sutton.

19 Abbeyfield – William Jennings

A Pension Card records that William Jennings was born on 6th June 1882 and his Royal Navy service sheet records birth on 6th June 1883 at Clonmel in County Tipperary. He joined the Royal Navy (Number 203127) straight from school on 6th June 1901 for a twelve-year engagement and his first posting was to HMS *Black Prince*. The 1911 England & Wales census records that Able Seaman William Jennings was 27 years old and was single. He transferred to the Royal Australian Navy (Number 7312) on 1st January 1913 and took part in operations in German New Guinea in 1916. On the RAN record sheet, his next-of-kin is recorded as his sister, Agnes Griffin, of Doyle Street in Waterford. The register of the marriage between Thomas Griffin and Agnes Jennings in 1900 records her father as being Patrick Jennings, a police pensioner, and the register of births records her mother as being Bridget Jennings (née Sexton). Able Seaman William Jennings was demobilised on 16th October 1919 and received a £29 War Gratuity from the Royal Australian Navy in December 1920. He married Ellen Harris on 15th February 1920 at Rathgormack Roman Catholic Church, Waterford, and they were living at 28 Upper Fitzwilliam Street in Dublin when he submitted a claim for a disability pension in respect of nervous debility. William was a widower and living at 19 Abbeyfield when he died of cancer and pneumonia at St Kevin's Hospital on 23rd

March 1967, aged 85, and is buried in Rathgormack Church Graveyard in Waterford.

20 Abbeyfield – Daniel Thomas Brady

In the 1926 Thom's Directory, the occupant is just recorded as 'Farrelly' and the 1928 directory records the occupant as 'Brady, D T' who was still recorded as the occupant in the 1947 directory.

Daniel Thomas Brady was born on 14th February 1885 at Glenpoole Cottages in Terenure to John Brady and Mary Brady (née Farrell) and he was living at Duke Road in Chiswick, London, when he enlisted with the Royal Fusiliers (Number G/25549) on 9th December 1915, his next-of-kin being recorded as his father, John Brady of 12 Whitton Road in Terenure. He was posted to 5th Battalion on 1st March 1916 (Number 5293) and was transferred to the London Regiment (Number 682536) on 6th June 1916. He served on the Western Front with 22nd (The Queen's) Battalion from 17th June 1916 to 1st January 1917. Private Brady had sustained gunshot wounds to both legs on 24th November 1916, necessitating the amputation of both limbs and was discharged on 15th June 1919 with Silver War Badge Number 480751. On the same day, he married Esther Daly in the temporary Roman Catholic Chapel in the Duke of Connaught's Military Hospital in Rathdown. They were living at Glen Lodge at Ashford, County Wicklow after his discharge and were living at Verdun Cottage at Sunnybank in Bray in October 1920. Daniel Thomas Brady was awarded a 100% Disability Pension for life at the rate of twenty-seven shillings and sixpence per week. In September 1939, Daniel Brady won the Morgan Mooney Cup for the best front and back garden in the competitions promoted by the Killester Horticultural Society and the Killester branch of the National Garden Guild. He also won a Gold Medal, presented by Alderman Byrne TD, in the 'Best Front Garden' category. Esther Brady died of cancer at the Royal City of Dublin Hospital on Baggot Street on 8th November 1938, aged 56, and Daniel Thomas Brady was living at 20 Abbeyfield when he died of nephritis and renal failure at the Meath Hospital on 29th July 1945, aged 60. Daniel and Esther Brady are buried in Mount Jerome Cemetery.

21 Abbeyfield – John Farrell

John Farrell was born on 20th April 1893 at Spring Hill near Carlow to James Farrell, a labourer, and Kate Farrell (née Fenton). Whilst details of John's war service have not been verified, information from Frank Farrell indicates that he served with the Royal Irish Regiment. After the war, he joined Guinness on 7th June 1920, and was a charger in the Brewhouse Department when he left the firm. John was a labourer and living at Carlow when he married Margaret Prendergast on 26th September 1921 at the Roman Catholic Church in Tullow. John died at 21 Abbeyfield on 12th August 1975, aged 82, and Margaret Farrell was living at 21 Abbeyfield when she died on 24th October 1986, aged 86. John and Margaret Farrell are buried in Balgriffin Cemetery (Section N Graves 24/25). Also buried in the plot is Kathleen Farrell, a single woman, who was living at Abbeyfield when she died on 4th July 2013, aged 87.

22 Abbeyfield – Michael Francis Campbell

In the 1926 Thom's Directory, the occupant is just recorded as 'Wallace, J', the 1929 directory records the occupant as 'Cummins, J', and the directories from 1930 to 1947 record the occupant as 'Campbell, M' Michael Campbell was born on 10th October 1888 at Sheephouse in St. Mary's Parish in County Meath to Michael Campbell, an agricultural labourer, and Jane Campbell (née Kelly). He enlisted with the Royal Field Artillery (Number 55964) on 19th March 1909 and was deployed to France on 11th September 1914. Driver Michael Francis Campbell was serving with 42nd Brigade when he was discharged as being 'Surplus to military requirements (having suffered impairment since entry into the service)' on 20th February 1919 with Silver War Badge Number B300407.

Michael was recorded as being a postman and residing at Castle Hospital when he married Mary Breslin of Ferns on 30th December 1918 at Boolavogue Roman Catholic Church in County Wexford. They were living at 17 Railway Avenue in Baldoyle when Michael was awarded a 30% Disability Pension in respect of gunshot wounds to the right hip at the rate of twelve shillings per week. A son, Michael, was born on 9th May 1920 in Baldoyle and a daughter, Annie, was born on

24th July 1921 at Carrigeen in the Ferns townland of County Wexford. The family was living at 4 Seaview Terrace in Baldoyle when Annie died of tubercular meningitis at the Meath Hospital on 21st October 1923 at the age of two years and three months. Mary Campbell died the following day, aged 29, of pulmonary tuberculosis at Our Lady of Lourdes Hospital in Blackrock. Michael Campbell junior died of meningitis at the Meath Hospital on 29th October 1923 at the age of three years and six months. Michael was a postman and still living at Seaview Terrace when he married Nora Tobin on 1st June 1925 at St Michael's Roman Catholic Church in Dun Laoghaire. He was a retired postal sorter when he died of coronary thrombosis at 22 Abbeyfield on 2nd April 1967, aged 78, and is buried in Kilbarrack Cemetery (Section DI Grave 18) along with his first wife and their two infant children.. Nora Campbell died at the St Clare's Nursing Home on 16th March 1968 and is buried in Fingal Cemetery (Section C Grave 539).

23 Abbeyfield – Joe Clifton

The occupant was recorded as 'Clifton J' in the 1926 Thom's Directory and was still recorded as the resident in the 1947 directory. Frank Farrell recalls that Joe Clifton was the Caretaker of the Legion Hall.

In 1954, Joan Clifton was one of twelve Sisters of the Medical Missionaries of Mary who were professed at a ceremony in the Chapel of Our Lady of Lourdes Novitiate in Drogheda by the Right Reverend Monsignor J F Stokes.

Charlotte Conlon (née Clifton) was living at 23 Abbeyfield when she died on 4th September 1986, aged 60, and her husband was living at the same address when he died on 9th April 1998, aged 71. Charlotte and Gabriel Conlon are buried in Fingal Cemetery (Section B Grave 243).

24 Abbeyfield – Denis Hayden

In the 1926 Thom's Directory, the occupant is just recorded as 'Hyland, P', the 1927 directory records the occupant as 'Hayden, D'. The bungalow was vacant in the 1939 directory and 'Moloney, P' was recorded as the occupant in the 1940 directory.

Denis Hayden was a labourer and living at Upper Gloucester Street when he married Ellen Kiernan of Garden Lane on 25th April 1909 at St

Nicholas Roman Catholic Church on Francis Street. They were living at 7 Cumberland Street South in Trinity Ward in 1911. Ellen Hayden was recorded as being the wife of a clerk when she died of Cancer at 24 Abbeyfield on 6th June 1933, aged 40. Denis Hayden was a labourer and living at Lower Kevin Street when he died of bronchopneumonia at the Dublin Union Infirmary on 14th April 1934, aged 53. Denis and Ellen Hayden are buried in Glasnevin Cemetery. In the Register of Marriages, the father of Denis Hayden was recorded as Loftus. Based on the ages recorded in 1911 and 1934, Denis was born around 1881 and the 1911 census recorded that he was born in Dublin City. The only viable Birth Registration was for a Denis Owen Haydon who was born on 22nd October 1885 at Naas to Loftus Haydon and Julia Haydon (née Bollard). Loftus and Hayden were living at Main Street East in Naas in 1901 and at Main Street North in 1911 – Denis is not recorded on either census return. Loftus was recorded as being a grocer when Denis was born but later as wholesale bottler (1901) and publican (1911). It is possible the Denis Hayden served with 7th Battalion Royal Inniskilling Fusiliers (Number 27701) being posted overseas after December 1915.

Mary Maloney died of cancer at 24 Abbeyfield on 4th March 1958, aged 63, and Patrick Maloney, who had suffered from mitral stenosis and chronic bronchitis for twelve years, died of a pulmonary embolism at 24 Abbeyfield on 1st September 1963, aged 68. Patrick and Mary Maloney are buried in Glasnevin Cemetery.

25 Abbeyfield – Charles Proudfoot

Charles Proudfoot was born on 25th January 1892 in Salford, Lancashire, and his father, James, was a shoemaker. James Proudfoot was a widower when he married Alice Delaney on 5th April 1900 and the family was living at Little Ship Street in Wood Quay, Dublin, in 1901. James Proudfoot died on 11th October 1903 and Charles was a cabinet maker and living with his widowed stepmother and his step siblings at 14 Coleraine Street in

Charles and Christina Proudfoot
25 Abbeyfield
(source: Christina Large)

Arran Quay in 1911. Charles was a machinist and living at Royal Canal when he married Christina Ryan of Upper Dominick Street on 24th September 1914 at St Michan's Roman Catholic Church. He enlisted with the Royal Engineers (Number 200570) on 24th August 1917 and served on the Western Front, where he was gassed. Sapper Charles Proudfoot was serving with the Inland Waterways and Docks (Number WR/503333) when he was discharged due to sickness on 15th August 1918 with Silver War Badge Number 43196. He was living at 8 Middle Gardiner Street when he was awarded an 80% Disability Pension at 32 shillings per week in respect of tubercle of lung, with a supplement of eleven shillings and ninepence in respect of two children. The family was living at the same address when Charles Proudfoot junior was born in 1918 and Patricia Proudfoot was born in March 1920. The family was living at 25 Abbeyfield when Charles Proudfoot junior married Kathleen Doyle in December 1942. In the 1945 Thom's Directory, the occupant of 25 Abbeyfield is recorded as J Sullivan. The Proudfoot family had moved to London during the Second World War and lived at Tuffnell Park in North London. Christina Proudfoot's death was registered in Islington in the second quarter of 1960 – she was 67 years old. Charles Proudfoot's death was registered in Hendon in Quarter One of 1979 – he was 87 years old. Charles and Christina Proudfoot are buried in Highgate Cemetery in London. Christina Large summed up her grandfather, Charles Proudfoot, with these words, 'He was a quiet man but he loved to sing and play his mandolin and was always in demand at the many family parties.' The family remained lifelong close friends with the McGrane family, who also lived in Killester.

26 Abbeyfield – Patrick Smith

Patrick Smith (Smyth in some civil and military records) was born on 15th August 1894 at 58 Meath Street in the Merchants Quay district to Patrick Smith, a labourer, and Mary Smith (née Timmons) and the family was living at the same address when Patrick, a factory hand, married Margaret Byrne of Francis Street on 28th August 1918 at St Nicholas of Myra Roman Catholic Church in Francis Street, Dublin. Patrick enlisted with Royal Dublin Fusiliers (Number 8/14474) on 22nd September 1914 and was deployed to France with 8th Battalion in December 1915. He later served with the Labour Corps (Number 229556) and was serving with the Inland Waterways & Docks section of the Royal Engineers (Number WR/332185) when he was discharged due to sickness on 17th November 1918 with Silver War Badge Number B41620. (Note: the Silver War Badge Register records his age as 55.) Margaret Smith (late of 550 20th Street, Brooklyn, New York, and 26 Abbeyfield, Killester) died on 27th August 1966. Patrick's mother, Mary Smith (née Timmons) was living with him at 26 Abbeyfield when she died on 29th October 1970, aged 97. Patrick Smith died on 3rd October 1972 at Mercer's Hospital and is buried in St Fintan's Cemetery, Sutton.

27 Abbeyfield – Richard Phelan

Richard Phelan was stationed in India with 2nd Battalion Royal Irish Rifles (Number 2/6368) when he married Mary Worth on 8th January 1911 at Maymyo in Bengal. He held the rank of Sergeant when he was deployed to France on 6th November 1914. Richard was admitted to No 10 General Hospital in Rouen with concussion on 13th March 1915 and held the rank of Colour Sergeant when he was attached to the Gold Coast Regiment in September 1917. He was mentioned for distinguished services in operations in East Africa between May and December 1917 in Lieutenant-General Sir Jacob Louis van Deventer's despatch dated 21st January 1918. In September 1918, *The London Gazette* reported that Colour Sergeant Richard Phelan had been awarded the Long Service and Good Conduct Medal. Mary Phelan was living at Annavilla in Rathmines when their son, Richard Joseph, was born in June 1917 and when their daughter, Mary Teresa, was born in October 1919. Richard Phelan had post-war service with the Royal Ulster Rifles (Number 7006214) and was demobilised on 13th June 1922. Richard was a labourer when his son, John, died of Influenza and General Debility at 27 Abbeyfield on 6th August 1930, aged 6 years and 11 months, and is buried in Mount Jerome Cemetery. Mary Phelan died at 27 Abbeyfield on 19th July 1955, aged 69, and Richard Phelan was living at 27 Abbeyfield when he died of bronchopneumonia at St Laurence's (Richmond) Hospital on 8th February 1962, aged 78.

28 Abbeyfield – Arthur Mayne

Based on the recorded age at death (65 in 1959), Arthur Mayne was born around 1894 and there is only one likely match in the 1901 Census and the 1911 Census.

Arthur Jocelyn Joseph Mayne was born on 3rd August 1894 at 36 Aberdeen Street, Dublin, to Herbert Mayne, an electrician, and Catherine Mayne (née Kelly) and the family lived at Ballisk Common in Donabate in 1901 and at 36 Foster Terrace in the Mountjoy district in 1911, when Arthur was recorded as being an electrical apprentice. Based on his pre-war occupation, the most likely military match is Arthur J Mayne who was deployed overseas with the Royal Engineers (Number 259564) after December 1915 and later served with Royal Dublin Fusiliers (Number 28323). Arthur Mayne married a Florence Reed, the marriage being registered in the fourth quarter of 1914 at Newmarket in Cambridgeshire. Arthur Mayne was a soldier and living at West William Street when Mary was born in August 1919, Florence's maiden name being recorded as Reid. Arthur Mayne was a Pensioner and living at 28 Abbeyfield when he died of coronary thrombosis at the James Connolly Memorial Hospital in Blanchardstown on 3rd December 1959, aged 65. Florence Mayne (née Reedy) was living at 28 Abbeyfield when she died at St Mary's Hospital, Phoenix Park, on 16th August 1978. Arthur and Florence Mayne are buried in Mount Jerome Cemetery.

29 Abbeyfield – John Edward McDowell

John Edward McDowell was born on 13th February 1881 at 2 Henrietta Buildings in the Inns Quay district to Patrick McDowell and Eliza McDowell (née Courtney). John was a labourer and living at Upper Oriel Street when he married Bridget Logue, a confectioner, of Watling Street on 7th May 1899 at St James' Roman Catholic Church and they were living at Upper Gloucester Street in 1901. Bridget McDowell, wife of a railway porter, died at St Patrick's Hospital in Cork on 14th February 1911, aged 34, and John McDowell was a railway porter and living at Old Youghal Road in Cork in 1911. He enlisted with the Royal Fusiliers (Number 8765) and was posted to 13th Battalion on the Western Front on 31st December 1915. He received treatment for lumbago at No 2 General Hospital in July 1916 and was transferred to the 43rd (Garrison) Battalion on 25th August 1918 (Number GS/83971). He continued to serve in France until 9th October 1918 and he was transferred to the Class Z Army Reserve on 19th May 1919. John was a widowed soldier and living at Upper Oriel Street when he married Bridget Clarke of 170 North Strand on 25th June 1918 at St Laurence O'Toole Roman Catholic Church. They were living at 170 North Strand when he was awarded a 60% Disability Pension in respect of deafness in his right ear and gastritis at the rate of sixteen shillings per week and an allowance of seven shillings per week in respect of a qualifying child from his first marriage. His father, Patrick McDowell, died at 29 Abbeyfield on 2nd March 1929, aged 80. John was a railway porter and living at 29 Abbeyfield when he died of cancer and cardiac failure at Harold's Cross Hospital 4th July 1942, aged 61. His second wife, Bridget, was recorded as living at 28 Abbeyfield when she died at St Kevin's Hospital on 25th July 1954, aged 77. John Edward McDowell, Bridget McDowell, and Patrick McDowell are buried in Glasnevin Cemetery.

A later occupant, Mrs Eileen Doran won the Bolands Biscuits Popularity Poll and won an Austin Seven Mini in December 1961.

30 Abbeyfield – Arthur William Palmer

The Thom's directories from 1926 to 1929 record the occupant as 'Doyle, R' and the 1930 directory records 'Palmer, A' as the occupant.

Arthur William Palmer was born on 13th December 1896 at 33 South King Street in Royal Exchange, Dublin, to William Palmer, a bottler, and Christina Palmer (née Welsh) and the family was living at 4 Bella Street in Mountjoy in 1911. William Palmer was recorded as a door porter in 1901 and as a mineral water porter in 1911, when Arthur was listed as being a messenger. Arthur enlisted with the Royal Dublin Fusiliers (Number 26284) on 5th March 1916 and was posted to 11th Battalion when it was formed in July of the same year. He served overseas with the Royal Dublin Fusiliers before being transferred to the 673 Home Service Employment Company Labour Corps (Number 521087). Private Palmer was discharged due to Sickness on 12th March 1918, with Silver War Badge Number 322208. He was living at the family home in Bella Street when he was awarded a 30% Diasability Pension in respect of chronic bronchitis and hypertropic rhinitis at the rate of twelve shillings per week. Arthur was a sorting clerk when he married Alice Bradford of Lower Gloucester Street on 15th February 1920 at St Mary's Roman Catholic Pro-Cathedral on Marlborough Road. They were living at 30 Abbeyfield when their son, Ronald Francis, died of meningitis, aged eight months. Arthur was a retired postal sorter and had been suffering from chronic bronchitis and emphysema for 20 years when he died on 18th August 1965, aged 68, at the Leopardstown Park Hospital in Blackrock. Alice Palmer died at 30 Abbeyfield on 13th June 1966, aged 68. Arthur and Alice Palmer are buried in Balgriffin Cemetery (Section N Grave 25).

31 Abbeyfield – Francis Murray

Francis Murray was born on 24th July 1891 in Kingstown to James Murray, a militia man, and Eliza Murray (née Burroughs/Burrows) and the family lived at Scott's Lane in Glasthule in 1901 and at 67 Mulgrave Street in Kingstown in 1911. Francis was a labourer and living at Mulgrave Street in Kingstown when he married Dora Wills from Pim's Court in Kingstown on 25th May 1913 at St Michael's Church of Ireland, Kingstown. *The researchers have not been able to identify his military service.* Jane Murray was born at 9 Summerhill Parade on 6th January 1921. Dora Murray died at 31 Abbeyfield on 22nd October 1948, aged 53, and is buried in Dean's Grange Cemetery. A later occupant of 31 Abbeyfield was Michael Hyland who had served with the Northumberland Fusiliers (Number 4254335) in the Great War.

32 Abbeyfield – James Byrne

James Byrne was born on 25th March 1891 at 51 York Street in Royal Exchange to James Byrne, a painter, and Catherine Byrne (née Smith) and the family was living at Arthurs Lane in Wood Quay in 1901. James was a painter and living at Essex Quay when he married Mary Teresa King on 1st August 1909 at St Mary's Roman Catholic Pro-Cathedral on Marlborough Street. James Byrne enlisted with the Royal Dublin Fusiliers (Number 17763) and was posted to 1st Battalion on the Western Front after December 1915. He sustained a gunshot wound to the head, face, and left eye at Monchy on 28th May 1917, being initially treated at Number 19 Casualty Clearing Station. He received further treatment at Number 18 General Hospital at Camiers before being evacuated from France on 6th June 1917. He subsequently served with the Labour Corps (Number 547271) and the Royal Air Force (Number 302035). James was a soldier and the family home was at Camden Place when Rose Byrne was born in May 1918 and he was discharged on 12th April 1919. Aircraftsman Byrne was awarded a 50% Disability Pension at the rate of twenty shillings per week, with a weekly supplement of seventeen shillings and sixpence in respect of four children. The supplement was reduced to fourteen shillings and sixpence in 1921 as only three children still qualified. James was a painter when Christopher Byrne was born at Great Denmark Street in May 1921. One of his daughters, Agnes, was a factory worker when she died at 32 Abbeyfield on 10th July 1944, aged 19. His mother-in-law, Catherine King, died at 32 Abbeyfield on 5th April 1937, aged 71. Mary Byrne died at 32 Abbeyfield on 24th January 1959, aged 70, and James Byrne died in August 1972, aged 81. James and Mary Byrne are buried in Glasnevin Cemetery and the burial register records James as being 88 when he died.

33 Abbeyfield – George Joseph Pattison

George was born around 1888 in Dublin City and his father was called Joseph and worked as a plumber. He enlisted with the British Army on 27th January 1908 but, in 1911, he was a tailor and boarding with Moses and Norah Ennis at Market Street in Castlebar, County Mayo. George was a tailor and living at Castle Street in Castlebar when he married Bridget Murray from Chapel Street on 1st January 1912 at Castlebar Roman Catholic Church. He served with the Army Service Corps (Number M/26348) being posted overseas after December 1915 and being discharged due to sickness on 9th August 1919 with Silver War Badge Number B323162. He was living at Portobello Road in the Rathmines district when he was awarded a 30% Disability Pension at twelve shillings per week in respect of piles. He also received a supplement of five shillings and sixpence per week in respect of his wife and child. Gabriel Ann Pattison was a factory hand when she died of pulmonary tuberculosis and meningitis at 33 Abbeyfield on 17th

September 1936, aged 16. George Pattison was a tailor when he died of myocardial disease at 33 Abbeyfield on 18th May 1944, aged 54. Bridget Pattison was living at 33 Abbeyfield when she died at Harold's Cross Hospital on 7th April 1970, aged 80. George, Bridget, and Gabriel Ann Pattison are buried in Glasnevin Cemetery.

34 Abbeyfield – Alfred Trebble

Alfred Trebble was born on 17th February 1876 at Hounslow Barracks living quarters in Sunbury, Middlesex, to Alfred Trebble, a soldier, and Elizabeth Trebble (née Byrne). Two brothers were born in New Ross – William in 1881 and John in 1882. Alfred Trebble (16) of Church Lane was admitted to the South Dublin Union Workhouse on 14th September 1893 and discharged on 13th November 1893. Alfred Trebble was working as a messenger when he enlisted with the Royal Irish Fusiliers (Number 5227) on 30th January 1895 in Dublin, his place of birth being recorded as St Mary's Parish in Dublin. He was posted to 1st Battalion and was stationed in India (1897) and Egypt (1897-1899) before serving in the Second Anglo-Boer War, being awarded the Queen's South Africa Medal with three clasps (Orange Free State, Transvaal, and Talana) and King's South Africa Medal with 1901 Clasp.

He served at home from July 1901 to January 1912 and was stationed at Royal Barracks in Dublin when he married Elizabeth Faulkner, the daughter of an army pensioner from Benburb Street, on 5th October 1902 at St Paul's Roman Catholic Church at Arran Quay. He was stationed at Palace Barracks in Holywood, County Down when Alfred Lawrence Trebble was born in January 1904 and was stationed at Portobello Barracks in Dublin when George Joseph Trebble was born in July 1907. He was stationed at St Lucia Barracks in Bordon, Hampshire, in 1911 and was posted to 2nd Battalion in India in January 1912. Elizabeth

Alfred Trebble
34 Abbeyfield
(source: Amy Grace Trebble)

accompanied him to India where their third child, Elizabeth Lilian, was born in Quetta in July 1913. The 2nd Battalion Royal Irish Fusiliers was recalled from India in October 1914, arriving at Winchester in late November 1914. The battalion was allocated to 82nd Brigade in 27th Division and landed at Le Havre on 19th December 1914. Alfred was treated for myalgia at No. 2 General Hospital in Le Havre for six days in July 1915, being discharged to a convalescent camp. The battalion was re-deployed to the Mediterranean Expeditionary Force, arriving at Salonika in early December 1915. In November 1916, 2nd Battalion transferred to 31st Brigade in 10th (Irish) Division and moved to Egypt in September 1917 for service in Palestine. Alfred transferred to the Labour Corps (Number 485489) on 1st January 1918 and served with 968 Agricultural Employment Company. In 1918, he was awarded the Long Service and Good Conduct Medal and he remained in Egypt until April 1919. Acting Corporal Alfred Trebble was discharged on 14th May 1919 having completed his second period of engagement. He was approximately 42 and had served in the British Army for 24 years and 105 days. His character was recorded as 'Exemplary' and that he was 'honest, sober, hard-working, and reliable'. His discharge address was Iveagh Buildings, New Bride Street, Dublin.

35 Abbeyfield – Michael Cunniam

In the 1926 Thom's Directory, the occupant was recorded as 'Bickford, C' and the occupant in 1942 was listed as 'Cunniam, Mrs'.

Michael Cunniam was born on 6th January 1899 at 8 St David's Terrace in Glasnevin to Thomas Joseph Cunniam, a clerk with Dublin Corporation, and Elizabeth Mary Cunniam (née Cleary). The family was living at Brighton Avenue in Rathmines in 1901 and Elizabeth Cunniam died in childbirth at Brighton Avenue on 16th March 1903, with Thomas Cunniam dying shortly after birth. Thomas Cunniam senior married Mary Gertrude Healy on 26th April 1910. In 1911, Michael and his sister, Nora, were boarders at St Mary's School at the Dominican Convent in Rathdrum. An Ancestry family tree records that Michael worked at a Munitions Factory in Coventry between 1916 and 1918 before serving with the Royal Field Artillery (Number 261828) and the Royal Engineers (Number 367438). He was living at 1 Haigh Terrace in Kingstown when he was demobilised on 16th March 1920. After being discharged, Michael was a clerk with the Local Government Board in Dublin before taking up a similar position with Irish Soldiers and Sailors Land Trust (Dublin) in 1922. In 1939, Michael was a Post Office Clerk and living at 22A Grosvenor Garden Mews North in London – his family were not present in the England and Wales Register. In 1940, he was appointed as Superintendent for Killester Garden Village by the Irish Soldiers and Sailors Land Trust (Dublin) and allocated the bungalow at 228 Howth Road (formerly the home of Captain and Mrs De Lacy). On Saturday 8th March 1941, Gladys Cunniam left the house early in the morning with their children for a day out, possibly to visit her family. When she returned home in the evening, she found her husband in the sitting room with a tube from the gas pipe near his face. Michael was taken to hospital but was dead on arrival at the Jervis Street Hospital. Before Dr D A MacErlean, the City Corner, Gladys reported that her husband had been suffering from stomach trouble and was sometimes depressed but had never threatened to take his life. The inquest concluded that he had died of 'cardiac failure and asphyxia following inhalation of Coal Gas, said act being self-determined whilst of unsound mind'. Michael was 42 years old. Captain Burke became the new Superintendent for Killester Garden Village and moved in to 228 Howth Road. Gladys Cunniam was allocated the bungalow at 35 Abbeyfield and was recorded as the occupant in the 1947 Thom's Directory. This is possibly the only occasion in which the ISSLT allocated a dwelling directly to a non-veteran. Gladys Cunniam died on 12th December 1978 at Chelmsford in Essex.

35A Abbeyfield – Thomas Giles

The Thom's Directory of 1931 shows the resident as Thomas Bell however, the house was described as vacant in 1944 and the resident in 1945 was a T Giles. Research has been unable to identify any civilian or military records for Thomas Bell.

Thomas Giles was born on 6th May 1893 at 6 Clarence Street, Dublin, the son of Michael and Elizabeth Giles, née Dunne. At the time of the birth, Michael Giles was a sailor. Elizabeth Giles died on 2nd June 1899 and the 1901 Census shows Thomas as resident with his father and siblings at Clarence Street North. Michael Giles died on 5th April 1909 at his home of chronic enteritis. It is believed that Thomas enlisted in the Leinster Regiment (Regimental Number 9613) in 1911. He was based in Fyazabad, India, with the Regiment's 1st battalion at the outbreak of war and returned with them to the United Kingdom arriving at Plymouth on 16th November 1914. He embarked for active service in

Thomas and Margaret Giles
35A Abbeyfield
(source: Sinead Moran)

France on 19th December 1914 and was posted with the battalion to Salonika in December 1915. He later saw service with the battalion in Palestine. He was transferred to Section B Army Reserve on 13th July 1919. Thomas took up employment at the Guinness Brewery on 25th August 1919, being a charger in the Cooperage Department. On 4th March 1924, he married Cecilia Quinn at the Roman Catholic Church, Howth. At that time, Thomas was resident in Sutton. Tragically, Cecilia died aged 21 on 30th December 1924 of puerperal eclampsia after giving birth to a daughter, Elizabeth. At the time of her death, the couple were resident at Claremount Cottage, Howth. Thomas was still resident at that address on 9th July 1934 when he married Margaret Conway at the Roman Catholic Church, Howth. They were living at Claremount Cottage when a son, Thomas Richard, died of diptheria at Clonskeagh Hospital on 4th March 1943, aged five years and six months. In 1964, Michael Giles, a son, won £5 in the St Vincents Pools Daily Dip. Thomas died at 35A Abbeyfield on 20th February 1974 aged 80, and Margaret Giles died at 35A Abbeyfield on 21st January 1985, aged 82. Thomas and Margaret Giles are buried at Balgriffin Cemetery, grave N 237. Also buried in the same plot is one of their sons, Seamus Giles of 18 St Bridget's Grove in Killester, who died on 6th April 2001, aged 65.

36A Abbeyfield – Patrick Joseph Bray

This address first appears in the 1931 Thom's Directory, the occupant being recorded as 'McGowran, Michael'. However, the property was vacant in the 1933 edition and the occupant was recorded as 'Bray, P' in the 1934 edition.

Patrick Joseph Bray was born on 18th May 1893 at 7 Charles Street, Dublin, to Patrick Bray, a boot and shoe maker, and Johanna Bray (née Cassidy). He enlisted with the Royal Irish Fusiliers (Regimental Number 10581) on 29th October 1910 and was stationed with 1st Battalion at St Lucia Barracks in Bordon, Hampshire, in 1911. He held the rank of Lance-Corporal when he was posted to 2nd Battalion on the Western Front on 19th December 1914. He also served with 7th Battalion on the Western Front and with the Royal Irish Regiment (Regimental Number 2626) on the Home Front. He held the rank of Sergeant in the Royal Irish Fusiliers (now with Regimental Number 31308) when he was discharged due to wounds on 16th October 1918 with Silver War Badge Number B34924. He was living at Charles Street when he was awarded a 100% Disability Pension in respect of shell shock at the rate of forty-six shillings and eight pence per week. The degree of disability was assessed at 80% in 1920 and the pension rate was reduced to thirty-seven shillings and four pence per week. Patrick Bray, a provision dealer from Charles Street, married Susan O'Reilly, also of Charles Street, on 12th October 1919 at St Michan's Roman Catholic Church. Patrick was recorded as being a soldier when Johanna Bray was born on 16th July 1921. Susan Bray died at St Mary's Hospital at Phoenix Park on 19th February 1957, aged 60. Patrick Joseph Bray, a retired clerk, died of a cerebral thrombosis and chronic bronchitis at 36A Abbeyfield on 15th September 1967, aged 74. Patrick and Susan Bray are buried in Glasnevin Cemetery.

36 Abbeyfield – Richard Parkes

Richard Parkes was born on 2nd June 1888 at 5 Greenville Parade in Merchant's Quay to Alexander Parkes, a postman, and Eveleen Parkes (née Sheil) and the family lived at New Bride Street in Wood Quay in 1901 and at 16 Bishop Street in the Mansion House district in 1911. Richard was working as a druggist's messenger in 1911 but he was a Van Driver and living at Mount Pleasant Buildings when he married Mary Meredith of the same address on 30th July 1915 at Our Immaculate Lady of Refuge Roman Catholic Church in Rathmines. Richard enlisted with the Royal Irish Rifles (Number 8425) and was posted to France with 7th Battalion on 20th December 1915. He also served with the 1st Battalion before being transferred to Royal Irish Fusiliers (Number 42556) and posted to 9th Battalion. Private Richard Phelan sustained gunshot wounds to the left leg and was transferred to the Class Z Army Reserve on 19th March 1919 and was living at 58 Great Charles Street when he was awarded a 30% Disability Pension in respect of disordered action of the heart. The rate was twelve shillings per week with a supplement of seven shillings and one penny in respect of his two children. Mary Parkes died at Sir Patrick Dun's Hospital on 29th August 1949, aged 60, and Richard was living at 36 Abbeyfield when he died of chronic duodenal ulcer and ventricular failure at Jervis Street Hospital on 15th October 1953, aged 64. Richard and Mary Anne Parkes are buried in St John the Baptist Cemetery, Clontarf.

A younger brother of Richard, Samuel Peter Parkes, served with Royal Dublin Fusiliers (Regimental Number 31860) and Royal Munster Fusiliers (Regimental Numbers 15328 and 32272). In 1920, he was back with the Royal Dublin Fusiliers (Army Number 7211638) and later served with the Seaforth Highlanders and the Royal Army Medical Corps under the same Army Number. He was living at 36 Abbeyfield when he applied to the Not Forgotten Society for assistance and was living at Tower Hamlets in London when he died in 1964.

37 Abbeyfield – Patrick Francis Fitzgerald

Patrick Francis Fitzgerald was born on 7th October 1889 at 1 Crosses Green in Cork to Patrick Thomas Fitzgerald, a printer/compositor, and Bridget Fitzgerald (née Pearse) and the family was living at Denmark Place in the North City district in 1901. The family also lived at Jervis Street, Little Denmark Street, and Little Dominick Street. Patrick Francis Fitzgerald was a grocer's porter when he enlisted with the Royal Dublin Fusiliers (Number 9952) on 3rd December 1907, being posted to 2nd Battalion in March 1908 and transferred to 1st Battalion in

Patrick and Elizabeth Fitzgerald
37 Abbeyfield
(source: www.findagrave.com)

January 1909. He was stationed in Egypt throughout 1909 and was then stationed in India until December 1914, when the battalion was recalled home for war service. He took part in the landings at Cape Helles on the Gallipoli Peninsula on 25th April 1915 and was wounded in May 1915. After the withdrawal from Gallipoli in January 1916, the battalion moved to the Western Front in March 1916. He sustained gas poisoning in September 1918 and was awarded a 29th Division Gallantry Certificate for his actions between September and December 1916. He held the rank of Company Quartermaster Sergeant when he was mentioned in General Lord French's despatch which was published in *The London Gazette* in July 1919. Having completed his twelve-year period of engagement, Patrick was demobilised on 10th February 1919, but he re-enlisted the following day, being posted to Naas. He reverted to the rank of Sergeant at his own request in January 1920 and was discharged as being 'Surplus to military requirements' on 5th February 1920. He was living at Little Denmark Street when he was awarded a 20% Disability Allowance in respect of the effects of gas poisoning at the rate of nine shillings and fourpence per week. Although Patrick was recorded as being an electrician in various documents, he was a labourer and living at Lower Dominick Street when he married Elizabeth Frayne of Holles Street on 17th May 1920 at St Andrew's Roman Catholic Church. They already had three children when Rita was born prematurely at 37 Abbeyfield on 6th April 1933 and died 30 minutes later. Patrick and Elizabeth went on to have another five children. Patrick was a post office pensioner when he died of bronchopneumonia and pulmonary Tuberculosis at 37 Abbeyfield on 28th June 1967, aged 78 (but recorded as 77 in the Register of Deaths). Elizabeth Fitzgerald died on

27th April 1990, aged 94. Patrick and Elizabeth Fitzgerald are buried in Grangegorman Military Cemetery. Noreen O'Leary, the youngest child of Patrick and Elizabeth, was still residing at 37 Abbeyfield in 2023.

38 Abbeyfield – Robert George Butler

Robert was born on 13th December 1896 at Nuns' Island in County Galway to John Butler, a carpenter, and Caroline Louisa Butler (née Moore). His father died of typhoid fever on 21st June 1897 and Caroline and six children under 11 were living at Bowling Green in Galway City in 1901. Caroline married William Byrne, an RIC Constable, on 19th November 1901 at St Nicholas' Church of Ireland in Galway and the family was living on Nun's Island in 1911. Robert Butler enlisted with the Army Service Corps (Number S4/070188) and was a Private when he was deployed to France on 21st June 1915. He held the rank of Acting Sergeant when he was discharged on 22nd November 1919 and was living at Nun's Island in County Galway when he was awarded a 30% Disability Pension in respect of bronchitis and defective vision at twelve shillings per week. The pension was increased to sixteen shillings per week (40% Disability) in 1922 and twenty shillings per week (50% Disability) in 1923. The Pension Index Card records 320 North Circular Road in Phibsborough as a later address. Robert was a Clerk when he married Mary Margaret Curtin on 26th October 1921 at the Roman Catholic Church in Tipperary. Mary's surname was recorded as Curtin in the Register of Marriages and in the 1901 Census, but as McCurtin in the Register of Marriages. Robert Butler – along with John Haugh, Robert Leggett, and others – initiated the case at the High Court seeking to have it declared that:

> *. . . the Irish Sailors and Soldiers Land Trust was not entitled to accumulate a reserve fund for the purpose of building new cottages out of the proceeds of the cottages provided for the accommodation of men who served in any of His Majesty's naval, military or air forces in the late war or for any purpose other than the repair and the insurance of the existing cottages, and to pay the debts and expenses of managing the Trust.*

They also sought to have it declared that 'the existing rents are excessive and should only be sufficient to cover necessary outlay.' In April 1930, the ISSLT had issued an ejectment suit against Robert Butler as he owed the Trust £30 in rent arrears and Mr Justice Reddin granted the decree stipulating that the decree would be discharged if Robert Butler agreed to pay the current rent and three shillings per week off the arrears. In May, Robert Butler appealed the decision in the Dublin Circuit Court on the grounds that he should not be ejected as he was one of the plaintiffs in the case that had been brought before the High Court. The 1939 Thom's Directory records that the property was vacant, with 'McMenamin, J' being recorded as the occupant in 1940. In 1939, Robert and Mary Butler were living at 270 Cheveral Avenue in Coventry, where he died on 25th March 1956 leaving effects totalling £1,471 18s and 1d (approximately £29,170 in current terms). Mary Margaret Butler died on 20th February 1972 in Coventry, Warwickshire.

The next occupant was John McMenamin who served with the Irish Guards (Number 4614). He was a night watchman and living at 38 Abbeyfield when he died at St Kevin's Hospital on 4th September 1958, aged 65.

39 Abbeyfield – Robert Lawrence

Robert Lawrence was born on 24th May 1889 at 65 Havelock Square in Pembroke West to Thomas Lawrence, a clerk with the Army Ordnance Corps, and Agnes Lawrence (née Harman) and the family home was in Henrietta Street in Inns Quay in 1901 and 1911. Robert enlisted with the Lancashire Fusiliers (Number 745) on 5th August 1905 and was a Labourer and living at Henrietta Street when he married Catherine Brohoon of Upper Gloucester Street on 25th June 1914 at St Mary's Roman Catholic Pro-Cathedral on Marlborough Street. As he was an army reservist, he was mobilised at the start of the war and posted to 2nd Battalion Lancashire Fusiliers in France on 26th August 1914. He sustained gunshot wounds to the left arm which left him unfit for further military service and he was discharged on 29th December 1915 with Silver War Badge Number 4480. Robert was recorded as being an Army Pensioner when Thomas Patrick Lawrence was born at Ushers Quay in November 1915 and as a Clerk when Thomas James Lawrence was born at Temple Street in October 1917. Catherine Lawrence died at Jervis Street Hospital on 19th August 1959, aged 71, and Robert was still living at 39 Abbeyfield when he died at St Mary's Hospital, Phoenix Park, on 23rd November 1974, aged 85. Robert and Catherine Lawrence are buried in Mount Jerome Cemetery.

40 Abbeyfield – Vincent Clarke

Vincent Aloysius Clarke was born on 4th September 1896 at 67 Phibsborough Road in the Arran Quay district to Joseph Thomas Clarke, a GPO sorting clerk, and Sarah Jane Clarke (née O'Neill) and the family was living at 7 David Road in Drumcondra in 1911. Vincent was a shop assistant for a tobacconist and living at St Clements Road in Drumcondra when he enlisted with the King's Liverpool Regiment (Number 25405) in Dublin on 9th January 1915 and was deployed to France with 4th Battalion on 4th March 1915. He was attached to the 98th Brigade Machine Gun Company when he was hospitalised with synovitis (inflammation) of the left knee for fourteen days in October and November 1916 and he was treated for tonsilitis for twelve days in September 1917. On 17th April 1918, Vincent was admitted to 19 Field Ambulance with gunshot wounds to the chest, a lung having been pierced by a bullet. He was transferred to Number 36 Casualty Clearing Station the following day and then evacuated on Ambulance Train Number 9 to Number 2 Australian General Hospital at Rouen on 27th April. He was evacuated to the UK and admitted to Kitchener's Military Hospital in Brighton on 11th May and was also treated at the Brewery House Red Cross Hospital in East Grinstead.

Private Vincent Clarke was discharged due to wounds on 22nd July 1918 with Silver War Badge Number B8113. He was living at Seapoint Manor Lodge when he was awarded a 40% Disability Pension in respect of gunshot wounds to the chest at the rate of sixteen shillings per week, which was reduced to eight shillings per week in July 1922. Vincent was a GPO sorting clerk when he married Teresa Cooney, a salesgirl from Primrose Avenue, on 23rd April 1922 at St Joseph's Roman Catholic Church on Berkley Street. Teresa Clarke died of nephritis at her parents' house, 3 Primrose Avenue, on 4th May 1926, aged 26, and Vincent married Mary Belinda Long of Church Street on 20th

February 1928 at St Laurence O'Toole Roman Catholic Church. A son, Thomas Joseph Clarke, died of convulsions at 40 Abbeyfield on 16th January 1932 at the age of six months and is buried in Glasnevin. In February 1945, Vincent Clarke submitted a personal injury case for £250 against the Great Northern Railway for negligence when he sustained injuries alighting from a train at Killester Station. The judge dismissed the claim on the grounds of contributory negligence as Clarke should have noticed that the train had over-shot the platform. Vincent Clarke of 40 Abbeyfield was working for the Post Office at the parcels office when he died at Elm Park Hospital on 17th April 1973, aged 76, and is buried in Balgriffin Cemetery (Section F Grave 61).

41 Abbeyfield – Joseph Cox

Joseph Cox was born around 1890 and his father was John Cox. He was a porter when he married Catherine/Kate McCabe of Granby Place on 20th August 1908 at St Mary's Roman Catholic Pro-Cathedral on Marlborough Street. His father's occupation was recorded as a car man. In the birth registers for their children, the father's forenames are variously recorded as Patrick Joseph, Joseph P, or Joseph. In 1911, Kathleen Cox and Joseph Patrick Cox (1) were living at 23 North Great Georges Street in the Rotunda district. Joseph Cox enlisted with the Royal Army Medical Corps (Number 35327) and was posted to France on 24th April 1915. He subsequently transferred to the Royal Dublin Fusiliers (Number 43467) and served with 2nd Battalion and 8th Battalion. Private Joseph Cox was transferred to the Class Z Army Reserve on 24th March 1919 and was living at 7 Granby Place when he was awarded 50% Disability Pension in respect of deafness and gunshot wounds to the head and shoulders. The rate was twenty shillings per week with an allowance of twenty shillings and ninepence per week for his dependants, a wife and five children under the age of 16. A James Francis Aloysius Cox (son of John Cox, a fitter's helper) was born prematurely and died at 41 Abbeyfield of Spina Bifida after eight days on 23rd August 1940. It is probable that John Cox and Joseph Cox were brothers. Patrick Joseph Cox was a GPO sorter when he died of a stroke and cardiac failure at the Royal City of Dublin Hospital on 6th September 1939, aged 49, and is buried in Glasnevin Cemetery.

In the 1940s Thom's Directories, the occupants of 41 Abbeyfield are recorded as 'Cox, C, Mrs' in 1940, 'Whelan, K' in 1943, and 'Currie, F' in 1945.

42 Abbeyfield – Henry Brophy

The 1926 Thom's Directory recorded the occupant as 'Keane, M, Mrs' and 'Brophy, H' was listed as occupant in the 1927 directory.

Henry Brophy married Norah Doody, a native of Milltown in County Kilkenny, in 1922 in Chelsea. Nora Brophy (née Doody) died at 42 Abbeyfield on 19th June 1957, aged 70, and is buried in Carrigan Churchyard at Mooncoin, County Kilkenny. Henry Brophy was recorded as being present at death.

In September 1955, John O'Leary, a clerk, whose address was given as 42 Abbeyfield, was riding his motorcycle when he was struck by a car at the junction of Amiens Street and Store Street. His left wrist was fractured and dislocated, and he suffered pain across his chest. He could not resume work until January 1957 and would remain partially disabled. He took the car-driver, Peter McDonnell of Charlemount Street, to court and, in February 1957, a High Court jury awarded John £1,688 damages for personal injuries and £42 for damage to his motorcycle. In current terms, £1,730 pounds equates to nearly £35,000 (or 40,500 Euro).

William Brennan was a farm labourer from Tallaght when he married Ellen Murphy, a tailoress from Upper Dorset Street on 28th March 1937 at St Michan's Roman Catholic Church. Ellen Brennan (née Murphy) died at 42 Abbeyfield on 6th January 1977, aged 75, and was survived by her husband, Bill, daughters, Marie (and son-in-law, Patsy), and Eileen (and son-in-law, Terry). William (Bill) Brennan, formerly of 6 Frankfort Cottages on Amiens Street, was living at 42 Abbeyfield when he died on 27th December 1978, aged 71. Bill and Ellen Brennan are buried in St Fintan's Cemetery in Sutton (Section P Grave 14). It is not clear whether William Brennan had served in the Great War or whether he had purchased the bungalow.

43 Abbeyfield – James Murphy

James Murphy was a postman when he died of a cerebral haemorrhage and Cardiac Failure at 43 Abbeyfield on 11th June 1936, aged 55, and Elizabeth Murphy died at 43 Abbeyfield on 7th November 1957, aged 60. James and Elizabeth Murphy are buried in Grangegorman Military Cemetery.

44 Abbeyfield – Albert George Woodman

The Thom's directories record the occupant as 'Woodman, A J' but the occupant was Albert George Woodman, who was born on 30th October 1891 at 40 Whitworth Road in Drumcondra to William George Woodman, a GPO clerk, and Askin Hutcheon Woodman (née Grimwood) and the family later lived in Glasnevin – at Hollybank Road in 1901 and at 15 Lindsay Road in 1911. Albert was also a GPO clerk and he enlisted with the Royal Engineers (Number 75598) and was deployed to France on 4th August 1915. Albert married Nellie Mary Valentine Preston of St Alphonsus Road in Drumcondra on 17th December 1917 at St George's Church of Ireland in Dublin. Sapper Albert George Woodman was transferred to the Class Z Army Reserve on 20th July 1919.

In the 1931 Thom's Directory, the occupant of 44 Abbeyfield is recorded as 'Deane, A E'.

45 Abbeyfield – Andreas (Andrew) Burtenshaw

The 1926 Thom's Directory recorded the occupant as 'Keating, M' and the occupant in the 1934 directory was 'Burtenshaw, A'.

Andreas Burtenshaw was born on 15th December 1896 at Stradbally Hall in Queen's County to Alfred Burtenshaw and Andrea Burtenshaw (née Wolff) and the family lived at Dame Lane in South City, Dublin, in 1901 and 1911. Alfred Burtenshaw was variously recorded as being a servant (1896), a stableman (1901 and 1919) and as a caretaker in 1911. Andreas was recorded as being a page boy in 1911 but he was a bank porter when he enlisted as a trumpeter with the South Irish Horse (Number 1630) on 2nd November 1915 and was posted to the Western Front on 13th March 1916. He was with E Squadron when he was admitted to Number 3 Canadian General Hospital at Dannes-Camiers with bronchitis and pleurisy on 21st June 1916, being discharged three days later and evacuated to the UK. He received further treatment at Leith War Hospital from 25th June 1916 until 1st August 1916, being transferred to Craigforth Red Cross Hospital in Elie for convalescence and then re-admitted to Leith War Hospital with neurasthenia on 22nd September 1916.

His second spell on the Western Front commenced on 12th December 1916 and he was treated for tonsilitis for twelve days at Number 18 Field Ambulance in March 1917. He was admitted to 1/1st South Middlesex Field Ambulance with myalgia on 13th July 1917 and was subsequently diagnosed at a Casualty Clearing Station as having a heart condition. He was treated for disordered action of the heart at Number 3 Stationary Hospital, Number 10 General Hospital, and Number 2 Convalescent Depot. He was evacuated to the UK on 13th October 1917, being compulsorily transferred to the Royal Irish Regiment (Number 25087). He was initially serving with a Depot battalion but was recorded as 7th Battalion when he transferred to Cavalry Rates of Pay on 10th November 1917. He was treated for endocarditis for 96 days at the King George V Hospital in Dublin between October 1917 and January 1918 and was discharged on 11th February 1918 as being 'No longer physically fit for war service'. He was allocated Silver War Badge Number 323729 and was living at 7 Sussex Terrace in Rathmines when he was awarded a 40% Disability Pension in respect of bronchitis and neurasthenia at the rate of sixteen shillings per week. His father had enlisted with the Army Veterinary Corps (SE 30305) on 29th June 1917 but was discharged on 25th October 1917 as being 'No longer physically fit for war service'.

Alfred Burtenshaw was awarded Silver War Badge Number 257815 and he died of cancer at the Richmond Hospital on 23rd January 1920, aged 56, and is buried in Mount Jerome Cemetery, with a CWGC headstone marking the plot. Andreas was a sorting clerk at the General Post Office and living at Sussex Terrace when he married Catherine McGarvey of Barrow Street on 24th September 1919 at St Mark's Church of Ireland, Dublin. Andreas Burtenshaw, a retired civil servant, had been suffering from cancer for two years when he died of chronic bronchitis at 45 Abbeyfield on 24th March 1965, aged 68, and is buried in St Fintan's Cemetery in Sutton. The entry in the Register of Deaths records that the bronchitis was due to 'war gassing' but the extensive surviving military service and medical documents do not record that he was gassed. Catherine Burtenhaw died at Abbeyfield in October 1988 and Frederick Burtenshaw, a son of Andreas and Catherine, died at Abbeyfield on 19th February 2008.

46 Abbeyfield – James Joseph Condon

In the 1926 Thom's Directory, the occupant was recorded as 'Aston, R' with 'Condron, J' being recorded as the occupant in 1930.

James Joseph Condon was born on 21st March 1888 at 6 Abercorn Road in North Dock to Thomas Condon, a boilermaker, and Mary Condon (née Sunner) and the family lived at Sheriff Street in North Dock in 1901 and at 150 Upper Sheriff Street in 1911. James enlisted with the Royal Engineers (Number 18500) on 1st February 1909 and was stationed in Egypt with 2nd Field Company in 1911. He was deployed to France on 5th November 1914 with the same unit and was listed as wounded in the War Office Casualty List dated 20th March 1915. Lance-Corporal Condon was discharged due to wounds on 26th February 1919 with Silver War Badge Number B277605. He was living at 150 Upper Sherriff Street when he was awarded a 30% Disability Pension in respect of gunshot wounds to the back at the rate of sixteen shillings per week. James was a boilermaker when he married Josephine O'Keefe of Ross Road on 20th September 1922 at St Andrew's Roman Catholic Church. He was working for Brooks Thomas (Timber Merchants) and living at 46 Abbeyfield when he died at Jervis Street Hospital on 23rd March 1973, aged 85, and is buried in St Fintan's Cemetery in Sutton.

47 Abbeyfield – John Joseph McNulty

The 1926 Thom's Directory recorded the occupant as 'Cummins, J' and the occupant in the 1930 directory was 'McNulty, J J'.

John Joseph McNulty was born on 25th October 1892 at Meelin near Newmarket in County Cork to Patrick McNulty, an RIC Constable, and Abina McNulty (née Cronin) and the family lived at Grove Street in Birr in 1901 and 1911. He enlisted with the Irish Guards in May 1915 and was posted to 1st Battalion on the Western Front in January 1916. On 15th September 1916, Private McNulty was admitted to Number 34 Casualty Clearing Station, Somme, with gunshot wounds to the left arm and evacuated later the same day on 120 Temporary Ambulance Train. He was wounded a second time in 1917 (War Office Daily List Number 5462, dated 10th January 1918) and was entitled to wear two 'Wound Stripes'. He was living at Westport in County Mayo when he was transferred to the Class Z Army Reserve on 27th April 1919 and was awarded the Military Medal in the 'Peace Gazette' the following month.

John was a clerk and living at Nelson Street when he married Margaret Handley, also of Nelson Street, on 1st May 1925 at the Roman Catholic Church on Berkeley Street. In 1937, John McNulty appeared before District Justice Reddin at Kilmainham Courthouse, having been accused of sending threatening letters to James Walsh of 48 Abbeyfield and Mrs Mary Kelly of 16 Middle Third. Mary Kelly gave evidence that the letter, which read 'Your corpse will not be mourned in Killester', related to the refusal of her husband to join the Killester Tenants' Rights Association, which James Walsh had also refused to join. The letter to James Walsh of 48 Abbeyfield read 'Walsh, Soldiers' Colony, Killester, R.I.P.'. District Justice Reddin described the latter as being 'an obituary notice which would be equally suitable for the press or a tombstone'. He went on to say that a number of men acted like children in Killester, which had been described as 'the last outpost of the British Empire' and concluded that, 'It is pleasant to note that even if the people of Killester will not mourn of Walsh, they hope he will rest in peace.' John J McNulty was 'bound to keep the peace for six months, himself in £10 and one surety of £10.' Ten pounds in 1937 would be approximately £540 in current terms (or 612 Euros). John McNulty died of Myocarditis at the Royal City of Dublin Hospital on Baggot Street on 13th May 1940, aged 48. His son, Patrick McNulty, an Apprentice Fitter of 47 Abbeyfield, died of tubercular meningitis at the same hospital on 17th June 1944, aged 17. Margaret was living at 47 Abbeyfield when she died at the Mercer's Hospital on 11th February 1963, aged 75. John, Margaret, and Patrick McNulty are buried in Mount Jerome Cemetery.

48 Abbeyfield – James Walsh and John McCormack

The 1926 Thom's Directory recorded the occupant as 'Walsh, J' and the property was listed as vacant in 1944, with 'McCormick, J' being the occupant in the 1945 directory. Information from Tom Burke indicates that John C Byrne, who had served with the Royal Army Medical Corps (Number 36697), was an alias for John McCormick.

James Walsh enlisted with the Leinster Regiment (Number 4164) on 28th April 1911 and was deployed to 2nd Battalion on the Western Front on 26th October 1914. John sustained a gunshot wound to the right hand and was discharged as being 'no longer physically fit for war service' on 5th May 1915 with Silver War Badge Number 6472. After being discharged, John Walsh lived at 178 Phibsborough Road. His wife, Amy Phyllis Walsh, died at 48 Abbeyfield on 5th December 1935, aged 37.

John McCormack was born on 19th December 1896 to John McCormack and Lizzie McCormack (née Cummins) and the family lived at Irishtown Road in Pembroke East in 1901 and 1911. John enlisted with the Royal Army Medical Corps (Number 36697) under the name John Christopher Byrne and served overseas after December 1915. He was transferred to the Class Z Army Reserve on 5th March 1919 and was living at 11 Windmill Lane in Crumlin when he was awarded a 20% Disability Pension in respect of pulmonary tuberculosis at the rate of eight shillings per week. His degree of disability was upgraded to 50% (twenty shillings per week) in 1921 and then to 60% (twenty-four shillings per week) in 1922 before being reduced to 40% (sixteen shillings per week) in 1923. John McCormack joined Arthur Guinness and Company on 16th June 1919 and was awarded a £45 grant from the Military Service (Civil Liabilities) Department in November 1920 towards the purchase of a pony, cart, and harness.

John was a labourer and living at 11 Windmill Lane when he married Mary Burke of Upper Leeson Street on 28th August 1924 at Donnybrook Roman Catholic Church. John was employed at Guinness for the remainder of his working life and was a cleaner in the traffic department when he retired. On Sunday 3rd December 1978, Jack and Madge, as they were known, attended Mass at St Brigid's Church and seemed in good form to neighbours who met them on the way home. Shortly after their tea, Madge, who had recently suffered a stroke, collapsed while taking a cake out of the oven. Jack rushed to the house of Mrs Lewis for help but collapsed when he returned to his bungalow and died almost instantaneously. Madge was taken to the Mater Hospital where she died a short while later. (Information from an article in the Evening Herald, 4th December 1978). Jack and Madge were buried in Mount Jerome Cemetery following a Funeral Mass in St Brigid's Church.

49 Abbeyfield – William Joseph Halpin

William Joseph Halpin was married and a retired postman when he died of mitralvalvular disease at 49 Abbeyfield on 23rd November 1945, aged 66 (giving a probable birth year around 1879). The entry in the Register of Deaths records that 'A Halpin, Widow' was present at death.

In 1911, a William Halpin (30, born in Arklow, County Wicklow) who was a town postman was boarding at 3 Seville Place in North Dock. He is recorded as being Church of England. Ancestry family trees indicate that his parents were James Halpin, a butler, and Elizabeth Catherine Halpin (née Waldron) who lived at Harold's Grange in Whitechurch (1901) and 3 Circular Road in Wood Quay (1911). In the 1901 Census entry for Harold's Grange, William was recorded as being a 22-year-old Joiner born in County Wicklow but he is not present at the family home in the 1911 Census. He was recorded as being Church of Ireland in the 1901 Census. The family trees also record his wife's forename as Alice. It is possible that the William Halpin who was a joiner in 1901 is the William Halpin who was a Town Postman in 1911.

50 Abbeyfield – Ernest Henry Lawrie

Ernest Henry Lawrie was born on 4th December 1888 at 12 Havelock Square in Pembroke West, Dublin, to James Alexander Lawrie, a clerk of works, and Elizabeth Lawrie (née Manders) and the family lived at 'Willowbrook' on Strandville Avenue in Clontarf West in 1901 and 1911. Ernest was a joiner when he enlisted with the Royal Garrison Artillery (Number 64110) and was deployed to France with 139th Siege

Battery on 1st August 1916. Ernest Henry Lawrie married Florence O'Brien, the marriage being registered in the second quarter of 1918 in West Derby, Lancashire. Corporal Ernest Henry Lawrie was demobilised on 21st February 1920 and was living at his parents' address when he was awarded a 20% Disability Pension in respect of chronic nephritis. The rate was eight shillings per week, with a supplement of three shillings and sixpence for one child. Ernest Henry Lawrie and his brother, John, are commemorated on the Roll of Honour for Clontarf Presbyterian Church, although Ernest is recorded as 'RAF'. Ernest was a carpenter and living at 50 Abbeyfield when he died of cancer and haemorrhage at Dr Steeven's Hospital on 24th May 1941, aged 50. Florence Lawrie was still living at 50 Abbeyfield when she died at the Jervis Street Hospital on 12th March 1970, aged 67.

51 Abbeyfield – John Patrick Garrahan

John Patrick Garrahan was born on 1st October 1895 at Gilgarve near Rooskey, County Roscommon to Hugh/Hubert Garrahan, a licensed publican and farmer, and Catherine/Kate Garrahan (formerly McSherran, née Fallon) who lived at Bridge Street in Strokestown, County Roscommon. John was living with his maternal grandparents at Kilgarve in 1901 and at Strokestown with his parents in 1911, his occupation being recorded as an officer's servant. John enlisted as a Sapper with the Royal Engineers (Number 26698) and was posted to France on 6th September 1915. Whilst his discharge date is not known, John joined the Dublin Metropolitan Police (Warrant Number 11782) on 28th September 1921 and was stationed at Kevin Street Barracks when he married Agnes McVeigh of Parnell Street on 15th February 1922 at St Mary's Roman Catholic Pro-Cathedral on Marlborough Street. In the 1944 Thom's Directory, John Garrahan is recorded as the occupant of 61 The Demesne. On 14th March 1955, John Garrahan was a passenger in his brother's car when it struck the car in front of it, causing his head to hit the roof. He fractured the vault of his skull and lost power in his right arm and right leg. As a consequence, he was discharged from An Garda Síochána as medically unfit on 10th April 1956 and he subsequently sued his brother for damages, being awarded £3,000 at the High Court in October 1956. Agnes Garrahan died at 61 The

Demesne on 16th July 1963, aged 68, and John Garrahan was living at 61 The Demesne when he died of cancer at St Joseph's Nursing Home in Raheny on 28th December 1966, aged 71. John and Agnes Garrahan are buried in Glasnevin Cemetery (St Paul Section).

In 1945, the Thom's Directory recorded the occupant of 51 Abbeyfield as being 'Hoare, J'. This was John Hoare who enlisted with the Leinster Regiment (Numbers 56460) on 1st December 1916, served with 2nd Battalion on the Western Front in 1917 and 1918, being taken prisoner in 1918, when his regimental number was 35171. He was transferred to the Class Z Army Reserve on 13th February 1919 and was working as a plate polishing packer when he attested with the Leinster Regiment (Army Number 7177991) on 31st March 1919 at Birr. He married Edith Brennan on 29th May 1919 and a daughter, Eviline, was born on 3rd April 1919 at the Rotunda Hospital but died the following day. He was living in Manchester when he was discharged from the army on 15th June 1922 at Warwick, when the Leinster Regiment was disbanded.

52 Abbeyfield – John Reginald Harvey

John Reginald Harvey was born around 1892 in Dublin to John Reginald Harvey and Helen Harvey (née Huddard) and the family lived at Fairview Strand in Clontarf West in 1901 and Belvedere Avenue in Rotunda in 1911. The occupation of John Reginald Harvey senior is variously recorded as house assurance and cycle agent (1901), insurance agent (1911), and traveller (1912). John was a waiter at the Ross Hotel in Kingstown when he married Annie Halpin on 23rd September 1912 at St Michael's Roman Catholic Church in Rathdown. They were living at John Street in Sligo in February 1915. Whilst it has not been possible to establish details of John's war service, he was serving as a Sergeant in the Irish Army when Hilda Harvey died of laryngeal diptheria at 52 Abbeyfield on 25th February 1927, aged one year and three months, and when Walter Harvey

John Reginald and Ann Harvey, 52 Abbeyfield (source: www.findagrave)

died of diptheria at Cork Street Fever Hospital in Dublin on 8th November 1931, aged 1. John was a chef when he died of cancer at 52 Abbeyfield on 24th January 1975. John, Ann, Hilda, and Walter are buried in St. John the Baptist Cemetery, Clontarf.

53 Abbeyfield – James Arthur Hill Waters

James Arthur Hill Waters was born on 6th October 1886 at St John's Road in Merrion to Samuel Abraham Walker Waters, a Deputy Inspector in the Royal Irish Constabulary, and Margaret Helen Waters (née Macnab). Samuel Waters retired with the rank of Assistant Inspector General and was a Justice of the Peace in 1911. James Waters was appointed as a Second Lieutenant with 4th Battalion Royal Irish Rifles with effect from 31st March 1906 and was appointed to the Office of the Registrar of Petty Sessions Clerks for Ireland with effect from 4th November 1910. He commenced his law studies in 1911 and was called to the Irish Bar in June 1914. James was appointed as a Temporary Second Lieutenant with effect from 24th September 1914 and posted to the Army Service Corps in France on 7th October 1914. He held the rank of Major when demobilised on 13th June 1919 and was a civil servant living at 'Woodview' in Stillorgan when he married Rachel Louie Orr of Ulster Terrace in Stillorgan on 21st September 1920 at Stillorgan Church of Ireland. Major Waters gave his address as 'The Dugout, Abbeyfields' when he applied for a pension in respect of rheumatism. A son, Samuel Arthur Wentworth Waters was born on 2nd July 1921 at 2 Ulster Terrace in Blackrock. He was commissioned into the Royal Naval Volunteer Reserve as a Sub-Lieutenant and served as a Pilot with the Fleet Air Arm. He was killed when his Fairey Firefly aircraft from HMS *Implacable* was shot down by German submarine U-1060 on 27th October 1944. He was 23 years old and is commemorated on the Lee-on-Solent Memorial. James Arthur Hill Waters was living at 'Bracken' at Delgany when he died of

James Arthur Hill Waters
53 Abbeyfield
(source: Ancestry Family Tree)

cancer at the Adelaide Hospital on 6th January 1965, aged 78, and is buried in Christ Church Cemetery in Delgany, County Wicklow. On the headstone he is recorded as being a 'Barrister at Law'. Rachel Louie ('Punchie') Waters died on 28th September 1974 and is buried in the same plot. James Arthur Hill Waters was the Killester Garden Village veteran with the most senior military rank.

54 Abbeyfield – Thomas George Pope

Thomas George Pope was born on 12th August 1882 at St Osyth near Clacton in Essex to James Pope (bootmaker) and Jemima Pope (née Pavelin) and the family home was at Bridge Street in Witham in 1901 and at Spring Road in St Osyth in 1911. Thomas George was a grocer's porter when he enlisted with the Royal Garrison Artillery (Number 28889) on 18th July 1898 and served in the UK for twelve years, being discharged on 17th July 1910 at the end of his term of engagement. Thomas George Pope was stationed at Magazine Fort, Phoenix Park, when he married Mary Kate McHugh of Kenilworth Square on 14th September 1904 at St Peter's Church of Ireland in Dublin. In 1911, he was a postman and living at 25 Swords Street in the Arran Quay district with his wife and five children. Another two children were born in 1913 and 1915 and the family was living at Manor Street when Thomas re-enlisted with the Royal Garrison Artillery (Number 8553) on 29th May 1916. He was posted as a cook to the Heavy Artillery HQ at Bordon, Hampshire, in September 1916 and held the rank of Sergeant when he was transferred to the Tank Corps on 23rd September 1918. He was appointed as a Transport Sergeant in June 1919 and transferred to the Class Z Army reserve on 29th September 1919. The family home was at 55 Manor Street when Thomas was awarded a 40% Disability Pension at the rate of sixteen shillings per week in respect of piles and bronchitis. There was also a weekly allowance of eighteen shillings and eleven pence in respect of his wife and seven children. The occupant of 54 Abbeyfield was recorded as 'Dent, G' in the 1931 Thom's Directory and the Pope family was living at 255 Park Avenue in Southall, London, in 1939. Thomas George Pope was a clothing agent collector when he died of an intestinal obstruction at Hillingdon County Hospital in Uxbridge on 16th June 1942, aged 59. Thomas left effects totalling £722 12s 10d to his widow, Kate – this equates to just under £27,000 in current terms.

55 Abbeyfield – Bernard Christopher Clarke

A Mr Woodhead is recorded as the occupant in the 1926 Thom's Directory, but 'Clarke, B' is the occupant in the 1927 edition.

Bryan Christopher Clarke was born on 27th December 1893 at 18 Connaught Street to Joseph Thomas Clarke, a post office sorter, and Sarah Clarke (née O'Neill). The family lived at Phibsborough Road in

Bernard/Bryan/Brian Clarke
55 Abbeyfield
(*source: Evening Herald, 1916*)

Arran Quay in 1901 and at 7 in David Road in Drumcondra in 1911. He enlisted with the Connaught Rangers (Number 3/7404) as Bernard Clarke and was posted to 5th Battalion after December 1915. He later served overseas with a Garrison Battalion of the Royal Fusiliers (Number G/112774) and with the Labour Corps on Home Service. He was demobilised on 31st March 1920 and was living with his brother, Vincent Aloysius Clarke, at 40 Abbeyfield before being allocated the bungalow at 55 Abbeyfield. Bernard Christopher (Brian) Clarke was an insurance official when he died of bronchial asthma and chronic myocarditis at 55 Abbeyfield on 30th January 1947, aged 53, and Bridget Clarke was living

at 55 Abbeyfield when she died at Mercer's Hospital on 14th November 1964, aged 73. Bernard/Brian and Bridget Clarke are buried in Mount Jerome Cemetery.

56 Abbeyfield – John William Devereaux

John William Devereaux was born on 1st October 1895 at Cappagh near Dungarvan in County Waterford to Police Sergeant John William Devereaux and Catherine Devereaux (née Dowling). His mother died on 28th March 1901 at the age of 40 and his father and his siblings were living at Mitchell Street in Dungarvan in 1901. In 1911, John was living with his aunt, Jane Devereaux, at 11 Park Place in the New

Kilmainham district. John was a soldier and living at Park Place in Islandbridge when he married Annie Keane of Rutledge Terrace on 28th August 1918 at St Catherine's Roman Catholic Church in South Dublin. John was a supervisor, when Anne Devereaux gave birth to Mary Catherine Devereaux at 29 Rialto Cottages in February 1921. Michael Joseph Devereaux was born prematurely at 56 Abbeyfield on 18th April 1925 and died of cardiac failure two days later. He was recorded as being the son of John Devereaux, a customs officer, and is buried in Glasnevin Cemetery.

John Devereaux
56 Abbeyfield
(source: www.findagrave.com)

John Devereaux is not recorded as the occupant in the 1927 Thom's Directory and J Griffin is recorded as the occupant in 1928. John William Devereaux was a customs and excise officer when he died of a coronary thrombosis at 96 Lower Kimmage Road in the Rathmines district on 23rd December 1951, aged 56. Annie Devereaux died at the same address on 30th November 1959, aged 63. John and Annie Devereaux are buried in Glasnevin Cemetery (St Paul's Section – PC 89).

57 Abbeyfield – John Joseph Rice

The 1926 Thom's Directory records the occupant as 'Hankey, F' and the occupant in the 1931 directory was 'Rice, J'.

John Joseph Rice was born on 10th March 1892 at the Rotunda Hospital, Dublin, to Patrick Rice and Delphine/Delia Rice (née Maguire) who were living at 9 Lower Sheriff Street in North Dock. The family lived in the Rotunda district – at Williams Place Upper in 1901 and 10 Lower Dorset Street in 1911, when John was a butcher's porter. He enlisted with the Royal Dublin Fusiliers (Number 19797) and was deployed to France with 8th Battalion on 20th December 1915. Lance-Corporal Rice was transferred to the Class Z Army Reserve on 14th April 1919 and was living at Phibsborough when he was awarded a 20% Disability Pension in respect of rheumatism and deafness at twelve shillings per week. John was working as a storekeeper when he married Mary Ellen Mahoney of Lower Gardiner Street on 27th June 1920 at St Mary's Roman Catholic Pro-Cathedral on Marlborough Street. John Joseph Rice was living at 57 Abbeyfield when he died of prostate enlargement at St Brendan's Hospital on 12th January 1962, aged 69, and Mary Rice died at the Mater Hospital on 26th November 1962, aged 68. John Joseph and Mary Ellen Rice are buried in St Fintan's Cemetery, Sutton.

58 Abbeyfield – William Field

The 1926 Thom's Directory recorded the occupant as 'McCam, P' but 'Field, W' was recorded as the occupant in 1930. I was unable to find any military documentation for 'McCam' and the entry in Thom's directory might be a misprint of McCann.

William Field was born on 13th August 1883 at Kilbarrack Junction in Coolock, Dublin, to John Field, a railway signalman, and Margaret Field (née Flood). William was an engine driver when he married Margaret L Green on 1st June 1924 at St Agatha's Roman Catholic Church. He was a pensioner and was suffered from cancer for four years when he died of a pulmonary embolism at 58 Abbeyfield on 16th October 1947, aged 63.

59 Abbeyfield – Roger Reddin

In the 1926 Thom's Directory, the occupant is recorded as 'Reddin, R', the occupant in 1930 directory being 'Naughton, V C', and the occupant in the 1940 Directory being 'McCabe, J'.

Roger Reddin (registered as Redden) was born on 29th December 1870 at Newtown Park in Stillorgan, Dublin, to Timothy Redden and Jane Redden (née Maney). He was living at 70 Cook Street when he married Margaret Fitzpatrick on 28th March 1896 at St Michan's Roman Catholic Church. In 1911, Roger and Margaret and their three daughters were living at 71 Cook Street and Roger was a plasterer. He enlisted with the Royal Dublin Fusiliers (Number 5/23681) but does not seem to have served overseas and was discharged on 18th February 1916. Margaret Reddin of 18 Back Lane died on 12th June 1918, aged 37, and Roger was living at that address when he was awarded a 100%

Disability Pension in respect of pulmonary tuberculosis aggravated by army service at the rate of forty shillings per week. Roger Reddin died of pulmonary tuberculosis at 18 Back Lane on 4th December 1925, aged 46, his eldest daughter, Jane Reddin, of the same address being present. Although Roger died at the same address as he was living at in 1918/1919, it is possible that the house in Back Lane had been transferred to Jane Reddin when Roger was allocated the bungalow in Abbeyfield and that he was staying with his daughter when he died.

The second occupant was Victor Cornelius Naughton who served with the Army Service Corps (Number S4/070303) and the Royal Inniskilling Fusiliers (Number 43303) and was transferred to the Class Z Army Reserve on 19th February 1919. He was born in Guernsey around 1887 to John Naughton, a soldier, and Annie Naughton and the family were living at Harrow Street in Belfast in 1901. Victor was a Railway Clerk and was lodging at Blessington Street in Inns Quay in 1911 and he married Jessie Moore on 11th November 1922 at St Mary's Roman Catholic Pro-Cathedral, Marlborough Street.

Joseph McCabe
59 Abbeyfield
(source: www.findagrave.com)

The veteran who occupied the bungalow for the longest period of time was Joseph Gerald McCabe, who was born on 9th December 1899 at 23 Richmond Place in Mountjoy to Joseph McCabe, a clerk, and Martha McCabe (née Maher). A son, Thomas McCabe, an engine driver for CIE, and Patricia McCabe (née Curran) were living with his parents at 59 Abbeyfield when they died at the Mater Hospital on 26th June 1972 following a head-on collision between two cars near the J F Kennedy Stadium at Santry. Maria McCabe died on 7th September 1973 and Joseph McCabe died on 15th August 1977, aged 77, and they are buried in Balgriffin Cemetery (Plot D 95).

60 Abbeyfield – John Joseph Redmond

The 1926 Thom's Directory records the occupant as 'Reevey, C' and the occupant in the 1930 directory was 'Redmond, J'.

John Joseph Redmond was born on 29th March 1895 at 4 Upper Buckingham Street in Mountjoy, Dublin, to John Redmond, a carter, and Margaret Redmond (née Earl) and the family lived at Summerhill in Mountjoy in 1901 and at 4 Great Charles Street in Mountjoy in 1911, when John junior was recorded as being a dairyman. According to family accounts, John served with the Royal Dublin Fusiliers, but this has not been verified. After the war, John joined Guinness as a labour-

John and Mary Redmond
60 Abbeyfield
Source: www.findagrave.com)

er in the engineering department on 23rd April 1920. He was a labourer and living at Lower Gloucester Street when he married Mary Rogers (21) of St Ignatius Road on 5th December 1923 at St Joseph's Roman Catholic Church, Berkeley Road (recorded as Church of Glas Caonog). John Redmond was recorded as being a labourer and living at 60 Abbeyfield when he died of inoperable cancer at the Rialto Hospital on 7th November 1953, aged 58. Mary Redmond of 60 Abbeyfield died on 13th February 1985 at The Richmond Hospital. John and Mary Redmond are buried in St. John the Baptist Cemetery in Clontarf.

61 Abbeyfield – William Breen

William Breen was born around 1888 and his father was a blacksmith with the same name. William enlisted with the East Lancashire Regiment on 28th January 1908 and was stationed with 2nd Battalion at Wijnberg in South Africa in August 1914. The battalion was recalled for war service, landing at Southampton on 30th October 1914, and was allocated to 24th Brigade in 8th Division. William Breen landed at Le Havre with 2nd Battalion on 6th November 1914 and later served with 11th Battalion. Private William Breen was discharged due to wounds on 1st June 1918 with Silver War Badge Number 393452, his age being recorded as 29 years and 187 days. He was living at Gallanstown in Chapelizod when he was awarded a 40% Disability Pension in respect of gunshot wounds to the left arm at the rate of sixteen shillings per week. William was a clerk with the GPO and living at Spencer Terrace in North Strand when he married Lucia (or Lucy) Butler of Tyrconnell Road on 23rd September 1919 at St James' Roman Catholic Church. They were living at Salem Terrace in Merchant's Quay when their first child, Joseph Patrick Breen, was born at Holles Street Hospital on 15th March 1921. Lucy Breen's father William Butler, a golf professional, was living with the family when he died on 1st February 1940, aged 73. William was a post office sorter when he died of cardiac failure at St Kevin's Hospital on 17th November 1957, aged 69, and Lucy Helen Breen was living at 61 Abbeyfield when she died at St Kevin's Hospital on 29th March 1958, aged 65.

62 Abbeyfield – John Edward Halpin

John Edward Halpin was born on 14th November 1897 at 11 Blackhall Parade in Arran Quay, Dublin, to Joseph Halpin, a van driver and later a hotel porter, and Mary Ellen Halpin (née Connell) and the family home was at Coleraine Street in the Arran Quay district. John enlisted with the South Irish Horse (Number 1666) and was living at North King Street when he married Sarah O'Neill of Upper Kevin Street on 27th December 1915 at St Nicholas of Myra Roman Catholic Church on Francis Street. He was deployed to the Western Front after December 1915. As part of a reorganisation of the cavalry regiments, John was transferred to 7th Battalion Royal Irish Regiment (Number 25335) in September 1917. He was taken prisoner around May 1918 and was repatriated to England after six months imprisonment, arriving at Dover on 22nd November 1918. Private John Halpin was transferred to the Class Z Army Reserve on 27th March 1919 and took up employment at the Dolphin Hotel, where he would be employed for 43 years. John Halpin was the head waiter in the grillroom at the Dolphin Hotel and had been suffering from gastric ulceration for four years when he died at 62 Abbeyfield on 2nd February 1962, aged 64. Sarah Halpin was living at 62 Abbeyfield when she died at the Mater Hospital on 11th December 1965, aged 68, and is buried in Kilbarrack Cemetery.

63 Abbeyfield – Thomas Thompson Prestage

Thomas Thompson Prestage was born on 21st September 1894 at Trim in County Meath, to John Prestage, an RIC Constable, and Johanna Prestage (née Thompson) and the family home was at Knockrea near Blackrock in County Cork in 1901 and at 64 Hibernian Buildings in Cork in 1911. Thomas was educated at Kilkenny College and Mountjoy School in Dublin. In June 1914, *The London Gazette* reported that Thomas had obtained a position in the Customs and Excise Department after an open competition. Thomas Prestage was living at Oxmantown Road when he enlisted with the Inns of Court Officers' Training Corps (Number 11616) on 30th June 1917 and was accepted for admission to Number 11 Officer Cadet Battalion at Pirbright on 9th November 1917.

Thomas married Veronica Mary Gaffney, the marriage being registered in Quarter 2 1918 at Birmingham in Warwickshire, and he was an Officer Cadet when he was appointed as a Second Lieutenant with 17th Battalion King's (Liverpool Regiment) in May 1918. The battalion left Glasgow in October 1918 for service in Northern Russia, returning to the UK in September 1919. He was promoted to Lieutenant on 1st November 1919, was released from active service on 6th November 1919, and relinquished his commission with effect from 7th January 1921. His address in 1919 was the Customs and Excise building at

Thomas Thompson Prestage
63 Abbeyfield
(source: Simon Prestage)

Victoria in Liverpool but he was transferred to the Dublin Customs and Excise in 1920 and was living at Phibsborough Road. His Medal Index Card recorded his address as 1 Cecil Avenue in Clontarf when he applied for his medals in 1922 but Thomas and Veronica were living at Toxteth Park in Liverpool when their first child was born in 1929. Victor Prestage, who had served with the Royal Engineers, was living with his brother at 63 Abbeyfield when he applied for a disability pension and he was a Customs & Excise clerk when he died of pulmonary tuberculosis at Crookling Sanatorium on 28th May 1924, aged 23. Stephanie, a daughter of Thomas and Veronica, died at 63 Abbeyfield on 19th December 1926 at the age of six weeks, Thomas being recorded as being a civil servant in the Register of Deaths. The Prestage family lived at 20 Marguerite Road in Glasnevin from 1930 (when J J Quirke became the occupant of 63 Abbeyfield) until at least 1947. According to an Ancestry family tree, Thomas Prestage was part of the team that negotiated the Republic of Ireland's entry to the Common Market. Thomas Thompson Prestage was living at 3 Ascal Brugha in Drogheda when he died on 21st September 1978, aged 84. Veronica Mary Prestage died on 1st December 1981 in Drogheda.

64 Abbeyfield – Thomas William Cooney

Thomas Cooney was born on 27th March 1890 at 12 Prehend Street in the Arran Quay district to John Henry Cooney, a railway ticket collector, and Mary Cooney (née Nicholson) and the family home was at Oxmantown Road in Arran Quay, Dublin, in 1901. In 1911, John Henry Cooney was the station master at Ashtown in the Castleknock district and the family lived in the stationmaster's house. Thomas Cooney joined Guinness on 21st February 1910 and he married Annie Dorothy Doherty on 23th November 1912 at St Stephen's Church of Ireland, Upper Mount Street. Thomas and Annie were living at 76 South Circular Road when their daughter, Annie Elspeth, was born on 18th November 1914 at Holles Street Hospital. Annie Cooney developed a series of infections and died of endocarditis at the same hospital on 30th November 1914, aged 32, and is buried in St. John the Baptist Cemetery, Clontarf. Thomas was a widowed joiner's machinist and living at Brian Boru Avenue when he enlisted with the Army Cyclist Corps (Number 6648) on 16th April 1915 and was posted to the 36th Divisional Cyclists, being deployed to France on 3rd October 1915. He subsequently served with Cyclist Battalions in X Army Corps and XI Army Corps, being appointed as Lance-Corporal in February 1917. He was compulsorily transferred to the Bedford Regiment (Number 30612) on 15th November 1918, being posted to 13th Battalion. He was transferred to the Class Z Army Reserve on 19th March 1919 and was living at Brian Boru Avenue when he was awarded a 20% Disability

Pension in respect of Debility at five shillings and sixpence per week, with an allowance of one shilling and fourpence for his child. At some stage, Thomas remarried (the Guinness Archive records her name as Ethel) and one of their children, Gerard Thomas Cooney, died at 64 Abbeyfield on 4th September 1927, aged one year and seven months, and is buried in St. John the Baptist Cemetery. Thomas Cooney was a Guinness pensioner when he died of coronary thrombosis, chronic myodcardial degeneration, and arterio-sclerosis at 64 Abbeyfield on 22nd April 1963, aged 79, and is buried in St. John the Baptist Cemetery, Clontarf.

65 Abbeyfield – Patrick Joseph Flanagan

In the Thom's Directories, the occupants were 'McCarthy' in 1926, 'Mallett, J' in 1927, 'Flanagan, P' in 1930, and 'Taylor, R' in 1944.

Patrick Joseph Flanagan was born around 1884 and he enlisted with the Royal Field Artillery (Number 44909), being deployed to the Western Front on 9th September 1914. He later transferred to base detail duties with the Royal Garrison Artillery (Number 226033). Patrick Flanagan was a soldier from Lower Gloucester Street when he married Teresa Jones of Upper Gloucester Street on 8th January 1917 at St Mary's Roman Catholic Pro-Cathedral, Marlborough Street. He was discharged on 16th July 1919 and was living at 17 Gloucester Street when he was awarded a 20% Disability Pension in respect of bronchitis at the rate of eight shillings per week. Patrick and Teresa were living at Temple Street when Mary Frances was born at the Rotunda Hospital in December 1920. In 1921, the degree of disability was re-assessed at 30% and the pension was paid at twelve shillings per week, plus a weekly allowance of five shillings and thruppence in respect of a wife and one child. Patrick Flanagan was a packer when he died of bronchitis and asthma at 65 Abbeyfield on 30th August 1940, aged 52, and Teresa Flanagan died at 65 Abbeyfield on 16th September 1941, aged 46. Patrick and Teresa Flanagan are buried in Glasnevin Cemetery. After Teresa's death, Patrick's sister, Mary Flanagan, became the guardian for Theresa (born 1931), Michael (born 1933), and Bridget (born 1936). Mary Flanagan married Patrick Bibby in October 1946.

66 Abbeyfield – Patrick J Kearney

In the 1926 Thom's Directory, the occupant was 'Johnston, J' but 'Kearney, P J' was recorded as the occupant from 1928 until at least 1947.

Patrick Kearney was a waiter with militia experience when he enlisted with the Royal Irish Regiment (Number 6225) on 27th December 1897 at Clonmel. He served with 1st Battalion as a Lance-Sergeant during the Second Boer War, being awarded the King's South Africa Medal with the South Africa 1901 and 1902 clasps. Sergeant Kearney was admitted to hospital in June 1904 having sustained a gunshot wound in an accident. Sergeant Patrick Kearney was stationed in India with 2nd Battalion when he married Mary Anne Clare on 12th February 1907 in Karachi and their first child, Patrick Joseph Kearney, was born in Rawalpindi. Patrick Kearney was a Militia Sergeant when Edward Michael Kearney was born at The Barracks in Kilkenny in October 1910. He was mobilised in September 1914 and posted to 6th Battalion on the Western Front in February 1917. He held the rank of Company Quartermaster Sergeant with 3rd Battalion when he was discharged on the termination of his second period of engagement on 26th March 1919. He was living at Elizabeth Fort in Cork when he was awarded a 40% Disability Pension in respect of debility and deafness at the rate of eleven shillings per week, with a supplement of nine shillings and five pence for his wife and two children. His Medal Index Card records Arbour Hill Barracks as a contact address. Mary Ann Kearney died at 66 Abbeyfield on 25th January 1936, aged 61, and Patrick was a pensioner and living at 66 Abbeyfield when he died of congestive heart failure at Dr Steeven's Hospital on 3rd March 1951, aged 73. Patrick and Mary Anne Kearney are buried in Glasnevin Cemetery.

67 Abbeyfield – Patrick Joseph Reynolds

Patrick Joseph Reynolds was born on 21st December 1885 at George's Street in Gort, County Galway, to Patrick Reynolds, a grocer, and Mary Ann Reynolds (née Kelly). His forenames were registered as John Patrick but he was recorded as Patrick in the 1901 Census. Patrick was a Civil Service clerk and boarding with Constable John Teeling and his family at Killarney Avenue in the North Dock district in 1911. ***Research has been unable to identify Patrick's war service.***

Patrick was a clerk and living at Eccles Street in Dublin when he married Mary Margaret Smyth, a draper from Derrynane Parade, on 22nd August 1921 at St Joseph's Roman Catholic Church, Berkeley Road (recorded as Church of Glas Caonog). Patrick Reynolds was living at 67 Abbeyfield when he died of myocardial failure and arteriosclerosis of coronary arteries at the Royal City of Dublin Hospital on 25th November 1946, aged 58, and Mary Reynolds died at 67 Abbeyfield on 27th October 1981, aged 89. Patrick and Mary Reynolds are buried in Glasnevin Cemetery.

68 Abbeyfield –

The pension card for Private Patrick Joseph Barrington, Royal Dublin Fusiliers, reports that he was living at 68 Abbeyfield in Killester when he was demobilised in July 1922, making him the original occupant. In the 1926 Thom's Directory, Patrick Joseph Barrington is recorded as the occupant of 54 The Demesne. A biography for Patrick Barrington has been included in the section for The Demesne.

The occupant of 68 Abbeyfield was listed as 'O'Donnell, P' in the 1926 Thom's Directory and as 'Newburn, H' in the 1928 directory. The bungalow was listed as Vacant in 1933 and the occupant was listed as 'Smith, J' from 1934 to at least 1947.

Margaret Smith, wife of William Smith of 68 Abbeyfield, died at Our Lady's Hospice at Harold's Cross on 27th December 1966, aged 80. William Smith was living at 68 Abbeyfield when he died on 30th March 1973, aged 86. William and Margaret Smith are buried in Balgriffin Cemetery (Section G Grave 248).

Percival Owen Roberts, a porter, was living at 68 Abbeyfield when he died at St Laurence's Hospital on 14th May 1971, aged 43, and is buried in Mount Jerome Cemetery. He was survived by his wife, Patricia, who was probably a daughter of William and Margaret Smith.

69 Abbeyfield – Hugh Bernard McGrath

Hugh Bernard McGrath was born around 1887 in Dublin to Hugh McGrath, a harness maker, and Frances McGrath (née Coffey) and the family lived at Upper Liffey Street in North City in 1901. His forename was recorded as Bernard when he married Mary Quinn on 17th March 1910 at St Joseph's Roman Catholic Church on Berkeley Road in Dublin. They lived at 10 Hardwicke Street in Rotunda district in 1911 and Hugh Bernard was a mechanical engineer. He was recorded as Bernard McGrath, chauffeur, in the birth register entries for sons born in 1913 and 1915 when the family homes were at Halliday Square and South Dock Road respectively. It has not been possible to identify

Great War service for Hugh but he served as a Driver with the Royal Army Service Corps (Number T/125897) in the Second World War. He was a storeman when he died of pulmonary tuberculosis and heart failure at 69 Abbeyfield on 13th April 1944, aged 56, and Mary McGrath was still living at 69 Abbeyfield when she died at Sir Patrick Dun's Hospital on 19th August 1964, aged 80. Hugh Bernard and Mary McGrath are buried in Grangegorman Military Cemetery in Cabra (Grave 270) and a CWGC headstone marks the grave. It should be noted that the Thom's Directory records 'McGrath, J' (James, a son) as the occupant of 69 Abbeyfield from 1928.

Hugh Bernard McGrath
69 Abbeyfield
(source: www.findagrave.com)

70 Abbeyfield – Joseph Holland

Whilst the occupant is recorded as 'Allen' in the 1926 Thom's Directory, the occupant is recorded as 'Holland, J' in 1927. The property was recorded as vacant in the 1933 Directory and the recorded occupant in 1934 was 'Beatty, J'.

Joseph Holland was born on 14th April 1892 at 43 Great Clarence Street to James Holland, then a sanitary officer, and Catherine Holland (née Corbett) and the family lived in the Fitzwilliam district – at Hatch Lane in 1901 and at 13 Charlemont Place in 1911. James Holland is recorded as being a Dublin Metropolitan Police pensioner in 1901 and 1911 and he also worked as a rent collector. *The researchers have not been able to confirm the war service details for this occupant.*

Joseph was a motor mechanic and living at High Street in Dublin when he married Margaret Murphy, a draper's assistant from Mill Street, on 10th November 1921 at Thomastown Roman Catholic Church. Joseph and Margaret were living at Thomastown when Joseph Alphonsus Holland was born in 1924 and were living at 70 Abbeyfield when he died of scarlet fever at Cork Street Hospital on 15th July 1926, aged 2 years. Joseph was a mechanic in 1926 but was a salesman when another son, Francis Holland, died at 70 Abbeyfield on 7th February 1927, two days after being born. Joseph had been suffering from pulmonary tuberculosis for twelve years when he died of heart failure at Kilquade Farm in Dalgenny on 18th November 1932, aged 40, and is buried in Mount Jerome Cemetery. An obituary published in the Irish Independent on 22nd November 1932 recorded that he was a manager for W F Poole of Westland Row and was a member of the Shelbourne Social Club. In the 1920s, W F Poole assembled Morris trucks and vans.

71 Abbeyfield – Osmond Thomas Taylor

Whilst the occupant is recorded as P O'Brien in the 1926 Thom's Directory, the occupant is recorded as Osmond Taylor in 1928 and as Leslie Friary in 1947.

Osmond Thomas Taylor was born on 12th February 1895 at 12 Brighton Square in Rathmines to Thomas William Taylor, a bank official, and Susan Jane Taylor (née Keegan) and the family was living at 76 Rathmines Road in 1911, when Thomas William Taylor was a bank manager. Osmond Thomas Taylor was educated at St Andrew's College in Dublin and was an insurance clerk when he enlisted with the Black Watch (Number 2156, later re-numbered as 265618) on 13th September 1914. He was posted to 6th Battalion on the Western Front on 2nd May 1915 and was treated for debility at No. 4 Stationary Hospital between 20th and 28th June 1915, returning to duty on 9th July. He sustained gunshot wounds the thigh on 13th November 1916 and was treated at 5th Field Ambulance and Number 20 General Hospital in Camiers before being evacuated to England. He was admitted to Number 7 Officer Cadet Battalion at Fermoy in September 1917, being commissioned as a Second Lieutenant in the 3rd (Special Reserve) Battalion Royal Irish Fusiliers on 29th January 1918. He was subsequently posted to 1st Battalion, part of 108th Infantry Brigade of the 36th (Ulster) Division.

Lieutenant Osmond Thomas Taylor was demobilised on 4th September 1919 at Crystal Palace and relinquished his commission on 1st April 1920. He was recorded as 'Gentleman' and was living in Greystones when he married Dorothy Victoria Higgins of Islandbridge on 1st June 1922 at St Jude's Church of Ireland. Osmond was a clerk with the Alliance & Dublin Consumer Gas Company when he applied for ISSLT house in Kingstown in August 1923. At the time, he and his wife and two children were living in lodgings at 102 Marlborough Road in Donnybrook which consisted of two-rooms, the rent being £1 per week. The application is endorsed, 'Good type s-in-law of Col. Higgins'. The application was unsuccessful, and Osmond Taylor submitted a second application in February 1926 for a bungalow in Killester. At this time the family was living in one room at Seafield House on Merrion Road and Taylor received notification that he had been placed on the 'special list' and would be considered in the event of a vacancy. Osmond and Dorothy Taylor took possession of the bungalow at 71 Abbeyfield on 19th November 1926 and the rent was ten shillings and sixpence per week (exclusive of rates). In January 1928, the ISSLT issued a 'Notice to Quit' against Osmond Taylor but the notice was cancelled when he paid the outstanding rent. In September 1928, Osmond Taylor applied for a transfer to one of the new ISSLT cottages at Milltown in County Dublin, but the transfer request was rejected in March 1929 as the Taylors had fallen into considerable arrears with the rent. He continued to be in arrears with his rent and ejectment proceedings

Osmond Thomas Taylor
71 Abbeyfield and 238 Howth
Road (The Demesne)
(source: Ancestry Family Tree)

were started by the Trust in January 1933. By the end of the month, Osmond Taylor had paid the full amount of arrears (£5-12-0) to the Trust. He again fell into arrears and owed £2-0-6 by July 1933. In October 1945, Osmond Taylor, aware that a bungalow in The Demesne would become available soon, wrote to the Trust requesting a transfer. He cited mobility issues connected to his war wounds and the distance of his Abbeyfield bungalow from the train and bus routes to support his request. The request was passed to Captain Burke, the ISSLT Superintendent, for his observations, which were positive. At this time, Osmond Taylor was Secretary to the Seaton Association, a military charity in Dublin, and one of his colleagues wrote to Sir George Franks, an ISSLT Trustee, on Taylor's behalf.

The Taylor family moved to 238 Howth Road, formerly 65 The Demesne, on 19th January 1946. In March 1953, Osmond Taylor made an application to purchase the bungalow, which was valued at £620 but the ISSLT approved a sale price of £558. The Trust rescinded the offer in November 1957 as Osmond Taylor had not completed the process. Osmond Taylor died at the Mater Hospital on 27th April 1976, aged 80, and is buried in the graveyard at St John's Church in Clondalkin. Although Osmond Taylor had first expressed an interest in purchasing the bungalow at 238 Howth Road, it was not until after his death that Dorothy Taylor bought the Type G semi-detached bungalow and plot (c26 perches or 0.1625 acres) for £1,950 in January 1977. The Type G Bungalow had a floor area of 841 square feet and three bedrooms.

72 Abbeyfield – John McMullen

John McMullen was born on 20th August 1867 at Mill Street, Newtownards, County Down, to John McMullen and Grace McMullen (née Busbey) and he enlisted with the Royal Inniskilling Fusiliers (Number 1034) on 8th August 1884, being posted to 2nd Battalion. His next-of-kin was recorded as his father, John McMullen of Mill Street in Newtownards. He served in South Africa from October 1885 to January 1889 and in India from December 1890 to February 1898. He was recalled from the Army Reserve on 9th October 1899 and served with 1st Battalion Royal Inniskilling Fusiliers during the Second Anglo-Boer War. From this period of service, John was awarded the India Medal

1895 (with Punjab Frontier, Caw (1897-98), and Tirah (1897-98) clasps), the Queen's South Africa Medal with nine clasps (Belmont, Modder River, Cape Colony, Orange Free State, Transvaal, Tugela Heights, Relief of Ladysmith, Laing's Nek, and South Africa 1901). After being discharged, he was living at Sultan Street in Belfast when he married Mary McIlroy, a stitcher from Irwin Street, on 16th October 1901 at St Peter's Roman Catholic Chapel. They were living at John Street in Newtownards when James was born in 1902 and at Irwin Street in Belfast when Mary Theresa was born in 1906.

John McMullen was living at 8 Irwin Street in Belfast when he enlisted with the Connaught Rangers (Number 2301) on 14th November 1914, giving his age as 37 years and six months when he was actually 47. He was promoted to Sergeant eight days after he enlisted and was deployed to France with 6th Battalion on 18th December 1915. The 6th Battalion Connaught Rangers was largely made up of men from Belfast who enlisted from John Redmond's Irish National Volunteers. He left the Western Front Theatre of War on 23rd September 1916 and was initially posted to a Depot unit of the Connaught Rangers and then to 4th (Reserve) Battalion before being transferred to the 3rd Garrison Battalion of the Royal Irish Fusiliers (Number G/19573) on 11th January 1917. Sergeant John McMullen was transferred to the Class Z Army Reserve on 7th May 1919 and was living at 8 Irwin Street in Belfast when he was awarded a 30% Disability Pension in respect of bronchitis, nephritis, malaria, and gunshot wounds to the arm at the rate of rate twelve shillings per week. A weekly allowance of seven shillings and one penny in respect of his wife and two children was paid until 27th October 1920, when it was reduced to five shillings and three pence per week for his wife and a child. The degree of disability was re-assessed at 20% in May 1921 and the rate was eight shillings per week, with three shillings and sixpence for his wife and child. In 1922, the dependents element was reduced to two shillings per week as he had no dependent children under the age of 16. The family was living in Belfast when John received a grant of £40 from the Military Service (Civil Liabilities) Department towards the establishment of a coffin-making business. In 1923, the family was living at 161 North

Strand Road in Dublin. In the 1930s, Alice McIlroy (or McElroy), a sister of Mary, was living with the McMullen family at 72 Abbeyfield and worked for the Sheila Manufacturing Company on Lower Abbey Street. John McMullen was recorded as being a coffin-maker when he died at Meath Hospital on 30th May 1949. His age was recorded as 73 but he was actually 81 years old. Mary McMullen died at 72 Abbeyfield on 5th April 1959, aged 75.

73 Abbeyfield – Thomas Nolan

Whilst the occupant is recorded as 'Burrett' in the 1926 Thom's Directory, the occupant is recorded as 'Nolan, T' in 1930

Thomas Nolan was born on 21st October 1880 at Coombe Cottages in Merchants Quay to Patrick Nolan and Ellen Nolan (née McGuinness) and the family was living in Wentworth Place in South Dock in 1901. He was a labourer when he enlisted with the Connaught Rangers (Number 7378) on 28th February 1902 and was posted to 2nd Battalion in October 1902. Thomas was a Drummer stationed at Renmore Barracks when he married Mary Josephine McGreal of St Patrick's Avenue on 27th April 1912 at St Nicholas' Roman Catholic Church in Galway. In February 1914, he re-engaged with the same regiment to serve for such a term as to complete 21 years' service. Thomas Nolan was posted to the 5th Battalion in Salonika in January 1917 and was treated for malaria at 32nd Field Ambulance in August 1917 and served with the Egyptian Expeditionary Force from September 1917 to May 1918. Thomas served on the Western Front from June 1918 and was hospitalised with malaria for a second time two months later. Following a period of service in the UK from March 1919 he served with 1st Battalion in India, where he was awarded the Long Service and Good Conduct Medal in November 1921, along with a £5 Gratuity. In 1920, under the replacement of Regimental numbers, he was allocated Army Number 7143053 and the battalion left India in March 1922, arriving back in the UK the following month. Lance Corporal Thomas Nolan was discharged on 25th August 1922 with over 20 years' service and his character was recorded as 'Exemplary'. The following is recorded in his service record, 'Is trustworthy, reliable and absolutely sober. Has been employed in charge of the Recreation Room and can be thoroughly recommended for a position of trust.' The family was living at Clarence Street in Dublin when Sheila Nolan was born in June 1917 and at 21 Fairview Avenue in Clontarf in 1923. Thomas was a retired hospital orderly when Mary Nolan died at 73 Abbeyfield on 3rd August 1960, aged 68. Thomas was recorded as being a retired labourer when he died of an inoperable cancer at 73 Abbeyfield on 6th December 1964, aged 84, and is buried in St Fintan's Cemetery in Sutton. His son-in-law William Carrick was present at death and was living at 73 Abbeyfield when he died in February 1981.

74 Abbeyfield – Thomas Taylor

Thomas Taylor was born on 2nd April 1877 at Main Street in Strabane, County Tyrone, to John Alexander Taylor, a foundry proprietor, and Margaret Taylor (née McGhee) and the family home was at Lifford in County Donegal in 1901 and 1911. Thomas enlisted with the Royal Inniskilling Fusiliers (Number 4592) at the age of 18 on 9th May 1894 and was posted to 1st Battalion, being discharged on 25th January 1896. He had re-enlisted in the army and was a Sergeant with the Royal Inniskilling Fusiliers stationed at Portobello Barracks when he married Norah Bell at North Strand Church of Ireland on 10th November 1909 and was recorded as being a soldier when Florence Taylor was born in 1910 at the Rotunda Hospital and when Norah Taylor was born in May 1915 at Lower Gardiner Street. Quartermaster Sergeant Thomas Taylor was on attachment to the School of Musketry when he received a commission as a Second Lieutenant with effect from 13th November 1915. The entry in the Presbyterian Church of Ireland's Roll of Honour book for the Strabane congregation records that a Captain T Taylor of Lifford served with the School of Musketry. Thomas Taylor and Ben Griffith of 8 Abbeyfield were on a bus which collided with a tram standard near Clontarf Railway Station on 25th August 1931. They made personal injuries claims of £200 and £50 respectively against Thomas J P Murphy (trading as the Pirate Bus Company). The case was heard at the Dublin Circuit Court on 9th December and Judge Shannon dismissed both cases holding that 'the accident was due to a latent defect in the steering-gear and not to any negligence on the part of the defendant or his driver'. Norah Taylor died at 74 Abbeyfield on

10th March 1959, aged 70, and Thomas Taylor, a retired Clerk, was still living in the bungalow when he died of hypostatic pneumonia at Leopardstown Park Hospital in Blackrock on 22nd March 1963, aged 83.

75 Abbeyfield – John Christopher Brown

John Brown (sometimes Browne) was born around 1895 and he enlisted with the Royal Irish Regiment (Regimental Number 10834) on 6th February 1913. He was posted to 2nd Battalion on the Western Front on 11th January 1915 and was treated at No. 2 General Hospital at Le Havre in May 1915 for gunshot wounds to the right thigh and evacuated to England on HMHS *Asturias*. He was serving with 5th Battalion when he was discharged due to wounds on 26th February 1917 with Silver War Badge Number 144767. He was living at Belvedere Place when he was awarded a 30% Disability Pension in respect of disordered action of the heart at the rate of twelve shillings per week. John was recorded as an ex-soldier and living at Parkgate Street in Dublin when he married Margaret Tallant of Royal Canal on 17th April 1917 at Drumcondra Roman Catholic Church. His father was recorded as John Brown, a blacksmith. John Christopher Brown was a bus driver when his daughter, Dympna, died of laryngeal diptheria at 75 Abbeyfield on 4th August 1929 when she was 23 months old. John Brown was a bus driver and living at 75 Abbeyfield when he died on 9th May 1973, aged 77, and Margaret died on 11th September 1973, aged 80. John, Margaret, and Dympna are buried in Glasnevin Cemetery. It is possible that John Christopher Brown was a driver with the Old Contemptibles Omnibus Company operated by veterans living at Killester Garden Village.

76 Abbeyfield – Joseph Michael Brennan

Joseph Michael Brennan was born on 12th February 1884 at Enniscorthy Workhouse Infirmary to Richard Brennan, a flour miller, and Mary Anne Brennan (née McCormick). His father's forename and occupation is recorded as 'Patrick, Miller' in the birth register entry for Joseph but as 'Richard, flour miller' when he married in 1865. The family home was at Royal Canal Bank in the Arran Quay district in 1901. Joseph was a plumber and living at Phibsborough Road when he married

Elizabeth Angela Black of Whitworth Road on 23rd December 1908 at St Columba's Roman Catholic Church in Drumcondra. In the marriage register, his father is recorded as 'Richard, Miller'. In 1911, Joseph and Elizabeth were living at 148 Phibsborough Road in the Arran Quay district with two children and Joseph's widowed mother. Joseph enlisted with the Royal Engineers (Number 89815) and was posted to France on 10th August 1915. He was transferred to the Class Z Army Reserve on 3rd April 1919 and was living at Munster Street when he was awarded a 40% Disability Pension in respect of malaria-induced debility at the rate of sixteen shillings per week with an additional allowance of four shillings per week for four children. Joseph returned to his trade as a plumber and died of bronchitis and cardiac failure at 76 Abbeyfield on 23rd October 1945, aged 61, and Elizabeth Brennan died at 76 Abbeyfield in 1975, aged 89. Joseph and Elizabeth Brennan are buried in Glasnevin Cemetery.

77 Abbeyfield – William Alfred (Bill) Hadden

The Thom's directories record the occupant as 'Fletcher' (1926) and as 'Fletcher, J' (1928, 1929) and as 'Hadden, W A' in 1930.

William Alfred (Bill) Hadden was born on 26th September 1894 at 13 Gordon Street in Ringsend to William Henry Hadden, a plumber, and Marion Hadden (née Porteous), being the eldest of their three children. His father had been afflicted with pulmonary tuberculosis for four years when he died of the disease at 19 South Dock Street on 18th January 1900, aged 35. Marion and her three children then lived with her widowed father, William Porteous, in Pembroke West – at Howard Street in 1901 and South Dock Street in 1911. William Hadden was appointed as a temporary boy clerk in the Department of Agriculture in Dublin in 1910, the appointment being reported in *The London Gazette* on 1st November. William Alfred Hadden enlisted with the Royal Army Medical Corps (Number 60781) and held the rank of Staff Sergeant when he was posted to France sometime after December 1915. He was serving with 94th Field Ambulance, part of the 31st Division, when he was awarded the Military Medal, the announcement being reported in *The London Gazette* in November 1916. Although Bill never talked about the war, the family understand that the Military Medal was awarded for rescuing injured solders from a battlefield whilst under fire. Bill wrote about fifty letters to May Hepburn, this being an extract from one dated 26th December 1916:

> *I hope my little souvenir from France reached you safely. The little piece of ribbon which I pinned on will, I suppose, have you guessing by now. Well Dear, it is simply a piece of the German Iron Cross Ribbon given to me by a Hun prisoner who had worn it. Whether he took a sudden fancy to me or not I cannot say but I had charge of a party in which he was working when he came to me and handed it over. I thought it would interest you as a souvenir, so I sent it along. I hope to be able to send you along another little bit of ribbon of my own soon as I know you will be pleased to hear that I have won a Military Medal. The news came to me about a week ago but being somewhat busy I could not write. I am naturally very proud of the distinction and my comrades have all been nice about it.*

After being discharged from the army, Bill returned to the Department of Agriculture, where he was employed for the rest of his working life. Bill was living at Bath Avenue when he married Mary (May) Hepburn of Holles Street, who had served with the Voluntary Aid Detachment during the war, on 19th April 1920 at Dublin Registrar's Office. Bill and May started married life at 18 Church Avenue, where their first daughter, Ethel, was born. They later moved to 27 Upper Mount Street, where they had five more girls – Irene, Marion, twins Pearl and Evelyn, and Joan. Around 1929, they moved to 77 Abbeyfield, where their final child, and only son, William Edward was born. However, tragedy struck the family when little Billy died of bronchitis and cardiac syncope at the family home on 9th August 1931, aged 3 years and 11 months. During the Second World War, the residents of Killester established an Air Raid Precaution unit and Bill Hadden was an instructor in the Civilian Anti Gas School and was also part of a fire extinguishing unit. In the late 1950s, Bill was instrumental in the amalgamation of two local association football teams – Woodside United & St Bridget's – to form Killester United Football Club. The club is now called Killester Donnycarney Football Club and its ground, Hadden Park, was named after Bill Hadden of Abbeyfield. Bill Hadden was a statistician for the Department of Agriculture and was living at 77

Abbeyfield when he died of a cerebral haemorrhage and hypertension at Mercer's Hospital on 9th August 1962, aged 67. May Hadden was living at 77 Abbeyfield when she died on 27th March 1974 at St Mary's Hospital, Phoenix Park. Bill, May, and Billy are buried in Mount Jerome Cemetery. Ironically, Bill and Billy share the same birth date (26th September) and the same death date (9th August). An obituary in the Killester Sports and Social Club's 'Back Room Bulletin' (Number 49, September 1962) paid tribute to Bill (the club scribe). The following is a brief extract from the bulletin:

> *. . . one clubman who we will never be able to replace as regards the administration of the administration of Club affairs or work in general. Two months after the formation of our club in 1957, Bill was instrumental in obtaining for us, from our Landlords, the Irish Sailors and Soldiers Land Trust, permission to enclose the playing field. In the same month he was responsible for the negotiations with the Church Authorities which finally led to the purchase of our present headquarters. Again, it was Bill who was solely responsible for the opening talks with our Landlords regarding the sale of the ground, and which were successfully concluded in October 1960.*

William Alfred (Bill) Hadden
and Mary Hadden (née Hepburn)
77 Abbeyfield
(source: Lesley Hepburn)

The above biography incorporates contributions from the grand-children of Bill and May who all share such wonderful memories of family, Abbeyfield and Killester.

78 Abbeyfield – Thomas Kinahan

Thomas Kinahan was born on 21st October 1885 to James Kinahan and Anne Kinahan (née Kinahan) who farmed land at Fearboy near Kilcumreragh in King's County. The surname is recorded as Keenaghan in the Register of Births but Kinahan in 1901 Census. Thomas married Jessie Hopley on 18th September 1909 at St Wilfred's Hulme Church at Chorlton in Lancashire, and they were living at 28 Windsor Street in Pendleton in 1911, when he was recorded as being a warehouse man. He was recorded as being a clerk when he enlisted with the Irish Guards (Number 8672) in Sheffield on 5th June 1915. He was posted to 2nd Battalion on the Western Front on 10th November

Thomas and Jessie Kinahan
78 Abbeyfield
(source: Eoin Roe)

1915. He was attached to a Trench Mortar Battery in October 1916 and sustained gunshot wounds to the face in April 1918, being treated at No 2 Casualty Clearing Station at Ebblinghem. Private Thomas Kinahan was transferred to the Class Z Army Reserve on 9th April 1919. Jessie Kinahan died on 13th September 1974 and is buried in St Fintan's Cemetery, Sutton, and Thomas Kinahan died on 27th January 1980, aged 94.

79 Abbeyfield – Joseph Phelan

Joseph Phelan was born on 11th April 1896 at Borris-in-Ossory near Roscrea in Queen's County to Michael Phelan, a cattle dealer, and Elizabeth Phelan (née Bennett). Michael Phelan died on 23rd August 1897 and Elizabeth was living at Main Street in Borris-in-Ossory with five children under the age of 16. Joseph Phelan enlisted with the

Irish Guards in July 1912 and was serving with 1st Battalion when he was admitted to Queen Alexandra's Military Hospital at Millbank in London with a cheek wound on 25th November 1913, being discharged two days later. He was deployed to France with 1st Battalion on 21st August 1914. On 18th March 1917, he was admitted to No. 34 Casualty Clearing Station at Grovetown, Somme, with pyrexia (a fever), being transferred to a base hospital on No.5 Ambulance Train the following day. Joseph was transferred to the Class Z Army Reserve on 7th April 1919 and was awarded a 20% Disability Pension at the rate of eight shillings per week. One pension card records his address as 79 Manor

Joseph Phelan
79 Abbeyfield
(source: Ancestry Family Tree)

Street, whilst a second records Merrion Road, which is stroked out and replaced with 79 Abbey Field, Killester. Joseph Phelan, a porter living at Merrion Road, married Bridget Grant (20) of Templemore in County Tipperary on 10th September 1919 at the Star of the Sea Roman Catholic Church in Donnybrook. He joined Guinness as a machinery man in the Engineering Department on 5th July 1920. Stephen Phelan was born on 31st July 1920 at the Rotunda Hospital to Joseph and Bridget Phelan of 79 Manor Street in Dublin and was serving as a Sapper with 2 Field Company Royal Engineers when he died on active service on 31st December 1941, aged 21, and is buried in the Knightsbridge War Cemetery at Acroma in Libya. Bridget Phelan died at 79 Abbeyfield on 30th March 1954 at the age of 55 and Joseph Phelan died on 15th January 1986 at the age of 90. They are buried in Glasnevin Cemetery.

80 Abbeyfield – Dennis Murphy

Denis Murphy was born around 1890 and his father was called Michael Murphy. Denis was a tailor and living at Ashford Street when he married Elizabeth Hollywood of Royal Canal on 13th August 1909 at St Joseph's Roman Catholic Church, Berkeley Road. In 1911, they were living at 23 Royal Canal Bank in Arran Quay. Whilst his military service details have not been identified, Denis was recorded as tailor when a son, Denis, was born in March 1916, and when a daughter, Elizabeth, was born in November 1918 at 1 Villa Park in Royal Canal. It is possible that 'tailor' was his army trade and that he served on the Home Front. Bridget Dorothy Murphy died at 80 Abbeyfield on 19th May 1930 aged one year and four months, her sister, Nancy, being recorded as present at death. Denis Murphy was a tailor with premises at South William Street and living at 80 Abbeyfield when he died of cerebral thrombosis and hemiplegia at Mercer's Hospital on 5th February 1952, aged 62, and is buried in Glasnevin Cemetery.

81 Abbeyfield – John Peter O'Connor

John Peter O'Connor was born on 6th August 1881 at Terenure Village to Peter O'Connor, a cooper, and Honor (known as Nora) O'Connor (née Rutledge). John joined his father at the Guinness Brewery on 9th Jun 1900 and was living at Viking Road when he married Agnes Sherry of Sarsfield Street on 27th April 1904 at St Paul's Roman Catholic Church in Arran Quay. The Guinness Brewery was one of the first firms in Ireland to have an on-site branch of the St John of Jerusalem Ambulance Brigade and it is probable that John was a member as he had a First Aid Certificate when he joined the army. He was living at 21 Aberdeen Street when he enlisted with the Royal Army Medical Corps (Number 103608) on 12th November 1915 in Dublin, being posted to 16th Company. He served in the Egyptian Theatre of War from September 1916 until May 1919, and he was transferred to the Class Z Army Reserve on 5th August 1919. Although he declared that he was not suffering from a disability due to military service (Army Form Z.22, 'Statement as to Disability'), John subsequently submitted a pension claim in respect of malaria contracted whilst serving at Famagusta Prisoner of War Hospital. He was living at 2 Fitzwilliam Place in Grangegorman when he was awarded a 40% Disability Pension at the rate of sixteen shillings per week, with a supplement of six shillings and fourpence per week for three children under the age of 16. Agnes O'Connor died at Harold's Cross Hospice on 11th May 1920, aged 39, and John married Mary O'Keefe (née McMahon) of Blacklace Street on 28th February 1922 at St Paul's Roman Catholic Church in Arran Quay. John Peter O'Connor returned to Guinness after the war and was a foreman in the Cooperage Department when he retired. He died of pulmonary congestion and chronic bronchitis at 81 Abbeyfield on 22nd December 1950, aged 69, and is buried in Glasnevin Cemetery. The death was registered by A H Fenton of 81 Abbeyfield, who was present at death.

82 Abbeyfield – William McGowan

The Thom's directories from 1926 to 1942 record the occupant as 'Collins, M' and the 1943 directory records 'Cowan, W' as the occupant – the surname was McGowan.

Cornelius Joseph Collins, a former GPO telegraphist, was living at 82 Abbeyfield when his drowned body was found in the Grand Canal on 29th November 1941. He was 72 years old and is buried in Glasnevin Cemetery. Cornelius Joseph Collins was born on 18th April 1869 at Bandon Workhouse to Jeremiah Collins (cutter) and Jude Collins (née Mahony). He was recorded as being a civil servant and was living at Ashfield Avenue in Ranelagh when he married Mary Katherine Byrne, a telegraphist from Seafield Lodge, on 1st June 1898 at the Roman Catholic Church in Sandymount. They lived at 4 Florence Villas, Botanic Avenue, Drumcondra in 1911 but the only son recorded was Jerome Anthony (3). The relationship between Cornelius Joseph Collins and 'M Collins' has not been determined.

William McGowan was born around 1887 and his father, a farmer, was also called William. He enlisted as a Pioneer with the Royal Engineers (Number 163627) on 18th May 1916 and served overseas with the Royal Engineers, the Labour Corps (Number 348370), and the South Lancashire Regiment (Number 50729). Private McGowan was discharged as being 'Surplus to military requirements (having suffered impairment since entry into the service)' on 20th August 1919 with Silver War Badge Number B288824. William McGowan was living at 22 Lower Dominick Street when he was awarded a 40% Disability Pension in respect of dysentery, bronchitis, and malaria at the rate of sixteen shillings per week. The degree of disability was reduced to 30% in 1921, at a rate of twelve shillings per week. William was a warder living in Maryborough when he married Bridget Mary Farrelly of Rutland Square on 12th November 1923 at St Mary's Roman Catholic Pro-Cathedral on Marlborough Street. William McGowan of 82 Abbeyfield died of myocardial degeneration and broncho-pneumonia at Leopardstown Park Hospital in Stillorgan on 12th May 1959, aged 71. Brigid was admitted to the Mater Hospital in November 1970 with fractures to both femurs. She underwent an operation but died of Pneumonia on 20th November 1970, aged 79. William and Brigid McGowan are buried in St Fintan's Cemetery in Sutton (Section P Grave 104).

83 Abbeyfield – Patrick McCormack

Patrick McCormack was born on 1st July 1881 at 19 Aldborough Place in Mountjoy to Christopher McCormack, a railway porter, and Mary McCormack (née Murtagh). He was a van driver and living at Empress Terrace when he married Elizabeth Anderson from Jardine Street on 8th September 1907 at St Mary's Roman Catholic Pro-Cathedral on Marlborough Street. They were living at Empress Terrace, Portland Row in Mountjoy in 1911 and Patrick enlisted as a driver with the Royal Field Artillery (Number 100950). He was posted overseas after December 1915 and was demobilised on 31st March 1920. Patrick was awarded a 20% Disability Pension at eight shillings per week, plus a supplement of seven shillings and a penny for his dependants – a wife and four children. Patrick was recorded as being a labourer when he died of pulmonary tuberculosis at Dublin Union Workhouse on 21st March 1933, aged 41. A son, Vincent Patrick McCormack, died of tubercular meningitis at 83 Abbeyfield on 22nd April 1933, aged one year and five months. Another son, Patrick James McCormack was a telegraph messenger when he died of pulmonary tuberculosis at 83 Abbeyfield on 11th December 1934, aged 19. Elizabeth McCormack died of a cerebral haemorrhage at 83 Abbeyfield on 14th December 1939, aged 53. Patrick, Elizabeth, and two of their children are buried in Glasnevin Cemetery.

84 Abbeyfield – Patrick O'Loughlin

Patrick O'Loughlin
84 Abbeyfield
(source: www.findagrave.com)

Patrick O'Loughlin was born around 1882 at Ennis in County Clare, his father being Peter O'Loughlin. He enlisted with the Connaught Rangers (Number 8336) at Ballinasloe on 14th October 1904, his age being recorded as 22. He was transferred to Section A Army Reserve in March 1908 and was mobilised for war service in Galway on 6th August 1914. He was deployed to France with 2nd Battalion on 14th August 1914 and was reported missing on 26th August 1914. Patrick spent the remainder of the war as a prisoner, being repatriated on 14th June 1918. He fractured his right tibia in an accident a week later and was discharged as being 'No longer physically fit for War Service' on 29th October 1918 with Silver War Badge Number B56634. The Silver War Badge Register records that he was 36 years old. Whilst awaiting his discharge, Patrick was living at Buckingham Buildings in Mountjoy district when he married Margaret O'Gorman of Charles Street on 20th August 1918 at St Mary's Roman Catholic Pro-Cathedral on Marlborough Street. He was living at Great Charles Street when he was awarded a 50% Disability Pension in respect of gunshot wounds, deafness, and debility at the rate of twenty shillings per week. Daniel O'Loughlin, a son of Patrick and Margaret, was serving with the Irish Army when he died of Meningitis at Clonmel Fever Hospital on 28th July 1942. Patrick O'Loughlin was recorded as being a 'Retired British Army Soldier' when he died of renal failure and chronic bronchitis at St Kevin's Hospital on 12th August 1969, aged 84. Margaret O'Loughlin died at 84 Abbeyfield on 7th December 1971, aged 80. Patrick and Margaret are buried in Grangegorman Military Cemetery (RC Ground Grave 38). The shape of the headstone at their grave resembles a Commonwealth War Graves Commission headstone, but with different dimensions.

85 Abbeyfield – Peter Markey

Peter Aloysius Markey was born on 31st May 1885 at 10 Queen Square in South Dock to Nicholas Markey, a van man, and Catherine/Kate Markey (née Wasser) and was baptised at Westland Row church on 5th June 1885. The family lived at Leitrim Street in Pembroke in 1901, when Nicholas was a lavatory attendant for Dublin Corporation, and at 45 St. Joseph's Place in Inn's Quay in 1911, when Peter Markey was a corporation labourer. Nicholas Markey, who died in January 1914, had been tutored in the uilleann pipes as a child and he provided classes for the Dublin Piper's Club [sic] at the rate of five shillings per session. His pupils included Bill Andrews, John Potts (grandfather of Sean Potts of the Chieftains), and Jimmy Ennis, father of Séamus Ennis. Peter was a member of the City of Dublin Royal Garrison Artillery militia when he enlisted with the Royal Irish Rifles (Number 7413) on 9th January 1904 and was posted to 2nd Battalion in July. Peter transferred to the Army Reserve in January 1907 and was transferred to the Royal Army Medical Corps (Number 4030) in September 1909. He was a labourer when he married Margaret Fitzpatrick on 26th November 1911 at St Nicholas of Myra Roman Catholic Church on Francis Street – 70 Bride

Peter and Margaret Markey
85 Abbeyfield
(source: Ancestry Family Tree)

Street was recorded as the address of both parties. He was recalled from the army reserve on 5th August 1914 and was posted to 15th Field Ambulance. He served overseas from 18th August 1914 until 12th February 1919, with two periods on the Western Front (August 1914 to November 1917 and April 1918 to February 1919) divided by a period of service in Italy. Private Peter Markey was transferred to the Class Z Army Reserve on 13th March 1919 and discharged from the British Army on 31st March 1920. He was living at 70 Bride Street when he was awarded a 20% Disability Pension in respect of disordered action of the heart at the rate of sixteen shillings per week. On 17th July 1935, Catherine Mary (known as Kathleen) Markey, a machinist from 85 Abbeyfield, was cycling at Killester Lane when she was knocked down by a Great Northern Railway omnibus (a Leyland Lion 2LT, registration number AZ 7644). Kathleen (21) died later the same day at Jervis Street Hospital and is buried in Glasnevin Cemetery. The Coroner's Inquiry concluded that the bus driver, Arthur W Gray of Holmpatrick, Skerries, was negligent and he appeared in court in October 1935 charged with manslaughter and dangerous driving, the case being adjourned. In 1939, Peter Markey was one of a group of ex-servicemen from various parts of the Irish Free State who brought a court case against the ISSLT to determine who was responsible for executing repairs on the ISSLT properties. Peter Markey, who was frequently successful in garden competitions, was a Dublin Corporation pensioner when he died of bronchopneumonia and vascular heart disease at 85 Abbeyfield on 11th December 1953, aged 69. Margaret Markey died on 25th May 1968, aged 83, at Jervis Street Hospital. Peter and Margaret Markey are buried in Mount Jerome Cemetery.

86 Abbeyfield – William Graham

William John Graham was born on 30th November 1877 at 14 Mackie's Terrace in the Mansion House district to John Graham, a coachman, and Kate Graham (née Ryder) and the family was living at Lad Lane in the Fitzwilliam district in 1901. William was a car driver when he married Harriet Pakenham of Ballycumber in King's County on 18th December 1902 at St Stephen's Church of Ireland in Dublin South and they were living at 6 Toft's Lane in the South Dock district in 1911. The Thom's directories record 'Graham, Mrs' as the occupant from 1928 to 1947.

The researchers have not been able to identify war service details for William John Graham or the death details for William John or Harriet Graham.

87 Abbeyfield – John Masterson

John Masterson was born on 29th June 1880 at Street near Granard in County Longford to John Masterson and Jane Masterson (née

John Masterson
87 Abbeyfield
(source: Gary McKane)

O'Donnell) and was a labourer when he married Ellen O'Brien on 15th June 1902 at St Mary's Roman Catholic Pro-Cathedral on Marlborough Street. Ellen died of pulmonary tuberculosis on 14th April 1909 at Artane, and John was living at Clark's Bridge Cottages in Summerhill when he married Ellen Whelan on 6th November 1910 at the Church of St Laurence O'Toole in Dublin. John and Ellen Masterson were living at 22 Guild Street in the North Dock district in 1911 and at 16 Guild Street in 1915. John was recorded as being a carter in birth register entries for most of their children. John was recorded as being a shoemaker in the Register of Births when Elizabeth Teresa Masterson was born in November 1916. *The researchers have not been able to identify war service details for John Masterson.* John and Ellen were living at Commons Street when their daughter, Catherine, was born in June 1921. Ellen Masterson died on 25th September 1956, aged 72, at St Kevin's Hospital, where John Masterson died of a coronary thrombosis on 16th October 1957, aged 77. The ISSLT bungalow remained in the Masterson family and, in September 1974, the Drogheda Independent reported that John Masterson (40) of Abbeyfield, Killester, had died when the lorry that he was driving crashed off a bridge into the River Boyne. This John Masterson was a son of Patrick Masterson and Josephine Lewis and a grandson of the John Masterson to whom the ISSLT bungalow had been allocated.

88 Abbeyfield – Thomas Cannon

Thomas Cannon was born on 13th October 1886 at Balscaddan in Balbriggan to Richard Cannon, a farmer, and Mary Anne Cannon (née Connolly) and was baptised on 18th October 1886. The surname was recorded as Kinane in the birth and baptismal registers and in the register of the marriage between Richard and Mary Anne. The family was living at 20 Commons, Balscadden in 1911, when Thomas was recorded as being a Private in the Royal Horse Artillery. He married Margaret Larkin on 19th July 1915 at the Roman Catholic Church in Drumcondra. Thomas Cannon joined the Mounted Military Police Corps (Number 784) and served on the Western Front from 16th September 1914 to 6th April 1916 and in the Egyptian Theatre of War from 30th December 1916 until 11th November 1918. He held the rank of Lance Corporal in 1914 and was an Acting Sergeant in 1917. He was commended for 'gallant and distinguished service in the Field' in despatches dated 31st May 1915 (Field Marshal Sir John Denton Pinkstone French) and 21st July 1917

Thomas Cannon
88 Abbeyfield
(source: Ancestry Family Tree)

(Lieutenant-General George Francis Milne, Commander in Chief of the British Salonika Force). The 'Peace Gazette' published on 30th May 1919 reported that Acting Sergeant Thomas Cannon had been awarded the Meritorious Service Medal. Thomas Cannon was recorded as being a foreman when the births of a son (Richard) and daughter (Catherine Mary) were registered in 1920 and 1921 respectively. The family was living at Brown Hill in the Whitehall district in 1921. Thomas Cannon was recorded as being an ex-Serviceman when he died of chronic bronchitis and emphysema at 88 Abbeyfield on 8th January 1948, aged 61. Margaret Cannon was living at 88 Abbeyfield when she died at Clonskeagh Fever Hospital on 26th August 1955, aged 69. Thomas and Margaret Cannon are buried in graveyard at the Church of the Assumption of Our Lady in Balscadden.

89 Abbeyfield – John Darker

John Darker was born on 27th April 1893 at the Rotunda Hospital and was baptised at Westland Row on 5th May 1893, with his parents being recorded as George and Bridget McMahon. However, the register also records that his father was Peter Darker. It is probable that John was adopted at birth by the McMahons. John Darker is recorded with the surname McMahon in census and marriage records. The McMahon family lived at Bishop Street in the Mansion House District in 1901 and at Little Fitzwilliam Place in South Dock district in 1911. Based on the birth records for the other children of George and Bridget, her maiden name was either Leeson or Gleeson. John McMahon was a labourer and living at Fitzwilliam Lane when he married Mary Lenihan of Powerscourt on 31st August 1913 at St Andrew's Roman Catholic Church. John enlisted with the Royal Dublin Fusiliers (Number 21843) under the surname Darker and was posted to France on 20th December 1915 with 8th Battalion. He was reported as wounded in the War Office Casualty List No.5374 dated 2nd October 1917. He held the rank of Sergeant when he was transferred to the Class Z Army Reserve on 9th May 1919. John was living at 7 East James Place, off Baggot Street, when he was awarded an 80% Disability Pension at thirty-two shillings per week in respect of bronchitis and tuberculosis. There was a weekly supplement of eighteen shillings and ten pence for his wife and two children. He received treatment for tuberculosis at the Newcastle Sanitorium in County Wicklow. In September 1920, the pension was suspended as John Darker was in prison. Although he married under the surname McMahon, the births of his children with Mary were registered with the surname Darker – John Joseph Darker (22nd March 1916) and Mary Darker (21st July 1918) were born at East James Place, and George Darker (25th March 1920) was born at 7 James Street. A later son, William, died at 89 Abbeyfield on 26th February 1931 at the age of five months. John Darker had a general goods shop whilst he was living in Abbeyfield and he was associated with Basin View Celtic AFC. The 'Darker Memorial Cup' was awarded for the 'Best Front Garden' by the Killester Horticultural Society. In the 1939 Thom's Directory, the occupant of 89 Abbeyfield is recorded as 'Lawrence, J'. The 1939 England & Wales Register, records that the Darker family was living in Tottenham in Middlesex and John Darker was living at Haringey in London when he died in 1965, aged 72.

90 Abbeyfield – John Joseph (Jack) Brophy

The 1926 Thom's Directory records the occupant as 'Marks' and the occupant was recorded as 'Brophy, J' in the 1928 directory and as still the occupant in the 1947 directory.

Jack Brophy was the eldest child of Thomas Christopher and Catherine Brophy, née Martin, born on 7th September 1894 at Finger Post, Malahide. The 1911 Census shows the family as resident at Feltrim, Kinsealy. At that time, John was in employment as a labourer. He enlisted in The Highland Light Infantry (Regimental Number 12150) and was posted to the regiment's 2nd battalion. He embarked for active service on 13th August 1914 and was wounded on 7th November near Ypres in a German attack on the battalion's positions. He was evacuated to the United Kingdom and treated at Stobshill Hospital, Glasgow, before re-joining the battalion in May 1915. He was again wounded at the Battle of Loos on 25th September 1915 and evacuated to the United Kingdom, where he was treated at Bangour Military Hospital, Linlithgowshire. Jack married Agnes Clelland, a domestic servant at the hospital, on 23rd October 1916 at 116 Hanover Street, Edinburgh. No longer fit for active service, Jack was transferred to the Military Foot Police (P14283) in February 1918 and was discharged as 'no longer fit for military service' on 13th December 1918. As he was honourably discharged, he was awarded the Silver War Badge (B72216). Jack was living at Couper Street, Leith when he was awarded a Disability Pension in 1919. Assessed as 20% disabled with neurasthenia, he was initially awarded a pension of eight shillings per week for himself and three shillings and sixpence per week for Agnes and one eligible child. In February 1921, this

Sgt. John Brophy
90 Abbeyfield
(source: Aaron Crampton)

was reassessed, and he was awarded a pension of nine shillings and sixpence per week for a period of 70 weeks as a final award.

Jack was a railway porter when two of his infant children died at 90 Abbeyfield in 1928 – Christina Euphemia died of bronchopneumonia on 22nd September, aged two and a half months, and Kenneth died on 15th December at the age of 20 months. Jack also worked as a ticket collector for the Great Northern Railway and following the outbreak of the Second World War, travelled to Belfast and enlisted in the 12th battalion Warwickshire Regiment (5115120). He was deployed to France in March 1940 and was involved in the retreat to Dunkirk, being evacuated in June 1940. In October 1941, he was transferred to the Military Provost Staff Corps and posted to the Military Detention Centre, Northallerton, Yorkshire. He remained on the staff there until discharged on 3rd May 1944 in the rank of Sergeant. Jack did not return to his family at Abbeyfield and resided initially with another woman in Hull. Jack died aged 70 on 19th February 1965 of cancer at Kilmarnock Infirmary, Ayrshire. At the time of his death, he was resident at Hamilton Street, Saltcoats, Ayrshire.

91 Abbeyfield – William Hoey

Thom's Directory recorded the occupant as 'Duffley, J' in the 1926 and as 'Hoey, Mrs' in the 1932 edition.

A John Duffley served with the Royal Army Medical Corps (Number 11095) and the Royal Field Artillery (Number 272281) but the researchers could not establish a connection to Ireland for this man.

William Hoey was born on 30th September 1892 at 30 Cumberland Street in Kingstown to William Hoey and Mary Hoey (née Byrne) of Summerhill. He enlisted as a militiaman with the 4th (Special Reserve) Battalion of the Royal Irish Rifles (Number 8297) on 6th January 1911 and was a baker with Noblett's of Sackville Street when he enlisted in the regular army with the Royal Irish Rifles (Number 1/9699) on 1st August 1911.

William was living at Cumberland Street when he married Elizabeth Oglesby on 28th January 1913 at St Mary's Roman Catholic Pro-Cathedral on Marlborough Street. He was stationed in India with 1st Battalion from December 1913 until October 1914, when the battalion was recalled for war service. He spent four periods on the Western Front, his first deployment being from 6th November 1914 to 26th December 1914. He returned to the Western Front on 23rd March 1915 and sustained shrapnel wounds to the left arm on 25th September 1915, being treated at Number 2 General Hospital before being evacuated to the UK. He remained on Home Service until 31st January 1916, when he was posted to 2nd Battalion on the Western Front. He sustained gunshot wounds to the face on 7th July 1916, being treated at Number 34 Casualty Clearing Station before being evacuated home. He remained on Home Service until 5th October 1916 when he was posted to 1st Battalion on the Western Front. He sustained gunshot wounds to the skull on 23rd October 1916, being treated at Number 34 Casualty Clearing Station before being evacuated home from the continent for the final time on 17th November 1916. He was a Lance-Sergeant with 3rd Battalion when he was discharged due to wounds on 19th August 1917 with Silver War Badge Number 124926. Patrick was living at 16 Summerhill when he was awarded a 70% Disability Pension in respect of gunshot wounds to the head and epilepsy at the rate of thirty shillings and four pence per week, with a supplement of seven shillings for one child.

Elizabeth Hoey died of pulmonary tuberculosis at 7 Lower Gloucester Place on 23rd July 1919, aged 23, and William was living at Lower Gardiner Street when he married Christina Ridgeway of Henrietta Street on 3rd March 1920 and St Michan's Roman Catholic Church. In 1921, the disability factor was increased to 100%, with the weekly rates being forty-three shillings and four pence and ten shillings respectively. William and Christina Hoey were living at 11 Hendrick Street when their son, Brendan, died at the Hardwick Hospital on 14th February 1931, aged 1. Another son, Christopher, died of congenital debility at 91 Abbeyfield on 4th September 1934, aged four months, and a third son, John David, died of meningitis and cardiac failure at 91 Abbeyfield on 8th June 1935, aged 2. William Hoey died of epilepsy at 91 Abbeyfield on 15th May 1944, aged 50. The entry in the Register of Deaths recorded that his death was related to gunshot wounds to the head sustained in the Great War, Christina Hoey died at 1 Brackenstown in Swords on 14th April 1977 and is buried in St Colmcille's Church Graveyard.

92 Abbeyfield – Thomas Farrell

Thomas Farrell was born on 1st January 1884 at 45 Lower Clanbrassil Street in Merchants' Quay to Michael Farrell, a compositor, and Louisa Farrell (née Montford) and the family was living at Inns Quay in 1901 and at Usher's Quay in 1911. Thomas was a compositor and living at Oxmantown Road when he married Agnes White on 23rd February 1909 at St Mary's Roman Catholic Pro-Cathedral on Marlborough Street, and they were living at 34 Mountjoy Square in 1911. *The researchers have not been able to identify military service for Thomas Farrell.*

Thomas was employed by Cahill & Company, a printing firm based on Parkgate Street, and for *The Irish Press* newspaper from 1931. He died of a cerebral embolism at 92 Abbeyfield on 30th October 1957, aged 72. The death was registered by his son-in-law, Patrick O'Dowd, who was a soldier when he married Agnes Frances Farrell in July 1941. Kathleen Farrell was living at 92 Abbeyfield when she died on 11th February 2003, aged 79, and is buried in Balgriffin Cemetery (Section K Grave 47).

93 Abbeyfield – James Patrick Murphy

James Patrick Murphy was born on 15th March 1894 in Liverpool to James Murphy, an insurance inspector, and Margaret Murphy (née Harding) and was baptised on 18th March at St Francis de Salle Church in Liverpool. The family moved to Ireland in the late 1890s and lived in the Clontarf district – at Windsor Avenue in 1901 and 1911 and at Fairview Avenue in 1917. James Patrick was a clerk in an Estate Agent's office when he enlisted with the Royal Dublin Fusiliers (Number 26832) on 15th April 1916. He was posted to 10th Battalion on the Western Front on 19th August 1916 and was serving with 'A' Company when he was taken prisoner at Miraumont in the Somme department on 16th February 1917. He was held at Minden PoW Camp and repatriated to the UK on SS *Londonderry*, arriving at Hull on 2nd December 1918. Private James Patrick Murphy was transferred to the Class Z Army Reserve on 27th September 1919 and was a clerk and living at Fairview

Avenue when he married Minnella East of Ravensdale Road on 21st November 1921 at St Laurence O'Toole Roman Catholic Church. James and Minnella lived at 93 Abbeyfield until about 1933, the occupant being listed as 'Turner, T' in the 1934 Thom's Directory. They were living at Marine Drive in the Sandymount district when Minnella Murphy died of bronchopneumonia and cardiac failure at St Vincent's Hospital on 30th November 1937, aged 37.

94 Abbeyfield – John Egan

The 1926 Thom's Directory records the occupant as 'Mullett' and the occupant was recorded as 'McCarthy, C' in the 1930 directory and he was still the occupant in the 1947 directory. *The researchers have not been able to positively identify information relating to either occupant.*

The bungalow was later allocated to John Egan who had enlisted with the Leinster Regiment (Regimental Number 1898) and was deployed to France with 7th Battalion on 17th December 1915. He was listed as 'Wounded' in the War Office Casualty List dated 16th October 1916, which indicates that John was injured in either the Battle of Guillemont or the Battle of Ginchy in early September 1916. He held the rank of Corporal and was serving with 2nd Battalion when he was taken prisoner at Epehy on 22nd March 1918 during the German Spring Offensive with a sprained right ankle. The PoW documentation records that he was born 15th May 1881 in Limerick and that his next of kin was Mrs Flynn of 8 Graham's Row. The War Office Daily List Number 5774, dated 17th January 1919, reported that John had been repatriated to England and recorded that he was from Caherconlish, a village in County Limerick. John Egan married Mary Flynn of Graham's Row on 2nd March 1919 at St Joseph's Roman Catholic Church and he was transferred to the Class Z Army Reserve on 27th March 1919. John was awarded a 15% Disability Pension in respect of gunshot wounds to the shoulder and a sprained ankle at six shillings per week. The degree of disability was reassessed at 20% in 1921 and the rate was increased to eight shillings and eightpence per week. In 1922, the pension rate was reduced to eight shillings per week for 104 weeks. John Egan was living at 94 Abbeyfield when he died at the Mater Hospital on 14th

July 1979 and is buried in Tuam Cemetery in County Galway (Section H Plot 42). He was survived by his wife, Mary.

95 Abbeyfield – William Henry Evans

William Henry Evans was born on 29th February 1884 at 142 Phibsborough Road to Thomas Evans, a law clerk, and Margaret Evans (née Power) and the family home was at Lower Tyrone Street in the North Dock district. William was a van driver when he married Annie Carroll of Hardwicke Street on 6th March 1907 at St Mary's Roman Catholic Pro-Cathedral on Marlborough Street and they were living at 4 Fitzgibbon Street in the Rotunda district in 1911. William was recorded as being a carter when he enlisted with 4th Battalion Royal Dublin Fusiliers (Number 9523) on 30th September 1914 and his wife's address was recorded as 23 Queen's Square. He was posted to the 2nd Battalion on the Western Front on 2nd May 1915 but was serving on the Home Front with 4th Battalion a month later. He spent a further year with 2nd Battalion on the Western Front between November 1915 and November 1916. In mid-July 1916, he was treated for self-inflicted wounds to the left hand for eight days at 12th Field Ambulance, No. 2 South Midland Casualty Clearing Station, and No 39 Casualty Clearing Station. In October 1916, he sustained gunshot wounds to the head and shoulders and subsequently served on the Home Front with 4th Battalion before being transferred to the Labour Corps in July 1917, serving with 506 Employment Company. He was transferred to the Royal Defence Corps (Number 48725) in June 1918 and served with 168 Company guarding a Prisoner of War Camp. Private William Evans was discharged due to wounds on 16th March 1919, aged 34, with Silver War Badge Number 479369. There are also references to gas poisoning in his service papers. He was living at Upper Gardiner Street when he was awarded a 50% Disability Pension in respect of gunshot wounds to the head and disordered action of the heart. The pension rate was twenty shillings per week, with a supplement of eleven shillings and ten pence per week for his dependants, a wife and three children. Annie Evans died at 95 Abbeyfield on 26th January 1934, aged 50, and William Henry Evans was living at the ISSLT bungalow when he died of cerebral thrombosis and arteriosclerosis at Sir Patrick

Dun's Hospital on 18th March 1966, aged 82. William and Annie Evans are buried in Glasnevin Cemetery.

96 Abbeyfield – Paul Peter Ryan

Paul Peter Ryan was born on 5th October 1895 at 3 Portland Place in Rotunda to Paul Peter Ryan, a tailor, and Mary Jane Ryan (née Edge) and the family lived at Carlingford Road in Drumcondra in 1901 and at 2 Upper Rutland Street in Mountjoy in 1911, when Paul was a messenger. Paul Ryan enlisted with the Royal Army Medical Corps (Number 11306) on 6th February 1915 and was posted to France on 22nd September 1915. Acting Corporal Paul Ryan was discharged due to sickness on 26th October 1918 with Silver War Badge Number B36207 and was living at 2 Upper Rutland Street in Summerhill when he was awarded a 30% Disability Pension in respect of epilepsy at the rate of twelve shillings per week. Paul was a railway porter when he married Johanna Reynolds of Lower Gardiner Street on 2nd November 1921 at St Thomas Church of Ireland. Paul Ryan had the same job and was living at 96 Abbeyfield when he died of toxaemia at Grangegorman Mental Hospital on 5th March 1941, aged 45.

97 Abbeyfield – William Henry Carthy

In the 1926 Thom's Directory, the occupant was recorded as 'O'Reilly, H' with the occupant being 'Carthy, W' in the 1930 directory. The bungalow was vacant in the 1933 directory and 'Breen, J' was recorded as the occupant in the 1934 directory.

William Henry Carthy was born in 1880 to Timothy Edwin Carthy and Margaret Carthy of Hannah Street and later of Artillery Street, both being in Blackburn. William was already serving in a militia battalion of the East Lancashire Regiment when he enlisted with the Regular Army (Number 5608) on 22nd April 1898 at Burnley. He served with 1st Battalion in South Africa from January 1900 to November 1902, being awarded the Queen's South Africa Medal with three clasps (Johannesburg, Cape Colony, and Orange Free State) and the King's South Africa Medal with the 1901 and 1902 clasps. He served in the United Kingdom from 1902 and was stationed at Portobello Barracks when he married Amelia Agnes Kenny on 9th August 1903 at St

Mary's Roman Catholic Pro-Cathedral on Marlborough Street. In 1911, he was a Corporal and was stationed at Inkerman Barracks in Woking. Sergeant Carthy was posted to 1st Battalion in France on 12th May 1915 but was evacuated to the UK on 18th October 1915, spending 20 days at the West Lothian Hospital.

After being discharged to duty, he served on the Home Front until he was posted to 9th Battalion in Salonika in November 1917. Whilst in the Balkans, he was compulsorily transferred to the Hampshire Regiment (Number 43791) in April 1918, serving with 12th Battalion before being posted to Malta in October 1918, where he remained until January 1919. Sergeant Carthy was discharged on 27th August 1919 as being 'No longer physically fit for war service', being awarded Silver War Badge Number B290808. He was living at 92 Upper Dorset Street in Dublin when he was awarded a 20% Disability Pension in respect of malaria and bronchitis at the rate of five shillings and sixpence per week, with a weekly supplement of three shillings and sixpence for his wife and one child. William Henry Carthy, a labourer, was living at 'Rathmoyle' in Abbeyfield when he died of tuberculosis and degeneration of the liver at the Mater Hospital on 5th March 1930, aged 50. Amelia Agnes Carthy later lived at 23 Warbeck Moor, Aintree, Liverpool.

98 Abbeyfield – Edwin Bridge

Edwin Bridge was born on 4th September 1899 at Old Youghal Road in Cork to Rifleman Samuel Bridge of the King's Royal Rifle Corps and Mary Bridge (née Ryan). The family lived in army barracks in Cork (1901) and Woolwich (1911). His father, Rifleman Samuel Bridge, 2nd Bn. KRRC was killed in action on 31st October 1914, aged 39 and is commemorated on the Menin Gate Memorial, Ypres. Edwin's widowed mother was living at 93 Montague Road at Cape Hill near Smethwick in Staffordshire. Edwin Bridge was a soldier and stationed at Ballykinlar Camp in County Down when he married Elizabeth Johnston from the Falls Road on 20th March 1921 at St Paul's Roman Catholic Church in Belfast. *The researchers have not been able to identify the regiment with which Edward Bridge served in the Great War.* Edwin Bridge was recorded as being a seaman when their daughter, Florence, died of bronchopneumonia and Convulsions at 98 Abbeyfield on 6th February 1927. The 1928 Thom's Directory records that the occupant of 98 Abbeyfield was a J Murray. Edwin and Elizabeth were living at Smethwick in Staffordshire in 1932 when a son, Philip Edwin Bridge, was born.

99 Abbeyfield – Christopher John Doyle

Christopher Doyle was born on 13th December 1891 at 14 Rialto Buildings in Ushers Quay to Andrew Doyle, a labourer, and Mary Doyle (née O'Brien) and he joined Guinness on 13th March 1906 at the age of 14. The Guinness Roll of Honour records that Christopher Doyle was employed in the Engineering Department when he enlisted with the Royal Army Medical Corps (Number 42660). He was deployed to the Western Front on 31st July 1915. Private Doyle was transferred to the Class Z Army Reserve on 25th March 1919 and was living at 172 James Street when he was awarded a 19% Disability Pension in respect of gunshot wounds to the right arm at the rate of five shillings and six pence per week. Christopher returned to employment at Guinness and was a boat engine driver in the Traffic Department when he left the firm. Christopher Doyle was living at 99 Abbeyfield when he died of cancer at St Luke's Hospital in Rathgar on 23rd March 1959, aged 66 and Eva Doyle was living at 99 Abbeyfield when she died at St Mary's Hospital, Phoenix Park, on 26th September 1971, aged 78. Christopher John and Eva Doyle are buried in St Fintan's Cemetery in Sutton.

100 Abbeyfield – Robert Henry Leggett

Robert Henry Leggett was born on 25th March 1889 at the Rotunda Hospital to Robert Leggett and Jane Leggett (née McClean) of 33 Watling Street and was baptised on 3rd April 1889 at St. Paul's Church of Ireland in Dublin. In 1911, he was a shop assistant for a licensed vintner called John McGrath and boarded with the family at George's Quay in Trinity Ward. Robert enlisted with 3rd Battalion Royal Irish Rifles (Number 3/25030) but was transferred to 18th (London Irish Rifles) Battalion of the London Regiment (Number 4815) before being posted to the Western Front after December 1915. Robert was a serving soldier when he married Isabella Lynch from St James' Avenue on 7th

November 1917 at North William Street Roman Catholic Church. He was living at Saint James Avenue off Clonliffe Road when he was demobilised on 23rd September 1919 and was awarded a 20% Disability Pension at the rate of eight shillings per week, with a supplement of two shillings per week in respect of his wife and child. In 1921, the family was living at the same address and Robert was working as a furniture remover when Sylvia Jane Leggett was born. Robert Leggett, along with Robert Butler (38 Abbeyfield) and John Haugh, initiated a case at the High Court seeking to have it declared that:

> *. . . the Irish Sailors and Soldiers Land Trust was not entitled to accumulate a reserve fund for the purpose of building new cottages out of the proceeds of the cottages provided for the accommodation of men who served in any of His Majesty's naval, military or air forces in the late war or for any purpose other than the repair and the insurance of the existing cottages, and to pay the debts and expenses of managing the Trust.*

They also sought to have it declared that 'the existing rents are excessive and should only be sufficient to cover necessary outlay.' The Supreme Court subsequently found in favour of the tenants. Maud Leggett, the eldest daughter of Robert and Isabella, was working as a factory hand when she died of intestinal obstruction at the Mater Hospital on 3rd November 1941, aged 22, and is buried in Mount Jerome Cemetery. According to information in an Ancestry Family Tree, Robert later worked as a tea blender for Lyons Tea in Dublin. Following a brief illness, Robert Leggett died at 100 Abbeyfield on 27th November 1976, aged 87, and is buried in Mount Jerome Cemetery. Isabella (or Isabel) died at 100 Abbeyfield in May 1980, aged 90.

101 Abbeyfield – Joseph Church

Although the occupant's name is consistently recorded as 'R Church' in the Thom's directories, the researchers believe the occupant to be Joseph Church, who was born on 4th February 1888 in County Sligo to Charles Church and Margaret Church (née Henry) who farmed land at Carrowgavneen near Coolaney. Joseph was a farm labourer when he joined the Royal Irish Constabulary (RIC Number 65935) in June 1911 and he subsequently enlisted with the Irish Guards (Number 10185) on 3rd November 1915. Around 200 RIC men enlisted with the Irish Guards. Joseph was posted overseas after December 1915 and he sustained gunshot wounds to the right hand, losing several fingers. He was discharged on 25th April 1918 with Silver War Badge Number 408977, his age being recorded as 26 years and six months. He was living at Coolaney when he was awarded a 60% Disability Pension at the rate of twenty-four shillings per week. Despite the injuries to his right hand, Joseph returned to police work and, on the disbandment of the force, was stationed at Gormanstown Camp when he was awarded an Annual Pension of £107~0~8 from 6th May 1922, with an Advance of

Joseph and Ellen Church
101 Abbeyfield
(source: www.findagrave.com)

Pension payment of £10. Joseph Church married Ellen Deasy and they had six children – Astrid Church was still living in Abbeyfield in 2023. Ellen died at 101 Abbeyfield on 26th July 1973 and Joseph died at 101 Abbeyfield on 17th November 1977, aged 89, and they are buried in Balgriffin Cemetery (Section D Grave 32).

In 1936, two schoolboys – Valentine Kennedy of 101 Abbeyfield and Owen Fitzsimmons of Blessington – were hunting for rabbits at Three Rocks Mountain with their ferret when they discovered a very rusty pistol embedded in clay. On 8th July 1936, the Irish Press reported that the British cavalry pistol, probably dating to the 1798 United Irishmen rebellion, had been presented to the National Museum. Valentine Kennedy was a cousin of Ellen Church and his father worked in Tara Street Fire Station. After his father's death, the Kennedy family had to leave the fire station accommodation and stayed with the Church family in Killester for a while.

102 Abbeyfield – Albert William Heffernan

The 1926 Thom's Directory records the occupant as 'Nolan' and as 'Nolan, Mrs' in the 1928 and 1929 directories. It is possible that the

1926 occupant is Thomas Nolan who is recorded as the occupant of 73 Abbeyfield in the 1930 Thom's Directory, when 'Heffernan, F' is recorded as the occupant at 102 Abbeyfield.

Albert William Heffernan was born on 3rd May 1887 at 40 Jervis Street in North City to William Heffernan, a painter, and Mary Heffernan (née Gore). In 1911, he was a painter and lodging with the Galvin family at River Street in Clara, King's County. He was living at the Iveagh Buildings on Bride Street when he married Frances Payne of Lower Denmark Street on 4th July 1913 at St Mary's Church of Ireland. Winifred Frances Heffernan was born at the Rotunda Hospital in September 1915. Albert enlisted with the Royal Dublin Fusiliers (Number 19494) and was deployed to France with 8th Battalion on 20th December 1915. Private Heffernan was discharged due to wounds on 14th June 1918 with Silver War Badge Number 412762 and was awarded a 40% Disability Pension in respect of gunshot wounds to right thigh at the rate of sixteen shillings per week, with a weekly supplement of seven shillings per week for his wife and one child. Albert William Heffernan of 102 Abbeyfield died of pulmonary tuberculosis at the Home of Rest for Protestant Dying on Camden Row on 23rd March 1929, aged 41. Frances Heffernan was recorded as the occupant of the ISSLT bungalow in the Thom's directories up to at least 1947.

103 Abbeyfield – John Joseph Whelan

John Joseph Whelan was born on 1st April 1886 at 8 O'Brien's Place on Haddington Road to John Whelan, a carpenter, and Mary Whelan (née Murray) and the family was living at Lower Gloucester Street in North Dock in 1901. John was a carpenter when he married Elizabeth/Lizzie Costello on 19th June 1907 at St Andrew's Roman Catholic Church in Dublin and they were living at 2 Grattan Court in South Dock in 1911. John enlisted with the Royal Dublin Fusiliers (Number 19829) and was a Corporal when he was deployed to France with 9th Battalion on 19th December 1915. John was recorded as being a Sergeant with the Royal Dublin Fusiliers when Elizabeth died of acute pneumonia at the Holles Street Hospital on 21st October 1918, aged 30. Sergeant John Joseph Whelan was serving with the Labour Corps (Number 613815) when he was transferred to the Class Z Army Reserve on 28th March 1919.

John was a widower when he was awarded a pension in respect of dyspepsia at six shillings and sixpence per week, with a supplement of two shillings and fourpence per week in respect of his two children. At some stage, John remarried a lady called Mary. John Joseph Whelan was a fitter with the Dublin Gas Company when he died of chronic myocardial degeneration and chronic bronchitis at 103 Abbeyfield on 28th March 1969, aged 82, and is buried in Balgriffin Cemetery (Section I Grave 52).

104 Abbeyfield – Patrick Burke (sometimes Bourke)

The 1926 Thom's Directory recorded the occupant as 'Briggs, W E' and as 'Burke, P' in the 1944 directory.

Patrick Burke was born on 22nd February 1883 at 4 James' Terrace in South Dock to John Burke, a porter, and Catherine Burke (née Breslin) and the family was living at Grattan Court in South Dock in 1901, when Patrick was a messenger and his father was a grocer's porter. Patrick was a van driver and a reservist with the Royal Garrison Artillery (Number 21295) in 1911, when he was boarding with the Curran family at Swan Place in Rathmines. Patrick was a van driver living at Sussex Place when he married Annie Byrne of Pembroke Cottages in Donnybrook on 4th August 1912 at Donnybrook Roman Catholic Church. They were living at Havelock Square when Carmel Rose Burke was born at the Holles Street Hospital in July 1913. Patrick was posted to the Western Front as a Gunner with 58th Heavy Artillery Group in 1916 and was transferred to the Class Z Army Reserve on 25th March 1919. He was living at Pembroke Cottages when he was awarded a 20% Disability Pension in respect of a fractured left wrist at the rate of eight shillings per week. Annie Burke died in 1919 and Patrick was living at Pembroke Cottages when he married Ellen Merriman of Ailesbury Road on 12th April 1920 at Donnybrook Roman Catholic Church. Patrick Burke was working as a bread van driver for Peter Kennedy Limited when he died of a coronary thrombosis and arteriosclerosis at 104 Abbeyfield on 30th November 1957, aged 74, and is buried in Dean's Grange Cemetery.

105 Abbeyfield – Matthew McCreary

The 1926 Thom's Directory records the occupant as 'Coady, Wm' and the occupant was 'McCreary, M' in the 1932 directory.

Matthew McCreary was born around 1892 to Michael McCreary, a gardener, and Mary McCreary and the family home was at Seaview Avenue in Clontarf East in 1901. He enlisted with the Royal Army Medical Corps (Number 35467) and was posted to France on 10th July 1915. He was awarded the Military Medal with the notification being reported in *The London Gazette* in June 1917. Acting Corporal McCreary was transferred to the Class Z Army Reserve on 16th March 1919 and a rejected application for an army pension records his address as 9 Dawes Park in Clontarf. Mathew was a railway worker living at Brian Boru Street in Clontarf when he married Mary E Murphy of Raheny on 18th June 1928 at Coolock Roman Catholic Church. Mathew McCreary was a railway porter when he died of liver disease at 105 Abbeyfield on 14th April 1945, aged 51, and is buried in Kilbarrack Cemetery (Section DF Grave 2).

106 Abbeyfield – James Joseph Stafford

James Stafford was born on 19th December 1871 at 12 Great Clarence Street to Stephen Stafford and Ellen Stafford (née Nolan) and was baptised three days later at St. Andrew's Roman Catholic Church on Westland Row. He was a labourer and living at James Street when he enlisted with Royal Inniskilling Fusiliers (Number 2944) on 17th July 1889 and served in India from December 1890 to April 1897, being discharged to the Class A Reserve. He married Mary Hanlon on 15th August 1897 at St Andrew's Roman Catholic Church. James was recalled to active service in October 1899 and served with 1st Battalion in South Africa from November 1899 until June 1902, being awarded the Queen's South Africa Medal (with Belfast, Cape Colony, Tugela Heights, and Relief of Ladysmith clasps) and King's South Africa Medal with the 1901 and 1902 clasps. James Stafford was discharged on 30th June 1902 with 12 years and 349 days service. In April 1911, James, Mary and their six children were living at 11 Sandwith Place, but their youngest child, Eileen, was one year old when she died in August 1911. In 1911, James was recorded as being a 'caster at works' but his occupation was recorded as 'carter' when he re-enlisted for war service with the Royal Inniskilling Fusiliers (Number 21109) on 15th April 1915. He was 44 years old with a wife and five children ranging in age from 15 to 6. A month after he enlisted, a younger brother was killed in action on 16th May 1915 during the Battle of Festubert whilst serving with 2nd Battalion Royal Inniskilling Fusiliers.

Private Patrick Joseph Stafford, the husband of Elizabeth Stafford of 22 Clarence Place, was 40 years old and is commemorated on the Le Touret Memorial in France. James was posted to the 7th Battalion on the Western Front on 16th February 1916 and eight months later, his eldest son was killed in action on the Salonika Front. Private Peter Stafford (23048, 6th Battalion, Royal Dublin Fusiliers) died on 3rd October 1916, just three days before his 17th birthday and is commemorated on the Doiran Memorial in Greece. James Stafford was mentioned in General Sir Douglas Haig's Despatch dated 9th April 1917. On 21st March 1918, he was reported as missing during the Battle of St Quentin and was later confirmed as having been taken prisoner. He spent 250 days in captivity before being repatriated to the UK on 26th November 1918. Sergeant James Stafford was transferred to the Class Z Army Reserve on 6th March 1919, with 3 years and 328 days war service. James was living at Sandwith Place when he was awarded a 20% Disability Pension in respect of bronchitis at the rate of nine shillings and four pence per week, with a supplement of five shillings and eleven pence per week in respect of his wife and three children under the age of 16. James and Mary Stafford were living at Killester when a daughter, Kathleen (or Catherine), married Christopher Russell, an Irish Army soldier stationed at Portabello Barracks, on 29th April 1925. James Stafford was recorded as being a government messenger when he died of arteriosclerosis and a cerebral haemorrhage at 106 Abbeyfield on 29th October 1942, aged 70, and is buried in Glasnevin Cemetery. The Death Register records his age as 64 and that Catherine Russell, daughter, was present at death.

107 Abbeyfield – Thomas Wade

Thomas Wade was born on 24th December 1889 at 13 Coombe Street in the Merchant's Quay district to William Wade, a blacksmith, and

Honora Wade (née Flaherty). His mother was known as Norah and the family home in 1901 was at Henrietta Street in Inn's Quay district. Norah Wade died on 25th January 1904, aged 49, and William Wade died on 16th April 1908, aged 53. Thomas was working in Liverpool when he enlisted with the Cheshire Regiment (Number 30464) on 3rd November 1915 and was transferred to the Machine Gun Corps as transport driver in March 1916. One document records his occupation at enlistment as a groom, whilst another records his trade as a painter.

Thomas was posted to 122nd Company Machine Gun Corps on the Western Front on 16th May 1916 and, during a period of home leave, he married Rachel Duffy, a hem stitcher from Ross Street, on 24th September 1916 at St Patrick's Roman Catholic Church in Belfast. He overstayed his period of leave and had to be escorted under guard to Southampton on 11th October 1916. Thomas was posted to a depot company in the UK on 16th March 1917. He was posted back to the to the Western Front on 2nd April 1918 but returned to Home Front duties on 12th May 1918. Throughout his time in the army, there were periods when Thomas absented himself from duty without leave, being declared as a deserter in 1917 and again in 1918. He forfeited pay as punishment for most of the absences but was also placed in military detention on two occasions. Thomas was transferred to the Labour Corps in February 1919 and was posted to 177 POW Company and was a transport Corporal when he was discharged in September 1919. Thomas Wade was a painter when he died of pulmonary tuberculosis and cardiac failure at 107 Abbeyfield on 25th January 1932, aged 42 (although his age was registered as 37). His son, also called Thomas, died of tuberculosis and meningitis at 107 Abbeyfield on 9th May 1933, aged 10. Rachel/Rachael Wade was living at 107 Abbeyfield when she died on 6th March 1977, aged 82. The Wade family grave is in Glasnevin Cemetery.

108 Abbeyfield – John Warnock

John Warnock was born on 23rd August 1883 at the Rotunda Hospital to Michael Warnock, a labourer, and Mary Warnock (née Talbot) who were living at 13 Coles Lane. The family home was at Gloucester Street South in the Trinity district in 1901 and John Warnock was a general labourer when he enlisted with the Royal Irish Rifles (Number 7771) on 28th December 1904 at the age of 19, having previously served with a militia battalion of the Royal Dublin Fusiliers. He served in India from 1905 until 1912, being transferred to the Army Reserve on 15th March 1912. John was mobilised for war service on 5th August 1914 and was deployed to France as a Lance-Corporal with 2nd Battalion on 14th August 1914. He was a Corporal when he sustained gun-shot wounds to the chest on 7th May 1915 near Hill 60 and was posted to depot duties in the UK later that month.

Corporal John Warnock was stationed at Portobello Barracks with 3rd Battalion when he married Kate Kavanagh of Seaview Terrace in Howth on 22nd September 1915 at the Church of the Assumption in Howth. (His family name was recorded as Warlock in the Register of Marriages.) He was a Drill Instructor with 5th Battalion when he was promoted to Sergeant in December 1916. John was transferred to the 3rd (Home Service) Garrison Battalion of the Northumberland Fusiliers (Number 52379) in September 1917 and then transferred to the Class Z Army Reserve on 3rd March 1919. He re-enlisted with the Royal Irish Rifles (Number 25791) on 14th August 1919 for a two-year term of engagement and was stationed at Palace Barracks in Holywood when he was discharged as being 'no longer fit for war service' on 1st April 1920. He had served in the British Army for over 15 years, his character was recorded as very good, and his home address was re-corded as 20 High Street in Holywood. John Warnock was living at 30 City Quay in Dublin when he was awarded a 30% Disability Pension in respect of olitis media and gunshot wounds to the back at the rate of twelve shillings per week. He also received a weekly supplement of eight shillings and ten pence for his wife and three children. John Warnock received a grant of £20 for a boat building business from the Military Service (Civil Liabilities) Department. Catherine Warnock died at Grangegorman Mental Hospital on 8th April 1951, aged 58, and John Warnock was living at 108 Abbeyfield when he died of cor-onary pulmonale, chronic bronchitis, and emphysema at Jervis Street Hospital on 18th November 1958, aged 75.

109 Abbeyfield – Patrick Joseph Drea

Patrick Joseph Drea was born on 18th January 1886 at Knocktopher near Thomastown in County Kilkenny to James Drea and Margaret Drea (née Byrne) and was baptised on 20th January 1886 at Ballyhale Parish Church. Patrick was a railway porter when he married Anastasia Power on 7th June 1909 at Ferrybank Roman Catholic Church in Waterford and they were living at 27 Dock Road in Waterford in 1911. Their first two children were born at Ferrybank, but they were living at Thomastown when Ellen was born in December 1914. *The researchers have not been able to identify military service for Patrick Joseph Drea.*

After being discharged, Patrick was employed as a labourer in the Guinness Cooperage Department from 28th May 1919 and the family home was at 8 Kearns Place in Dublin when Thomas Drea was born in July 1919. Dermot Augustine Drea died of acute lobar pneumonia at 109 Abbeyfield on 13th April 1927, aged seven months. Patrick was a Guinness Brewery pensioner when he died of bronchogenic cancer at Dr Steeven's Hospital on 7th March 1951, aged 65. Anastasia Drea died at 109 Abbeyfield on 18th September 1957, aged 74.

110 Abbeyfield – Montague Alexander Strudwicke

The Thom's directories record three occupants for this bungalow in the 1920s – 'Murphy, J' in 1926, 'Strudwick, M A' in 1927 and 'Duignan, J' in 1928. The latter was recorded as the occupant in 1944 but not in 1945, when the bungalow was vacant.

The second occupant was Montague Alexander Strudwicke who was born on 25th May 1894 at Bournemouth in Hampshire to Alexander Gould Strudwicke and Emily Elizabeth Strudwicke (née Barker). The family lived at Ashley Road in Branksome (1901) and at 5 Park Terrace, Bournemouth Road, Parkstone (1911). His father was recorded as being a sanitary and electrical engineer in 1901 and as being a plumber in 1911, when Montague was assisting in the business. He was a member of the Officers' Training Corps at Bournemouth School and spent three years with 7th Battalion Hampshire Regiment. He emigrated to Canada in March 1912, travelling on SS *Ivernia* from Liverpool to Boston, Massachusetts, his destination being British Columbia. He was a draughtsman when he enlisted with the Canadian Expeditionary

Force (Number 24791) on 25th September 1914 at Valcartier in Quebec. He was serving with 13th Battalion Canadian Infantry (also known as the Royal Highlanders of Canada) when he sustained knee injuries in April 1915, having been blown around ten feet by an exploding shell. He was admitted to the Australian Base Hospital at Wimereaux on 26th April 1915, being transferred to the Castle Red Cross Hospital in Dublin four days later. He was also treated at the King George V Hospital in Dublin and at the Royal Victoria Hospital in West Hampshire before being transferred to the Canadian Convalescence Home in Hythe in September.

In November 1915, he was commissioned into the British Army and was a Lieutenant with the 105th Mahrattas (Indian Army) when he married Cecilia Boa Wilson of Frankfort Avenue in Rathgar on 14th August 1919 at Rathgar Presbyterian Church. His medal index card also records service with the Dorsetshire Regiment and records addresses in Skerries and Rathgar. After relinquishing his commission, Montague worked as a civil engineer in Dublin and was living at 62 Frankfort Avenue when Cecilia gave birth to Alexander Wilson Strudwicke in February 1921. In 1939, Montague was a departmental superintendent at a steel factory and the family home was at 9 Wharfedale Street in Wednesbury, Staffordshire. Montague Alexander Strudwicke died on 10th March 1951 at Acton Road in Whitstable, Kent.

111 Abbeyfield – Francis Smyth

Francis Smyth was born in Dublin around 1881 to Francis Smyth and Mary Smyth and lived in the Mountjoy district – at Summerhill in 1901 and at 52 Great Charles Street in 1911. Francis Smyth junior was recorded as being a wine porter in 1901 and a commercial porter in 1911. He was a hotel porter when he married Margaret Tuite on 18th July 1912 at St Mary's Roman Catholic Pro-Cathedral on Marlborough Street. Francis Smyth enlisted with the Royal Dublin Fusiliers (Number 12013) and landed at Suvla Bay on the Gallipoli Peninsula with 6th Battalion on 7th August 1915. He was transferred to the Class Z Army Reserve on 4th April 1919 and was living at 52 North Great Charles Street when he was awarded a 30% Disability Pension in respect of Bronchitis and Malaria at the rate of twelve shillings per week, with a weekly allowance of seven shillings and one penny for three dependent children. The degree of disability was reduced to 20% in 1922, making a total weekly pension of thirteen shillings and eleven pence. Francis had been suffering from pulmonary fibrosis for nine years when he died of bronchitis at 111 Abbeyfield on 12th December 1929, aged 47.

112 Abbeyfield – Thomas Milner

Thomas Milner was born on 14th August 1874 at Coombe Hospital to Henry Milner, a blacksmith and later a coachsmith, and Margaret Milner (née Smith) of 34 South King Street. Thomas was baptised on 17th August 1874 at St Nicholas of Myra Roman Catholic Church on Francis Street. He was a coachsmith and living at Ossory Road when he married Christina Sheffield of Holles Row on 19th February 1898 at Dublin Registrar's Office. In 1901, they were living at 66 Walnut Tree Walk in Lambeth and Christina was recorded as being an upholsterer working from home. They had returned to Dublin later the same year as their first son, Thomas, was born at the Rotunda Hospital on 7th December 1901. In 1911, the family was living at 22 Temple Street in the Rotunda district and the census records that Christina had given birth to ten children but that only five were still living. They had a fur-

Thomas Milner
112 Abbeyfield
(source: Ancestry Family Tree)

ther three children, the last child being Thomas who was born on 6th May 1920 at 11 Lower Northbrook Avenue.

Thomas Milner enlisted with the Army Service Corps (Number M2/074611) and was posted to the Western Front on 29th August 1915 at the age of 41. He later served with 360 Motor Transport Company, part of the 4th Bridging Train, stationed at Pontoon Park in Aldershot. Corporal Thomas Milner was transferred to the Class Z Army Reserve on 27th March 1919 and does not appear to have been in receipt of a disability pension. After they moved to Abbeyfield, they named their bungalow 'Mount St Eloi'. Thomas Milner was a committed trades unionist being a member of the National Union of Vehicle Builders (NUVB). Thomas and Christina Milner were keen gardeners and were regular winners in garden competitions, a picture of the bungalow and garden being published in the Saturday Herald in September 1936. In 1939, Christina won the Darker Memorial Cup for 'Best Front Garden' in the competitions organised by the Killester Horticultural Society and the Killester Branch of the National Garden Guild. Thomas died of liver failure at Mercer's Hospital on 22nd April 1952, aged 76, and is buried in Glasnevin Cemetery. Christina Milner died at Mercer's Hospital on 25th May 1952 aged 72 and is buried in St. John the Baptist Cemetery in Clontarf.

113 Abbeyfield – Henry Alexander Jones

The 1926 Thom's Directory recorded the occupant as 'Lomansey, P' and in the 1928 directory, the occupant is recorded as 'Jones, H A'.

Henry Alexander Jones was born on 4th April 1890 at St Fintan's in Sutton to Robert Jones, an RIC Sergeant, and Elizabeth Jones (née Kehoe) of Lisheens in County Wicklow. The family lived at Donard Town in County Wicklow in 1901 and at Clownings near Bodenstown in County Kildare in 1911, by which time Robert had retired from the police force and was a postmaster, Henry Alexander Jones was recorded as being a clerk in 1911 and he enlisted with the Royal Engineers (Number 31834). Sapper Jones was posted to the Western Front on 3rd December 1915 and was transferred to the Class Z Army Reserve on 10th July 1919. Henry was a civil servant and living at Clonliffe Road in Dublin when he married Clarissa Jane Climo Baird on 27th July 1920 at Hill Street Presbyterian Church in Lurgan. Henry Alexander Jones, a retired civil servant, had been suffering from bronchitis and asthma for twenty years when he died of a pulmonary oedema at 113 Abbeyfield on 19th April 1959, aged 69. Clarissa Jane Climo Jones died at 113 Abbeyfield on 20th February 1963, aged 71. Henry and Jane Jones are buried in St Fintan's Cemetery in Sutton.

114 Abbeyfield – Patrick White

The 1926 Thom's Directory recorded the occupant as 'Lawlor, W' and the 1931 directory records 'White, P' as the occupant.

Patrick was born on 26th June 1884 at 86 Great Britain Street to Thomas White, a compositor, and Mary White (née O'Brien). In 1911, he was a club waiter at the Hibernian United Services Club on St. Stephen's Green North in Royal Exchange. He married Alice Stoney of Holles Street on 21st June 1911 at St Andrew's Roman Catholic Church. Patrick was recorded as being a valet when Gerard Thomas White was born at 'Lucerne' on Castle Avenue in Clontarf and as a waiter when Alice White was born at 49 Upper Rutland Street in June 1919. *The researchers have not been able to specifically confirm Patrick's military service.*

After being discharged, Patrick continued to work as a waiter and he died of a pulmonary embolism at 114 Abbeyfield on 29th May 1942, aged 57. Alice White died at 114 Abbeyfield on 23rd October 1972. Patrick and Alice White are buried in Dean's Grange Cemetery.

115 Abbeyfield – Francis J Lawlor

Thom's Directory recorded the occupant as 'Lawlor, W' in the 1926 and 1928 editions, but as 'Lawlor, F' in the 1929 edition.

Francis Lawlor was born on 23rd February 1895 at 14 Eustace Street in South City to Michael Lawlor, a painter, and Ann Lawlor (née Dolan). The surname was recorded as LAWLER in the Register of Births. In 1911, Frank was in domestic service as a page boy and living with his maternal grandparents, Simon and Jane Dolan, at 19 Temple Bar in South City. Francis enlisted as a Driver with the Royal Field Artillery

Francis and Christina Lawlor
115 Abbeyfield
(source: www.findagrave.com)

(Number 35036) and was posted to France on 10th September 1915. The War Office Daily List No.5559 (7th May 1918) reported that Francis had been wounded. He was still in the army and was living at Queen's Square when he married Christina Stowell of Temple Bar on 12th December 1918 at SS Michael and John Roman Catholic Church. Francis Lawlor was living at 3 Temple Bar when he was transferred to the Class Z Army Reserve on 10th March 1919. He was working as a waiter when Christina Lawlor gave birth to their first two children – James Vincent in 1919 and

Annie in 1921. Christina Mary Lawlor died at 115 Abbeyfield on 17th May 1967, aged 70, and Francis was living at 115 Abbeyfield when he died of bronchopneumonia at Mercers Hospital on 12th October 1970, aged 70. Francis and Christina Lawlor are buried at Plot 255-G in Balgriffin Cemetery.

116 Abbeyfield – William Cummins

William James Cummins was born on 17th October 1894 to William Cummins, a house painter, and Honoria Cummins (née Lyons) of Stephen Street and baptised at SS Michael and John Church on 22nd October 1894. His mother died in August 1899, aged 26, and William Cummins and his widowed father were living at Bishop Street in the Mansion House district with his maternal grandparents, John Joseph Lyons and Bridget Lyons in 1901. William Cummins senior married Margaret Kavanagh in 1907 and the family home was at 34 South King Street in the Royal Exchange district in 1911, when William Cummins junior was a messenger.

William enlisted with the Royal Irish Fusiliers (Number 11068) on 7th July 1912 and married Mary Caldwell, a machinist from Little Longford Street, on 26th November 1913 at SS Michael and John Roman Catholic Church. Private William Cummins was deployed to France with 1st Battalion on 22nd August 1914. In April 1915, a War Office Casualty List reported that he had been subjected to gas poisoning. He remained on the Western Front until 23rd June 1916, by which time he held the rank of Sergeant. William was stationed at Ebrington Barracks, Londonderry, when William Joseph Cummins was born on 19th May 1917 at Ebrington Street in the city. He was transferred to the Royal Flying Corps (Number 133269) on 20th February 1918 and incorporated into the Royal Air Force on 1st April 1918. He was a Drill Instructor and his rate of pay in the RAF was three shillings and thruppence per week. William was transferred to the Class F Reserve 5th October 1919. When Hugh Anthony Cummins was born on 4th April 1920 at the Rotunda Hospital, William was recorded as being a soldier and living at 8 Charlemont Mall. He was living at the same address when he was awarded 50% Disability Pension in respect of debility at twenty-three shillings and fourpence per week, with a supplement of eight shillings and ninepence in respect of one child. In 1921, the pension was amended to 70% Disability and the rate was thirty-two shillings and eightpence per week, with a supplement of twenty shillings and eightpence in respect of three children. William Cummins senior was living with his son when he died at 115 Abbeyfield on 3rd January 1944, aged 70, and is buried in Glasnevin Cemetery. William Cummins junior was a timekeeper with Brown Thomas of Grafton Street and living at 116 Abbeyfield when he died of chronic bronchitis and myocardial infarction at Jervis Street Hospital on 13th September 1959, aged 65. Mary Cummins was living at 116 Abbeyfield when she died at St Mary's Hospital, Phoenix Park, on 3rd March 1968, aged 74.

117 Abbeyfield – James McKenna

James McKenna was born around 1893 but the researchers have not been able to identify his military service. James was a clerk living at St Mary's Place when he married Alice Kavanagh of Brian Boru Street on 17th February 1920 at St John the Baptist Roman Catholic Church in Clontarf. In the Register of Marriages, his father is recorded as James McKenna, a commercial traveller.

James and Alice McKenna
117 Abbeyfield
(source: www.findagrave.com)

On 3rd July 1928, James McKenna was walking along the North Circular Road towards Phoenix Park with his son, Jim. As they approached the railway bridge, James Mckenna said, 'Good-bye Jim', and jumped over the wall. He was taken to the Mater Hospital with serious injuries, developed pneumonia and died on 14th July 1928, aged 35. His widow, Alice, gave evidence at the Coroner's Inquiry before Dr L A Byrne, the City Coroner. She stated that James had been attended by a doctor for the previous couple of years and the doctor had declared that James was 'off his head' and should be committed to an asylum. Alice said that James had never threatened to take his own life. Dr Byrne told Mrs McKenna that, 'It was a pity you did not take the doctor's advice.' The jury returned a verdict that the 'deceased died from pneumonia following injuries received by jumping over the wall on to the railway line while insane.' Alice McKenna continued to live in the ISSLT bungalow at 117 Abbeyfield until her death at her daughter's home in Phibsborough Terrace on 19th May 1974. James and Alice McKenna are buried in the Kavanagh plot at St. John the Baptist Cemetery in Clontarf.

118 Abbeyfield – Frederick Christopher Sharpe

Frederick Christopher Sharpe was born on 25th December 1886 at 40 Charleville Avenue in the Mountjoy district to Frederick Sharpe, a clerk with HM Customs and Excise, and Ellen Sharpe (née Davis). The family lived at Ulster Terrace in Mountjoy in 1901 and at 128 North Strand Road the North Dock district in 1911. Whilst Frederick's occupation was recorded as typist in the 1911 Census, he was recorded as being a Civil Service clerk when he married Mary Behan, a dressmaker from the Shankill district, on 16th September 1913 at Little Bray Roman Catholic Church in Rathdown. Frederick was recorded as being a clerk when Lilian Maria Sharpe was born at 33 Royal Canal on 19th December 1916 but as a soldier when Lilian died at 18 Berkeley Road on 8th December 1917. Frederick enlisted with the Royal Irish Regiment (Number 11594) and was posted to the Western Front with the 7th (South Irish Horse) Battalion, which had been formed the previous month. The medal entitlement documentation records that his service number was 35554 when his service terminated. This implies that two periods of service overseas with the Royal Irish Regiment were split by a period of home service with another regiment. They were living at Berkeley Road when Frederica Sharpe was born on 6th April 1920. Frederick was a retired civil servant when he died of coronary occlusion at 118 Abbeyfield on 24th June 1965, aged 79. Mary Teresa Sharpe, late of 118 Abbeyfield, died at her son's home at Kilshane Road in Finglas on 27th December 1972. Frederick Christopher and Mary Teresa Sharpe are buried in Glasnevin Cemetery.

119 Abbeyfield – Hugh Callan

Hugh Callan was born on 10th June 1886 at Calga near Ardee in County Louth to John Callan, a shoesmith and later a farmer, and Alice Callan (née Durnin). In 1901, Hugh was living at Calga with his maternal grandparents, Owen and Margaret Durnin. He enlisted with the Royal Irish Fusiliers (Number 10557) on 9th December 1910 and he was awarded a certificate for mastering one of the dialects of Hindustani whilst stationed in India. He held the rank of Lance-Corporal when he was posted to the 2nd Battalion on the Western Front on 19th December 1914. Hugh married Mary Jane Cash of Main Street in Buncrana, on 27th November 1916 at St Mary's Roman Catholic Church in that town. Lance-Sergeant Hugh Callan was transferred to the Section B Reserve on 20th February 1919 and discharged due to illness on 6th November 1919 with Silver War Badge Number 450670. He was living at 2 Merchants Road in East Wall when he was awarded a 20% Disability Pension in respect of rheumatism and frostbite at the rate of eight shillings per week, with a supplement of four shillings and eight pence per week for his wife and two children. John Joseph Callan was born in August 1917 at Clonmany and Joan was born in June 1920 in Dublin. After being discharged, Hugh passed an examination for the Civil Service and served in the Land Commission and the Army Audit Department, being subsequently transferred to the Free State Army in a civilian capacity.

Hugh and Mary Jane Callan took possession of 119 Abbeyfield on 4th August 1923. In 1925, Hugh was convicted of defrauding the Ministry of Defence of £5,000 (£231,548 in current terms) and he was sentenced to five years' penal servitude, serving one year and three months. Whilst in Portlaoise Prison, where he mastered the Gaelic language, the ISSLT commenced proceedings to eject him from the Abbeyfield bungalow and the bungalow was let to Joseph McCann from 8th January 1927. Hugh Callan was a teacher and living at Phibsborough Road in 1934 when he commenced a legal action against the ISSLT. The Supreme Court in the Irish Free State had ruled that the Irish Land (Provision for Sailors and Soldiers) Act of 1919 did not entitle the charging of rent. In his case against the ISSLT, Hugh Callan wanted the rents that he had paid to be refunded. He also wanted the current occupant of 119 Abbeyfield, Joseph McCann, evicted and his occupancy reinstated. The High Court and the Court of Appeal both rejected his claim. The family home was at Clonmacnoise Road in Crumlin when Mary Jane Callan died on 12th September 1840, aged 52. Hugh Callan was a clerk and living at 63 Charleville Avenue in North Strand when he died of congestive heart failure and renal failure at St Kevin's Hospital on 13th October 1954, aged 68. Hugh and Mary Jane Callan are buried in Killbarrack Cemetery (Section BA Grave 23).

119A Abbeyfield – Joseph Coleman

This address first appears in the 1931 Thom's Directory, the occupant being recorded as 'Coleman, J' and the 1947 edition records the occupant as 'Coleman, Joseph'.

Based on his age at death, Joseph Coleman was born around 1898 and his father's name was William. Joseph enlisted with the Royal Dublin Fusiliers (Regimental Number 8798) and landed at Cape Helles with 1st Battalion on 25th April 1915, the start of the Gallipoli land campaign. He was wounded and left the Theatre of War on 27th July 1915. He saw further overseas service between 25th November 1915 and 11th November 1918. Joseph was a soldier and living at Lower Mayor Street when he married a widow called Margaret Baker (née Skingle) from St Mary's Road on 21st March 1918 at St Laurence O'Toole Roman Catholic Church. Lance Corporal Joseph Coleman was serving with the Military Foot Police (Regimental Number P/6735) when he was discharged on 28th February 1919. He was living at 32 Guild Street in the North Wall district when he was awarded a 20% Disability Pension in respect of rheumatism and malaria at the rate of eight shillings per week. There was also an allowance of three shillings and sixpence per week for his wife and one child. Joseph Coleman, a building labourer, died of gangrene of the lower limbs, arteriosclerosis and heart disease at St Kevin's Hospital on 11th October 1954, aged 56, and is buried in Grangegorman Military Cemetery. In 1966, Eileen Russell was living at 119A Abbeyfield.

120A Abbeyfield – Fred Smith

This address first appears in the 1931 Thom's Directory, the occupant being recorded as Fred Smith. It has not been possible to identify this man but one person with the surname SMITH was living at the bungalow when he died and at least one person with the surname SMITH died at 120A Abbeyfield.

Joseph Smith, a son of John and Agnes Smith of 120A Abbeyfield, died of bronchopneumonia at the Cork Street Hospital on 25th June 1952, aged 19 months, and is buried in Glasnevin Cemetery. Margaret Smith died at 120A Abbeyfield on 15th December 1978 and is buried in Mount Jerome Cemetery.

120 Abbeyfield – J Connor

'Connor, J' is recorded as the occupant in the Thom's directories from 1926 until at least 1947 but the researchers have not been able to identify either family or military information relating to the occupant.

121 Abbeyfield – Walter Harrison

Walter Harrison was born in London on 3rd June 1876 to Walter Harrison and Mary Ann Harrison (née Kenniff) and the family home was at Temple Lane in Dublin in 1901 and at Winetavern Street in Belfast in 1911. His father's occupation was recorded as rubber stamp maker in 1901 and as a stereotyper in 1911. Walter Harrison junior was a printer when he enlisted with Royal Irish Regiment Militia in April 1896 (No 2970) and transferred to the regular army in July 1896 with number 5850. He served in South Africa from 16th December 1899 until 10th February 1905, being awarded the Queen's South Africa Medal (with Cape Colony, Orange Free State, Johannesburg, and Diamond Hill clasps) and the King's South Africa Medal (with 1901 and 1902 clasps). He was stationed in India from February 1906 until December 1906 and again from February 1909 until October 1914.

Walter was a Sergeant in the Royal Irish Regiment and stationed at Longford when he married Constance Edith Crampton of Molesworth Street on 26th December 1914 at St Anne's Church of Ireland in Dublin.

Walter and Connie Harrison and family, 121 Abbeyfield
Source: Marion Moore (née Bell)

He was posted to the 2nd Battalion on the Western Front on 23rd October 1916 at the age of 40, and remained on the Western Front until August 1918. Walter Harrison was a porter at Trinity College, Dublin and living at 121 Abbeyfield when he died of prostatectomy mesenteric thrombosis at the Adelaide Hospital on 30th December 1942. The Register of Deaths records his age 64 and he was buried in Mount Jerome Cemetery. Constance Harrison was living at 121 Abbeyfield when she died of bronchopneumonia at St Mary's Hospital, Phoenix, on 25th July 1970 at the age of 89. This bungalow has stayed in the extended family and the current occupant, Marion Moore, a grand-daughter of Walter and Connie Harrison, has contributed a piece to Chapter 7.

122 Abbeyfield – William Freeny

William Freeney (recorded as FRENEY in the Register of Births) was born on 26th August 1897 at 92 Lower Dorset Street in the Inns Quay area of Dublin to James Freeney, a painter, and Agnes Freeney (née Lynch). In the 1901 Census, Agnes was recorded as being a dressmaker and the family was living at 71 St. Ignatius Road in Inns Quay in 1911. William Freeney enlisted with the Royal Irish Fusiliers (Number 18459) and was posted to 6th Battalion in the Balkans on 21st September 1915. William was living at Fitzgibbon Street when he married Mary Anne Ryan of Grenville Street on 27th October 1918 at St Mary's Roman Catholic Pro-Cathedral on Marlborough Street. (Note: his father's forename was recorded as John.) William was still in the army when Clare Josephine Freeney was born on 8th October 1919 at Barrack Street in Armagh and when Mary Freeney was born on 8th January 1921 at Grenville Street in Dublin. His post-war army number was 7040620. William Freeney was the Chief Port Officer for the Automobile Association and living at 122 Abbeyfield when he died of myocardial infarction at the Mater Hospital on 5th July 1969, aged 71. Mary Anne Freeney was living at 118 Abbeyfield when she died at the Mater Hospital on 16th October 1974. William and Mary Anne Freeney are buried in Glasnevin Cemetery.

123 Abbeyfield – Salvator Ludien Gavillet

The 1926 Thom's Directory records the occupant as 'Nolan, K' and 'McLoughlin, W' is recorded as the occupant in the 1930 directory and the 1941 directory. The McLoughlin family moved from Abbeyfield to The Demesne in the early 1940s with 'McCullough, W' being recorded as the occupant of 254 Howth Road (formerly 73 The Demesne) in the 1941 Thom's Directory. The next occupant listed for 123 Abbeyfield was 'Gavelliet, W' in the 1943 Thom's Directory.

Salvator Gavillet
123 Abbeyfield
(sources: Evening Herald, 1917,
and www.findagrave.com)

Salvator Ludien Gavillet was born on 21st June 1888 in Dublin to Charles Francois Gavillet, a hairdresser and later a chiropodist, and Susan Gavillet (née Dougherty) and his mother died of cancer at Clonturk Avenue in Drumcondra on 10th April 1898, aged 40. Charles Francois Gavillet, who was born in Geneva, married Annie Curtis on 29th August 1900. The family home was at North Frederick Street in Rotunda (1901) and 12 Hawthorn Terrace in North Dock (1911) but Salvator was not living at the family home on either occasion. Salvator enlisted with Royal Dublin Fusiliers on 29th October 1908 and was stationed in India with 1st Battalion in 1911. When the war started, the battalion was recalled to the UK from India, arriving in late December 1914. The battalion became part of the 86th Brigade in 29th Division and sailed from Avonmouth for the eastern Mediterranean in mid-March 1915, stopping at Alexandria before disembarking at Mudros on 9th April. The division landed from the converted coaster SS *River Clyde* at Cape Helles on 25th April 1915, sustaining heavy casualties. He was reported as wounded in a War Office Casualty List dated 4th August 1915. After the withdrawal from

Gallipoli in January 1916, the 29th Division sailed from Port Said in mid-March, bound for Marseilles and service on the Western Front. In March 1917, *The Evening Herald* reported that Salvator had been seriously wounded and hospitalised at Rouen.

Private Gavillet was discharged due to wounds on 28th December 1917 at the age of 27 years and seven months with Silver War Badge Number 297034. His Pension Index Card records that he had sustained gunshot wounds to the face causing the loss of an eye. He was living at Cook Street in Coventry when he married Mary Ann Conway in late 1918 and they were living in Coventry when Alice Theresa Gavillet was born in April 1922. They later lived at Moore Street in Dublin. Salvator Gavillet died of bronchopneumonia at 123 Abbeyfield on 7th March 1956, aged 67, and the entry in the Register of Deaths records that he had been suffering from chronic bronchitis and war injuries for 38 years. Mary Gavillet was living at 123 Abbeyfield when she died at St Kevin's Hospital on 23rd January 1963, aged 66. Salvator and Mary Gavillet are buried in Grangegorman Military Cemetery.

124 Abbeyfield – James Martin

James Martin was born on 3rd July 1883 at 101 Leeson Street, Belfast, to James Martin, a van man, and Margaret Martin (née Gorman) but the family home was at Kirwan Cottages in the Arran Quay district of Dublin in 1901. James was a postman when he married Teresa Brown from Casper Street on 20th July 1902 at St Michan's Roman Catholic Church and they were living at 23 St. Benedict's Gardens in the Inn's Quay district in 1911. James Martin enlisted with the Royal Garrison Artillery (Number 76171) and was posted to 177 Siege Battery on the Western Front after December 1915. Gunner James Martin was listed as wounded in the

James and Teresa Martin
124 Abbeyfield
(source: Catherine Murphy)

War Office Casualty List dated 30th October 1917. In August 1918, his medical fitness grading was amended to Category B III (sedentary work, light duties) by the Regimental Medical Officer, Captain R W Mackintosh, RAMC. At that time, he was stationed at Milton Range in Gravesend, Kent.

Gunner James Martin was demobilised on 25th September 1919 and was living at 84 Lower Dorset Street when he was awarded a 50% Disability Pension in respect of gunshot wounds to the right chest at the rate of twenty shillings per week. In 1942, James Martin was the Honorary Secretary of the Killester Branch of the British Legion of Ex-Servicemen. Charles Anthony Martin, who was born on 13th September 1910, became a career soldier in the British Army and was stationed in Egypt when the Second World War started. He was badly injured when his glider crash-landed during the D-Day Landings and had to have a metal plate inserted in his skull. He spent the rest of the war as a batman for Desmond Windham Otho FitzGerald, the 28th Knight of Glin, who employed Charles as a driver after the war. Teresa Martin died at Jervis Street Hospital on 9th June 1965, aged 80, and James Martin died in 1976, aged 92/93 – they are buried in Mount Jerome Cemetery. Their youngest son, Kevin, lived in the Abbeyfield bungalow up until his death in recent years.

(Additional information from Catherine Murphy and Kevin Martin)

125 Abbeyfield – Patrick Morrin

The 1926 Thom's Directory recorded the occupant as 'O'Kane, B' (although the list compiled by St Brigid's Church recorded the forename initial as 'R') and he was recorded as the occupant in the 1937 directory. The bungalow was vacant in the 1939 directory and the next occupant was 'Morrin, P' in the 1942 directory.

Patrick Joseph Morrin was born on 6th February 1892 at Mountmellick in Queens County to Francis Morrin, a farmer, and Ellen Morrin (née Conroy) and was baptised three days later. The family lived at Knocknagroagh near Borris in Queen's County in 1901 and at Shaen in Queen's County in 1911. Patrick enlisted with the Army Service Corps (Number M2/150789), serving with a Mechanical

Transport company and being posted to a theatre of war after December 1915. The circumstances of his discharge are not known but he was an engineer living at Aberdeen Street when he married Elsie Jacob of Wicklow Street on 25th June 1921 at St Andrew's Roman Catholic Church, Westland Row. Elsie Morrin died at Mercer's Hospital on 18th February 1963, aged 63, and Patrick was living at 125 Abbeyfield when he died of cancer at St Kevin's Hospital on 5th September 1964, aged 72. Patrick and Elsie Morrin are buried in Mount Jerome Cemetery.

125A Abbeyfield (later 126 Abbeyfield) – Michael Leech

This address first appears in the 1931 Thom's Directory, the occupant being recorded as 'Leech, Michael'.

Michael Leech was born on 7th July 1885 at 5 Synott Place to Christopher Leech, a coachman, and Mary Leech (née Ennis) and was baptised three days later at St Michan's Church. Both his parents died of tuberculosis when Michael was growing up – Mary died in March 1892 and Christopher died in April 1899, their surnames being recorded as Leetch in the registers of death. Michael Leech was a tailor when he enlisted in the Royal Engineers (Regimental Number 16820) on 14th October 1907 but he was discharged on 16th November having been 'irregularly enlisted'. It has not been possible to identify details of war service. However, he was a tailor and was living at Hardwick Street when he married a widow called Mary O'Reilly (née McCormack) from North Frederick Lane on 22nd June 1919 at St Mary's Roman Catholic Pro-Cathedral. When Sarah Leech was born at the Rotunda Hospital on 2nd July 1920, Michael's occupation was recorded as 'ex-soldier'. Michael Leech, a tailor, of 126 Abbeyfield died of congestive heart failure at the Mater Hospital on 5th August 1952, aged 67. Mary Leech of Abbeyfield died in 1978, aged 94. Michael and Mary Leech are buried in Glasnevin Cemetery, as are two people named Thomas Leech from Abbeyfield. Thomas Leech, a tailor, of 126 Abbeyfield died at St Kevin's Hospital on 26th July 1955, aged 63, and Thomas Leech of Abbeyfield died in 1985, aged 62. It is not known how these men are related to Michael Leech, but it is possible that they were his brother and nephew.

41A Abbeyfield (127 Abbeyfield) – Charles John O'Toole

When the six bungalows were added to Abbeyfield in the early 1930s, two were originally numbered 41A/125A but had been re-designated as 127 and 126 by 1938. The occupant was recorded as 'O'Toole, C J' in the Thom's directories from 1931 to 1941 inclusive and the occupant was recorded as 'Rowden, C T' in the 1942 edition. In 1945, the occupant was 'Downey, P'

Charles John O'Toole was born on 24th September 1889 at 38 Molesworth Street to Loughlin Laurence O'Toole and Marion O'Toole (née Ryan). In 1901, the family was living at Jervis Street in North City and Loughlin was a 'commercial traveller in horse outfitting'. Loughlin died in 1910 and the family was living at Usher's Island in 1911, Charles being recorded as being a railway labourer. Charles was a fitter when he enlisted with the Royal Flying Corps (Regimental Number 942) in Dublin on 18th October 1913 and was posted to 5 Squadron as an Aircraftman First Class on 1st July 1914. He was deployed to France on 14th August 1914 and was promoted to Corporal in February 1915 and then to Sergeant seven months later. On 1st November 1915, he was appointed as a Flight Sergeant with Number 8 Reserve Aeroplane Squadron and appointed as an Acting Warrant Officer three months later. He served in the UK from 24th September 1915 until 6th March 1917.

Sergeant Major Charles O'Toole married Cherry Bryans from Drumcondra on 19th August 1916 at the Anglican Parish Church of North Cerney in Gloucestershire. In October 1916, he extended the term of engagement to complete seven years of service. When their first child, Cherry, was born at 15 Richmond Cottages in Summerhill on 20th July 1917, Charles' address was recorded as 'In the Field in France'. Charles was transferred to the Royal Air Force on its establishment on 1st April 1918 and was posted to 48 Squadron. In July 1918, he was awarded the Meritorious Service Medal and he extended his term of engagement to complete twelve years of service. In January 1919, 48 Squadron was stationed at Bickendorf Aerodrome in Cologne as part of the Army of Occupation. On 1st November 1919, 48 Squadron was posted to India and Charles was stationed at Deolali with 5 Squadron in October 1921. Charles was discharged on 17th January 1922, with eight years and three months service, having purchased his release for £35 (approximately £1,600 in current terms). On 14th June 1922, Charles was appointed as an aero ground engineer at Baldonnell Aerodrome by the Irish Free State's Civil Aviation Department. Charles and Cherry had two more children – Maria on 3rd April 1923 and Kenneth on 1st July 1932. Charles was a motor engineer when he enlisted as an Aircraftman Class 2 in the RAF's Class E Reserve for a four year engagement on 4th July 1939, being promoted to Sergeant the following day. Charles John O'Toole died in Leicester in 1960, aged 70. Additional information from Avril Tynan, a great-grand-daughter of Charles and Cherry O'Toole, who informed the project that Charles was a member of 'The Magic Circle' and recalls her grandmother relating that she was often 'sawn in half' by Charles.

Charles and Cherry O'Toole
127 Abbeyfield (formerly 41A Abbeyfield)
(source: Avril Tynan)

Chapter 6

Occupants of The Orchard

The 1931 Thom's Directory records that 32 houses for Orchard Road and the names of the householders for 31 of the dwellings were recorded. Although newspapers were using 'The Orchard' as early as 1936, Thom's directories recorded the street name as Orchard Road until at least 1947. Unlike the original dwellings in Killester Garden Village, these were two-storey dwellings, with four sets of six-dwelling blocks, one four-dwelling block, and two sets of semi-detached houses.

1 The Orchard – Joseph William Bergin

Joseph William Bergin was born on 1st March 1895 at 43 Beresford Street in North Dock, Dublin, to Joseph Bergin, a labourer, and Catherine Bergin (nee Daly). He enlisted with the Royal Dublin Fusiliers (Regimental Number 11548) as William Bergin on 22nd May 1913 and was deployed to France on 23rd August 1914 with 2nd Battalion. Sergeant Bergin was serving with 2nd Battalion Royal Irish Regiment (Regimental Number 1218) when he was discharged due to wounds on 28th February 1919 with Silver War Badge Number B157488. He was living at Grattan House on Lower Mount Street when he was awarded a 30% disability pension in respect of gunshot wounds to the left forearm at the rate of fourteen shillings per week. Joseph was a clerk and living at Lower Mount Street when he married Alice Cooper of East James Street on 15th August 1923 at St Andrew's Roman Catholic Church. Joseph was a tram driver and had suffered from tubercular peritonitis for twenty-one months when he died of acute obstruction toxaemia at Jervis Street Hospital on 10th February 1933, aged 37. Joseph William Bergin is buried in Glasnevin Cemetery.

2 The Orchard – Frederick Synnott

Frederick Synnott was born on 12th February 1895 at Glasnevin to Samuel Synnott, a gardener, and Mary Synnott (nee Fagan) and the family was living at Kennycourt near Gilltown in County Kildare in 1911. Frederick was a groom when he enlisted with the Royal Dublin Fusiliers (Regimental Number 16177) on 5th November 1914. He held the rank of Lance-Corporal when he was deployed to France on 19th December 1915 with 9th Battalion. He was promoted to Corporal on 17th January 1916 and to Sergeant on 18th February of that year. He was mentioned in Field Marshal Sir Douglas Haig's Despatch dated 9th April 1917. He returned from the Western Front on 9th December 1917, being posted to 3rd Battalion on Home Service in August 1918. He relinquished his rank when he was transferred to the Royal Engineers (Regimental Number 328556) in September 1918, being posted to P5 Company and later serving with 11th Anti-Aircraft Company. Frederick was living at St David's Terrace in Glasnevin when he was transferred to the Class Z Army Reserve on 11th April 1919. He was awarded a 20% disability pension in respect of bronchitis at the rate of eight shillings per week, which was increased to twelve shillings a week (30% disability) in August 1920. Norah Sinnott, the daughter of M Sinnott (a mental hospital attendant), died of tubercular peritonitis at 2 Orchard View on 31st March 1932 at the age of one. Frederick Synnott of 2 The Orchard was a widower when he died of coronary heart disease at St Vincent's Hospital on 8th May 1969, aged 74.

3 The Orchard – Robert Ferguson

Robert Ferguson was born on 26th March 1885 at St Rollox in Glasgow, his parents were Malcolm Ferguson, an iron roofer, and Marion Miller (Minnie) Ferguson (nee Horsborough). The family had moved to Dublin by 1888, when Robert's brother, John, was born and were living at Henrietta Street in Inns Quay in 1901 (Robert was an apprentice painter) and at Brighton Terrace in Pembroke West in 1911 (Robert was an iron roofer). Robert enlisted with the Royal Navy (Naval Number K25479) on 22nd April 1915, his date of birth being recorded as 26th March 1887. Although his rank is recorded as Stoker, his war service

Robert Ferguson
3 The Orchard
(source: Leroy Keller)

was restricted to shore bases in England, and he was discharged on 21st February 1919. His character was recorded as 'Very Good' and his ability was recorded as 'Satisfactory'. Robert was a steel erector and living at Hastings Street, Dublin, when he married Sarah Jane Hopkins of York Street on 26th November 1919 at St Peter's Church of Ireland. Sarah Jane Ferguson died at the Adelaide Hospital on 1st February 1945, aged 62, and is buried in Mount Jerome Cemetery. Robert Ferguson died at Livingstone in West Lothian on 26th December 1967, aged 82.

4 The Orchard – Michael Foley

Michael Foley was born around 1886 and his father was also called Michael, but it has not been possible to confirm his military service in the Great War. He was a stevedore and living at Queen's Square when he married Mary O'Neill of Mountpleasant Terrace on 29th September 1920 at the Church of Our Immaculate Lady of Refuge. Michael Foley was an engine driver when he died of locomotor ataxia at 4 The Orchard on 26th July 1946, aged 60, and is buried in Glasnevin Cemetery (Plot No: JJ 130 1/2 St Patrick's Section).

5 The Orchard – Joseph English

Joseph English was born on 18th June 1886 at 1 Whitworth Place in Drumcondra to Joseph English, a customs official, and Margaret English (nee English). His father died in 1896 and Margaret English was living at George's Place in Rotunda in 1911 with eight children ranging in age from ten to 25. In 1911, Joseph was a house painter and lodging with his married sister, Ellen Williams, at Hardwicke Street in Rotunda. Joseph was living at Hardwick Place when he married Annie Lawlor of Stafford Street on 31st January 1914 at St Mary's Roman Catholic Pro-Cathedral on Marlborough Street. He enlisted as a Driver with the Royal Field Artillery (Regimental Number 40215) and served overseas after December 1915 and was treated at 4th Stationary Hospital, St Omer, in September 1916. Joseph English was discharged on 25th September 1919 and was living at 109 Summerhill when he was awarded a 30% disability pension in respect of debility at the rate of twelve shillings per week. Ann English died at Mercer's Hospital on 8th October 1962, aged 68, and Joseph was living at 5 The Orchard when he died of myocardial infarction at Meath Hospital on 21st June 1964, aged 78. Joseph and Ann English are buried in Glasnevin Cemetery (Plot Number JJ 130-132 in St Patrick's Section). Their son, Joseph Vincent English, was

Joseph and Annie English
5 The Orchard
(source: www.findagrave.com)

a traffic manager and living at 5 The Orchard when he died on 13th December 1969, aged 47, and is also buried in Glasnevin Cemetery.

6 The Orchard – Charles William Brown

In the Thom's directories, William Brown is recorded as the occupant from 1931 until at least 1947. However, his full name was Charles William Brown, and he was a son of Alfred Frank Brown of the Dublin Metropolitan Police. (Some military documents record his name as Charles William, whilst others record William Charles.) Charles enlisted with the Army Service Corps (Regimental Number T/25347) and was a saddler when he married Ellen Crane of Fairview on 1st July 1913 at Drumcondra Church of Ireland. He was deployed to France on 10th August 1914 and was serving with 6th Battalion Royal Dublin Fusiliers (Regimental Number 30939) when he was demobilised on 18th November 1919. Charles and Ellen were living at 44 Upper Rutland Street when Charles applied, unsuccessfully, for a disability pension. Ellen Brown died at the Royal City of Dublin Hospital on 31st March 1959, aged 68, and Charles was a retired motor driver and living at 6 The Orchard when he died of bronchitis at Mercer's Hospital on

31st July 1965, aged 72. The house passed to his son, Leonard Brown and his wife, Eileen.

7 The Orchard – John Reginald Fisher

John Reginald Fisher was born on 14th December 1882 at 4 Russell Buildings on Church Road to William Fisher, a clerk, and Mary Fisher (nee Whelan). John enlisted with the Army Service Corps (Regimental Number R4/091309) and was posted to Salonika on 1st November 1915. He was demobilised on 9th February 1920 and was living at Manor Place when he was awarded a 15% Disability Pension in respect of injury to his right hand at the rate of six shillings per week. John was a chauffeur and living at Duke Street when he married Elizabeth (Lizzie) Keenan of Brian Boru Street on 17th February 1920 at St John's Church of Ireland in Clontarf. Elizabeth Fisher died on 31st October 1943, aged 47, at the Harold's Cross Hospice and John was a court usher and living at 7 The Orchard when he died of tuberculosis and arteriosclerosis at St Kevin's Hospital on 9th October 1952, aged 61. John and Elizabeth Fisher are buried in Mount Jerome Cemetery.

John Reginald Fisher
7 The Orchard
(source: Ancestry family tree)

8 The Orchard – James Donnelly

The occupant named in the 1931 Thom's Directory was 'Radican, J' but it has not been possible to confirm information for this occupant. The occupant in the 1940 directory was James Donnelly.

James Donnelly was a son of James Donnelly, a postal official, and Elizabeth Donnelly and the family lived at Upper Erne Terrace in South Dock in 1901, when James was recorded as being ten years old. The family home was at Gordon Street in Pembroke West in 1911. James Donnelly junior was a labourer when he enlisted as a militiaman with 3rd Battalion Royal Dublin Fusiliers (Regimental Number 7389) on 6th

December 1905. He gave his age as 18 years and two months old when he enlisted with the Royal Irish Rifles (Regimental Number 8383) on 17th November 1906. He was stationed in India with 1st Battalion from January 1909 until his battalion was recalled to the United Kingdom for war service in October 1914. His battalion was deployed to France on 6th November 1914 and he was reported as having been wounded in the Casualty List issued by the War Office on 23rd May 1915. Lance-Corporal Donnelly was awarded the Distinguished Conduct Medal, the citation being published in the London Gazette on 1st June 1915:

For conspicuous gallantry and great daring near Neuve Chapelle on 12th March 1915. When we decided to attack it was found that the wires in front were still intact, and before any advance could be made they had to be cut. Lance-Corporal Donnelly and another man at once volunteered and succeeded in cutting down the wires, under very heavy machine-gun and rifle fire.

On 25th August 1915, *The London Gazette* reported that Lance-Corporal Donnelly had been awarded the Cross of the Order of Saint George (3rd Class) by Imperial Russia. He was subsequently transferred to the Royal Irish Regiment (Regimental Number 2G/19) on 11th March 1916, being posted to 2nd (Home Service) Garrison Battalion. Lance-Sergeant (unpaid) James Donnelly was discharged due to wounds on 3rd July 1916, with Silver War Badge Number 79157. James had to have his right arm amputated and was living at 4 Belvedere Avenue when he was awarded a permanent 70% disability Pension at the rate of twenty-one one shillings and eight pence per week. James was a porter and living at Gordon Street when he married Delia Lalor on 18th February 1917 at St Agatha's Roman Catholic Church. He was recorded as being an 'Ex British Army Pensioner' when he died of bronchopneumonia at Jervis Street Hospital on 7th October 1962, aged 71. Delia Josephine Donnelly died at 8 The Orchard on 11th November 1967, aged 78. James and Delia Donnelly are buried in Glasnevin Cemetery and the cemetery register records that James had a second forename, Theobold.

9 The Orchard – Robert Patrick Byrne

Robert Patrick Byrne was born around 1888 to John Byrne, a carpenter and cabinet maker, and the family lived at Portland Place North in Rotunda in 1911. He enlisted with the Leinster Regiment (Regimental Number 7845) on 25th November 1905 was stationed in India with 2nd Battalion in 1911. He was deployed to France with the same battalion on 8th September 1914 and was discharged due to wounds on 13th September 1915 with Silver War Badge Number 14621. He was living at 20 Middle Gardiner Street when he was awarded a 40% disability pension in respect of gunshot wounds to the thigh at the rate of sixteen shillings per week. The degree of disability was increased to 50% (twenty shillings per week) in 1921. Robert was a motor man when he married Lucy Hackett on 23rd November 1919 at St Mary's Roman Catholic Pro-Cathedral on Marlborough Street. Lucy Byrne died on 1st May 1946, aged 43, at the Mater Hospital. John Byrne was working as a motor man for CIE and living at 9 The Orchard when he died of pulmonary tuberculosis at Alan Ryan Hospital on 10th May 1952, aged 64. John and Lucy Byrne are buried in Glasnevin Cemetery.

10 The Orchard – John Thomas Timpson

The 1931 Thom's Directory records the occupant as 'Timpson, John', but in 1933 the occupant is recorded as 'Simpson, John'.

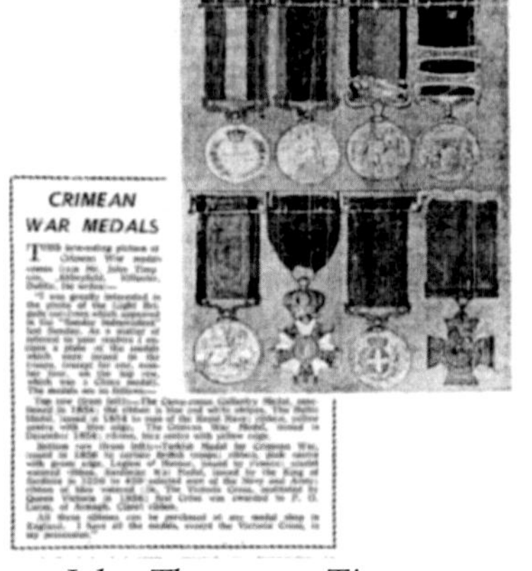

*John Thompson Timpson
10 The Orchard and
1 Abbeyfield
(source: Ancestry family tree)*

John Thomas Timpson, who was born on 11th January 1885 at Blackparks in Athy, County Kildare to Patrick Timpson and Mary Timpson (nee Leonard). He was serving with the 8th (King's Royal Irish) Hussars and stationed in Colchester when he married Julia Whelan of Blackparks in Athy on 21st February 1909 at Athy Roman Catholic Church. In 1911, he was stationed in India, but it has not been possible to confirm his Great War service, which might have been on the Home Front. The Timpson family had moved to 1 Abbeyfield in the early 1950s and the Sunday Independent printed a photograph of John's collection of Crimean War medals on 16th January 1955. In addition to British medals, his collection included medals issued by Turkey, France, and the King of Sardinia. John Timpson was a docker when he died of pneumonia and myocardial degeneration on 3rd January 1962, aged 77. Julia Timpson was living at 1 Abbeyfield when she died at St Mary's Hospital at Phoenix Park, on 15th August 1976. John and Julia Timpson are buried in Grangegorman Military Cemetery (Section RG Grave 303).

11 The Orchard – Patrick Carroll

The occupant for this address is recorded as James Carroll in the Thom's directories from 1931 until at least 1947. Whilst no information has been found for James Carroll, references have been found for Patrick Carroll at 11 The Orchard. It is probable that the incorrect forename is recorded in the various Thom's directories. Patrick was born on 12th June 1895 at 16 North Brunswick Street, Dublin, the son of Patrick, a tailor, and Alice Carroll, nee Burke (although his mother's forename is recorded as Catherine in the Register of Births). The 1901 Census shows Patrick as resident with his parents and his siblings at the home of his maternal grandmother, Mary Bourke/Burke, at Dominick Street. In 1911, he was resident with his family at Marlborough Street. At that time, he was employed as a carter. No military records can be identified for Patrick however, it is known that he married Kathleen Nolan at Stoke on Trent in the third quarter of 1920. A daughter, Alice Hilda Carroll was born in August 1921 in Stoke on Trent. Patrick and Kathleen were successful in competitions, Patrick won two newspaper horse racing sweepstakes in the 1930s and Kathleen won second prize for crochet work at Killester's inaugural Flower Show and Garden Fete, which was held in the grounds of St Brigid's Schools in August 1933. Patrick was living at 11 The Orchard when he died at Peamount Hospital on 26th November 1975, aged 80, and is buried in St Mary's Church Graveyard in Saggart. He was survived by his widow Kathleen, who was known as May, who died in 1988. Patrick's elder brother, James Patrick, was killed in action on 29th April 1916, aged 26, with 8th Battalion Royal Dublin Fusiliers (Regimental Number 18894) and is buried at Noeux-les-Mines Communal Cemetery, France.

Patrick and Kathleen Carroll on Their Wedding Day
11 The Orchard
(source: Ancestry family tree)

12 The Orchard – Albert Green and Richard O'Keefe

In the 1931 Thom's Directory, the occupant was recorded as 'Murry, Thomas' and the occupant was recorded as 'O'Keefe, Richard' in 1940.

Albert Green enlisted with Royal Dublin Fusiliers (Regimental Number 10594) on 24th May 1909 and was stationed in India with 1st Battalion at the outbreak of the Great War. His battalion was recalled to the UK, arriving in January 1915 and Albert was stationed at Torquay Barracks in Devon when he married Annie Fitzgerald of Upper Jane Place on 4th January 1915 at St Laurence O'Toole Roman Catholic Church. His father, also called Albert, was serving with the Army Service Corps. His battalion departed for the eastern Mediterranean in March 1916 and Albert took part in the landings at Cape Helles on the Gallipoli Peninsula on 25th April 1915. The battalion was withdrawn from Gallipoli in January 1916 and re-deployed to the Western Front, arriving at Marseilles in March. Lance-Corporal Green was discharged due to wounds on 27th December 1916 with Silver War Badge Number 105756. He was living at Wall's Square when he was awarded a 70% Disability Pension in respect of gunshot wounds to the forearm and back at the rate of twenty-eight shillings per week, with an allowance of seven shillings for his wife. In 1922, the degree of disability was reduced to 40% but was changed from being conditional to being a permanent pension for life. The rate was sixteen shillings per week, with an allowance of four shillings per week for his wife. Annie Green (42) of 12 The Orchard was knocked down by a motor car at the junction of Amiens Street and North Strand on 28th February 1936 but was dead on arrival at the Jervis Street Hospital.

Richard O'Keefe was born around 1877 but it has not been possible to identify further family or military details. Richard was a labourer and living at 12 The Orchard when he died of coronary arteriosclerosis at St Kevin's Hospital on 11th February 1958, aged 83. His widow, Jane O'Keefe, died at 12 The Orchard on 20th July 1968, aged 88. Richard and Jane O'Keefe are buried in Grangegorman Military Cemetery.

13 The Orchard – Thomas Michael Ryan

Thomas Michael Ryan was born on 26th September 1887 at 52 Jervis Street in North City to Philip Patrick Ryan, a fitter and later a Sergeant in the Dublin Metropolitan Police, and Sarah Mary Ryan (nee Phelan). He was baptised on 28th September 1887 at St Mary's Pro-Cathedral and the family lived at Warrenmount Place in Merchants Quay in 1901 and at Courtney's Place in Mountjoy in 1911. Thomas enlisted with the Royal Engineers (Regimental Number 495395) and was posted to a Theatre of War after December 1915. Sapper Ryan served with a Signals Company attached to the 63rd (Royal Naval) Division and was evacuated to Etaples on 31st Ambulance Train on 5th November 1918. He was discharged on 22nd February 1919 and, on 20th August 1919, *The London Gazette* reported that he had been awarded the Military Medal. Thomas was awarded a 30% disability pension in respect of neurasthenia at the rate of twelve shillings per week, with the disability degree being reduced to 20% (eight shillings per week) in 1922. Thomas was a carpenter and living at North Clarence Street when he married Mary Murphy, a waitress from Grattan Street, on 25th October 1919 at St Columba's Roman Catholic Church in Drumcondra. He was

Thomas Ryan
13 The Orchard
(source: Ancestry family tree)

a retired carpenter when he died of an oesophageal ulcer at Mercer's Hospital on 19th September 1962, aged 74. Mary Ryan was living at 13 The Orchard when she died at St Brigid's Hospital in Crooksling on 7th January 1970, aged 78. Thomas and Mary Ryan are buried in St Fintan's Cemetery in Sutton.

14 The Orchard – Frederick Alexander Dyas

Frederick Alexander Dyas was born on 6th January 1895 at 28 Longwood Avenue in Wood Quay to Edward Dyas, a clerk and later an accountant, and Helen Edith Dyas (nee Howard) and the family lived at Havelock Square in Pembroke West in 1901 and at 69 Cabra Road in Glasnevin in 1911. Frederick was a druggist's assistant in 1911 but he was living in Liverpool when he was 'called up for Service' with the King's (Liverpool Regiment) on 29th April 1916. (This indicates that he was conscripted under the Military Services Act rather than enlisting voluntarily). He was posted to 5th Battalion (Regimental Number 38543) and was deployed to the Western Front in March 1917, joining the regiment's Labour Company. In May 1917, he was transferred to the Labour Corps (Regimental Number 42828) as a Medical Orderly and served in 42nd Company and 70th Company. He served on the Western Front until November 1917 and was transferred to the Royal Army Medical Corps (Regimental Number 139402) in February 1918 and posted to 8th Company. He qualified as a Nursing Orderly and worked at the Huddersfield War Hospital from May 1918 until August 1919.

Private Frederick Alexander Dyas was transferred to the Class Z Army Reserve on 18th September 1919 and was living at the family home on Cabra Road when he was awarded a 30% disability Pension in respect of bronchitis and trench fever at the rate of twelve shillings per week. The degree of disability was re-assessed at 20% in 1922 and the pension was reduced to eight shillings per week. Frederick was a civil servant when he married Mary Eileen Robinson of Bengal Terrace on 1st March 1921 at St Mobhi's Church of Ireland in Glasnevin. In February 1939, he was undergoing a course of ARP lectures with a view to joining a First Aid Squad. Frederick Alexander Dyas was working at the Department of Social Welfare when he retired from the Civil Service and was living at 28 Finglas Road when he died of cancer at St Laurence's Hospital on 19th February 1963, aged 68. Mary Dyas was living at 28 Finglas Road when she died at Sir Patrick Dun's Hospital on 21st February 1966, aged 67. Frederick and Mary Dyas are buried in Mount Jerome Cemetery.

15 The Orchard – Peter McCormack (McCormac)

Peter McCormack was born on 26th December 1882 at 20 Aldborough Place to Christopher McCormack, a railway porter, and Mary McCormack (nee Murtagh) and the family lived at Aldborough Court in North Dock in 1901. Peter was a labourer when he enlisted with the Royal Garrison Artillery (Regimental Number 12407) on 10th October 1902 and transferred to the Section B Army Reserve on 9th October 1905. In 1911, the family home was at Portland Row in Mountjoy, Christopher being recorded as being a labourer with the Telephone Engineering Department NIC and Peter being recorded as a GPO postman. Peter was mobilised for war service on 19th October 1914 and posted to 121 Heavy Battery RGA. He was deployed to France on 13th February 1915 and was serving with the Armoured Cars Section in September 1915. He also served with other units, including trench mortar batteries, before returning to the UK on 8th April 1918. Peter was serving with 2nd Reserve Battery when he was discharged as 'No longer physically fit for war service' with Silver War Badge Number B62546 on 16th December 1918. He was living at Richmond Cottages in Summerhill when he was awarded a 50% Disability Pension in respect of rheumatism at the rate of twenty shillings per week. The degree of disability was reduced to 40% (sixteen shillings), then 30% (twelve shillings), before being raised to 60% (twenty-four shillings) in 1922.

Peter was a labourer when he married Teresa Reddin of Upper Rutland Street on 3rd June 1919 at St Mary's Roman Catholic Pro-Cathedral on Marlborough Street. On 28th July 1936 a son, Desmond McCormack (10) was playing with friends at a fifteen-foot-deep water-filled quarry hole at The Stiles in Howth when he slipped off their raft at about 9:30 pm. In order to help the searchers, motor cars lined up near the quarry edge and directed headlights onto the water. His body was recovered at about 1.00 am on 29th July. Peter McCormack died of pulmonary tuberculosis at 15 The Orchard on 6th March 1944, aged 61 (although the Register of Deaths records his age as 58). Teresa Maria McCormack died at 15 The Orchard on 29th February 1972, aged 87, and the death was registered by James Byrne, who was recorded as the occupier at 15 The Orchard. Peter, Teresa, and Desmond McCormack are buried in Glasnevin Cemetery.

16 The Orchard – Norman Halstead

Norman Halstead was born on 29th June 1895 at Lockwood in Yorkshire to Allen Halstead, a cloth miller, and Mary Hannah Halstead (nee Wrigglesworth). The family was living at Burbeary Street in Lockwood, and Norman was employed by the Post Office. It is not known when Norman enlisted with the King's Own Scottish Borderers (Regimental Number 11576) but he was deployed to France with 2nd Battalion on 15th August 1914. He was taken prisoner eleven days later during the Retreat from Mons and was hospitalised at Lazarett Alexandrinenstrasse in Berlin and Lazarett Merzdorf. It is not known when Norman was released from captivity, but he was still serving with the KOSB when he was allocated Army Number 3179972 in 1920 and there is evidence that he also served with the Military Foot Police (Regimental Number P/19125). Norman was a soldier when

Norman Halstead
16 The Orchard
(*source: Ancestry family tree*)

he married Margaret Anne Woods of Sarsfield Quay on 28th September 1919 at St Paul's Roman Catholic Church on Arran Quay. Norman was a postman when their first child, John Joseph, was born at Sarsfield Quay in March 1921. They were still living at Sarsfield Quay when a second son, Leonard Christopher, was born in June 1926. A third child, Eileen, was born in May 1931 and a third son, Norman, was born in 1932. Margaret Ann Halstead died at 16 The Orchard on 18th October 1974 and Norman was living at 16 The Orchard when he died at the Richmond Hospital on 6th July 1977, aged 82. Norman and Margaret Ann Halstead are buried in Mount Jerome Cemetery.

17 The Orchard – George Henry Johnston

George Henry Johnston was born on 8th May 1888 at Harristown near Naas, County Kildare, to James Johnston, a blacksmith, and Hannah Rebecca Johnston (nee Hawkins) and the family lived at Forgney in County Longford in 1901 and at Cambridge Place in Pembroke East in 1911. George was a van man when he married Jane Smyth of Bride Street on 3rd July 1914 at St Werburgh Church of Ireland. *The researchers have not been able to confirm war service details for this occupant.*
George joined Guinness on 25th August 1919 and worked as a tapman in the Brewhouse department. Jane Johnston died at 17 The Orchard on 19th April 1965, aged 79, and George died of bronchopneumonia at 17 The Orchard on 8th April 1969, aged 81. George and Jane Johnston are buried in Dean's Grange Cemetery.

18 The Orchard – James Kealy

Although the surname is recorded as **Kelly** in the Thom's directory, the correct surname is **Kealy**.

James Kealy was born on 24th December 1879 at 127 Dorset Street in Inns Quay to James Kealy, a carpenter, and Bridget Kealy (nee McAuley) and he served with the Army Service Corps (Regimental Number 16731) from 26th September 1900 to 5th June 1905 and then with the Royal Irish Rifles (Regimental Number 8022) from 20th September 1905 to November 1910. He was living in Glasgow when he enrolled with the Royal Naval Reserve (Naval Number SD/3139) on 6th November 1915, giving 24th December 1887 as his date of birth, but was invalided from the service due to rheumatism and heart disease on 13th May 1916, being issued Silver War Badge Number 28162 in June 1918. James was living at Upper Gardiner Street when he was awarded a Disability Pension in respect of valvular disease of the heart and rheumatism at the rate sixteen shillings per week, which was increased to twenty shillings per week (50% disability) in 1922. James was a labourer and living at Francis Street when he married Mary Keegan, a match maker from Braithwaite Street on 5th August

1923 at St Catherine's Roman Catholic Church. James was recorded as being a naval pensioner when he died of valvular disease of the heart and cardiac failure at 18 The Orchard on 18th February 1940, aged 53, and is buried in Glasnevin Cemetery. In his research on grants issued by the Not Forgotten Society, Tom Burke records that Richard Kelly, who had served with the Royal Irish Rifles (Regimental Number 8779) and the Labour Corps (Regimental Number 513320) lived at 18 The Orchard. Richard Kelly, a retired postman, died of influenza and pneumonia at 18 The Orchard on 25th January 1961, aged 70, leaving a widow, Mary E Kelly.

19 The Orchard – Michael Butler

Michael Butler was born on 19th January 1885 at 28 Holles Street in South Dock to Edward Butler, a labourer, and Mary Butler (nee Carty). He enlisted with the Royal Dublin Fusiliers (Regimental Number 5/5267) on 21st June 1908 and was stationed in India with 1st Battalion in 1911. He was recalled from the reserves and posted to 2nd Battalion on the Western Front on 2nd May 1915. He was hospitalised with gas poisoning on 1st June 1915 and evacuated to the UK, being discharged from Charing Cross Hospital on 9th July 1915. He was discharged from the army due the effect of gas poisoning on 24th August 1916 with Silver War Badge Number 24716. Michael was a postman when he married Elizabeth Maloney on 30th November 1916 at St Catherine's Roman Catholic Church. They were living at Longford Lane in Royal Exchange when Michael was awarded a 40% Disability Pension at the rate of sixteen shillings per week, with an allowance of four shillings per week for his wife. In 1922, his disability was reassessed as being 60% and the pension rate was increased to twenty-four shillings per week. Michael resumed working for the Post Office and was employed at the Pearse Street Sorting Office when he retired. Elizabeth Butler died at St Kevin's Hospital on 1st October 1968, aged 70, and Michael Butler, a dairyman, died of bronchitis and emphysema at St Kevin's Hospital on 26th March 1969, aged 76. Michael and Elizabeth were both living at 19 The Orchard when they died and are buried in Balgriffin Cemetery (Section: K Grave 271).

20 The Orchard – Cyril White Warburton

Cyril White Warburton was born on 27th July 1898 at 121 Leinster Road in Rathmines to John Warburton, a solicitor's clerk, and Marie Hilda Warburton (nee White) and the family lived at Harolds Cross Road in Rathmines in 1901 and at Beach Road in Pembroke East in 1911. Cyril enlisted with the Royal Engineers and served overseas under three regimental numbers – 254473, 314806, and 1856889). Sapper Warburton was demobilised on 14th August 1921 and, in addition to the British War Medal and the Victory Medal, was also awarded the Indian General Service Medal with Waziristan 1919-21 and Mahsud 1919-20 clasps. Cyril was a civil servant and living at Lower Mount Street when he married Georgina Lyster of Wellington Street on 26th August 1926 at St Michael's Roman Catholic Church in Dun Laoghaire. He was living at 20 The Orchard when Georgina Warburton died at St Laurence's Hospital on 25th April 1969, aged 71, and is buried in Balgriffin Cemetery (Section I Grave 94).

21 The Orchard – John Joseph Elliott

There is no entry for Number 21 in the 1931 Thom's Directory and it is recorded as being vacant in the 1932 edition. From 1933 to 1939, the directories record the occupant simply as Mrs Hughes. The occupant is recorded as Mrs Rosanna Elliott from 1940 to at least 1947. However, research shows that the Elliott family were the occupants in 1934.

22 The Orchard – Henry Long

Henry Long was born on 21st June 1894 at Stillorgan to Henry Long, a policeman, and Ellen Long (nee Lawlor). *The researchers have been unable to confirm the war service for this occupant.* Henry was a GPO telegraphist and living at Clonliffe Road when he married Mary Anastasia Harvey of Russell Avenue on 25th July 1925 at St Agatha's Roman Catholic Church. In the marriage register, his father's occupation was recorded as 'Inspector, Dublin Metropolitan Police''. The Long family was living at 22 The Orchard when Mary died at the Richmond Hospital on 12th August 1935, aged 38. Henry was a GPO linesman when he married Annie Fleming of Hagans Court on 15th November 1937 at St Andrew's Roman Catholic Church. He was recorded as being a test clerk at the

Gerald and Bridget Desmond
22 The Orchard
(source: www.findagrave.com)

GPO when he died of coronary thrombosis, arteriosclerosis, and hypertension at 22 The Orchard on 11th March 1954, aged 59. Annie Long was still living at the ISSLT bungalow when she died at St Kevin's Hospital on 11th June 1965, aged 66. Mary, Henry, and Annie Long are buried in Glasnevin Cemetery.

After the Long family, the occupant was Gerald Desmond, a brother of John Desmond of 6 Abbeyfield. Gerald Joseph Desmond was born on 12th September 1895 to Edward Desmond, a basket maker, and Mary Desmond (nee Dunsworth). Gerald Desmond enlisted with the Royal Dublin Fusiliers (Regimental Number 11303) and was deployed to France with 2nd Battalion on 23rd August 1914. Gerald Desmond was serving with A Company when he was taken prisoner at Cigny four days later during the Retreat from Mons and held prisoner at the Limburg, Giessen, and Meschede POW camps. He was transferred to an internment camp in Holland on 13th June 1918 and the Weekly Casualty List dated 21st January 1919 reported that he had been repatriated to the United Kingdom. He was discharged on 19th August 1919 but subsequently enlisted with the South Lancashire Regiment (Army Number 7075291). In the Second World War, he served with the Auxiliary Militia Pioneer Corps (Army Number 13031374). Gerald Desmond was living at 22 The Orchard when he died on 21st January 1983, aged 87, and Bridget Desmond died on 15th March 1991. They are buried in Grangegorman Military Cemetery and the shape of the black marble memorial at the grave, which records that he served with 1st Battalion Royal Dublin Fusiliers, resembles a CWGC headstone.

23 The Orchard – Michael Hayden

Michael Joseph Hayden was born on 17th August 1893 at 19 Upper Tyrone Street in North Dock to Loftus Hayden, a quay labourer, and Frances Hayden (nee Boston) and the family was living at Marlborough

Street in North Dock, Michael's occupation being recorded as messenger. He enlisted with the Royal Irish Regiment (Regimental Number 2/10551) on 6th August 1912 and was mobilised for war service on 4th August 1914. He was deployed to France with 2nd Battalion nine days later and was taken prisoner at Le Pilly on 20th October 1914, being held at Limburg POW Camp. Michael was transferred to the Class B Army Reserve on 8th September 1919 but returned to regular army service with Regimental Number 7109332, being finally dis-

Michael and Mary Hayden
23 The Orchard
(source: www.findagrave.com)

charged on 6th September 1922, following the disbandment of the Royal Irish Regiment. Michael was a motor driver and living at Lower Oriel Street when he married Mary Lyons on 1st October 1922 at St Laurence O'Toole Roman Catholic Church. He was a CIE bus driver based at Clontarf Garage when he retired and he died of acute renal failure and cardiac failure at Jervis Street Hospital on 16th June 1960, aged 66. Mary Hayden was living at 23 The Orchard when she died on 29th May 1979 at Richmond Hospital. Michael and Mary Hayden are buried in Grangegorman Military Cemetery.

24 The Orchard – Edward P McGuire

Note: the surname is recorded as **Maguire** in the registers for his birth, marriage, and death but as **McGuire** in the military records and on the gravestone. Whilst there is no second forename recorded in the official civil registers, some military records have **Preston** as a second forename whilst others have Edward **Patrick** Maguire.

Edward McGuire was born on 4th August 1882 at Cullovill near Crossmaglen, County Armagh, to Peter Maguire, a fowl dealer, and Bridget Maguire (nee Traynor). He enlisted as Edward McGuire with the King's Royal Rifle Corps (Regimental Number 5599) in Liverpool on 23rd October 1903 and was posted to 2nd Battalion. He was stationed in Bermuda (March 1904 to October 1905) and India from (January 1907

Edward and Catherine McGuire
24 The Orchard
(source: www.findagrave.com)

to October 1910) before being transferred to Class A Army Reserve on 7th May 1911 and then to the Class B Army Reserve on 6th February 1912. In October 1912, he was recorded as 'illegally missing' and was struck off the regimental strength. Meanwhile, Edward was a dealer when he married Catherine McNamee of Crossmaglen on 23rd May 1911 at the Roman Catholic Church in the town. Edward Preston McGuire was a labourer when he enlisted with the Loyal North Lancashire Regiment (Regimental Number 2919) on 19th August 1914 in Liverpool and was posted to 1st Battalion on the Western Front on 22nd September 1914. He re-joined the King's Royal Rifle Corps 'from absence' on 25th November 1914 and was posted to 2nd Battalion. He was awarded the Distinguished Conduct Medal, with the citation being published in *The London Gazette* on 1st April 1915:

> *For conspicuous gallantry and ability on 30th January 1915, at Cuinchy. With great ingenuity he occupied a position which dominated a German dugout, and by his accurate fire cleared the occupants into the open, where, as he had previously arranged with his Battalion, they came under our destructive fire. Subsequently he went out into the open (he had been already slightly wounded) and killed four of the enemy in another dugout.*

His first stint on the Western Front lasted until August 1915, when he was posted to the Depot. In the same month, *The London Gazette* reported that Sergeant Edward Preston McGuire had been awarded the Cross of St George (4th Class) by the Russian Imperial authorities. He was transferred to 5th (Reserve) Battalion on 10th December 1915 and returned to the 2nd Battalion on the Western Front at the end of the month. He sustained gunshot wounds to the head and right leg on 1st July 1916 and was evacuated to the UK, being posted to the Depot five days after being wounded. He was posted to the 6th (Reserve)

Battalion in September 1916 and returned to the 2nd Battalion on the Western Front for the final time in February 1917. He was taken prisoner at Nieuport in Belgium on 10th July 1917 and was initially held at Termonde in Belgium before being transferred to Dulmen Camp in the autumn of 1917.

On 30th August 1918, Edward was transferred from Bayreuth in Bavaria to Switzerland and interned at Chateaux D'Oex. There was an agreement amongst the belligerent countries that prisoners with certain medical conditions could be interned in Switzerland where they sat out the war at the expense of their home country. Edward McGuire was repatriated to the UK on 6th December 1918 and was immediately admitted to hospital. Corporal Edward McGuire was transferred to the Class Z Army Reserve on 20th March 1919. Despite having spent seventeen months as a prisoner of war, Edward enlisted with the King's Own Yorkshire Light Infantry (Army Number 4683377) around 1920 and the date of his final discharge is not known. Edward McGuire was a fireman when he died of cancer and cardiac failure at St Kevin's Hospital on 24th March 1944, aged 61 (although the death register records his age as 55). Catherine McGuire was living at 24 The Orchard when she died at Mercer's Hospital on 24th April 1964, aged 80. Edward and Catherine McGuire are buried in Grangegorman Military Cemetery.

25 The Orchard – Frederick Impey

Frederick Impey was born around 1896 in England and he enlisted with the Royal Field Artillery (Regimental Number 1356) and was posted to France as a Gunner on 6th March 1919. He was serving with A/230 Brigade (Regimental Number 806677) when he was discharged due to sickness on 31st July 1919, with Silver War Badge Number 500625. He was living at 16 Ivar Street in Dublin when he was awarded a 30% disability Pension at the rate of twelve shillings per week. The degree of disability was increased to 40% in 1922, the payment rate becoming sixteen shillings per week. Frederick married Bridget Colmey (or Comey) at Paddington in London in mid-1919 and they had two children – Adrian Dennis Impey was born in Leeds in 1924 and Elizabeth Impey was born in Dublin in 1928. Frederick was a railway foreman when he died of cardiac failure and toxaemia at 25 The Orchard on 9th August 1945, aged 48, and is buried in Mount Jerome Cemetery.

26 The Orchard – Matthew Nolan

Matthew Nolan was born on 15th Feb 1893 at 5 Cooke Street to Owen Nolan, a fireman with the Dublin Fire Brigade, and Ellen Nolan (nee Dingle, but recorded as Mack in the birth register) and the family was living at Henrietta Street in Inns Quay in 1901. Matthew worked as a carter for Plunket's of Portmarnock in 1909, before becoming a storeman for Eason's on Abbey Street in 1910. In March 1912, he moved to Glasgow and worked as a steel worker at the Singer Sewing Machine Factory in Clydebank until September 1914. Matthew was a carter when he enlisted with the Royal Dublin Fusiliers (Regimental Number 13778) in Dublin on 18th September 1914. He was posted to 9th Battalion and deployed to France on 19th December 1915.He was posted to 1st Battalion on 24th April 1918 and was gassed in August 1918 and sustained gunshot wounds to the right leg and left arm two months later. He was attached to a Depot unit on 23rd October 1918 and married Bridget Maguire on 16th May 1919 at St Mary's Roman Catholic Pro-Cathedral. Matthew was discharged due to wounds on 14th August 1919, with Silver War Badge Number B285713. They were living at North Portland Street when Matthew was awarded a 40% Disability Pension in respect of gunshot wounds and bronchitis at the rate of eleven shillings per week. He was re-assessed as 20% disabled in 1921, the pension being reduced to 8 shillings per week. In 1922, the pension was reduced to seven shillings and sixpence per week for two years. Matthew and Bridget were living at Carrick Street in Kells when their first child, Eileen, was born in January 1920 and at Mountjoy Square when their second daughter, Margaret, was born in February 1921. Matthew and Bridget had two further daughters – Bridget and Kathleen Patricia. Bridget Nolan died at 26 The Orchard on 1st July 1954, aged 58, and Matthew was a hospital porter and living at 26 The Orchard when he died of pulmonary tuberculosis and coronary insufficiency at the James Connolly Memorial Hospital in Blanchardstown on 9th September 1960, aged 67.

27 The Orchard – Christopher Joseph Moffitt

Christopher Joseph Moffitt was born on 30th December 1880 at 53 Bolton Street in Inns Quay to William Moffitt, a porter, and Annie Moffitt (nee Kirk). Christopher was an organ builder and a militia-man with 3rd Battalion Royal Dublin Fusiliers when he enlisted with 8th (King's Royal Irish) Hussars (Regimental Number 5252) on 23rd November 1900 at Dundalk. He transferred to the 15th (The King's) Hussars (Regimental Number 4263) in February 1902 and was stationed in India until December 1908, when he transferred to the army reserve. He was mobilised on 4th August 1914 and was deployed to France on 13th August. He was treated at Number 3 General Hospital in St Nazaire in September 1914 for an unspecified reason. He sustained wounds to the head and arm and was treated at Number 13 General Hospital in Boulogne, being recorded as dangerously ill in November 1916. He was evacuated to the UK and posted to the 8th Cavalry Depot on 12th December 1916, and then to Number 3 Cavalry Depot on 21st February 1917. Due to his wounds, Private Christopher Moffitt's left arm was amputated at the shoulder and he was discharged as 'No longer physically fit for war service' on 20th August 1917, with Silver War Badge Number 253435.

Christopher was a lift attendant and living at Poole Street when he married Annie McCormack from Sandymount on 28th April 1919 at St Mary's Roman Catholic Church on Haddington Road. They had four

Christopher Moffitt
27 The Orchard
(source: Annie and Sandra Hughes)

daughters – Annie, Mona, Betty, and Chrissie. Whilst the latter three emigrated to England or the United States, Annie remained in Dublin. Christopher was still working as a lift attendant when he died of chronic bronchitis, asthenia, and cardiac failure at 27 The Orchard on 18th June 1939, aged 58. Annie Moffitt died at 27 The Orchard on 25th February 1978. Christopher and Annie Moffitt are buried in Grangegorman Military Cemetery. The Honourable Discharge Certificate is in the possession of Annie Hughes and her daughter, Sandra, who currently live at 27 The Orchard. They are grand-daughter and great-grand-daughter of Christopher Moffitt.

28 The Orchard – John Henry Evans

In the 1932 Thom's Directory the occupant was recorded as 'Evans, John H' and 'Walsh, J' was recorded as the occupant in the 1944 edition.

John Henry Evans was born on 16th November 1896 at Dowagh near Cong in the Ballinrobe Poor Law Union, County Mayo. His parents were John Henry Evans, who had served with the Royal Artillery, and Emily Evans (nee Canty). In 1901, the family was living at Northcourt Avenue in Dublin's North Dock district and John Henry senior was an unemployed blacksmith. In 1911, the family was living at Philipsburgh Avenue in Clontarf West and John Henry senior was employed as a general labourer. John Henry Evans junior was an engineer's assistant and living at Killarney Street when he enlisted with the Royal Army Medical Corps (Regimental Number 55999) in Dublin on 20th February 1915. He was transferred to the Royal Irish Fusiliers (Regimental Number 18898) on 3rd June 1915 and posted to the 3rd (Reserve) Battalion. John Henry Evans was posted to the 5th Battalion, part of the 10th (Irish) Division, on the Salonika Front on 5th November of the same year. Whilst in the Balkans, he contracted malaria and was to suffer the effects for the rest of his life. In the Autumn of 1917, the 10th (Irish) Division was transferred from the Mediterranean Expeditionary Force to the Egyptian Expeditionary Force (EEF). On 1st December 1917, John was transferred to the Royal Engineers (Regimental Number WR/288736) and posted to the Railway Operations Division as a fitter's mate. He remained with the

EEF for the remainder of his active war service, embarking for the UK from Port Said on 15th March 1919.

Sapper John Henry Evans (now with Regimental Number 353643) was living at 92 Aughrim Street in Dublin when he was transferred to the Class Z Army Reserve on 30th April 1919. In the discharge documents, John was recorded as being sober, reliable, and intelligent. John Henry Evans was an engine fitter and living at Aughrim Street when he married Dora Ward of St Stephen's Green on 28th June 1924 at St Ann's Church of Ireland. His father was recorded as being an engineer. The Evans family was living at St. Barnabas Gardens in 1926 when John wrote to the army authorities to request a certificate of character. In the 1944 Thom's Directory, John H Evans is recorded as the occupant of 18 Middle Third, John Walsh having been allocated 28 The Orchard. John Henry Evans later worked at the CIE Broadstone Depot, and he died at the Adelaide Hospital on 23rd November 1976, aged 80. Dora was living at 18 Middle Third when she died at Jervis Street Hospital on 3rd January 1980, aged 83. John and Dora Evans are buried in Mount Jerome Cemetery. Additional information provided by Mike Lee and Sally Dunne.

29 The Orchard – Patrick Joseph Lawlor

The Thom's directories record the occupant as 'Mulcahy, J J' from 1931 to 1941. In 1942, the occupant was recorded as 'Lawlor, J J' and as 'Smith, W' in the 1943 edition. No records can be found for either Mulcahy or Smith.

Patrick was born on 6 March 1883 at 10 Marrowbone Lane, Dublin, the son of Martin and Mary Lawlor, nee Devereux. The 1901 Census shows Patrick as resident at Echlin Street in the Usher's Quay area. At that time, he was employed as a general labourer. Patrick gained employment at the Guinness Brewery in 1909. The 1911 census shows him as a resident at Echlin Street with his wife of one year, Annie. Unfortunately, no record of the marriage can be located. Patrick was employed in the Guinness Forwarding Department at the start of the war. It is likely that Patrick was an Army Reservist mobilised at the outbreak of war, as he was posted to 2nd battalion Royal Dublin Fusiliers in France on 12th September 1914, regimental number 7504.

In November 1916 in the rank of Sergeant, he was awarded the Military Medal for gallantry in the field. Patrick was transferred to Class Z Army Reserve on 17th March 1919. He applied for a Disability Pension citing myalgia and a gunshot wound to the right hip. His military service is commemorated on the Roll of Honour for the St James' Gate Brewery. He was assessed as 20% disabled and awarded a pension of nine shillings and fourpence for himself, and three shillings and sixpence for Annie and one eligible child. The pension for Annie stopped in 1921 and it is believed that she died, although no death register entry can be found. Patrick resumed employment with Guinness and on 30th September 1928 married Elizabeth Smyth at the Roman Catholic Church, Coolock. At the time of the marriage, Patrick was a foreman at Guinness. Elizabeth was the daughter of a salesman and was living at 26 The Demesne, Killester. (Note: A John Downes was resident in 26 The Demesne in 1926 and a Francis Lees from 1930). Patrick was later a foreman in the Guinness Traffic Department, and he died at his home address aged 56 on 5th October 1940, of asthma and cardiorespiratory failure. His next-door neighbour, Charles D'Arcy was present at the death. Patrick is buried at Glasnevin Cemetery. When Patrick died, a death notice in the Irish Independent recorded that he 'died at his residence, 29 The Orchard' but the Thom's directory for 1940 and 1942 recorded Mr Mulcahy as the occupant. It is possible that Patrick and his family were lodging at 29 The Orchard with the Mulcahy family but, as there are known to be errors in the Thom's directories, it is also possible that Patrick Lawlor was the official ISSLT tenant in 1940.

30 The Orchard – Charles Leech D'Arcy

Charles Leech D'Arcy was born on 14th August 1893 at 31 Lower Clanbrassil Street in Merchants Quay to John D'Arcy, a chemist, and Jane D'Arcy (nee McCloud) and the family was living at Wellington Quay in South City in 1901. In 1911, Charles was an apprentice druggist to his uncle, Hyacinth D'Arcy, and was boarding with the family at Berkeley Road in Inn's Quay. *The researchers have not confirmed military service details for this occupant.*

Charles was a labourer and living at Berkeley Road when he married Jessie Donaldson of Thorncastle Street on 18th September 1922 at the Roman Catholic Church in Ringsend. Jessie May D'Arcy died at St Luke's Hospital in Rathgar on 13th March 1955, aged 65, and Charles was living at 30 The Orchard when he died of congestive cardiac failure at the Mater Hospital on 22nd May 1967, aged 73. His occupation was recorded as traffic warden in the death register but a death notice in the Irish Press recorded that Charles was 'late of W & R Jacob and Company'. Charles and Jessie D'Arcy are buried in Dean's Grange Cemetery.

31 The Orchard – Edward McCullagh

Edward McCullagh was born on 12th September 1891 at Wellpark in Drumcondra to Charles McCullagh, a gardener, and Mary McCullagh (nee Quinn). He enlisted with the Irish Guards (Regimental Number 3224) on 5th January 1909 and was stationed at Chelsea Barracks in London in 1911. He was transferred to the army reserve and joined Guinness on 8th November 1913 at the age of 22, being employed in the Forwarding Department. Edward was recalled from the reserve and posted to 1st Battalion Irish Guards in France on 23rd November 1914. In September 1917, *The London Gazette* reported that Corporal McCullagh had been awarded the Military Medal. He sustained gunshot wounds to right hand in October 1917 and was treated at Number 46 Casualty Clearing Station and 18th General Hospital at Camiers before being evacuated to the UK on 21st November. Corporal McCullagh was discharged due to wounds on 14th September 1918 with Silver War Badge Number B1775. He was living at Tolka Cottages in Drumcondra when he was awarded a 50% Disability Pension in respect of gunshot wounds to the right hand at the rate of twenty-one shillings and eight pence per week. Edward returned to work for Guinness and was a porter when he married Catherine Segrave on 31st January

Edward McCullagh
31 The Orchard
(source: Ancestry family tree)

1923 at the Roman Catholic Church in Fairview. Edward was a gate porter in the Guinness Brewhouse Department when he died of cancer and heart failure at Dr Steeven's Hospital on 9th January 1950, aged 58. Catherine McCullagh was living at 31 The Orchard when she died on 2nd October 1952, aged 61. Edward and Catherine McCullagh are buried in Glasnevin Cemetery.

32 The Orchard – John James Timmins

John James Timmins was born in England around 1891 to John James Timmins, a cabinet maker, and Jane Timmins (nee Reilly) and the family was living at Gaelic Street in North Dock in 1901 and at Charleville Avenue in Mountjoy in 1911. In the 1901 census return, father and son are recorded as **James** but in 1911, the father is listed as **John** and the son is not present in the household. It is unclear whether the son's name was registered as **John James** or as **James John**, which has hampered research. A John Timmins is recorded in the England & Wales Census as being stationed in India with 1st Battalion Leinster Regiment in 1911. There is medal entitlement documentation for a John Timmons who was posted to the Leinster Regiment (Regimental Number 8968) on the Western Front on 20th December 1914. This man later served with the Army Cyclist Corps (Regimental Number 5745) in the 27th Divisional Cyclist Company and the 16th Corps Cyclist Battalion. He was transferred to the Section B Army Reserve on 21st April 1919. John James Timmins was a cabinet maker and living at West Road when he married Anne Reilly of Viking Place on 1st June 1920 at the Roman Catholic Church in Aughrim Street. In January 1953, John was a winner in the annual singing contest of the Irish Roller Canary Club. He was recorded as being an old age pensioner when he died of bronchopneumonia and parkinson's disease at 32 The Orchard on 1st March 1968, aged 75, and Anne Timmins died at 32 The Orchard on 2nd December 1970, aged 84. John and Anne Timmins are buried in Mount Jerome Cemetery. The Timmins family was still living at 32 The Orchard in 1979 when Deirdre won a transistor radio in a competition organised by the Savoy Cinema and the manufacturers of Tayto products.

Chapter 7

Reminiscences of Killester

In 2011 and 2012, Jan Glover interviewed descendants of some of the early or long-term residents of Killester Garden Village and this chapter is largely compiled from those interviews. One exception is the memories of Marion Moore (nee Bell) of 121 Abbeyfield.

22 Demesne – Jimmy Magee

I am a son of Richard Magee who was a painter from Ship Street before the war and served with the Royal Dublin Fusiliers. He was just out of his time when he signed up for a steady wage and adventure. My father rarely spoke about the war but once, when a WWI documentary was on the TV, he commented that the water in the trenches was not realistic as, in reality, the water was red! Jimmy felt that his father developed a real will to live after the war, especially considering local suicides. Many men were very troubled and some committed suicide, including Mr Stack of 24 the Demesne. There were also some grumpy old men, for example McDonnell and Powderly, and I was afraid of them as a kid. My dad got a job as a painter and decorator with Dublin Corporation after the war but always suffered with chest problems as a result of mustard gas. When he applied to the ISSLT for a house, he was offered Drimnagh from the Corporation the same week. He spent a couple of nights in Killester and decided to stay and moved to Killester 1939. I did not move with the family and stayed with my grandmother in Capel Street. Eventually, I moved out and settled in fairly quickly, changed schools and went to St Brendan's. We moved in amongst Army captains – de Lacey and Hunt and English. I noticed the poppies and medals around Armistice Day but nothing else. We were always out playing football, riding bikes, exploring in Dollymount and St Annes, and getting chased by wardens. There were fields, orchards, and freedom. I remember that the Scout's Hall was a wooden structure and that Father Kenny was in charge. There were dances, socials, classes, knitting, dancing, cookery. There was also a full-size boxing ring. There were also dances, shows, and socials at the Legion Hall. Soccer was a major part of life in Killester and Bill Hadden, a civil servant, pushed the ISSLT to allow the residents to purchase the scrub land, which was cleared to make pitches. I remember the shops. Mick O'Rourke's chipper had fabulous chips, prepared at his house (14 Abbeyfield), and a wood burning stove. Mick Gaffney sold vegetables from his horse and cart and there were always Corner Boys hanging around the shops. The British authorities treated us well and my father got good medical treatment. He was hospitalised 23 times in Jervis Street and was offered treatment at Leopardstown and Chelsea. However, it took a long time to get his pension, lots of letters, took months to sort out. Our bungalow had a smaller garden than most houses, but we still grew veg. My Dad had to get others to show him as he was a Dub and lived in the city all his life.

46 The Demesne – Bernie Kelly

I am a daughter of Michael Gabriel Kelly who was recorded as the occupant of 46 The Demesne in the 1941 Thom's Directory. My father was born in 1890 at Howth and was a son of a fisherman and joined the British Army in 1908 straight after leaving O'Connell's school. He had a distinguished military career, being commissioned in Gallipoli and later served as an officer in India, where he spoke the language. He returned home to Dublin in 1918, his family having moved from Howth to Seville Place after his father's death. His mother trained as a midwife in order to support her young family. After the war, he had difficulties finding work and approached Lord Howth, who promised him work as a labourer in Guinness. My father declined the offer of labouring work as he had an education and he later got work as a clerk in the ICC, where he remained until retirement in 1960s. He married a girl from Seville Place when he was in his 40s and they lived in Seville Place and then Clontarf. He never spoke about his wartime experiences and never considered himself a 'soldier' once he left the army as that part of his life was over and he just moved on. He got several promotions in ICC and occasionally met with snide remarks in work over his time in the army but nothing that he could not handle. He pestered the ISSLT for a house and was offered one in Ballinteer but refused. Our family moved to Killester in 1940 but my father did not get involved with the Anti Rates committee. I was aware of the cruelty of the Trust, stories of evictions of children, and was aware of various issues and disputes over the years. My father held strong Republican views and was a supporter of de Valera. He did not participate in any WWl commemorations and did not join the RBL. He just kept to himself and his family. I remember a bonfire on the green when I was five but was not allowed to go. I recall Armistice Day/Remembrance Sunday when some of the men would dress up with medals and poppies and go to mass, but my father did not wear medals or poppies.

I have very happy memories of living in Killester, there were lots of children to play with and plenty of food and homegrown vegetables. There was no shortage of food during WWll and normal vegetables were so abundant that my father took to growing artichokes and his neighbours grew marrows. There were good neighbours in a close community, and some worked in Guinness or for the Gas Company, and there were also civil servants and fireman. We were aware that they were younger than the original families and we were more conscious of that than any religious differences. I only became aware that neighbours like McCleans, Hurseys and Gordons were Protestants in later years. The only shop was Mrs Donnellan's, a Monaghan woman who ran the grocers shop and post office. We went to Belgrove school as we had lived in Clontarf before Killester. I remember Captain de Lacey, Captain Burke, Captain Holt and Dr Buchanan was the local GP and also worked in Leopardstown Hospital. I remember the shell-shocked men. I did not go to local dances and my parents did not drink or frequent Egans or Harry Byrnes. The highlight of week was the Miraculous Medal at church on Monday nights because of the 'Non-stop Draw' held afterwards. I recall trips out to family in Howth and staying overnight in summer huts owned by the family. My father eventually bought the house for £630 in the 1950s, mainly to secure the home for his family. The Cobbledick sisters, who were both army nurses, bought the family home back years later.

7 Middle Third – Paul and Catherine Browne

We are the grandchildren of John Browne from Golden in Tipperary and Catherine Quigley and he worked for Guinness, as did his sons, John and Paddy. John Browne Jr founded Killester United Football Club in the 1950s with George Hadden. Our parents lived in Summer Street until the 1960s when we moved to a family home in Killester. We remember the big gardens with lots of veg, potatoes, and beetroot. There were also allotments where St Brigid's houses were built. Killester House was the home to the Caffrey family and later the Bramblings. We remember men wearing poppies and men in wheelchairs due to war injuries. Our fathers and grandfathers spoke very little and never about the war.

12 Middle Third – Frank Clarke of Coolock

I remember that the bungalows were different sizes and we referred to them as 'guinea houses, pound houses, etc'. The Legion Hall was used by the ex-servicemen for meetings but was also used for bingo and dances. We played football on the greens, and I remember the Scout hall. We explored the woods and raided orchards in Dollymount and St Anne's. I remember the sound of hobnail boots as the Artane Boys were marched down to Dollymount and girls called at the doors selling poppies. I never had a problem wearing a poppy then or one now. All the kids played together, Catholic and Protestant. It was a tight knit community with lots of green spaces and huge gardens where vegetables were grown. We always knew that the houses were owned by the Trust and I remember my father and our neighbours constantly trying to buy their houses. On the downside, I remember the eviction of widows and children which was terribly sad, especially the eviction of the eight Flanagan children. Those who were well connected with the Trust got the better houses, but my father felt he had been well treated by the Brits, he got a house, a pension, and medical care. There was no discrimination, but I got the odd jibe in work about living in a free house, but they weren't free, they had had to fight for them! There were wounded men in the estate and many of the neighbours worked on the railway or for Guinness. My father never spoke about the war, he said he was glad that part of his life was over and the main thing was that we won. Killester was a new start, a new house, new part of his life. Like Jimmy Magee and Frank Farrell, I was very involved in Killester United even after moving to Coolock.

28 Middle Third and 93 Abbeyfield – Kathleen Turner (née Lindsay)

I am a daughter of Richard Lindsay of 28 Middle Third and the daughter-in-Law of William Turner who lived at 93 Abbeyfield from around 1934. Richard was a quiet man and my mother died in 1925 and relatives and friends helped to mind the children. My father then married Elizabeth Leonard in 1930 and she was a fantastic stepmother and looked after all of us. My stepmother's sister, Mary, was married to Benjamin Griffiths of 8 Abbeyfield but they moved to England in the late 1930s. I remember that Captain De Lacey had a maid who answered the door when you called to him if there was a problem. There was no church in early days and we had to walk through fields to mass in Coolock. I also remember the freezing cold school and the cruel nuns. There were flower shows organised by De Lacey and I remember all the shops in Killester – Egans pub, Kincaids for petrol, Lucky Coady for sweep tickets. Donnellans, and Byrnes (Needler). I socialised with all local kids and later worked in Lemon's factory and Player Will (?) I married Patrick Turner from 93 Abbeyfield on 5th July 1954 in Killester Church.

Kathleen Turner (nee Lindsay) was living at 93 Abbeyfield when she was interviewed by Jan Glover in 2012.

21 Abbeyfield – Frank Farrell of Armstrong Walk

Frank Farrell, a son of John Farrell from Carlow, is a local historian who has written a history of Killester United Football Club. His grandfather had already enlisted when his father signed up after hearing his parish priest telling all able-bodied young men to go and help the souls in Catholic Belgium. He had no secure employment (just labouring), he was thinning strawberries when he decided to go. He joined the Royal

Irish Regiment, went to France in Sept 1916, was sent to Somme and was under attack at Guillemont. He got hit twice, in the neck and the eye and crawled to a shelter where he stayed overnight with the rats until he was picked up the next morning. He was sent to hospital in London and then back to Dublin. He re-enlisted and was sent to Greece to fight the Turks. Sent to Egypt (Jaffa and Haifa), where he got malaria and was sent to hospital in Cairo. Nurse told him there was another Farrell in the hospital which turned out to be his father. My father went to work in Guinness on his return, who were very good employers with good wages and free medicals. He cycled to James Street every day but often got hassled by the Black and Tans. My parents settled in quickly at Killester and tried to move to a bigger house in the scheme but were not well connected. We kept hens, ducks, pigeons and had an aviary. We also had pets – a rabbit, two cats, and a dog. We were called 'West Brits' but it didn't bother us. I remember men like Mr Brady of 20 Abbeyfield who had no legs. I played with Jimmy Magee and we were always out on our bikes or playing football. There were loads of fields, trees, and big houses. We played in the ice-house at Killester House, in Killester Avenue graveyard, Nuns' walk, and our meeting place was the water tower. The tower was built on public land and when it was demolished, Freddie Burtenshaw took the land to add to his garden at 45 Abbeyfield and he eventually got title to the land. Joe Clifton of 23 Abbeyfield was the caretaker of the Legion Hall. Playing football was a big part of living at Killester as the men had played soccer during the war, which could explain why Killester never had a GAA football team. In 1928, local men cleared scrubland to make a pitch and the owner of 128 Howth Road (Mr Kelburne) donated the first kits and the team were called Kelburne United.

60 Abbeyfield – Joe Redmond

I am a son of John Redmond who joined Royal Dublin Fusiliers at 16, possibly using his brother's name, and served for four years. His wife, who was 'good with pen and paper', wrote to Lord Howth and John got a job in Guinness. His wife also wrote looking for an ex-service-man's house and the family moved into 60 Abbeyfield around 1928. They had a total of nine kids, two of which died in childbirth. His father grew veg and kept a cow, two pigs, and hens. I remember the day the Flanagan children were evicted; the furniture was out on the path and all the neighbours were out trying to help. It was a very sad day. I remember three men who had been Captains in the British Army and I reckon they all loved the authority, they thought they were still in the army – Captain Bourke, agent for the Trust, Captain de Lacy, and Captain Griffin of 56 Abbeyfield. There was never any problems socialising outside Killester, just the odd comment about getting a free house. It was a tight community, which looked out for each other. Four or five of our neighbours were in the Irish army, others worked for the post office or as labourers. Mr Harvey of 52 Abbeyfield was a cook in the army. I went to St Brendan's school, and we played in the woods, robbing orchards and timber, playing football, boxing, and riding on our bikes to Dollymount. One time about ten of us were playing up at the bridge in a barn with about 10 altogether and one of us got caught sliding down the hay and we were all arrested. We were marched up to Kilmainham court and fined six shillings each by Justice Reddin, an IRA man who hated ex-servicemen. We never wore poppies and my father was not in the RBL. There were three halls – Legion, Abbey, and Scouts – and there was always loads going on, socials, dances. The women met up on a Monday night and organised outings to places like the Skerries. My dad left Guinness around WWll and went to London with my eldest brother as there was plenty of work. When he came back, he bought a horse and cart and delivered coal and logs and turf. He also gave people lifts to the boats, anything to make a few bob as money was scarce. Two Redmond brothers joined the British army, and my father was not impressed, he said that the only thing that should be joined are hands. One brother joined the paratroopers, served in Egypt in WWll, and settled in Leeds. The other was in the Royal Air Force. I remember Father Traynor and visited his grave in Gouganbarra.

65 Abbeyfield – John Bibby

I am a grandson of Patrick and Teresa Flanagan, who lived at 65 Abbeyfield with their eight children. After the deaths of Patrick (1940) and Teresa (1941), the children were 'turfed out' by the ISSLT.

It caused a major furore in Killester, but neighbours were powerless to prevent the eviction, although there were attempts to intervene on the children's behalf. The children were taken in by a childless aunt and uncle who had a big house on Richmond Road, where they had a strict upbringing. Patrick Flanagan junior applied to the Dublin Corporation Housing Department and got a house on Collins Avenue in Donnycarney. The family was reunited, but some eventually moved to England. The family felt very bitter about their treatment by the ISSLT.

119 Abbeyfield – Jim Byrne

Both my grandfathers were in the British Army and lived in Killester – they were James Byrne of 49 Middle Third and Joseph McCann of 119 Abbeyfield. My wife was related by marriage to Hubert McGowan of 1 The Demesne. James Byrne was a stationmaster at Arklow before the war and came from a family of railway men. He also lived at Rugby Road and lived in Dolphins Barn after the war. He ran a local shop with his wife and was a quiet man who did not speak about the war. His son, David met his wife at the Dance Hall in Killester. Joseph McCann worked in the Post Office after the war and was allocated the bungalow that had previously been occupied by a man called Callan. I was aware of the Trust and I remember the Stanley family of 46 Abbeyfield. There was a granny who was blind, a grandad, their daughter, her husband and their kids. The Grandad died and the husband ran off, leaving the women and kids to fend for themselves. They had no money and were living in terrible poverty. Their children, including my best friend, Billy, were sent to Artane in 1950s. No-one helped them and they shouldn't have been allowed to reach such a level of poverty. I used to bring stuff home from my Grandad's shop for them. In general, my memories of Killester are happy, there was great freedom and there loads of veg from the garden. I remember there was a treehouse, playing cowboys and Indians, and exploring at St Annes and the river at Kilmore Road. I went to St. Brendan's primary school and Joey's secondary. Both my grandfathers considered themselves very lucky to have been given the houses and I was always aware that we lived in the 'ex-servicemens' houses. There were no problems and no discrimination. I helped out in the shop a lot and it was a very lively meeting place. In the 1950/60s, Killester was very lively and busy. My grandfathers were not involved with the RBL. I remember playing with a bayonet in the house and finding a grenade in the fields with my friends.

121 Abbeyfield – Memories by Marion Moore (née Bell)

My name is Marion Moore (née Bell), and I feel incredibly fortunate to call 121 Abbeyfield my home. This house holds a special place in my heart because it was not only my childhood home but also the home of my grandparents, Walter and Connie Harrison. They lovingly raised their six children within these walls. After them, my parents, Victor and Connie Bell, took ownership of the house, and they raised the six of us here. And now, my husband Ken and I have the privilege of living in this cherished family home, where we have raised our own five children. It brings me great joy to have three generations of our family residing at 121 Abbeyfield. One of my earliest memories takes me back to what we fondly referred to as the 'tin shops.' The shop I am referring to is now the location of Heaven Hairdressers and was once owned by the Gaffney family. Carmel, Babs, and Mick were the friendly faces that greeted customers. They offered a variety of food items, but what stands out in my memory are the broken biscuits, the twopenny wafers, and the loose cigarettes that I was occasionally allowed to purchase for my parents. Another vivid recollection is the arrival of traveling families with their horse-drawn caravans, as they made themselves at home on the green area near the entrance to the football ground. If my memory serves me correctly, they stayed for the entire summer, and surprisingly, we all got along quite well. During those summer months, the children on our road engaged in games of skipping and beds, while the boys played marbles. We had an incredible time playing outside on the road, as cars were not as prevalent back then. From morning until night, laughter and camaraderie filled the air. Back then there was a strong sense of community and neighbourliness that permeated daily life. We knew all our neighbours by name and would often gather for community events and celebrations. There was a strong sense of camaraderie and support among residents, with people looking out for one another. I also recall the visits from the rag and bone man, who would come around every couple of weeks, searching for jam jars. If you were fortunate enough to have one, you'd receive a balloon on a stick in exchange. Furthermore, I remember when the area where the apartments and houses in Venetian Hall now stand was nothing but open fields. One of the residents in Abbeyfield even had a couple of goats grazing there, adding a unique touch to the landscape. Lastly, I must mention the scorching summers we experienced in the early sixties. I distinctly remember the heat of the sun causing the tarmac on our road to melt, which ended up staining my clothes. It serves as a testament to the remarkable weather we enjoyed during those times. I hope these memories provide you with as much joy as they do for me. Thank you for allowing me to share these cherished moments from my childhood at 121 Abbeyfield.

123 Abbeyfield and Howth Road – Ursula McLoughlin

I am a daughter of William McLoughlin who lived at 123 Abbeyfield from about 1929 to the early 1940s, when the family moved to 254 Howth Road (formerly 73 The Demesne). My father worked in the Post Office as a Telegraphist both before and after the war. He was very friendly with Captain de Lacey and the move to 254 Howth Road was very quick. We were given no prior warning, we just packed and moved. Our new neighbours were the Switzers and the Pykes. The gardens were fabulous, with fresh vegetables and fruit. We had plum trees and apple trees. My mother used to say that they couldn't eat all the cabbage and lettuce that my dad grew. My mother was not keen on moving from Howth to Killester, she cried bitterly as Killester had a bad name. I do not recall any discrimination, just very happy memories with lots of school friends at St Brigid's. I was not aware that I lived in a 'Soldier's house' until later in life. Church played a large part of our lives. My father never spoke of any discrimination and considered himself extremely lucky to have been given a house and a pension after such a short army career. The bungalow was bought from the ISSLT for £750 –and my brother built a house on the side garden which was eventually sold for €1.6 million.

9 Abbeyfield – Val Cronin

I am a grand-daughter of William Thomas Edwards who served with the Connaught Rangers and my dad was Cecil Edwards, who was well known in Killester. My mam, Rita, still lives in Abbeyfield. My dad was born in 9 Abbeyfield in 1942 and died in 9 Abbeyfield 2008. So, he was born, reared, lived, and died in the same house. My dad worked in Merville dairy in Finglas and also Premier in Killester. He got to know many of the lads from Artane and Donnycarney and I am sure have many fond memories of him. He married my mam, Rita, in 1968. Dad rarely went far from his pals in Killester, he spent many a Saturday night upstairs in the Beachcomber with a few regulars, solving the problems of the world. A lot of my pals will remember him from the Killester Summer Project, where lots of locals helped out, trying to keep us on the straight and narrow and out of trouble. After he retired, Dad worked for P R Reilly, who owned the petrol station on Howth Road. If dad was alive, he would have lots of memories of local heroes and characters who lived in Killester - Duggy who helped Mr Barry with the horses, Mr Fox, Carmel Gaffney, Paddy the butcher, and Jimmy Byrne who all had local businesses in the tin shops. My dad is buried in Glasnevin and my grandparents are buried in Mount Jerome Cemetery. I am happy to be able to share my memories with the project as dad was a proud Killester man all his life who loved his community and the people in it. A lovely community with lovely people in it.

Chapter 8

Killester Through the Lens

3 Abbeyfield
Mrs Hannan

18 Middle Third
John Henry Evans and family

28 Middle Third
The Lindsay family

38 Abbeyfield
The McMenamin family

73rd Scout Troop Killester marching down the Howth Road

A dinner inside the Legion Hall
(source Linda Byrne)

34 The Demesne
The Murphy family

70 Abbeyfield
Peadar Ball and family

Capt Dick Burke MC
228 Howth Rd (source Tom Burke)

Leonard and Margaret Atkin of
2 Abbeyfield (source: Jan Kelleher)

Wedding day at St Brigid's Church

Abbeyfield under construction

1923 Armistice Day in Killester Garden Village: veterans of the Boer War and the Great War and children from the Killester community (source: British Pathe newsreel)

Killester Village in the 1920s

Killester Halt in the 1920s (source: National Library of Ireland)

Labourers of the Killester Scheme who were also ex-servicemen, 1922

Local men of Killester at the Legion Hall 1940s

Middle Third in the 1920s

The ARP Unit of Killester during The Emergency

Founding members of the Killester Football Club

Construction of St Brigids Church, 1926

'Singing in the Rain': Killester Ladies Singing Club

Cecil Edwards at St Mary's Convent

The Legion Hall Christmas Party, 1940

*The First Killester Remembrance
Ceremony, 2021*

*Mr Kevin Martin, Ms Linda Byrne, Mr Paddy O'Reilly, Ms Marion Martin,
Ms Aoife Byrne, Mr Tom Burke, Mr Gerry Leigh, Mr Aaron Crampton in 2022*